L. RUSH H

A LAWYER'S GUIDE TO
ELDER LAW

WITH FORMS

AMERICAN**BAR**ASSOCIATION

Solo, Small Firm and
General Practice Division

Cover design by Kelly Book/ABA Design

Printed in the United States of America.

24 23 22 21 20   5 4 3 2 1

A catalog record for this book is available from the Library of Congress.

Discounts are available for books ordered in bulk. Special consideration is given to state bars, CLE programs, and other bar-related organizations. Inquire at Book Publishing, ABA Publishing, American Bar Association, 321 N. Clark Street, Chicago, Illinois 60654-7598. www.ShopABA.org

CONTENTS

Acknowledgment xiii
Preface. xv

Chapter 1
Client Interview and Ethical Considerations 1
     I.   Interviewing the Client. 1
    II.   Basic Drafting. 2
   III.   Limited Capacity Considerations. 3
   IV.   Living Arrangements 4
    V.   Paying for Housing. 5
   VI.   Ethical Considerations 5
         A. Maintaining Confidentiality 5
         B. Multiple Representation. 7
         C. Estate Planning Conflicts. 8
         D. Accepting Payment of Fees from Non-Client 8
         E. Setting Fees. 9
         F. Competency of Elder Client 9
Appendix A: Family Questionnaire 11
Appendix B: Asset Questionnaire. 16
Appendix C: Engagement Letter for Individual 21
Appendix D: Engagement Letter for Couple 23
Notes. 25

Chapter 2
Health Care and Financial Decision Making 27
     I.   Overview. 27
    II.   Right to Be Informed 28
   III.   Unwanted Medical Treatment. 28
   IV.   Patients' Rights 29
    V.   Case Law on Withholding Medical Treatment. 30
   VI.   Factors That Courts Consider in Determining Life-Sustaining
         Treatment 31
  VII.   Advance Directives. 31
         A. Durable Health Care Power of Attorney 32
         B. Durable Health Care Power of Attorney Form 34
         C. Appointment of an Agent 39
         D. Revocation of Durable Health Care Power of Attorney 39
         E. Second State Residency 39
 VIII.   Living Will 40

     A. Revocation of Living Will 41
  IX. Do Not Resuscitate (DNR)............................. 41
   X. Guardianship and Conservatorships 44
  XI. Joint Ownership of Assets 46
 XII. Durable Power of Attorney 47
XIII. Living Trust 53
XIV. Simple Will 59
Notes... 65

Chapter 3
Social Security 67
    I. Overview.. 68
   II. Social Security Basics 69
     A. Persons Eligible for Social Security 69
     B. Payment Procedures 70
     C. Rules for Representative Payee......................... 70
     D. Rules for Overpayments 71
     E. Rules for Underpayments 71
     F. Lump Sum Death Benefit 72
  III. Insured Status... 72
     A. Insured Individuals................................. 72
     B. Fully Insured Individuals 72
     C. Currently Insured Individuals 73
     D. Disability Insured Individuals 73
     E. Earning Credits 73
  IV. Calculating Benefits.................................... 74
     A. Determining the Primary Insurance Amount (PIA) 74
     B. Determining the PIA by the Average Indexed Monthly
        Earnings Method..................................... 75
     C. Alternate Methods of Calculating PIA 75
     D. How the Family Maximum Rule Affects the
        Benefit Amount 75
     E. Grounds for Reduction of Benefits 76
   V. Social Security Retirement (Old-Age Benefits)................. 76
     A. Background... 76
     B. How Excess Earnings May Reduce Social Security
        Retirement Benefit Amount............................. 78
  VI. Husband's and Wife's Benefits............................ 78
     A. Introduction 78
     B. Deemed Valid Marriages 79
     C. How a Spouse Qualifies for Husband's and Wife's Benefits... 79
     D. How a Divorced Spouse Qualifies for Husband's or
        Wife's Benefits 79
     E. When Husband's and Wife's Benefits Terminate 80
 VII. Widow's and Widower's Benefits 81
     A. Introduction 81

     B. How a Spouse Qualifies for Widow's or
       Widower's Benefits 81
     C. How a Divorced Spouse Qualifies for Widow's
       or Widower's Benefits 82
     D. When Widow's or Widower's Benefits Terminate 83
  VIII. Mother's or Father's Benefit 83
     A. Introduction 83
     B. How a Divorced Spouse Qualifies for Mother's or
       Father's Benefit 83
     C. When Mother's or Father's Benefit Terminate 84
   IX. Parent's Benefits. 84
     A. Introduction 84
     B. How to Qualify for Parent's Benefits 85
     C. When Parent's Benefits Terminate 85
    X. Child's Benefits 85
     A. Introduction 85
     B. How to Qualify for Child's Benefits 86
     C. How the Dependency Requirement Is Satisfied 86
     D. Rules for Adopted Children 86
     E. Rules for Grandchildren and Step-Grandchildren 87
     F. When a Child's Benefits Terminate 87
   XI. Disability Insurance Benefits. 88
     A. Introduction 88
     B. How an Individual Qualifies for Disability Benefits 89
     C. Substantial Gainful Activity (SGA) 89
     D. What Constitutes SGA for Blind Individuals. 89
     E. Drug Addiction and Alcoholism Are No Longer Basis
       for Disability. 90
     F. When Disability Benefits Terminate. 90
  XII. Appeals Procedure 90
     A. The Initial Determination Stage 90
     B. The Reconsideration Stage. 91
     C. The Administrative Law Judge (ALJ) Stage. 91
     D. The Appeals Council Stage 91
     E. Judicial Review in Federal Court. 92
     F. Expedited Appeals Process 92
     G. Attorney's Fees 92
Appendix A: Social Security Retirement Checklist 93
Notes. 96

Chapter 4
Veterans Benefits **101**
    I. Overview. 102
   II. Introduction to Veterans Benefits 103
  III. Disability Compensation Benefits. 103
     A. Introduction 103
     B. Eligibility for Disability Compensation Benefits 103

     C. "Service Connected" and "Line of Duty" Defined 103
     D. Grades of Disability 104
     E. Amount of Payments 104
  IV. Pension Benefits. 104
     A. Introduction 104
     B. Eligibility for Pension Benefits 105
     C. Wartime Service Defined 105
     D. Non-Service Connected Defined 105
     E. Resource Limits 106
     F. Excluded Resources 106
     G. Treatment of Income. 106
     H. Exclusions from Income. 107
     I. Amount of Payments 108
     J. Aid and Attendance (A&A) Benefits for
        Pension Recipients. 108
     K. Housebound Benefits for Pension Recipients 108
     L. Election of Benefits 109
   V. Dependency and Indemnity Compensation (DIC) Benefits 109
     A. Introduction 109
     B. How a Surviving Spouse Qualifies for DIC Benefits 109
     C. How a Child Qualifies for DIC Benefits. 110
     D. How a Parent Qualifies for DIC Benefits 110
     E. Eligibility Requirements for DIC Benefits. 110
     F. Amount of DIC Benefits for a Surviving Spouse 111
     G. Effect of Remarriage of Surviving Spouse 111
     H. Amount of DIC Benefits for Dependent Child
        or Children 111
     I. Amount of DIC Benefits for a Surviving
        Dependent Parent 112
  VI. Improved Survivors Pension Benefits (Death Pension) 112
     A. Introduction 112
     B. Eligibility for Survivors Pension Benefits. 112
     C. How a Surviving Spouse Qualifies for Survivors
        Pension Benefits. 113
     D. Amount of Survivors Pension Benefits for a
        Surviving Spouse. 113
     E. Amount of Survivors Pension Benefits for
        Surviving Child 114
 VII. Aid and Assistance and Homebound Benefits 114
VIII. Medical Benefits. 114
     A. Introduction 114
     B. Enrollment Requirement 114
     C. Medical Benefits for Dependents 115
  IX. Burial Benefits 115
   X. Claims for Benefits 116
     A. Introduction 116
     B. The Board of Veterans' Appeals 117

C. The Court of Veterans Appeals..........................117
D. U.S. Court of Appeals for the Federal Circuit.............118
Appendix A: VA Benefits Checklist................................118
Notes...119

Chapter 5
Medicare **123**
I. Overview..124
II. Introduction 124
III. Medicare Part A..124
A. Introduction 124
B. Hospital Services Covered by Medicare Part A............125
C. Skilled Nursing Facility Services Covered by
Medicare Part A......................................126
D. Home Health Care Services Covered by
Medicare Part A......................................126
E. Hospice Services Covered by Medicare Part A............127
IV. Medicare Part B...128
A. Introduction 128
B. Services Covered by Medicare Part B 129
C. Preventive Services Covered by Medicare Part B..........129
D. Additional Services Covered by Medicare Part B..........130
E. Services Not Covered by Medicare Part B 130
V. Assignment...130
A. How Assignment Works 130
B. The Limiting Charge...................................131
C. Private Contracts......................................131
VI. Medigap Insurance 132
A. Medigap Insurance for Original Medicare Participants......132
B. When Medigap Insurance Can Be Purchased 132
VII. Medicare as Primary or Secondary Payer...................133
A. Medicare as Primary Payer.............................133
B. Medicare as Secondary Payer 133
C. Medicare and Workers' Compensation and Federal
Black Lung Program..................................134
D. Medicare and No-Fault Insurance 134
VIII. Medicare Advantage Plans—Part C.........................134
A. Introduction 134
B. Medicare Advantage Plans 134
IX. Medicare Part D..135
X. Appeals Procedures.......................................136
A. Appeals Procedures for Entitlement to Medicare
Benefits 136
B. Appeals Procedures for Claims 137
Appendix A: Overview of Medicare Benefits 138
Appendix B: Medicare Checklist for New Beneficiaries 140
Notes...141

Chapter 6
Supplemental Security Income. 143
  I.   Overview. 144
  II. Introduction to Supplemental Security Income. 144
  III. Eligibility Requirements. 145
       A. How an Individual Qualifies for SSI on the Basis
          of Age 145
       B. How an Individual Qualifies for SSI on the Basis
          of Disability 145
       C. How an Individual Qualifies for SSI on the Basis
          of Blindness 146
       D. Persons Who Are Ineligible for SSI Benefits 146
  IV. Treatment of Income. 146
       A. Introduction 146
       B. What Constitutes Earned Income. 147
       C. Earned Income That Does Not Count. 147
       D. What Constitutes Unearned Income 148
       E. Unearned Income That Does Not Count 148
       F. In-Kind Support and Maintenance 150
       G. The One-Third Reduction Rule. 150
       H. Presumed Value Rule 151
       I. Deeming of Income. 151
       J. Types of Income That SSA Does Not Deem. 152
       K. Other Rules for Deeming Income. 153
       L. Rules for Changes in the Status of a Spouse 154
       M. What Is Not Considered Income 154
  V.   Treatment of Resources. 156
       A. Introduction 156
       B. Resources Defined. 156
       C. When Resources Are Counted 157
       D. Rules for Jointly Held Assets 157
       E. Assets That Are Not Considered Resources. 158
       F. Disposition of Resources 160
       G. Transfer of Resources 161
  VI. The Application Procedure 162
  VII. Underpayment of Benefits. 163
  VIII. Overpayment of Benefits 163
  IX. The Appeals Procedure 164
       A. The Initial Determination. 164
       B. The Reconsideration Stage. 164
       C. The Administrative Law Judge Stage 165
       D. The Appeals Council Stage 165
       E. Federal District Court. 165
Appendix A: Overview of Social Security Disability Programs:
       SSI And SSDI 166
Appendix B: Supplemental Security Income Checklist. 168
Notes. 170

Chapter 7
Medicaid **175**
    I.   Overview. 176
   II. Introduction to Medicaid Eligibility. 176
       A. Individuals Who Are Covered by Medicaid 177
  III. Services Covered by Medicaid 177
       A. Mandatory Covered Services. 177
       B. Optional Services Covered by Medicaid. 178
  IV. Eligibility for Long-Term Care Benefits. 179
   V. Financial Qualifications 179
       A. Definition of Income. 179
       B. Income-Capped States 180
       C. Non-Income-Capped States. 180
  VI. Resources. 181
       A. Resource Exemptions 181
 VII. Spousal Impoverishment Rules 182
       A. The Fair Hearing Procedure 184
VIII. Five-Year Look-Back Rule 184
  IX. Planning for a Married Couple. 186
       A. Spend Down. 186
       B. Promissory Note or Purchase of Annuity. 187
   X. Transfers to Trusts. 188
       A. Introduction 188
       B. Medicaid Exemption for Transfers to Trusts 188
  XI. Estate Recovery 190
  XII. Appeals Procedure for Medicaid 192
Appendix A: Will with Testamentary Third Party Special Needs Trust
      for Couple with Handicapped Child/Person 195
Appendix B: Third Party Special Needs Inter Vivos Trust. 209
Appendix C: First Party Special Needs Inter Vivos Trust. 220
Appendix D: Qualifying Income Trust. 229
Appendix E: Income Only Trust 235
Notes. 243

Chapter 8
Retirement Plans and Benefits. **245**
    I.   Overview. 245
   II. Background. 246
  III. Types of Retirement Plans 247
       A. Pension Plans 247
       B. Profit-Sharing Plans 247
       C. Money-Purchase Plans. 247
       D. 401(k) Plans 248
       E. 401(k) SIMPLE Plans. 249
       F. Keogh or HR-10 Plans 249
       G. SEP. 250
       H. IRA. 250

I.   Simple IRA 251
J.   Roth IRA 251
IV.   Participation, Vesting, and Nondiscrimination 252
V.   Top-Heavy Plans 253
VI.   Penalty Taxes 253
A.   Premature Distributions 253
B.   Minimum Distributions 254
VII.   Taxation of Distributions 256
A.   Income Taxation of Distributions during Lifetime 256
B.   Estate Taxation of Distributions at Death 257
VIII.   Creditor Protection 257
Appendix A: Comparison of Plans 259
Notes 262

Chapter 9
Income, Estate, Gift, and Generation-Skipping Taxes 265
I.   Overview 266
II.   Introduction to Federal Income Tax 267
III.   Filing Status 268
IV.   Gross Income Exclusions 269
V.   Gross Income Inclusions 270
VI.   Adjusted Gross Income 271
VII.   Standard Deduction 271
VIII.   Itemized Deductions 272
IX.   Tax Rate Schedules 272
X.   Tax Credits 273
XI.   Alternative Minimum Tax 273
XII.   Common Tax Issues for Elder Clients 274
A.   Tax Credit for the Elderly or Disabled 274
B.   Social Security Exclusion 275
C.   Sale of Personal Residence 275
D.   Medical Expense Deduction 275
E.   Retirement Plan Distributions 276
F.   Cost Basis 276
XIII.   Introduction to Federal Estate Tax 276
XIV.   Gross Estate 277
A.   Gifts 277
B.   Transfers with Control Retained by Decedent 279
C.   Annuities and Retirement Benefits 281
D.   Joint Interests 281
E.   Powers of Appointment 282
F.   Life Insurance 283
XV.   Adjusted Gross Estate 284
XVI.   Taxable Estate 284
XVII.   Net Estate Tax 285
XVIII.   Filing and Payment 286

XIX. Introduction to Federal Gift Tax............................287
    A. Advantages of Gift Giving 287
    B. General Requirements 288
XX. Special Considerations 289
    A. Gifts of Services......................................289
    B. Disclaimers 290
    C. Assignment of Income 290
    D. Delivery of the Gift..................................290
XXI. Annual Exclusion and Split Gifts...........................291
    A. Annual Exclusion 291
    B. Gift Splitting...292
XXII. Income Tax Basis in Gift Property 292
XXIII. Transfers Not Subject to Gift Tax 293
    A. Marital Deduction...................................293
    B. Charitable Deduction 293
    C. Tuition and Medical Expenses 293
XXIV. Gifts for the Benefit of Children...........................294
XXV. Special Situations..294
    A. Net Gifts 294
    B. Gift Subject to an Indebtedness 295
XXVI. Introduction to Generation-Skipping Transfer Tax 295
XXVII. General Rules..295
    A. Skip Person...296
    B. Transferor 296
    C. Taxable Distribution 297
    D. Taxable Termination 297
    E. Direct Skip 298
XXVIII. Tax Apportionment...299
Appendix A: Tax Rate Schedule 300
Notes...300

The forms in this book will be found
as downloadable PDFs at
ambar.org/ElderGuideForms.

ACKNOWLEDGMENT

I appreciate the American Bar Association publishing this book on the growing field of elder law. I first authored a book for the ABA more than 25 years ago. That book, *A Lawyer's Guide to Estate Planning*, has been revised over the years and is in its fourth edition. I have had the pleasure of authoring three other books for the ABA. This book on elder law, in all likelihood, marks the end of my writing career for the ABA. It has been an association of many years for which I am most grateful. I have had the pleasure of working with Lorraine Murray on this current book. I appreciate her encouragement and patience as the project became a bit more tedious and time-consuming than I had anticipated.

PREFACE

This text is intended to provide a helpful introduction to the basics of what is today known as elder law. The text is written with an eye toward practitioners who need an easily accessible book on the basics of this area of law. With this objective in mind, the text provides references to other outstanding ABA elder law–related publications. Readers desiring to become more proficient in elder law should consider adding most or all of these publications to their libraries.

The text includes a number of useful legal documents, including wills, various trusts, powers of attorney, and advance directives, that are commonly used when drafting for elder clients. A word of caution is in order. The reader is reminded that the forms should not be used without being certain they meet the requirements of the lawyer's own state law. Additionally, because there are variations in the implementation and administration of Medicaid laws among the states, lawyers are reminded to be certain of their own state laws when using any of these forms. Minor modifications will often be needed. In addition to the forms, a number of checklists are provided throughout the text. The checklists simply provide a convenient way to summarize the laws and issues being discussed.

The reader will note that the chapters begin with an overview. The overviews are intended to give quick reference to particular sections of the chapter for which the lawyer will have the most use. Also, the reader will find references to helpful websites of the various government agencies administering programs that affect your elder clients. Each of these government agencies has excellent web pages that provide very useful information. These web pages are updated regularly, which makes them a valuable tool for an attorney working in this area of the law.

Social Security, SSI, Medicare, Medicaid, and Veteran's Administration laws and regulations are tedious to read and understand. On a personal note it is hoped that the reader will find this text useful in understanding this area of the law. The reader who wishes to practice in this area of the law is encouraged to not only read the publications from the ABA referenced in this book but also to take time to attend continuing education programs in the reader's own state in order to become well versed in the state-specific application of many of these laws.

CHAPTER 1

Client Interview and Ethical Considerations

   I. Interviewing the Client.. 1
  II. Basic Drafting 2
 III. Limited Capacity Considerations 3
  IV. Living Arrangements.. 4
   V. Paying for Housing 5
  VI. Ethical Considerations....................................... 5
        A. Maintaining Confidentiality............................ 5
        B. Multiple Representation................................ 7
        C. Estate Planning Conflicts 8
        D. Accepting Payment of Fees from Non-Client............. 8
        E. Setting Fees.. 9
        F. Competency of Elder Client 9
Appendix A: Family Questionnaire 11
Appendix B: Asset Questionnaire.................................. 16
Appendix C: Engagement Letter for Individual 21
Appendix D: Engagement Letter for Couple 23

I. Interviewing the Client

The client interview is the pivotal part of planning for your elder client. This text is written from the perspective that everything flows from that client meeting. It is not merely a data-collecting meeting. Rather, it is the beginning of a meaningful working relationship with your client, and an opportunity for you to demonstrate your technical expertise and your concern for your client's situation. Efficiency should not be the focus of this meeting. The client meeting is a time to solidify your working relationship with your client. It may be a springboard for future work with this client, or for future referrals to you made by this client because of the client's appreciation of your concern and expertise. Obviously, it is also the meeting in which you gather the important information you need to begin developing the estate plan for your elder client. It is also a time to be aware of any ethical issues that may need to be addressed in the meeting. A helpful ABA publication in this regard is Carolyn L. Rosenblatt, *Working with Aging Clients.*

This chapter focuses on five issues. The first issue concerns basic drafting for the elder client. The second issue covers limited capacity considerations that arise due to diminished capacity of your client, your client's children, and oftentimes your client's parents. Third, a common issue, is living arrangements. Where will the client, the client's disabled child, or the client's elderly parent live? Everyone wants to live at home, but the question becomes how can that be handled with safety, and if that is no longer possible, what are the possible housing options? The fourth issue is how to pay for housing. For example, how will housing costs be paid if your client can no longer take care of his or her needs without assistance? Finally, are there ethical issues to address?

II. Basic Drafting

In the initial interview there is some basic information that is always needed no matter what the client's unique situation is. The lawyer will find it helpful to have a good questionnaire to use to assist in data collection. See, for example, Appendix A, a family questionnaire, and Appendix B, an asset questionnaire. By addressing the issues raised in these two questionnaires, the lawyer should have good data with which to begin the planning process. Obviously, these questions and data can be supplemented as the lawyer deems appropriate. Sensitive matters, such as legal costs and ethical issues, should be addressed during the initial interview. Ethical issues are discussed later in the chapter (see Section VI). Appendix C is a sample engagement letter that deals with the ethical issues of dual representation for a single client, and Appendix D is an engagement letter for a married couple. The ABA, through its Commission on Law and Aging, offers an excellent brochure entitled *Understanding the Four C's of Elder Law Ethics.* Lawyers may find this a convenient brochure to give to clients to help them understand the ethical dilemmas lawyers face when other family members want to sit in on or participate in meetings with elder clients.

Most lawyers are familiar with the basics of estate planning. Typically, the client will need several legal documents. First, a durable power of attorney is almost always needed (see Chapter 2, Section XII, for more information and a sample form). Second, advanced directives are almost always needed (see discussion on these documents in Chapter 2, Section VII; forms are provided in Sections VII.B, VIII, and IX). Be sure to notice the ABA resources that are cited in the overview of Chapter 2, as they will aid you in your practice. Third, of course, is the client's will. A simple will form is provided in Chapter 2, Section XIV.

If more sophisticated will and trust instruments are needed, the author's ABA publication *Estate Planning Forms* will be helpful.

You may find it helpful to provide your client with a checklist of items they need to have readily available for their family at the time of estate settlement or in the case of diminishing capacity or declining health. The ABA has three excellent books by Susan Balch Hurme that include invaluable checklists for lawyers and for their clients: *Checklist for My Family: A Guide to My History, Financial Plans, and Final Wishes*; *Checklist for Family Caregivers: A Guide to Making It Manageable*; and *Checklist for Family Survivors: A Guide to Practical and Legal Matters When Someone Dies.*

III. Limited Capacity Considerations

Diminishing or limited capacity is almost always one of the issues you must deal with. You will find the ABA publication by Kerry Peck and Rick L. Law, *Don't Let Dementia Steal Everything*, helpful. In some cases, a client may be in the best of health but concerned about those issues in the long term. In that situation little is needed other than those documents that are part of basic drafting—powers of attorney and health care directives. In some situations, the client has an adult disabled child who may be receiving social security disability insurance benefits, or SSI benefits. The adult child will also be receiving Medicare in most situations and in other situations may also be receiving Medicaid to cover health care expenses. If the client's child is receiving SSI and Medicaid benefits then any inheritance will result in disqualification from those benefits, thus those clients will be either electing to disinherit that child, trusting that the other estate beneficiaries will provide any supplemental needs the child has, or, more commonly, their will or trust will involve a third party special needs trust. The terms *special needs trust* and *supplemental care trust* are often used interchangeably. For purposes of this writing we will use the term *special needs trust*. A third party special needs trust is one in which the source of the money is not the adult disabled child but rather the parents. Drafting of this type of trust is discussed in Chapter 7, Section X, and sample forms are provided in Chapter 7, Appendix A, and Appendix B. Appendix A is a will providing a testamentary trust and Appendix B is simply an inter vivos trust. Either is sufficient, depending on the client's needs and preferences.

In other situations, the child may have received an inheritance or in some situations a personal injury award. To avoid loss of the SSI and Medicaid benefits in these situations, a special needs trust is also needed; however, in this case it is more correctly termed a *first party special needs trust*. In other words the source of the funds is the adult disabled child (the first party) and not a third party. Special drafting is required for this type of trust. See Chapter 7, Section X, for a discussion on first party special needs trusts and Chapter 7, Appendix C for a sample form.

In some situations, the client in his or her elder years is concerned that the client's long-term housing needs may include living in a nursing home or other long-term care facility. The cost of these facilities for most middle-income Americans who do not have long-term care insurance is devastating. The client's life savings will often be consumed over a period of several years, leaving the client a pauper at death with nothing for their children or other loved ones to inherit, other than, hopefully, a lifetime of good memories. There are no simple solutions to this problem.

Some clients find that an income only trust is a preferred solution. This type of trust is referred to by different names, for example, Medicaid compliant trust, Medicaid asset protection trust, and so on. This type of trust is discussed in Chapter 7, Section X.B, and a form is provided in Chapter 7, Appendix E. This type of trust requires the client to transfer all property the client wants to preserve to a trust in which the client receives only the income. No principal may be expended. Other variations of this trust have the client not even receiving income, but rather the income is distributed to the children.

Either approach requires an irrevocable trust to be established, the assets that are to be protected transferred to the trust, and the five-year look-back period being satisfied. After the five-year look-back period has expired then the assets in the trust are not considered resources for purposes of Medicaid eligibility. Only the income payable to the client is considered a resource, if the trust is drafted to permit the client to receive the income. Many clients who own real estate find this option a solution to their desire to maintain some assets for their children to inherit. Be certain of your state Medicaid regulations for this and any of these trusts.

IV. Living Arrangements

The client will often raise the issue of living arrangements, but, if not, the lawyer may choose to raise this issue. All clients want to believe they will continue to live in their homes throughout their lifetimes. No client wants to think about, talk about, or plan toward times of diminished capacity or limited physical ability. Other than the wealthy, your older clients should consider this issue. Unfortunately, most clients delay dealing with this issue until they are at the crisis stage of declining health and needing to move to a long-term care facility. Options are limited at that time. The lawyer should, when possible, talk to the client about living arrangements while the client is in good health. In addition to this book, two excellent ABA publications deal with housing (and all other issues of elder law): Lawrence A. Frolik, *Elder Law and Later Life Legal Planning*, and *The Law of Later Life Health Care Decision Making*, second edition.

Client meetings concerning housing are difficult. The costs of home care and nursing home care are high. There are options. Possibly, the client can continue to live in his home with supervision from one or more of the children. In this case, you may want to remind the client's children of the need to be sure the home is safe for an elderly parent. Helpful checklists are in the earlier mentioned ABA publication *Checklist for Family Caregivers*. Other times, the solution is hiring caregivers to provide help during part of the day with the adult children helping during the remainder of the day. If the client is looking to employ caregivers, the checklists in the ABA publication *Checklist for Family Caregivers* will be helpful. If the lawyer knows of third party vendors who provide caregiver services, or knows of other individual caregivers in the community, providing that information to your client will be extremely helpful to them. Finally, if the only option is a long-term care facility, then the checklist in the ABA publication *Checklist for Family Caregivers* may be helpful to your client in considering which facility to use. Also, the aforementioned ABA publication *Working with Aging Clients* is helpful.

V. Paying for Housing

If your client is addressing housing issues for themselves and they are still in good health there are more options. The client may recognize that they have adequate financial resources. Otherwise, you need to acquaint your client with long-term care insurance. These policies are more broadly written than they were years ago. Most policies now include benefits in the event of an elderly client living in their home and are not restricted to nursing home care. See the ABA publication *Checklist for Family Caregivers* for a checklist that may prove helpful when shopping for long-term care insurance. For clients of limited financial means there may be VA benefits if the client is a war veteran or the spouse of a wartime veteran. Those qualifications are discussed in Chapter 4. Ideally, clients can pay privately or live at home with the help of family members or other caregivers. Some will be able to pay for their care with additional income from VA and Social Security benefits, or they may be able to supplement their financial needs with long-term care insurance. Otherwise, the only option is to spend one's assets until they qualify for Medicaid. The Medicaid eligibility rules are discussed in Chapter 7, Section II. Spend down options are discussed in Chapter 7, Section IX.A.

VI. Ethical Considerations

Attorneys representing elder clients often face ethical issues in determining competence, in properly representing the impaired or incapacitated client, and in determining who is actually the client. One of the first questions the attorney must ask is "who do I represent?" Is it the elderly person, is it the family member, or is it both? An excellent ABA resource is Roberta K. Flowers and Rebecca C. Morgan, *Ethics in Practice of Elder Law.*

The attorney must clearly understand who is represented, and must communicate that relationship to the other parties involved. If you represent the older family member, you must advise the other family members of your obligation of undivided loyalty to your client and the requirement of the confidentiality of lawyer-client communications. The professional judgment of a lawyer should be exercised, within the bounds of the law, solely for the benefit of the client and free of compromising influences and loyalties.

In this section we will look at the ABA Model Rules of Professional Conduct, focusing on Rule 1.5: Fees; Rule 1.6: Confidentiality of Information; Rule 1.7: Conflict of Interest: Current Clients; Rule 1.8: Conflict of Interest: Current Clients: Special Rules; and Rule 1.14: Client with Diminished Capacity.

A. Maintaining Confidentiality

A fundamental principle in the attorney-client relationship is the attorney's duty to maintain the confidentiality of information relating to the representation. The client is thereby encouraged to communicate fully and frankly with the attorney even as to embarrassing or legally damaging subject matter. And it is important to remember the duty of confidentiality continues after the attorney-client relationship has terminated. The American Bar Association Model Rules for Professional Conduct, Rule 1.6, provides guidance as it states:

> (a) A lawyer shall not reveal information relating to representation of a client unless the client gives informed consent, the disclosure is impliedly authorized in order to carry out the representation or the disclosure is permitted by paragraph (b).
>
> (b) A lawyer may reveal information relating to the representation of a client to the extent the lawyer reasonably believes necessary:
>
> (1) to prevent reasonably certain death or substantial bodily harm;
>
> (2) to prevent the client from committing a crime or fraud that is reasonably certain to result in substantial injury to the financial interests or property of another and in furtherance of which the client has used or is using the lawyer's services;
>
> (3) to prevent, mitigate or rectify substantial injury to the financial interests or property of another that is reasonably certain to result or has resulted from the client's commission of a crime or fraud in furtherance of which the client has used the lawyer's services;
>
> (4) to secure legal advice about the lawyer's compliance with these Rules;
>
> (5) to establish a claim or defense on behalf of the lawyer in a controversy between the lawyer and the client, to establish a defense to a criminal charge or civil claim against the lawyer based upon conduct in which the client was involved, or to respond to allegations in any proceeding concerning the lawyer's representation of the client;
>
> (6) to comply with other law or a court order; or
>
> (7) to detect and resolve conflicts of interest arising from the lawyer's change of employment or from changes in the composition or ownership of a firm, but only if the revealed information would not compromise the attorney-client privilege or otherwise prejudice the client.
>
> (c) A lawyer shall make reasonable efforts to prevent the inadvertent or unauthorized disclosure of, or unauthorized access to, information relating to the representation of a client.

The attorney must be careful if family members want to be present when the attorney is counseling the elder client. The question of undue influence can arise whenever the elder client has another person present at the interview. But you should also not automatically exclude everyone except the elder client from the interview. Consider the reasons why the elder client wants another person present. There may be legitimate reasons, for example, the client wants someone there for moral support; but at the other extreme it may be because the client is a victim of undue influence. How do you know? The burden on the attorney is significant though seldom appreciated by the client or the client's family. The confidentiality rule applies not merely to matters communicated in confidence by the client but also to all information relating to the representation, whatever its source.

An additional concern is the presence of a third party at the client meeting. The general rule is that by allowing a third party to be present the client has waived the privilege. There are exceptions, as when the third parties' presence is highly useful to the client and the client intends the communication to remain secret. Obviously, be careful and know your state's ethics ruling on this issue. You will find the ABA booklet *Why Am I Left in the Waiting Room? Understanding the Four C's of Elder Law Ethics* a convenient tool to give to the family members of your elder clients to enable them to better understand your ethical concerns.

B. Multiple Representation

Multiple representations are easy to fall into. The appointment is made by the adult child for the elderly parent to discuss wills, powers of attorney, and advance directives. The child drives the parent to the appointment and comes in to meet with the parent and attorney. The child may do most of the talking and is the one who writes the check to pay the legal fee. You may have done legal work for both the parent and the child in the past. They consider you the family's attorney. Who is your client? Oftentimes there is no problem, but what do you do when the child appears to pressure the parent into naming her as personal representative and power of attorney? This may appear to be the best decision, but it won't look so clear if at a later date another child contacts you complaining of possible improprieties by the child who now has power of attorney under the document you prepared and your secretary notarized. It is even worse if the child makes you aware of the parent's declining mental condition and you only spent 30 minutes interviewing the client because it was a boilerplate simple will, advanced directive, and power of attorney.

The watchword is be cautious. And make the ethical problems known at the beginning of the representation. Keep in mind the Rules of Professional Conduct, Rule 1.7, which states:

> (a) Except as provided in paragraph (b), a lawyer shall not represent a client if the representation involves a concurrent conflict of interest. A concurrent conflict of interest exists if:
>
> (1) the representation of one client will be directly adverse to another client; or
>
> (2) there is a significant risk that the representation of one or more clients will be materially limited by the lawyer's responsibilities to another client, a former client or a third person or by a personal interest of the lawyer.
>
> (b) Notwithstanding the existence of a concurrent conflict of interest under paragraph (a), a lawyer may represent a client if:
>
> (1) the lawyer reasonably believes that the lawyer will be able to provide competent and diligent representation to each affected client;
>
> (2) the representation is not prohibited by law;
>
> (3) the representation does not involve the assertion of a claim by one client against another client represented by the lawyer in the same litigation or other proceeding before a tribunal; and
>
> (4) each affected client gives informed consent, confirmed in writing.

When representation of multiple clients is undertaken, the consultation should include explanation of the implications of the common representation and the advantages and risks involved. The client engagement letter provided in Appendix D should be used any time there is multiple representation. The form is designed for husband and wife, which is the most common type of multiple representation. You should avoid a multiple representation that involves an elder client and one or more of his children. If multiple representation is required, then modify the engagement letter in Appendix D as is appropriate.

C. Estate Planning Conflicts

Conflict questions may also arise in estate planning and estate administration. An attorney may be called on to prepare wills for several family members, such as a husband and wife, and in some situations, a conflict of interest may arise. In estate administration, the identity of the client may be unclear under the law of a particular jurisdiction. Under one view, the client is the fiduciary (executor); under another view the client is the estate or trust, including its beneficiaries. The attorney must make clear the relationship to the parties involved.[1] Consider this possible problem.

An attorney in estate practice represents an older couple for whom she prepares "mirror wills" in which each leaves the estate to the other. Several days after the wills are executed, the husband alone visits the attorney, asks the attorney to prepare a new will leaving the bulk of his estate to the children of his prior marriage, and instructs the attorney to keep the visit confidential from his wife. How should the attorney respond? May she draft the new will? May she—indeed, must she—disclose the circumstances of the visit to the wife?

Taking a practical approach, the attorney's dilemma in this example was largely of the attorney's making. By appropriately counseling the clients at the outset of the representation, in a manner consistent with the Model Rules, the prudent estate attorney would ordinarily avoid having to act in a manner that one client or the other might reasonably regard as an act of betrayal. Thus, the attorney when asked to represent multiple family members should explain the possibility that a conflict of interest may arise. The more you put in writing the better.

The prospective clients should be told at the initial client conference that in a joint representation one client's disclosures will not be kept confidential from the other client if those revelations are relevant to another client's interest. In the context of estate planning for a married couple, the spouses should be told that there can be no secrets as to issues about the estate planning representation. Unless the family members agree in advance that confidences will be handled in this manner, they must seek separate attorneys. Having achieved an understanding of how confidences will be handled, the attorney can then act in accordance with that understanding without reasonably being accused of violating the duty of loyalty or confidentiality. For example, the husband who intended to alter his will without his wife's knowledge will be on notice that if he seeks the assistance of the estate attorney who had prepared the couple's "mirror wills," that attorney will be obligated to withdraw. The sample engagement letter will be helpful.

D. Accepting Payment of Fees from Non-Client

What ethical problems can the attorney face when another family member and not the client pays for the legal services given to the elderly client? The Model Rules of Professional Conduct, Rule 1.8(f), addresses this issue.

(f) A lawyer shall not accept compensation for representing a client from one other than the client unless:

(1) the client gives informed consent;

(2) there is no interference with the lawyer's independence of professional judgement or with the client-lawyer relationship; and

(3) information relating to representation of a client is protected as required by Rule 1.6.

If your services are being paid for by other family members, you must obtain consent for this arrangement from the elder family member who is the client. The mere fact the attorney is actually paid by a third party does not affect that relationship, so long as the client gives consent and the attorney is directly responsible to the client. On the other hand, if you choose to represent the other younger family members and not the elderly family member, be careful. You must explain your role to the older family member so that they know you are not their lawyer. You should avoid offering any advice to the older family member other than to obtain his or her own counsel.[2]

E. Setting Fees

Attorneys should keep detailed itemized statements of all charges for an elderly client. An attorney's fee must be reasonable. Rule 1.5 provides that factors to be considered in determining the reasonableness of a fee include the following:

(a) A lawyer shall not make an arrangement for, charge, or collect an unreasonable fee or an unreasonable amount for expenses. The factors to be considered in determining the reasonableness of a fee include the following:

(1) the time and labor required, the novelty and difficulty of the questions involved and the skill requisite to perform the legal service properly;

(2) the likelihood, if apparent to the client, that the acceptance of the particular employment will preclude other employment by the lawyer;

(3) the fee customarily charged in the locality for similar legal services;

(4) the amount involved and the results obtained;

(5) the time limitations imposed by the client or by the circumstances;

(6) the nature and length of the professional relationship with the client;

(7) the experience, reputation, and ability of the lawyer or lawyers performing the services; and

(8) whether the fee is fixed or contingent.

Determining a proper fee requires consideration of the interests of both client and attorney. An attorney should not charge more than a reasonable fee, because excessive costs of legal service will deter individuals from using the legal system in protection of their rights. Furthermore, an excessive charge abuses the professional relationship between attorney and client. On the other hand, adequate compensation is necessary in order to enable the attorney to serve his client effectively and to preserve the integrity and independence of the profession. Be wise. Don't be greedy.

F. Competency of Elder Client

Competent adults have the right to make decisions, whether or not the decision is the same as the one the attorney would make; and protecting the client's autonomy in making a decision is crucial in the attorney-client relationship. Attorneys should give thought to whether elderly clients have the mental capacity to make major legal decisions concerning their lives. If there is doubt, the attorney should be guided by the ABA Model Rules of Professional Conduct, Rule 1.14, and its comments and then take any reasonable steps needed to protect the client's interest. The attorney may find ABA resources to be helpful. One is a book entitled *Assessment of Older Adults with Diminished Capacity: A Handbook for Lawyers* and the other is *Practical Tools for Lawyers: Steps in Supporting Decision Making*. Both are excellent resources that are useful in dealing with clients with cognitive problems.

Today many of our elderly are facing the terrible disease of dementia. Dementia refers to degenerative diseases that result in the progressive deterioration of intellectual and emotional functions. This disease can destroy a person's mind and leave a person helpless. For more about dementia, you may want to read the earlier mentioned ABA publication *Don't Let Dementia Steal Everything*.

Appendix A: Family Questionnaire

1. Client Facts

a. Full Name	
b. Name Commonly Used	
c. Social Security No.	
d. Home Address	
e. Primary Telephone	
f. Secondary (Cell) Telephone	
g. E-mail Address	
h. Occupation	
i. Work address	
j. Birth date	
k. Birthplace	
l. Period of residence [state]	

2. Additional Information (Spouse)

    a. Do you have any physical or mental health conditions? Yes / No
        If yes, please explain: _____
        _____
        _____

    b. In what state do you vote, have your driver's license, car registered, own real estate, and file state income taxes?
        _____

    c. Have you ever lived in a community property state (AZ, CA, ID, LA, NV, NM, TX, WA, WI)?   Yes / No
        If yes, please list: _____

    d. Do you have a prenuptial or postnuptial agreement?   Yes / No
        If so, please provide a copy of that agreement with this questionnaire.

    e. Do you have a divorce decree affecting any of your property rights or imposing a current legal obligation to support a former spouse or child?   Yes / No
        If so, please provide a copy of that divorce decree, property settlement agreement, and any related court documents.

    f. Are you a U.S. citizen?   Yes / No
        If not, in what country are you a citizen?
        _____

3.   Children and Grandchildren

Is there a physical possibility of your having more children?   Yes / No
Please list all children, noting any who are illegitimate or non-U.S. citizens.

_____

_____

_____

If a child is not of your present marriage, please note the name of the other parent (your prior spouse/partner).

_____

_____

Child #1 Facts	Deceased? Yes / No Adopted? Yes / No Handicapped / Poor Health? Yes / No
Full Name	
Date of Birth	
Address	
Spouse's Name	
Child's Children	Name: _____ Date of Birth: _____
	Name: _____ Date of Birth: _____
	Name: _____ Date of Birth: _____
	Physical possibility of further children? Yes / No

Child #2 Facts	Deceased? Yes / No Adopted? Yes / No Handicapped / Poor Health? Yes / No
Full Name	
Date of Birth	
Address	
Spouse's Name	
Child's Children	Name: _____ Date of Birth: _____
	Name: _____ Date of Birth: _____
	Name: _____ Date of Birth: _____
	Physical possibility of further children? Yes / No

Child #3 Facts	Deceased?	Yes / No
	Adopted?	Yes / No
	Handicapped / Poor Health	Yes / No
Full Name		
Date of Birth		
Address		
Spouse's Name		
Child's Children	Name: _____ Date of Birth: _____	
	Name: _____ Date of Birth: _____	
	Name: _____ Date of Birth: _____	
	Physical possibility of further children? Yes / No	

Child #4 Facts	Deceased?	Yes / No
	Adopted?	Yes / No
	Handicapped / Poor Health?	Yes / No
Full Name		
Date of Birth		
Address		
Spouse's Name		
Child's Children	Name: _____ Date of Birth: _____	
	Name: _____ Date of Birth: _____	
	Name: _____ Date of Birth: _____	
	Physical possibility of further children? Yes / No	

4. Parents	Father	Mother
Client's Parents		
Name		
Address		
Age		
State of Health		
Financially Dependent?		
Expected Inheritance from Parent?		
Spouse's/Partner's Parents		
Name		
Address		
Age		
State of Health		
Financially Dependent?		
Expected Inheritance from Parent?		

5. Advisors	
a. Accountant	
b. Stockbroker	
c. Financial Advisor	
d. Insurance Underwriter	
e. Banker	
f. Other	
g. Other	

6. Additional Information

   a. Did you bring your existing estate planning documents? If not, please provide copies or originals for my review.

   b. Have you or your spouse/partner made any gifts to any other person that require the filing of a federal gift tax return? If so, please provide a copy of all gift tax returns.

   c. Are you or your spouse/partner beneficiaries under any trust agreements? If so, please provide a copy of those documents.

   d. Are you or your spouse/partner the holders of a power of appointment under any legal document? If so, please provide a copy of that document.

e. Do you or your spouse/partner anticipate receiving an inheritance or a large gift in the future? If so, in what amount, and please explain the details.

_____

_____

_____

f. Do you or your spouse/partner own any property in a foreign country? If so, please give full details.

_____

_____

_____

g. Are you or your spouse/partner subject to any existing or anticipated litigation; or are you in any business arrangements or occupations in which such liabilities are a possibility? If so, please explain.

_____

_____

_____

h. Do you or your spouse/partner have any relatives who are dependent on your for support? If so, please explain.

_____

_____

_____

i. Are you going to be disinheriting any family members? If so, please explain who and the reason for the disinheritance.

_____

_____

_____

j. Do any of your children or grandchildren, or other family members who are inheriting from you, have special needs either due to being of young age, mental or physical health problems, substance abuse, marital problems, or other factors that should be taken into account in determining how such person should inherit? If so, please explain.

_____

_____

_____

Appendix B: Asset Questionnaire

(If more space is needed for any section, continue at number 12.)

1. Cash Equivalents

Do you have any checking accounts and/or any other bank accounts or certificates of deposit?

	Name of Institution, Address, Account Number	Title in Whose Name	Approximate Balance
Checking Accounts	1.		
	2.		
	3.		
	4.		
Certificates of Deposit, Savings Accounts	1.		
	2.		
	3.		
	4.		
		TOTAL:	$
Safe Deposit Box no.			
Location			

2. Stocks

Do you own any stocks?

Number of Shares	Company	Title in Whose Name	Current Market Value
		TOTAL	$

3. Bonds

Do you own any bonds?

Maturity Value	Description	Title in Whose Name	Current Market Value
		TOTAL:	$

4. Mutual Funds

Do you own any mutual funds?

Number of Units	Company	Title in Whose Name	Current Market Value
		TOTAL:	$

5. Real Estate (please bring deeds)

Do you own a home or any other real estate? Indicate which is your residence.

Description and Location	Title in Whose Name	Current Market Value	Mortgage Amount
	TOTAL:	$	$

6.   Business

Do you own an interest in any business?

Description of Business	Percentage of Ownership	Name of Co-owners	Market Value
		TOTAL:	$

Is there an existing buy-sell agreement? If so, please provide a copy of that agreement.

7.   Retirement Benefits

Do you have any IRAs, 401Ks, or other retirement benefits?

Description	Beneficiary	Approximate Value
	TOTAL:	$

8.   Life Insurance

Do you have any life insurance policies and/or annuities?

Insurance Company	Policy Owner	Insured	First Beneficiary	Second Beneficiary	Death Benefit

9.   Other: Trusts, Anticipated Inheritance, Etc.

_____

_____

_____

10. Personal Property

Do you own any other titled property such as a car, boat, etc.?

Description	Title in Whose Name	Approximate Value	Amount of Lien
	TOTAL:	$	$

Do you own any other personal property that is not titled?

Description	Title in Whose Name	Approximate Value
Home Furnishings		
Jewelry		
Collections		
Other		
Other		
	TOTAL:	$

11. Liabilities

Description	Lender/Debtor	Approximate Value
Home Mortgage		
Other Mortgages		
Other Debts		

12. Continuation of Assets

Type of Asset	Description of Asset	Title in Whose Name	Current Market Value

Appendix C: Engagement Letter for Individual

Dear _____:

I am pleased that you have asked me and [name of firm] to assist you in developing your estate plan. This letter confirms my discussion with you regarding your employment of our firm and describes the basis upon which we will provide legal services to you. Accordingly, I submit for your approval the following provisions governing our employment. If you are in agreement, please sign a copy of this letter in the space provided below.

Scope of Representation. You have asked me to represent you with regard to the planning, preparation, and implementation of appropriate estate planning documents (such as wills, health care power of attorney, durable power of attorney, and revocable trust agreements). You may limit or expand the scope of my representation from time to time, provided that any substantial expansion must be agreed to by me. While our firm would be interested in assisting you in other matters, unless our firm is specifically engaged for some other future matter this letter shall confirm that our representation of you is limited to the foregoing matters and shall end when they are concluded.

Fees. Our fees are based primarily upon the time expended by our attorneys and paralegals on the engagement. Attorneys and paralegals have been assigned hourly rates based upon their experience and level of expertise. The present rates of those attorneys and paralegals likely to work on these matters range from $_____in the case of the paralegal who will work on this matter, $_____in the case of the associate who will work on this matter, and $_____ in my case. Our hourly rates are reviewed periodically and may be increased from time to time, but will remain at these rates during this representation. We do not consider any billing for our services final until you are satisfied as to both the quality of our services and the amount charged. If you have any questions about a billing, please contact me directly.

Potential Conflicts. Our firm represents other businesses and individuals. This can create situations where work for one client on a matter may preclude us from assisting other clients on unrelated matters. It is at least possible that during the time that we are representing you some of our present or future clients may have disputes or transactions with you. In order to avoid the potential problems that this kind of restriction could have for our practice, we ask you to agree that we may continue to represent (or may undertake in the future to represent) existing or new clients in any matter that is not substantially related to matters in which we have represented you, even if the interests of such clients in those other matters might be adverse to yours. We do not intend, however, for you to waive your right to have our firm maintain confidences or secrets that you transmit to our firm, and we agree not to disclose them to any third party without your consent. We will, of course, take appropriate steps to insure that such information is kept confidential.

Additional Standard Terms. Our engagement is subject to the policies included in the enclosed memorandum.

Privacy Policy. Enclosed is a copy of the firm's privacy policy. Please let us know if you have any questions about it.

If these terms of our engagement are acceptable to you, please sign a copy of this letter for my records. You may keep the original letter for your records.

Sincerely,
[name of firm]

_____
[name of attorney]
_____

The foregoing is understood and accepted:

_____

Date: _____

Appendix D: Engagement Letter for Couple

Dear _____,

I am pleased that you have asked me and [name of firm], to assist you in developing your estate plan. This letter confirms my discussion with you regarding your employment of our firm and describes the basis upon which we will provide legal services to you. Accordingly, I submit for your approval the following provisions governing our employment. If you are in agreement, please sign a copy of this letter in the space provided below.

<u>Scope of Representation.</u> You have asked me to represent you with regard to the planning, preparation, execution and implementation of appropriate estate planning documents (such as wills, health care power of attorney, power of attorney, and revocable trust agreements) for each of you concerning the management of your assets during your joint lives and the life of the survivor and the disposition of those assets to beneficiaries in connection with various contractual rights, such as life insurance policies and retirement plan accounts. You may limit or expand the scope of my representation from time to time, provided that any substantial expansion must be agreed to by me. While our firm would be interested in assisting you in other matters, unless we are specifically engaged for some other future matter this letter will confirm that our representation of you is limited to the foregoing matters and will end when they are concluded.

<u>Joint Representation.</u> Under the ethical rules that govern attorneys, I may represent both of you jointly so long as you are in agreement about your estate plan. It is normally quite beneficial for one attorney to represent both a husband and wife in the estate planning process, and my goal in doing so will be to help you implement a mutually agreeable plan for both the present and future. However, in the course of the estate planning process a husband and wife sometimes develop differences in their choices of beneficiaries, appointments of trustees, executors and representatives and in their overall interests and desires. Occasionally, couples initially agree on a plan and then later change their minds and go in different directions. Consequently, please understand that if I undertake to represent both of you jointly, I cannot take sides or favor one of you over the other, either now or in the future.

During the planning process, I will obtain confidential information from each of you, whether in conference with both of you together or with one of you alone. If I undertake to represent you jointly, please understand that I cannot withhold any such information from either of you even if one of you asks me to do so. The alternative is for me to represent only one of you separately without open sharing of information. The other one of you would then have to either engage separate counsel or choose not to be represented at all. Such separate representation is usually not practical and having one party unrepresented is usually not desirable. If during the course of my joint representation of you a conflict should develop that in my opinion would keep me from adequately representing both of you or if either of you asks me to take sides against the other, I will have no choice but to withdraw from further joint representation of the two of you and advise each of you to obtain separate counsel. By your signing this letter you are assuring me that you are comfortable with my representing both of you jointly.

Fees. Our fees are based primarily upon the time expended by our attorneys and paralegals on the engagement. Attorneys and paralegals have been assigned hourly rates based upon their experience and level of expertise. The present rates of those attorneys and paralegals likely to work on these matters range from $_____ in the case of the paralegal who will work on this matter, $_____ in the case of the associate who will work on this matter, and $_____ in my case. Our hourly rates are reviewed periodically and may be increased from time to time, but will remain at these rates during this representation. We do not consider any billing for our services final until you are satisfied as to both the quality of our services and the amount charged. If you have any questions about a billing, please contact me directly.

Potential Conflicts. Our firm represents other businesses and individuals. This can create situations where work for one client on a matter may preclude us from assisting other clients on unrelated matters. It is at least possible that during the time that we are representing you some of our present or future clients may have disputes or transactions with you. In order to avoid the potential problems that this kind of restriction could have for our practice, we ask you to agree that we may continue to represent (or may undertake in the future to represent) existing or new clients in any matter that is not substantially related to matters in which we have represented you, even if the interests of such clients in those other matters might be adverse to yours. We do not intend, however, for you to waive your right to have our firm maintain confidences or secrets that you transmit to our firm, and we agree not to disclose them to any third party without your consent. We will, of course, take appropriate steps to insure that such information is kept confidential.

Additional Standard Terms. Our engagement is also subject to the policies included in the enclosed memorandum.

Privacy Policy. Enclosed is a copy of the firm's privacy policy. Please let us know if you have any questions about it.

If these terms of our engagement are acceptable to you, please sign a copy of this letter for my records. You may keep the original letter for your records.

If you have any questions regarding any of the matters discussed in this letter, please feel free to give me a call.

Sincerely,
[name of firm]

_____
[name of attorney]

_____

The foregoing is understood and accepted:
_____

Date: _____

Notes

1. Model Rules of Prof'l Conduct R. 1.7 cmt. [29–33].
2. *Id*. at [13].

CHAPTER 2

Health Care and Financial Decision Making

     I. Overview 27
    II. Right to Be Informed 28
   III. Unwanted Medical Treatment 28
    IV. Patients' Rights 29
     V. Case Law on Withholding Medical Treatment 30
    VI. Factors That Courts Consider in Determining
         Life-Sustaining Treatment 31
   VII. Advance Directives 31
         A. Durable Health Care Power of Attorney 32
         B. Durable Health Care Power of Attorney Form 34
         C. Appointment of an Agent 39
         D. Revocation of Durable Health Care Power of Attorney 39
         E. Second State Residency 39
  VIII. Living Will 40
         A. Revocation of Living Will 41
    IX. Do Not Resuscitate (DNR) 41
     X. Guardianship and Conservatorships 44
    XI. Joint Ownership of Assets 46
   XII. Durable Power of Attorney 47
  XIII. Living Trust 53
   XIV. Simple Will 59

I. Overview

Advances in medical technology, especially in the control of acute life-threatening illness coupled with changing societal attitudes about a person's right to know and chose or refuse medical treatment places a new responsibility on the lawyer. An essential part of any estate plan is ensuring that health care decisions can be made if the client reaches a time of poor health in which the client is not able to make those decisions. The chapter first reviews the client's right to informed consent when receiving medical treatment, including the right to refuse treatment. Then the text considers substituted decision making once a client is unable to make those medical decisions. This involves the discussion of the durable health care power of attorney, living will, and do not resuscitate orders in Sections VII through IX, respectively. Sample documents are found in Sections VII.B, VIII, and IX. Next is a brief discussion of guardianships. As guardianships are specific to state law, attorneys will need to refer to their own state laws. The chapter concludes with a discussion of common ways of handling financial matters, including joint accounts, the durable power of attorney, and living trusts.

There are several excellent ABA resources. Lawrence A. Frolik, *The Law of Later-Life Health Care and Decision Making*, second edition, provides a comprehensive description of the manner in which the law regulates and reacts to health care and personal decision making for the elderly. Also of interest is *The Tool Kit for Health Care Advance Planning* (ABA 2005) and *ABA Advance Directive Counseling Guide for Lawyers*.

II. Right to Be Informed

Although it may be surprising to some, it was not that long ago that the right of the patient to be informed of medical treatment options was rather restricted. There was a common view of the "all-knowing doctor" who knows best what treatment a patient should receive. Those attitudes no longer prevail. Today it is clear that a patient has the right to be informed in order to make proper consent of the medical treatment he will receive. Generally, the right to be informed includes the physician informing the patient of the diagnosis and informing the patient of the treatment options. In considering treatment options the physician should make the patient aware of the risks associated with the treatment option and the probable short-term and long-term results of that treatment option. The physician should also explain the probable results if that treatment option is not pursued. Ideally, the physician will also explain to the patient any alternative treatments, including the risks of those treatments and the probable short-term and long-term results of those alternative treatment options. An interesting question—the answer to which depends on the state in which the lawyer practices—is whether the standard of informed consent is based on that of a reasonable physician, or that of a reasonable patient. Of course, even if the standard of informed consent is not met, there are no legal issues of any significant consequence if the failure to adequately inform does not result in injury to the patient. Delving more deeply into this issue is not the focus of this writing, as that involves the more complicated area of malpractice liability. Let's move now to the right of the patient to refuse life-prolonging treatment.

III. Unwanted Medical Treatment

Only a few decades ago, a competent individual had a limited right to refuse treatment. The belief was that refusal of treatment was tantamount to suicide. Many of the elderly do not want to have life-prolonging treatment. This is because of the many cases where an individual's life has been prolonged, but with no quality of life. People demanded the right to refuse "unwanted treatment." In response, the law has drastically changed regarding unwanted life-prolonging technology. The current belief is that the person who refuses life-prolonging treatment has died from the underlying disease and not as a result of suicide.

Today, a person's right to refuse treatment is constitutionally protected. In 1990, the U.S. Supreme Court, in the famous Cruzan case ruled that a competent individual's "liberty interest" to refuse unwanted treatment was protected by the Fourteenth Amendment under the due process clause.[1] Some states have also protected this right under state constitutional rights of privacy. Additionally, all states have since enacted laws clarifying this right. The lawyer should be familiar with her own state laws.

IV. Patients' Rights

The federal government following the Cruzan decision adopted the "Patients' Rights" Condition of Participation (CoP) which furnishes notice to each patient or the patient's representative that the patient has a right to discontinue care. The Patients' Rights CoP is amended from time to time and can be found at 42 C.F.R. § 482.12. In order to continue Medicare and Medicaid programs, all hospitals, including psychiatric, rehabilitation, long-term, children's, hospitals must satisfy the CoP. Generally, hospitals must meet the following requirements:

1. Notice of patient's rights must be given before caring for a patient.
2. The patient is allowed to participate in the development and implementation of his plan of care.
3. The patient's personal safety, including the freedom of abuse and harassment, must be protected.
4. Confidentiality of the patient's medical records and any access to those records must be protected.
5. Restraints or seclusion cannot be used to correct behavior or punish patients.
6. Restraints or seclusion when used for medical care must meet certain standards for staff training.
7. A grievance process for the patients must be in place.
8. The patient must be asked if he or she has prepared advance directives.

All patients are guaranteed these rights when seeking treatment. These rights are particularly important for the elder client to know that when she enters a medical facility that treatment will be provided with dignity and respect. These patients' rights ensure the elder person will have a voice in determining her care. Be sure your elder clients are aware of these rights. The rights are explained at hospital admissions, but in any given case the lawyer may wish to provide his client with a copy of the aforementioned federal regulation.

V. Case Law on Withholding Medical Treatment

If an individual is not competent or able to help make medical decisions and has not signed an advance directive, who should be the decision maker to determine what medical treatment will be given? Will it be the family, the physician, the hospital staff, or the courts? To withhold or terminate life-sustaining medical treatment is often a very difficult decision for a family member or guardian to make. There are a number of state cases that illustrate the trauma that families have endured in making the decision to withhold life-sustaining medical treatment. The following is a recap of three of the prominent cases that have developed our case law as to continuing, withholding, or terminating life-sustaining medical treatment when the patient is unable to make the decision.

In 1976, Karen Ann Quinlan's case came before the New Jersey Supreme Court. Karen Ann had severe brain damage and had been placed on a respirator. Her father, as her guardian, came before the lower court asking that the respirator be removed. The lower court approved removal. On appeal the New Jersey Court affirmed that decision ruling that Karen Ann had a right to privacy under state law and this allowed her, through her guardian, to refuse further medical treatment.[2]

Claire C. Conroy was an 84-year-old, bedridden incompetent who was living in a nursing home. A gastrostomy tube had been inserted in her body. Her nephew, as her guardian, came before the New Jersey Superior Court requesting that the tube be removed. The tube remained in while the case was litigated through the appellate process. She died before the Supreme Court ruled, but it nonetheless ruled to provide clarity on this issue. The state Supreme Court used three alternative approaches for allowing a discontinuation of treatment.[3]

The first alternative was a factual one of determining if the patient, if able, would have refused treatment under the circumstances. The second alternative approach (termed a *limited objective standard*) considered by the court was whether the net burden of life with the treatment would clearly and markedly outweigh the benefit of that life for the patient. The third approach (termed a *pure objective standard*) was if treatment negatively outweighs the benefits derived from life and if the patient's unavoidable and recurring severe pain from the treatment is such that administering life-sustaining treatment would be inhumane. Meeting any one of these three standards would allow a court to permit discontinuing life-prolonging treatment.

Nancy Cruzan was in a vegetative state due to an automobile accident. She was being provided nutrition and hydration through a surgically implanted feeding tube. Her parents, as co-guardians, requested the Missouri trial courts to allow them to disconnect these tubes. Nancy was not at the point of death. The trial court ruled that a person had a fundamental right under the Missouri constitution and the federal constitution to refuse or withdraw death-prolonging procedures. The Missouri Supreme Court reversed the trial court and found that under certain circumstances a surrogate acting for the patient may withdraw nutrition and hydration; however, Nancy's right to refuse treatment did not outweigh the fundamental policy of preservation of life. The Missouri Supreme Court noted:

1. There was no clear or convincing evidence of what she would desire under the circumstances,
2. She was not in a terminal condition, and
3. She was not in pain and the treatment was not burdensome to her.

The U.S. Supreme Court then heard the case and found that the Fourteenth Amendment protected a person's individual liberty in refusing unwanted medical treatment. However the Court upheld the Missouri Court limitations on a surrogate's power to decline medical treatment for a party who is incompetent and whose wishes were not sufficiently known.[4] Subsequent to this much publicized litigation, new evidence was presented at the trial court that Nancy had spoken to a co-worker of her decision not to be fed. Treatment was discontinued and Nancy died a few days later.

VI. Factors That Courts Consider in Determining Life-Sustaining Treatment

Courts will weigh many factors in determining whether life-sustaining treatment should be withdrawn or discontinued for an incompetent who has not signed an advance directive. Among these factors are the patient's diagnosis and prognosis (e.g., terminal illness, permanent coma, lack of cognitive brain function); the imminence of death if treatment is continued; whether treatment will merely prolong life or is likely to improve the patient's health; and the imminence of death.

A reading of this brief recap of state court rulings should be enough to convince any client of the need for a well-drafted advance directive.

VII. Advance Directives

Clients should be encouraged to make known to their lawyer what their wishes are when they have a serious illness or when death is imminent. The lawyer should listen carefully and address each concern. All 50 states have now enacted laws whereby the clients can make advance directives. No one wants to be tied up in the courts over such a difficult and personal matter. However, just following the state's statutory forms contained in these laws may not be sufficient to make the true desires of your client known.

Advance directives range from a Living Will or Directive to Physicians to Do Not Resuscitate Orders (DNR) and Durable Powers of Attorney for Health Care. Many clients do not understand advance directives or that the state allows them to make these decisions. Therefore, the lawyer should fully explain advance directives to the client. Spend time with the client to fully explore the client's ideas. Take care to avoid imposing your own values on the client, or simply printing out a standard form as if one size fits all.

Your clients may have questions about advance directives when they come into your office. Discussing their questions first will be very helpful in preparing a proper document for your client. Some pertinent questions for your client are:

- What are your beliefs about end of life medical treatment?
- How do your religious or personal ethical views impact your decision?
- Do you know what an advance directive is?
- What should be included in your advance directive?
- Do you understand what is included in a health care power of attorney and a living will?

Answering these questions will help you and your client determine how the document should be worded. Further, answering these questions opens communication between the lawyer and client ensuring the lawyer is drafting the document to meet the client's objectives.

The prospect of living an extended life in a state of serious incapacity is, in many respects, a far greater legal and ethical problem than death is to the elder client. Additional key questions you may ask the elder client may include the following:

- Who will make health care decisions for you?
- Will that person be able to carry out your wishes?
- Will there be family conflict over the implementation of your wishes?
- If you become seriously and terminally ill, can you be sure that your doctors will let you die naturally?

All 50 states and the District of Columbia now allow individuals to make advance directives. The elements of an advance directive vary from state to state, but the basic premise of all state laws is to ensure that the wishes of the individual are followed when the individual can no longer speak for himself. One should recognize that the term *advance directive* can refer to decision making for any medical treatment and not just a terminal illness.

A. Durable Health Care Power of Attorney

One of the advance directives that an attorney may use with an elderly client is a durable health care power of attorney. A durable power of attorney has traditionally been used for financial matters but now it is also being used for health care decisions. When using a power of attorney for health care decisions the lawyer should be mindful of the basic legal concepts of powers of attorney. Best practice is to have two separate documents—one a power of attorney for health care decisions and a second one for financial matters. The financial power of attorney is discussed beginning in Section XII.

Under common law, a power of attorney is a document in which one person, the "principal," grants authority to another, the "attorney-in-fact" or "agent," to act on the principal's behalf. For a power of attorney to be valid under common law, the principal must be competent at the time of its execution and must remain competent. If the principal becomes incompetent, the power of attorney ceases and a judicially supervised guardianship replaces it.

Today no one wants the common law result. States now allow powers of attorney to continue during the principal's incapacity—a so-called durable power of attorney. Under a durable power of attorney even if the individual becomes incapacitated, the document remains in effect. About the only requirement is that the person executing the durable power of attorney must be competent at the time the document is executed. In most states, the durable health care power of attorney must contain language that the principal intends that the powers granted to the agent will be effective upon the principal's incapacity. With these advances in state laws, powers of attorney have now become the solution to avoiding court intervention to end of life medical decision making. However, some *caveats* should be noted in drafting a durable health care power of attorney for health care decisions.

1. Because the principal must be competent to execute a valid directive, it is advisable to choose witnesses who are well acquainted with the client (declarant) so that they will later be available to establish the competency of the client (principal) at the time of execution, if that question should arise. This is not necessary in states whose laws provide for the document to be notarized and do not require any other witnesses. Many states exclude certain persons from serving as witnesses, such as those who will benefit from the principal's death and those who are involved with the person's care, such as health care facility personnel.

2. In those states which provide model forms, it is wise to follow the model as closely as possible. Modifications should be drafted with attention to any formalities required by state law.

3. The instrument should define the physical conditions under which the principal wants the agent to withhold or discontinue treatment, such as an irreversible coma or a terminal, incurable illness that is expected to result in death within a certain period of time.

4. The instrument should describe under what circumstances the agent may give consent on behalf of the principal, such as when the principal is unable to give consent or is unable to make or communicate decisions concerning medical treatment.

5. The document should describe the types of medical treatment and procedures that the principal wishes to forgo or discontinue, such as cardiopulmonary resuscitation, the use of a respirator, surgery, dialysis, feeding, or hydration.

6. The basic statutory formalities for executing a durable health care power of attorney should be followed if applicable.

7. Copies of the directive should be given, at a minimum, to the principal's physician, the appointed agent, the principal's attorney, and those family and friends who are expected to bring it to the attention of the principal's treating physician. The principal should keep the

original and at least one copy for her own records, but with notice to the agent and other family members as to where the original and copies can be found. It should be noted that the federal Patient Self-Determination Act of 1990 requires facilities to inquire of a patient at admission as to the existence of an advance directive and, if one is provided, to make it a part of the patient's medical record.

8. In almost all states, the directive will continue in effect indefinitely, but the principal should periodically reconfirm its validity. The principal may also limit its duration, but caution must be used in incorporating such limits because the document could lose validity while the patient lacked capacity, thus forfeiting the power to replace it.

There are several other issues that the client may want addressed. The agent may be granted the ability to make contracts with health care service providers or facilities such as a nursing home and home health care. The client may want the agent to have access to medical records and if so a provision should be made. If the client wants to make organ donations, then the client should address this issue in the power of attorney and empower the agent to be able to make anatomical gifts. These are very important decisions and the lawyer should be satisfied that the elderly client has thoroughly considered the ramifications of these decisions.

A durable health care power of attorney for health care is provided in the following section. For an excellent ABA resource that provides a thorough discussion of advance directives and multiple forms, see Carol Krohm and Scott Summers, *Advance Health Care Directives: A Handbook for Professionals* (Chicago: ABA 2002).

B. Durable Health Care Power of Attorney Form

The Uniform Health-Care Decisions Act (UHCDA), is a model act whose provisions allow an individual to complete a living will and to appoint a health care agent in one document. The act also establishes a helpful list of default decision makers when a person has not provided for a health care decision agent and has left no living will or other instructions. This act has not been adopted in all states. The lawyer will need to check her own state law to see if this act has been passed. It is an excellent and very comprehensive aid in health care decision making. The form that follows is based on the UHCDA form, though it has been modified. Most states now have statutory forms. The lawyer will need to decide whether to use that state's statutory form or add to the statutory form with additional provisions such as those in this form or from the UHCDA.

1. DESIGNATION OF HEALTH CARE AGENT.

I, _____, hereby appoint:
(Principal)

_____
(Attorney-in-fact's name)

_____
(Address)
Home: _____ Work: _____
as my attorney-in-fact (or "Agent") to make health and personal care decisions for me as authorized in this document.

2. EFFECTIVE DATE AND DURABILITY.

By this document I intend to create a durable health care power of attorney effective upon, and only during, any period of incapacity in which, in the opinion of my agent and attending physician, I am unable to make or communicate choice regarding a particular health care decision.

3. AGENT'S POWERS.

I grant to my Agent full authority to make decisions for me regarding my health care. In exercising this authority, my Agent shall follow my desires as stated in this document or otherwise known to my Agent. In making any decision, my Agent shall attempt to discuss the proposed decision with me to determine my desires if I am able to communicate in any way. If my Agent cannot determine the choice I would want made, then my Agent shall make a choice for me based upon what my Agent believes to be in my best interests. My Agent's authority to interpret my desires is intended to be as broad as possible, except for any limitations I may state below. Accordingly, unless specifically limited by Section 4, below, my Agent is authorized as follows:

A. To consent, refuse, or withdraw consent to any and all types of medical care, treatment, surgical procedures, diagnostic procedures, medication, and the use of mechanical or other procedures that affect any bodily function, including (but not limited to) artificial respiration, nutritional support and hydration, and cardiopulmonary resuscitation;

B. To have access to medical records and information to the same extent that I am entitled to, including the right to disclose the contents to others;

C. To authorize my admission to or discharge (even against medical advice) from any hospital, nursing home, residential care, assisted living or similar facility or service;

D. To contract on my behalf for any health care related service or facility on my behalf, without my Agent incurring personal financial liability for such contracts;

E. To hire and fire medical, social service, and other support personnel responsible for my care;

F. To authorize, or refuse to authorize, any medication or procedure intended to relieve pain, even though such use may lead to physical damage, addiction, or hasten the moment of (but not intentionally case) my death;

G. To make anatomical gifts of part or all of my body for medical purposes, authorize an autopsy, and direct the disposition of my remains, to the extent permitted by law;

H. To take any other action necessary to do what I authorize here, including (but not limited to) granting any waiver or release from liability required by any hospital, physician, or other health care provider; signing any documents relating to refusals of treatment or the leaving of a facility against medical advice, and pursuing any legal action in my name, and at the expense of my estate to force compliance with my wishes as determined by my Agent, or to seek actual or punitive damages for the failure to comply.

4. STATEMENT OF DESIRES, SPECIAL PROVISIONS, AND LIMITATIONS.

A. The powers granted above do not include the following powers or are subject to the following rules or limitations:

_____
_____
_____
_____
_____
_____

B. With respect to any **Life-Sustaining Treatment**, I direct the following:
(INITIAL ONLY ONE OF THE FOLLOWING PARAGRAPHS)

_____ REFERENCE TO LIVING WILL. I specifically direct my Agent to follow any health care declaration to "living will" executed by me.

_____ GRANT OF DISCRETION TO AGENT. I do not want my life to be prolonged nor do I want life-sustaining treatment to be provided or continued if my Agent believes the burdens of the treatment outweigh the expected benefits. I want my Agent to consider the relief of suffering, the expense involved and the quality as well as the possible extension of my life in making decisions concerning life-sustaining treatment.

_____ DIRECTIVE TO WITHHOLD OR WITHDRAW TREATMENT. I do not want my life to be prolonged and I do not want life-sustaining treatment:

a. If I have a condition that is incurable or irreversible and, without the administration of life-sustaining treatment, expected to result in death with a relatively short time; or
b. If I am in a coma or persistent vegetative state which is reasonably concluded to be irreversible.
____ DIRECTIVE IN MY OWN WORDS: _____
_____
_____
_____
_____

C. With respect to **Nutrition and Hydration** provided by means of a nasogastric tube or tube into the stomach, intestines, or veins, I wish to make clear that. . .
(INITIAL ONLY ONE)

_____ I intend to include these procedures among the "life-sustaining procedures" that may be withheld or withdrawn under the conditions given above.
_____ I do not intend to include these procedures among the "life-sustaining procedures" that may be withheld or withdrawn.

5. SUCCESSORS.

If any Agent named by me shall die, become legally disabled, resign, refuse to act, be unavailable, or (if any Agent is my spouse) be legally separated or divorced from me, I name the following (each to act alone and successively, in the order named) as successors to my Agent:

A. First Alternate Agent_____
Address: _____
Telephone:_____
B. Second Alternate Agent_____
Address:_____
Telephone_____

6. PROTECTION OF THIRD PARTIES WHO RELY ON MY AGENT.

No person who relies in good faith upon any representations by my Agent or Successor Agent shall be liable to me, my estate, my heirs or assigns, for recognizing the Agent's authority.

7. NOMINATION OF GUARDIAN.

If a guardian of my person should for any reason be appointed, I nominate my Agent (or his or her successor), named above.

8. ADMINISTRATIVE PROVISIONS.

A. I revoke any prior power of attorney for health care.

B. This power of attorney is intended to be valid in any jurisdiction in which it is presented.

C. My Agent shall not be entitled to compensation for services performed under this power of attorney, but he or she shall be entitled to reimbursement for all reasonable expenses incurred as a result of carrying out any provision of this power of attorney.

D. The powers delegated under this power of attorney are separable, so that the invalidity of one or more powers shall not affect any others.

BY SIGNING HERE I INDICATE THAT I UNDERSTAND THE CONTENTS OF THIS DOCUMENT AND THE EFFECT OF THIS GRANT OF POWERS TO MY AGENT.

I sign my name to this Health Care Power of Attorney on this _____ day of_____, 20__.

My current home address is: _____

_____

Signature:_____

Name: _____

WITNESS STATEMENT

I declare that the person who signed or acknowledged this document is personally known to me, that he/she signed or acknowledged this durable power of attorney in my presence, and that he/she appears to be of sound mind and under no duress, fraud, or undue influence. I am not the person appointed as agent by this document, nor am I the patient's health care provider, or an employee of the patient's health care provider. I further declare that I am not relate to the principal by blood, marriage or adoption, and, to the best of my knowledge, I am not a creditor of the principal nor entitled to any part of his/her estate under a will now existing or by operation of law.

Witness #1:

Signature: _____ Date: _____

Print Name: _____ Telephone: _____

Residence Address: _____

_____

Witness #2:

Signature: _____ Date: _____

Print Name: _____ Telephone: _____

Residence Address: _____

_____

OR
NOTARIZATION

STATE OF _____)

COUNTY OF _____)

On this _____ day of _____, 20__, the said _____, known to me (or satisfactorily proven) to be the person named in the foregoing instrument, personally appeared before me, a Notary Public, within and for the State and County aforesaid, and acknowledged that he or she freely and voluntarily executed the same for the purposes stated herein.

_____
NOTARY PUBLIC
My Commission Expires:_____

C. Appointment of an Agent

The most important element of an advance directive is the appointment of an agent who will make the health care decisions. It is very important that the lawyer be sure the person appointed will follow the wishes of the client. The lawyer must be certain the person selected is the choice of the elderly client and the elderly client is not under duress to appoint a certain individual.

D. Revocation of Durable Health Care Power of Attorney

Revocation of a durable health care power of attorney should be addressed with the client. Destroying the document and notifying the agent is the commonly used method. Practical revocation problems include the principal's need to gain access to all copies of the durable health care power of attorney and identify all third parties who may be relying on the document. Recording a revocation document may be a possibility depending on the state law, but the practical problem of notice to the third parties may not be solved with recording.

E. Second State Residency

If the lawyer has a client who spends a portion of her time in the home state and a portion of time in another state, the question arises as to whether the durable health care power of attorney is valid in the second state. Cautious practice is to advise your client as follows:

1. Take the durable health care power of attorney and have it reviewed by a lawyer in the second state to make sure it complies with the second state's laws, or;
2. Make a second durable health care power of attorney in the second state, or;
3. The lawyer can determine whether the second state has a reciprocal recognition.

These steps should also be followed for powers of attorney, living wills, and wills.

VIII. Living Will

Not only may your client need a durable health care power of attorney but the client may also need a living will. These two documents are usually used in conjunction with each other. The health care power of attorney concerns general medical treatment, and the living will concerns end of life decision making. In drafting a living will, the lawyer must be familiar with the state law requirements for living wills. State statutory forms should be reviewed to determine any limitations on the exercise of the power under the living will. In most cases, living wills are applicable when an individual has a terminal condition and the person's death is imminent. In the living will, individuals will want to address whether life-prolonging treatment such as respirators are to be used when death is imminent. The client must also consider whether nutrition and hydration will be administered. Many lawyers now combine living will provisions in a durable health care power of attorney.

Living Will Form[5]

My wishes regarding life-prolonging treatment and artificially provided nutrition and hydration to be provided to me if I no longer have decisional capacity, have a terminal condition, or become permanently unconscious have been indicated by checking and initialing the appropriate lines below. By checking and initialing the appropriate lines, I specifically:

____ Direct that treatment be withheld or withdrawn, and that I be permitted to die naturally with only the administration of medication or the performance of any medical treatment deemed necessary to alleviate pain.

____ DO NOT authorize that life-prolonging treatment be withheld or withdrawn.

____ Authorize the withholding or withdrawal of artificially provided food, water, or other artificially provided nourishment or fluids.

____ DO NOT authorize the withholding or withdrawal of artificially provided food, water, or other artificially provided nourishment or fluids.

____ Authorize the giving of all or any part of my body upon death for any purpose specified in KRS 311.185.

____ DO NOT authorize the giving of all or any part of my body upon death.

In the absence of my ability to give directions regarding the use of life-prolonging treatment and artificially provided nutrition and hydration, it is my intention that this directive shall be honored by my attending physician and my family as the final expression of my legal right to refuse medical or surgical treatment and I accept the consequences of the refusal.

If I have been diagnosed as pregnant and that diagnosis is known to my attending physician, this directive shall have no force or effect during the course of my pregnancy.

I understand the full import of this directive and I am emotionally and mentally competent to make this directive.

Signed this _____ day of _____, 20__.

_____
Signature of grantor

_____
Address of grantor

In our joint presence, the grantor, who is of sound mind and eighteen (18) years of age, or older, voluntarily dated and signed this writing or directed it to be dated and signed for the grantor.

_____   _____
Signature of witness   Address of witness

_____   _____
Signature of witness   Address of witness

OR

STATE OF KENTUCKY)
_____ COUNTY)

Before me, the undersigned authority, came the grantor who is of sound mind and eighteen (18) years of age, or older, and acknowledged that he voluntarily dated and signed this writing or directed it to be signed and dated as above.

Done this _____ day of _____, 20__.

_____
Signature of Notary or other Officer
Date commission expires:_____

A. *Revocation of Living Will*

Revocation of the living will can be done in several different ways. The living will can be revoked orally or in writing. If the living will is destroyed by the client, then all copies should be destroyed. The health care providers should be notified to note in the medical records that a living will has been revoked.

IX. *Do Not Resuscitate (DNR)*

Some clients are reluctant to rely only on a living will or health care power of attorney. Those documents authorize the health care decision maker to refuse or terminate treatment including respirators. The client's concern is that in a medical emergency, the emergency medical personnel will resuscitate the client and he will arrive at the hospital on a respirator. Many states allow a DNR order, which can be given to the emergency personnel upon arrival. Also, the client can wear a bracelet to put the emergency personnel on notice of this request. There follows a sample DNR used in the author's home state and the standard instructions accompanying the use of a DNR is provided.

Kentucky Emergency Medical Services
Do Not Resuscitate (DNR) Order

Person's Full Legal Name _____

Surrogate's Full Legal Name (if applicable) _____

I, the undersigned person or surrogate who has been designated to make health care decisions in accordance with Kentucky Revised Statutes, hereby direct that in the event of my cardiac or respiratory arrest that this **DO NOT RESUSCITATE (DNR) ORDER** be honored. I understand that DNR means that if my heart stops beating or if I stop breathing, no medical procedure to restart breathing or heart function, more specifically the insertion of a tube into the lungs, or electrical shocking of the heart or cardiopulmonary resuscitation (CPR) will be started by emergency medical services (EMS) personnel. I understand this decision will *not* prevent emergency medical services personnel from providing other medical care.

I understand that I may revoke this DNR order at any time by destroying this form, removing the DNR bracelet, or by telling the EMS personnel that I want to be resuscitated. Any attempt to alter or change the content, names, or signatures on the EMS DNR form shall make the DNR form invalid.

I understand that this form, or a standard EMS DNR bracelet must be available and must be shown to EMS personnel as soon as they arrive. If the form or bracelet is not provided, the EMS personnel will follow their normal protocols which could include cardiopulmonary resuscitation (CPR) or other resuscitation procedures. I understand that should I die, EMS personnel will require this form and/or bracelet for their records.

I give permission for information about this EMS DNR Order to be given to the prehospital emergency medical care personnel, physicians, nurses, or other health care personnel as necessary to implement this directive.

I hereby state that this **'Do Not Resuscitate (DNR) Order'** is my authentic wish not be resuscitated.

_____   _____
Person/Legal Surrogate Signature   **Date**

Commonwealth of Kentucky   County of _____
Subscribed and sworn to be before me by _____ to be his/her own free act and deed, this _____ day of _____, 20___.

_____, Notary Public
My commission expires:_____

In lieu of having this Form notarized, it may be witnessed by two persons not related to the individual noted above.

WITNESSED BY:
1. _____
2. _____

This EMS Do Not Resuscitate Form was approved by the Kentucky Board of Medical Licensure at their March 1995 meeting.

Complete the portion below, cut out, fold, and insert in DNR bracelet
I certify that an EMS Do Not Resuscitate (DNR) form has been executed.

Person's Name (print or type) _____

Person's or Legal Surrogate's Signature _____

KENTUCKY EMERGENCY MEDICAL SERVICES
DO NOT RESUSCITATE (DNR)
ORDER INSTRUCTIONS

PURPOSE

This standardized EMS DNR Order has been developed and approved by the Kentucky Board of Medical Licensure, in consultation with the Cabinet for Human Resources. It is in compliance with KRS Chapter 311 as amended by Senate Bill 311 passed by the 1994 General Assembly, which directs the Kentucky Board of Medical Licensure to develop a standard form to authorize EMS providers to honor advance directives to withhold or terminate care.

For covered persons in cardiac or respiratory arrest, resuscitative measures to be withheld include external chest compressions, intubation, defibrillation, administration of cardiac medications and artificial respiration. The EMS DNR Order does **not** affect the provision of other emergency medical care, including oxygen administration, suctioning, control of bleeding, administration of analgesics and comfort care.

APPLICABILITY

The **EMS DNR Order** applies only to resuscitation attempts by health care providers in the **prehospital** (i.e., certified EMT-First Responders, Emergency Medical Technicians, and Paramedics)—in patients' homes, in a long-term care facility, during transport to or from a health care facility, or in other locations outside acute care hospitals.

INSTRUCTIONS

Any adult person may execute an EMS DNR Order. The person for whom the Order is executed shall sign and date the Order and my either have the Order notarized by a Kentucky Notary Public or have their signature witness by two persons not related to them. The executor of the Order must also place their printed or typed name in the designated area and their signature on the EMS DNR Order bracelet insert found at the bottom of the EMS DNR Order form. The bracelet insert shall be detached and placed in a hospital type bracelet and placed on the wrist or ankle for the executor of the Order.

If the person for whom the EMS DNR Order is contemplated is unable to give the informed consent, or is a minor, the person's legal surrogate shall sign and date the Order and may either have the form notarized by a Kentucky Notary Public or have their signature witnessed by two persons not related to the person for which the form is being executed or related to the legal health care surrogate. The legal health care surrogate shall also complete the required information on the EMS DNR bracelet insert found at the bottom of the EMS DNR Order form. The bracelet shall be detached and placed in a hospital type bracelet and placed on the wrist or ankle of the person for which this Order was executed.

The original, completed EMS DNR Order or the EMS DNR Bracelet must be readily available to EMS personnel in order for the EMS DNR Order to be honored. Resuscitation attempts may be initiated until the form or bracelet is presented and the identity of the patient is confirmed by the EMS personnel. It is recommended that the EMS DNR Order be displayed in a prominent place close to the patient and/or the bracelet be on the patient's wrist or ankle.

REVOCATION
An EMS DNR Order may be revoked at any time orally or by performing an act such as burning, tearing, canceling, obliterating or by destroying the order by the person on whose behalf it was executed or by the person's legal health care surrogate.
IT SHOULD BE UNDERSTOOD BY THE PERSON EXECUTING THIS EMS DNR ORDER OR THEIR LEGAL HEALTH CARE SURROGATE, THAT SHOULD THE PERSON LISTED ON THE EMS DNR ORDER DIE WHILE EMS PREHOSPITAL ARE IN ATTENDANCE, THE EMS DNR ORDER OR EMS DNR BRACELET MUST BE GIVEN TO THE EMS PREHOSPITAL PERSONNEL FOR THEIR RECORDS.

X. Guardianship and Conservatorships

The guardianship and conservatorship laws vary among states, as each state has its own unique statutory scheme that must be followed, but the process is similar. Some states refer to these laws as a guardianship whereas other states use the term *conservatorship*. Thus in one state the client is applying to be a guardian but in another state it is a conservator. The Uniform Probate Code terms a conservator as the person appointed by the court to manage the estate; and a guardian is the person appointed by the court to make person decisions, including medical decisions for the ward. The ensuing discussion will use the term *guardian* for both. A helpful ABA resource is *The Fundamentals of Guardianships: What Every Guardian Should Know.*

A petition is filed with the local court, typically a probate or lower court, alleging incompetency, providing an inventory of the individual's assets, and requesting the appointment of the guardian. Notice is served on the alleged incompetent with a guardian ad litem appointed to represent him or her. One or more physicians and mental health professionals are required to examine the person, file reports with the court as to competency, and typically testify at a judicial hearing to determine the issue of incompetency. A hearing is held either before the court, or a jury, at which the petitioner, the incompetent (unless medically excused), the guardian ad litem, medical witnesses, and interested family members are present and may testify. Assuming incompetency is established, which it almost always is, then a court order to that effect is entered with the court next appointing the petitioner or another qualified person to be guardian. State laws vary, but they each provide various types of guardians, such as, a guardian of the person, a guardian of the property, a guardian of both, or a limited or temporary guardian who may serve over either the person, the property, or both.

After appointment as guardian, continuing oversight by the court is required. The guardian must post a bond when the guardian's power includes authority over property. Typically, an inventory must be filed providing more detail as to the incompetent's assets. The guardian must then file periodic settlements with the court, typically on an annual or bi-annual basis, reporting all financial transactions and the incompetent's current health condition. The guardian's authority over finances is usually limited, requiring court approval for extraordinary matters, such as selling real estate, borrowing or pledging assets as collateral, removing assets from the state, and making any extraordinary expenditures of the incompetent's estate.

This is an excellent system to protect a person from being improperly declared incompetent, and if declared incompetent, to ensure one's estate is not unwisely invested or spent. But it is a burdensome process for most families, unless the incompetent has become difficult to care for and the family needs the authority of the court to force the incompetent into institutional care against his or her own will. In these situations, the court process is a needed blessing; and to counsel elder clients and their families a thorough knowledge of the lawyer's own state guardianship laws is essential. But most people need another alternative. These alternatives are discussed shortly.

The need for a guardianship will typically arise in one of several situations. Your elder client may have a disabled adult child. A guardianship is necessary in this situation in order for the parents to continue to have the legal right to make health care decisions and handle financial matters for the disabled child. Typically, near the time that the child reaches 18 years of age, the parents will need to establish themselves as guardian for their adult child. The other situations in which a guardianship is needed either involve an elderly parent or other adult family member. If the person prior to incompetency or disability has executed a durable health care power of attorney and a durable financial power of attorney, nothing further is needed to make health care decisions and financial decisions for that person. Unfortunately, sometimes these documents have not been executed (or cannot be due to incompetency), in which case the guardianship is a necessity in order to have the legal authority to make health care decisions and to handle the persons finances. Other times, the situation is more heartbreaking, as the family member may have executed such documents, but they have become resistive to your client making their health care and financial decisions. Often times there can be a period of time prior to a judicial determination of incompetency in which the person becomes suspicious, resistive, and combative toward the client who is trying to care for their family member. Even with the appropriate powers of attorney in place, the person may revoke those documents and create an amazing amount of havoc in trying to care for themselves. At this point, the guardianship must be pursued in order to have the legal authority to care for the family member. Once a guardianship is in place, it overrides the powers of attorney, as all future health care and financial decisions are made by the guardian, subject to judicial oversight as required by the court and state law.

It is for these reasons that durable health care powers of attorney and durable financial powers of attorney are now widely used. As long as the person needing assistance is not resistive to the decisions being made for them, the power of attorney documents provide full legal authority to care for the person needing assistance. The ensuing discussion will deal with financial matters.

XI. *Joint Ownership of Assets*

The simplest and most common substitute for a guardianship to handle financial affairs is titling assets jointly with rights of survivorship in the name of the elder client and the person who is to handle his or her financial affairs. By simply being a co-owner of the elder client's checking account, most financial matters can easily be handled. There is no court supervision and no need for a lawyer to prepare legal documents. Many elder clients also title most of their other investments jointly so that the person handling their financial affairs can have immediate access to those assets if they must be sold to pay for living expenses. The simplicity is grand, but it comes at a great price.

Unless the elder client only has one beneficiary of his or her estate, joint ownership is a poor solution. What happens under state law if a judgment creditor levies on the assets an interest which is now owned by the elder client's joint owner? In some states at least one-half of the asset can be attached. If the joint owner predeceases the elder client or becomes ill, there is no one designated as a successor to handle the elder client's financial affairs. This can be quickly rectified if the client is still competent, but, if not, a guardianship is the only alternative. In states that levy an inheritance tax, the elder client may owe an inheritance tax on a portion of the jointly owned assets if the joint owner dies first. It is a bitter pill for elder clients to swallow when required to pay an inheritance tax on their own money.

The worst problem is when there are multiple estate beneficiaries, but the elder client's property is titled in the joint name of the elder client and only one of those beneficiaries. For example, assume a widow has written a will passing her estate equally to her three children, but has titled her estate assets jointly with the daughter who handles her financial affairs. Under the laws of most states, absent clear and convincing evidence to the contrary, the jointly owned assets will pass at death to the one daughter and only those assets owned in the elder client's individual name will pass in three equal shares under the will. This is seldom the elder client's intent, but it is the result unless the daughter is honest. Even then, honesty may have a price. In states that levy an inheritance tax, the jointly owned assets will be taxed as passing to the daughter, and due to the progressive rate schedule more inheritance tax will be owed than if the same assets had been divided equally among the three children and taxed at lower rates. There is also the possibility of a gift tax, or use of the daughter's estate tax exclusion amount, when the daughter transfers two-thirds of the jointly owned assets to the other two siblings to carry out the mother's testamentary intent. The potential problems with joint ownership are great, thus the preferred alternatives are either a durable power of attorney or a living trust. Let's look first to the durable power of attorney.

XII. *Durable Power of Attorney*

A power of attorney is merely a written form of an agency agreement. The elder client is the principal with the power of attorney named being the agent. Powers of attorney may be limited to a very specific purpose, such as to sell a parcel of real estate, or convey assets to a living trust, but for purposes of these discussions it is the general power of attorney that is needed. A general power of attorney is broad and seeks to authorize the agent to handle all types of financial matters that could otherwise be handled by the principal. Before looking to specific provisions of a general power of attorney, two points need to be remembered.

First, common law under the power of attorney terminated upon incompetency of the principal. Then a guardianship was required. To opt out of guardianship laws, each state now has a statute creating the "durable" power of attorney. The term *durable* simply means that a power of attorney that complies with the state statute will continue during disability. It is critical to be familiar with the laws of the attorney's own state. Some states have enacted the Uniform Durable Power of Attorney Act 1979; some the Uniform Statutory Form Power of Attorney Act 1998; and others the Uniform Power of Attorney Act 2006.

Be sure of the laws of your own state. For example, if your state law follows the 1979 act, the power of attorney must contain specific wording that the power continues during disability. Thus, care must be taken to insert that statutory wording. The 2006 act makes all powers of attorney durable. A trap, often not recognized by some attorneys who are not aware of the common law, is to assume that all powers of attorney are effective during disability. If the 2006 act has been adopted, that is correct. If your state has adopted the 1979 act, that may not be the case. In this case if the power of attorney omits the recital that it is effective during disability, then the power terminates at incompetency, with the unwanted guardianship the only alternative.

Second, in drafting a power of attorney, the attorney must be mindful of whether the client wants the power of attorney to become effective immediately or only upon disability. Because the document is being prepared to avoid a guardianship, the client will normally expect the power of attorney to become effective at disability. If this is the client's desire, then wording should be added to the power of attorney both to state that the effective date is upon incompetency and to define how incompetency is determined. Usually the document specifies that this decision is to be made by the client's then-treating physician, or a decision by two physicians, one of whom is

board certified in a specialty that includes the cause of the client's incompetency. To avoid this triggering mechanism, many elder clients prefer that the
power of attorney be effective immediately. This both avoids scrambling for a
physician's statement of incompetency and provides the convenience of the
document being used currently if the principal is unavailable to sign a legal
document but prefers for the transaction to be consummated in his or her
absence.

Those lawyers who live in states that have statutory powers of attorney
(the 1998 act) have a simpler task in preparing the power of attorney. For
them it is essentially a task of striking the provisions from the statutory form
that are not desired and adding any additional powers that are needed.

When drafting powers of attorney that specify the activities that are permitted by the agent, it is typical to include powers to handle real estate matters; bank and financial institution transactions; stock, bond, and mutual
fund transactions; access to safe deposit boxes; elections concerning retirement plans; representing the principal's interest in litigation; handling
employment benefits; operating a business owned by the principal; transactions concerning life insurance and annuities; handling tax matters; borrowing from financial institutions, including pledging assets; making gifts;
funding a living trust; and the naming of successors.

Rather than consider these powers as boilerplate provisions that must be
inserted in every power of attorney, ask the client about each provision. Does
the client really want the agent to have authority over life insurance, and if so
how much power. Is there any need for the agent to have the authority to
borrow money, or pledge the client's assets? Is there any need to grant the
agent authority to make gifts? Whether using a statutory form or one the
attorney prepares, consideration should be given to the extent of powers
granted by the principal to the agent. Obviously, the client will only name
individuals he or she trusts explicitly, yet ask some good questions.

A few concluding comments concerning gift giving may be helpful. First,
the law is unsettled in some states as to whether or not it is essential to have
provisions in a power of attorney that grant the agent power to make gifts. To
avoid any confusion, if gifting is desire, then specific provisions authorizing
gift giving should be inserted in the power of attorney, or if not desired, the
document should specify no gifting is allowed. The next question is whether
those provisions should be limited to the $15,000 annual gift tax exclusion, or
should larger gifts be permitted? Is the client comfortable with gifts being
given during his or her incompetency in excess of the $15,000 annual exclu-
sion amount? Just be thorough.

SAMPLE POWER OF ATTORNEY

I, _____, hereby appoint _____ as my attorney-in-fact (my "agent") to act for me and in my name (in any way I could act in person) with respect to the following powers:

I. POWERS OF ATTORNEY-IN-FACT

A. Real estate transactions. The agent is authorized to buy, sell, exchange, rent and lease real estate (which term includes, without limitation, real estate subject to a land trust and all beneficial interests in and powers of direction under any land trust); collect all rent, sale proceeds and earnings from real state; convey, assign and accept title to real estate; grant easements, create conditions and release rights of homestead with respect to real estate; create land trusts and exercise all powers under land trusts; hold, possess, maintain, repair, improve, subdivide, manage, operate and insure real estate; pay contest, protest and compromise real estate taxes and assessments; and, in general, exercise all powers with respect to real estate which the principal could if present and under no disability.

B. Financial institution transactions. The agent is authorized to open, close, continue and control all accounts and deposits in any type of financial institution (which term includes, without limitation, banks, trust companies, savings and building and loan associations, credit unions and brokerage firms); deposit in and withdraw from and write checks on any financial institution account or deposit; and, in general, exercise all powers with respect to financial institution transactions which the principal could if present and under no disability.

C. Stock and bond transactions. The agent is authorized to buy and sell all types of securities (which term includes, without limitation, stocks, bonds, mutual funds and all other types of investment securities and financial instruments); collect, hold and safekeep all dividends, interest, earnings, proceeds of sale, distributions, shares, certificates and other evidences of ownership paid or distributed with respect to securities; exercise all voting rights with respect to securities in person or by proxy, enter into voting trusts and consent to limitations on the right to vote; and, in general, exercise all powers with respect to securities which the principal could if present and under no disability.

D. Tangible personal property transactions. The agent is authorized to buy and sell, lease, exchange, collect, possess and take title to all tangible personal property; move, store, ship, restore, maintain, repair, improve, manage, preserve, insure and safekeep tangible personal property; and, in general, exercise all powers with respect to tangible personal property which the principal could if present and under no disability.

E. Safe deposit box transactions. The agent is authorized to open, continue and have access to all safe deposit boxes; sign, renew, release or terminate any safe deposit contract; drill or surrender any safe deposit box; and, in general, exercise all powers with respect to safe deposit matters which the principal could if present and under no disability.

F. Insurance and annuity transactions. The agent is authorized to procure, acquire, continue, renew, terminate or otherwise deal with any type of insurance or annuity contract (which terms include, without limitation, life, accident, health, disability, automobile casualty, property or liability insurance); pay premiums or assessments on or surrender and collect all distributions, proceeds or benefits payable under any insurance or annuity contract; and, in general, exercise all powers with respect to insurance and annuity contracts which the principal could if present and under no disability.

G. Retirement plan transactions. The agent is authorized to: contribute to, withdraw from and deposit funds in any type of retirement plan (which term includes, without limitation, any tax qualified or nonqualified pension, profit sharing, stock bonus, employee savings and other retirement plan, individual retirement account, deferred compensation plan and any other type of employee benefit plan); select and change payment options for the principal under any retirement plan; make rollover contributions from any retirement plan to other retirement plans or individual retirement accounts, exercise all investment powers available under any type of self-directed retirement plan; and, in general, exercise all powers with respect to retirement plans and retirement plan account balances which the principal could if present and under no disability.

H. Social Security, unemployment and military service benefits. The agent is authorized to prepare, sign and file any claim or application for Social Security, unemployment or military service benefits; sue for, settle or abandon any claims to any benefit or assistance under any federal, state, local or foreign statute or regulation; control, deposit to any account, collect, receipt for, and take title to and hold all benefits under any Social Security, unemployment, military service or other state, federal, local or foreign statute or regulation; and, in general, exercise all powers with respect to Social Security, unemployment, military service and governmental benefits which the principal could if present and under no disability.

I. Tax matters. The agent is authorized to: sign, verify and file all the principal's federal, state and local income, gift, estate, property and other tax returns, including joint returns and declarations of estimated tax; pay all taxes; claim, sue for and receive all tax refunds; examine and copy all the principals' tax returns and records; represent the principal before any federal, state or local revenue agency or taxing body and sign and deliver all tax powers of attorney on behalf of the principal that may be necessary for such purposes; waive rights and sign all documents on behalf of the principal as required to settle, pay and determine all tax liabilities; and, in general, exercise all powers with respect to tax matters which the principal could if present and under no disability.

J. Gift giving. To give my spouse, my children and my more remote lawful descendants so much of my property, including (but not limited to) any cash, securities, life insurance policies, and real property, as my attorney-in-fact deems appropriate for their comfort and care and to continue or implement a program of giving annually to each of my children and my more remote lawful descendants, amounts equal to the annual federal gift tax exclusion (presently fifteen thousand dollars ($15,000) per donee), under Internal Revenue Section 2503(b), or twice this amount if my spouse agrees to be treated as having made one-half of such gifts. All such gifts may be made outright, in trust, or to any legal guardian or custodian under any applicable Uniform Transfers or Gifts to Minors Act, as my attorney-in-fact deems appropriate, even if my attorney-in-fact is such Trustee, guardian, or custodian.

K. Claims and litigation. The agent is authorized to institute, prosecute, defend, abandon, compromise, arbitrate, settle and dispose of any claim in favor of or against the principal or any property interests of the principal; collect and receipt for any claim or settlement proceeds and waive agreements and other contracts as necessary in connection with litigation; and, in general, exercise all powers with respect to claims and litigation which the principal could if present and under no disability.

L. Business operations. The agent is authorized to organize or continue and conduct any business (which term includes, without limitation, any farming, manufacturing, service, mining, retailing or other type of business operation) in any for, whether as a proprietorship, joint venture, partnership, corporation, trust or other legal entity; operate, buy sell, expand, contract, terminate or liquidate and business; direct, control, supervise, manage or participate in the operation of any business and engage, compensate and discharge business managers, employees, agents, attorneys, accountants and consultants; and, in general, exercise all powers with respect to business interests and operations which the principal could if present and under no disability.

M. Borrowing transactions. The agent is authorized to borrow money; mortgage or pledge any real estate or tangible or intangible personal property as security for such purposes; sign, renew, extend, pay and satisfy any notes or other forms of obligation; and, in general, exercise all powers with respect to secured and unsecured borrowing which the principal could if present and under no disability.

N. Estate transactions. The agent is authorized to accept, receipt for, exercise, release, reject, renounce, assign, disclaim, demand, sue for, claim and recover any legacy, bequest, devise, gift or other property interest or payment due or payable to or for the principal; assert any interest in and exercise any powers over any trust, estate or property subject to fiduciary control; transfer assets to any revocable trust created by the principal; establish a revocable trust solely for the benefit of the principal that terminates at the death of the principal and is then distributable to the legal representative of the estate of the principal; and, in general, exercise all powers with respect to estates and trusts which the principal could if present and under no disability; provided, however, that the agent may not make or change a will and may not revoke or amend a trust revocable or amendable by the principal or require the trustee of any trust for the benefit of the principal to pay income or principal to the agent unless specific authority to that end is given, and specific reference to the trust is made, in the statutory property power form.

O. All other property powers and transactions. The agent is authorized to exercise all possible powers of the principal with respect to all possible types of property and interests in property, except to the extent the principal limits the generality of this category (o) by striking out one or more of categories (a) through (n) or by specifying other limitations in the statutory property power form.

II. COMPENSATION

My agent shall be entitled to reasonable compensation for services rendered as agent under this power of attorney.

III. EFFECTIVE DATE

This power of attorney shall become effective on this date, and such rights, powers, and authority shall remain in full force and effect, including during my disability or incompetency, and until I give notice in writing that such power is terminated.

IV. SUCCESSOR

If any agent named by me shall die, become incompetent, resign or refuse to accept the office of agent, I name _____ as successor to such agent.

V. GUARDIAN

If a guardian of my estate (my property) is to be appointed, I nominate the agent acting under this power of attorney as such guardian, to serve without bond or security.

I am fully informed as to all the contents of this form and understand the full import of the grant of powers to my agent.

This the _____ day of _____, 20__.

_____   _____
Witness   Address

_____   _____
Witness   Address

STATE OF _____   )
)SCT
COUNTY OF _____)

I, _____, a Notary Public within and for the State and County aforesaid, do hereby certify that the foregoing Power of Attorney was this day executed by _____, who executed and acknowledged the same before me to be _____ act and deed in due form of law.

Given under my hand and notarial seal on this the ____ day of _____, 20__.

_____
Notary Public, State at Large
My commission expires: _____

PREPARED BY:

_____
L. Rush Hunt
Attorney at Law
39 South Main Street
Madisonville, Kentucky 42431

XIII. *Living Trust*

The living trust simply refers to a revocable inter vivos trust created by a client during his or her lifetime. Typically, a client transfers some or all of his or her property to the trust during his or her lifetime. The client may act as trustee of the trust or name an individual or corporate trustee. The trust pays income for life to the client and to the client's spouse and children, as the client directs, or in the trustee's discretion if the client is incapacitated. Principal can also be expended as directed by the client, or by the trustee if the client is incapacitated.

Following the death of the client, the trust can continue for the benefit of the surviving spouse, children, and grandchildren. The trust then terminates at some later date, such as on the death of the surviving spouse. Because the trust is funded during the client's lifetime, there is no delay in paying income to the trust beneficiaries when the client dies. Of course, a delay would occur if the trust were not funded until during the settlement of the client's estate. Also, the living trust may save estate settlement costs such as executor and legal fees in states in which those costs are calculated as a percentage of the probate estate. This is because the assets that are already in the living trust do not make up a part of the probate estate on which those costs are calculated.

Rather than transfer assets into the trust when it is first established, some clients delay funding until a future time of disability or poor health. This variation of the living trust is sometimes termed a *standby trust*. Basically, the client establishes a revocable living trust that contains most of the same provisions as in any living trust. The primary difference between a standby trust and the typical living trust is that the standby trust is not funded until disability or poor health occurs. For example, the client establishes a standby trust naming a corporate or individual trustee but does not transfer any property into the trust. A relative, friend, or the trustee is given a limited power of attorney that will enable the agent (attorney-in-fact) to transfer the client's property to the trustee should the client become disabled or seriously ill. The determination of disability or serious illness is normally made by the client's treating physician. If the client never becomes disabled, the trust will not be funded and will remain inactive. The trust simply "stands by" until needed. Often the trust is funded following the client's death for the benefit of the surviving spouse, but this is not essential. The trust can terminate and pass to the client's estate to be distributed as provided in the client's will.

In this writer's opinion, the living trust has been over popularized by those vendors who sell trust forms designed to avoid the alleged horrors of probate. With that personal bias expressed, the living trust is nonetheless often a preferable alternative to the durable power of attorney for several reasons. First, if a financial institution is handling the elder client's financial affairs, most prefer acting as a trustee as the laws governing that relationship are more clearly defined. Second, there may be less difficulty with third parties relying on the action of a trustee than on the agent acting under the power of attorney. For example, some third parties, particularly some brokerage houses, are concerned over actions taken by an agent under a power of attorney that was executed a number of years ago. Some brokers insist on a current power of attorney. Obviously, this is impossible if the principal is incompetent, but some do make these requests. Interestingly the same institutions do not seem concerned about the "staleness" of a trust agreement. There is no logical distinction, but institutional third parties are used to transacting business with trustees and have less experience working with powers of attorney. Third, in estates in which the assets are going to pass into a trust at death, it is more efficient to go ahead and transfer assets now to the trust than to use a power of attorney. Finally, if the probate process will be simplified by placing the client's assets in trust then the trust should be used.

A sample pour-over will and a sample living trust follow. Several points should be recognized when using these forms. First, there are no provisions to lessen the federal estate taxes should the estate exceed the exclusion amount, which in 2019 is $11,400,000.[6] Second, note paragraph "N Estate Transactions" in the earlier power of attorney form for wording to transfer assets to the "stand by trust." Third, the pour-over will and the trust are both drafted to demonstrate the fundamentals of each document. You should customize the documents to your client's specific situation, including more specific provisions as to distribution of the estate, and of course, complying with requirements of your own state law.

Sample Pour-Over Will

I, John A. Roe, a resident of Madisonville, Hopkins County, Kentucky, make this my Last Will and Testament, hereby revoking all prior wills and codicils.

ARTICLE I

I direct that my just debts, funeral expenses, costs of administration and all estate, inheritance, or other transfer taxes which become payable by reason of my death, be paid out of my residuary estate as soon as practicable after my death.

ARTICLE II

I bequeath and devise all the rest, residue, and remainder of the property, real or personal, and wheresoever situated, which I own or in which I may have an interest at my death to the Trustee under a Trust Agreement executed by me on _____ day of _____, 20____, and in full force and effect on the date of the execution of this Will.

Comment: A pour-over will is normally a permissible testamentary instrument; however, the trust must be in existence before the execution of the will. This simply requires that the trust be executed first and then the will. The lawyer must be certain of the effect of a pour-over will under state law.

ARTICLE III

I nominate and appoint _____ as Executor of this my Last Will and Testament. I grant my Executor full power and authority to compromise or otherwise settle or adjust any and all claims, charges, debts or demands against or in favor of my estate, as fully as I could do if living, and with full power, without order of court, to sell, transfer, or convey any of my property, real or personal, for the purpose of administration, division or distribution in carrying out the terms of this Will.

I also expressly empower my Executor to sell to the Trustee under the Trust Agreement referred to hereinabove, for cash, any assets in my estate which in the sole discretion of my Executor may be necessary or expedient in order to produce cash for the payment of taxes or costs of administration, such sale to be at the prevailing market price or fair and reasonable market value at the time of said sale. My Executor may determine, without regard to any rule of law, what assets shall be sold in order to produce cash for the purposes hereinabove set out.

I nominate and appoint _____ to be the successor Executor. Either my Executor or my successor Executor shall be allowed to serve without surety on their bond and without performing any formalities in the settlement of my estate as are not mandatory under the law.

IN TESTIMONY WHEREOF, I have hereunto set my hand on this the _____ day of _____, 20____.

_____

John A. Roe

We, whose names are hereto signed as subscribing witnesses, have at the request of the Testator,_____, witnessed the execution of this Will, consisting of this page and _____ (___) preceding pages, and each has signed as subscribing witness in the presence of the Testator and in the presence of each other on the ____ day _____ of, 20____.

_____   _____
Witness   Address

_____   _____
Witness   Address

ADD SELF-PROVING NOTARIZATION AS PROVIDED BY STATE LAW

Sample Living Trust

THIS TRUST AGREEMENT is entered into by, JOHN A. ROE, of Madisonville, Kentucky, as both Settlor and Trustee.

WITNESSETH:

I have delivered or will deliver to the Trustee the property described in Schedule A. Upon receipt of this property, the Trustee agrees to hold it in trust and to manage and dispose of it according to the provisions of this Trust Agreement.

ARTICLE I

A. During my lifetime, the Trustee shall pay to me and my wife, Jane D. Roe, or pay for our benefit, as much of the net income and principal from the trust as I shall request. If I make no request, due to disability or otherwise, the Trustee may distribute to, or for the benefit of, my wife and me, such amounts of income and principal, as needed for our reasonable health, maintenance, and support. If any net income remains at the end of each trust year, the Trustee shall add it to the principal of the trust.

B. Upon my death, the Trustee shall pay all expenses and indebtedness of my estate, including the expenses of my last illness and funeral, unless other provisions have been made for their payment. Also, the Trustee shall pay any administrative expenses and any estate, inheritance, or other death taxes that are owed by my estate.

C. If my wife, Jane D. Roe, survives me, the trust shall continue and the Trustee shall manage and dispose of the Trust as follows:

1. The Trustee shall pay as much of the net income and principal as necessary to provide for the health, support, and maintenance of my wife, Jane D. Roe. If any net income remains at the end of the trust year, the Trustee shall add it to the principal of the trust.

2. Upon the death of my wife, the Trustee shall pay all expenses and indebtedness of the estate of my wife, including expenses for her last illness and funeral, as well as any administrative expenses and any real estate, inheritance, or other death taxes that are owed by the estate or my wife.

D. After the death of both my wife and me, the trust shall terminate and the Trustee shall divide the trust property into two equal shares, one for the benefit of each of our children, _____ and _____, and distribute each share outright to each child. In the event either of our children should die prior to receiving his or her complete distribution from the trust estate, then the share to which that deceased child would have been entitled had that child been living at the time of distribution shall be distributed outright and per stirpes to the issue of that deceased child. If the deceased child should have no issue surviving at the time of distribution from the trust estate, then that child's share shall be distributed by the Trustee to our other than surviving child, if living, and if not, to that child's issue, per stirpes.

ARTICLE II

I, or any other person, may at any time add property to the principal of the trust with the consent of the Trustee. Any additions to the trust shall be administered according to the provisions of this trust agreement.

ARTICLE III

I grant the Trustee all powers generally conferred upon a Trustee by state law. The Trustee shall have the following powers in addition to any other powers given to the Trustee in this trust or by law.

A. The Trustee may keep in the trust any original property received from me, or from any other source even though the property may not be the type of property prescribed by law for the investment of trust funds.

B. The Trustee may sell publicly or privately any property of the trust without a court order and upon such terms as it deems proper.

C. The Trustee may invest and reinvest any part or all of the principal of the trust in stocks, bonds, mortgages, shares in common trust funds, or other securities, as well as any other real or personal property.

D. The Trustee may exercise discretion as to diversification of trust property and shall not be required to reduce any concentrated holdings merely because of such concentration. The Trustee is also relieved from any requirements there may be as to the percentage of the trust to be invested in fixed income securities and may invest wholly in common stocks.

E. The Trustee shall have the full power to sell, exchange, lease, mortgage, repair, and improve and take any prudent steps with regard to any real estate that may be a part of the trust. Any contract on real estate in the trust which is made by the Trustee shall be binding for the full period of the contract if the period extends beyond the determination of the trust.

F. The Trustee shall have the power to vote shares of stock held in the trust, either in person or by proxy, and with or without the power of substitution.

G. The Trustee may participate in the liquidation, reorganization, incorporation, or any other financial readjustment of any corporation or business in which the trust is financially interested.

H. The Trustee shall have full power to borrow money from any source, including the Trustee in the Trustee's individual capacity, for any purpose connected with the trust property and to mortgage or pledge as security any property of the trust upon such conditions as the Trustee deems proper.

I. The Trustee shall have the right to hold any security in bearer form, in the Trustee's own name, or in the name of a duly appointed nominee.

J. Any time the Trustee is required to divide the principal of the trust, the Trustee may make such division in cash, or in kind, or both, and the judgment of the Trustee concerning the proper way to make such a division and to value the property being divided shall be binding on all parties.

K. During the incapacity of any beneficiary to whom income or principal may be spent, the Trustee may pay the income and principal in any one or more of the following ways: (1) to the legal guardian of the beneficiary; (2) to a relative of the beneficiary to be spent by the relative for the support, maintenance, and health care of the beneficiary; and (3) by making payments directly for the support, maintenance, and health care of the beneficiary. The Trustee shall not be required to see to the application of any money paid and the receipt from the person to whom the monies are paid shall be full acquittance to the Trustee.

L. In general, the Trustee shall have the same powers, authorities, and discretions in the management of the trust property as I would have in the management and control of my own property.

ARTICLE IV

If I cease to act as Trustee, or if I am incompetent, then my wife, Jane D. Roe, shall act as Trustee. If my wife fails or ceases to act as Trustee, then my children, _____ and _____, shall act as Co-Trustees. No bond or court reporting shall be required of my Trustees.

ARTICLE V

I declare this Trust Agreement to be revocable and I may alter, amend or revoke this trust at any time and in any way.

ARTICLE VI

This Trust Agreement shall be construed and regulated by the laws of Kentucky.

IN TESTIMONY WHEREOF, the undersigned have signed their names to this Trust Agreement consisting of this and _____ (___) preceding pages on the _____ day of _____, 20____.

_____
Settlor & Trustee

_____
Successor Trustee

_____
Witness

_____
Witness

STATE OF (State of Notary)   )
) SCT.
COUNTY OF (County of Notary))
    The undersigned, a Notary Public within and for the state and country aforesaid, does hereby certify that the foregoing trust agreement executed by _____(settlor's name) as Settlor and Trustee, was on this day produced to me in the county by _____ (settlor's name), who executed, acknowledged and swore the same before me to be (his or her) act and deed in due form of law.
    Given under my hand and notarial seal on this the _____ day of _____, 20___.
STATE OF (State of Notary)   )
) SCT.
COUNTY OF (County of Notary))
    The undersigned, a Notary Public within and for the state and country aforesaid, does hereby certify that the foregoing trust agreement executed by _____, (successor trustee's name) as Successor Trustee, was on this day produced to me in the county by _____, (successor trustee's name) who executed, acknowledged and swore the same before me to be (his or her) act and deed in due form of law.
    Given under my hand and notarial seal on this the _____ day of _____, 20___.

_____
Notary Public, State at Large
My commission expires:_____

STATE OF (State of Notary)   )
) SCT.
COUNTY OF (County of Notary))
    The undersigned, a Notary Public within and for the state and county aforesaid, does hereby certify that the foregoing trust agreement was witnessed by _____ and _____ on this day in due form of law.

Given under my hand and notarial seal on this the _____ day of _____, 20___.

_____
Notary Public, State at Large
My commission expires:_____

SCHEDULE A

ASSETS   DATE TRANSFERRED
Ten Dollars ($10.00)   January 1, 2019

XIV. Simple Will

This is a sample simple will. It would be used in those simple estate plans in which the entire estate passes from one spouse to the other and then to the ultimate beneficiaries, typically the children. This will would not be used in estate plans involving federal estate tax planning. Those types of legal documents are beyond the scope of this text. The author's two ABA books, *A Lawyer's Guide to Estate Planning*, Fourth Edition, and *Estate Planning Forms*, will be helpful. Also, in estate plans that do not involve estate tax planning, there still may be a need to have a trust to hold the beneficiary's inherited share due to either asset protection reasons or special life circumstances, such as addictions, that require the use of a trust to better provide for the estate beneficiary. Again, the two referenced publications will be helpful in those situations. Finally, many clients prefer to utilize a trust in order to simplify estate settlement. Again, that is not the focus of this text, thus the aforementioned publications will be helpful in those planning situations.

LAST WILL AND TESTAMENT OF [FULL NAME OF CLIENT]
I, [Full Name of Client], currently of [Client's City], [Client's State], make this my last will and testament, hereby revoking all wills and codicils previously made by me.

1. *Family Information.* My [husband/wife]'s name is [husband's/wife's name], and all references in this will to "my [husband/wife]" are only to [him/her].

OPTION 1: Naming of all children My [child is or children are] [names of children], and all references in this will to "my [child or children]" are only to [him/her/them].

OPTION 2: Inclusion of step-children Even though some of these children are step-children, it is my intent that each of the above-named children be treated for purposes of inheriting under this will as if they and their lineal descendants are my natural-born children and descendants.

OPTION 3: After-born children If subsequent to the execution of this will there shall be an additional child or children born to me, then such child or children shall share in the benefits of my estate to the same extent as my above-named children and their descendants; and the provisions of this will shall be deemed modified to the extent necessary to carry out this intent.

Comment: The full name of the other spouse and children should be inserted. If step-children are involved, Option 2 should be considered. Also, Option 3 may be appropriate if there is the possibility of additional children. The lawyer's state law should provide for this contingency, but it still may be appropriate to add this provision to the will.

OPTION 4: Adopted and illegitimately born children The words "child," "children," "descendant," or "descendants" shall exclude adopted persons unless they are adopted prior to [insert written age (numerical age)] years; and shall include only persons legitimately born unless a decree of adoption terminates the parental rights of the natural mother during her lifetime, or the natural father signs a written notarized instrument during his lifetime in which he irrevocably states that the child is to be considered legitimately born for purposes of inheriting under this will.

Comment: Some clients will want to restrict distribution for an adopted child to preclude a child adopted as an adult. Thus, many will use age 18 or perhaps a slightly older age such as 20 or 21. Other clients may wish to restrict the age to a younger adopted child, such as under the age of 10. The issue of illegitimate children should also be addressed. In many situations, a child or more remote descendant should be treated the same as any other child, in which case the portion of this paragraph that deals with illegitimate children can be deleted. In other situations there may be a limited or no relationship with the child, in which event no distribution should be made to that child. This form gives the father the right to allow the child to inherit by the father signing a written document allowing inheritance.

OPTION 5: Disinheritance I have made no provisions for the benefit of my [relationship], [name], for reasons that need not be expressed.

Comment: If a child is to be disinherited, then it is wise practice to mention the child's name to clarify the child is not to receive a share so that no claim can be made that the client intended for the child to inherit, but the lawyer drafting the document failed to name the child.

2. *Payment of Debts, Death Taxes, and Funeral Expenses.* I direct that all of my just debts, my funeral expenses, costs of estate administration, and death taxes, if any, be paid from the residue of my estate as soon as possible after my death. I further direct that any real property that is subject to a mortgage or lien shall pass under my will subject to such mortgage or lien, rather than such indebtedness being paid from my estate.

Comment: This paragraph first provides for the payment of all debts and final expenses, then imposes any death taxes on the residue to the estate. Any mortgage indebtedness is not to be paid from the residue but is to pass to the beneficiary who is the recipient of that property subject to the debt. If the debt is to be paid, then this second sentence should be deleted.

3. *Specific Gift.* **OPTION 1: Single gift** I give to my [relationship], [name], if [he or she] survives me, [gift], if owned by me at my death.

OPTION 2: Multiple gifts To the individuals listed below, I give the following:

a. To my [relationship], [name], if [he or she] survives me, [gift], if owned by me at my death.

b. To my [relationship], [name], if [he or she] survives me, [gift], if owned by me at my death.

4. *Advancements.* I have made gifts to various of my children and may make additional gifts in the future, all of which I have made record of in my personal papers.

OPTION 1: Gifts not considered None of these gifts shall be considered an advancement and thus these gifts shall not be taken into account in determining the distribution of my estate.

OPTION 2: Gifts considered These gifts shall be considered an advancement without interest to the recipient and shall be taken into account in determining the distribution of my estate.

Comment: Oftentimes, the testator has made gifts to a child or other beneficiary prior to death. If that is the case, a decision needs to be made whether those gifts are to be considered a gift or an advancement against the inheritance.

5. *Loans.* I have made loans to various of my children and may make additional loans in the future, all of which I have made record of in my personal papers.

OPTION 1: Loans forgiven I forgive these loans, thus these loans shall not be taken into account in determining the distribution of my estate.

OPTION 2: Loans collected These loans shall be considered an advancement without interest to the recipient and shall be taken into account in determining the distribution of my estate.

Comment: If the client has made loans to the children or other estate beneficiaries, then a clear statement in the will as to whether that loan is forgiven or is to be collected will avoid administrative problems for the personal representative and will ensure that the testator has given proper consideration to the effect of gifts.

6. *Disposition of Tangible Personal Property.* I give to my [husband or wife] all of my personal and household effects, including but not limited to furniture, furnishings, appliances, clothing, jewelry, automobiles, and any other similar tangible personal property. If my [husband or wife] does not survive me, I give all such tangible personal property to my [child or children] in as nearly equal shares as is possible.

OPTION 1: If no agreement personal representative decides If my children cannot agree upon this division within ninety (90) days after the appointment of my personal representative, then the division made by my personal representative shall be final and binding upon my children and shall not be subject to question by anyone or in any court.

OPTION 2: If no agreement sell and pass to residue If my children cannot agree upon this division within ninety (90) days after the appointment of my personal representative, then my personal representative shall sell all property with respect to which my children have not reached an agreement and the net sales proceeds shall be distributed as part of the residue of my estate.

Comment: Gifts of personal property can be the source of family disagreements and even litigation. While the initial gift of such property to the surviving spouse is not a problem, the problem arises when the personal property passes to the children. Options 1 and 2 provide two different approaches for handling distribution in the event of a disagreement. The lawyer may choose either of those options, write his/her own method of resolving the conflict, or leave out these options and let the probate court deal with the problem. This writer has found that going to court over grandmother's clock is not something most clients want their children to do. Thus, Option 1, Option 2, or some variation may be helpful.

I may leave with my will or among my papers a handwritten letter or handwritten memorandum concerning the distribution of certain items of my tangible personal property. If so, I direct my personal representative to distribute those items of my tangible personal property as I have provided in that letter or memorandum.

Comment: Some clients have numerous items of personal property that they want to give to family and friends. Rather than having a lengthy will naming these items, some lawyers prefer the use of a handwritten letter that is dated and signed at the bottom of the page by the testator. This approach allows the ease of changing the document over the years. It has the disadvantage of possibly not being an enforceable document depending upon state law. If the document qualifies under state law as a holographic codicil, or due to enactment of Section 2-513 of the Uniform Probate Code, then it is enforceable and the personal representative is required to account for those items named in the letter and to ensure their distribution to the correct beneficiary. A problem with the handwritten letter is that it is unlikely that it will be written so as to address the lapse of a gift if a beneficiary predeceases the testator and the applicability of the rule of ademption in the event the gift is no longer in existence at the testator's death.

7. *Residuary Estate.* I give the residue of my estate to my [husband or wife], if [he or she] survives me. If my [husband or wife] does not survive me, I give the residue of my estate in equal shares to my children. If a child should die before me, I give the share of my deceased child to such child's surviving lineal descendants, per stirpes. If a deceased child has no living lineal descendants, the share of my deceased child shall be given to my other descendants, per stirpes.

Comment: This is a basic provision that provides for the residue passing to the surviving spouse if living and, if not, then to the children or more remote living descendants if children are deceased. Care must be taken to be certain that the outright distribution to the non-spouse beneficiaries is properly defined.

8. *Default Provisions.* If all beneficiaries under this instrument are deceased, my estate or trust assets shall be distributed to [default provisions].

9. *Appointment of Personal Representative.* My [husband or wife] shall be the personal representative of my estate. If my [husband or wife] fails to qualify as personal representative, or having qualified, dies, becomes incompetent, resigns, or declines to continue to serve, then my [relationship of successor PR], [name of successor PR], shall serve as my successor personal representative. Neither my [husband or wife] nor my successor personal representative shall be required to furnish any surety bond for serving as my personal representative.

Comment: The full names of the personal representative and successor personal representative are required, as is a decision concerning the waiver of a surety bond. The form, as drafted, assumes the intent to waive such bond.

10. *Powers of Personal Representative.* I hereby grant to my personal representative (including my successor personal representative) the absolute power to deal with any property, real or personal, held in my estate, as freely as I might in the handling of my own affairs. This power may be exercised independently and without the approval of any court, and no person dealing with my personal representative shall be required to inquire into the propriety of the actions of my personal representative. Without in any way limiting the generality of the foregoing provisions, I grant to my personal representative in addition to those powers specified under state law the following powers:

a. To sell, exchange, assign, transfer, and convey any security or property, real or personal, held in my estate at public or private sale, at such time and at such reasonable price and upon such reasonable terms and conditions (including credit) as my personal representative may determine; and without regard to whether or not such sale is necessary in order to settle my estate.

b. To lease any real estate for such term, or terms, and upon such reasonable conditions and rentals and in such manner as my personal representative deems proper, and any lease so made shall be valid and binding for its full term even though such lease term extends beyond the duration of the administration of my estate; to make repairs, replacements, and improvements, structural or otherwise, to any such real estate; to subdivide real estate, dedicate real estate to public use, and grant easements as my personal representative deems proper.

c. To employ accountants, attorneys, and such other agents as my personal representative deems necessary; to pay reasonable compensation for such services; and to charge same to (or apportion same between) income and principal as my personal representative deems proper.

Comment: A statement of the powers of the personal representative is not essential, as those powers are specified by state law; however, those state laws may not be sufficiently broad. Often state laws do not include power to real estate. Paragraph 10.c may not be essential, but this writer prefers to clarify that the personal representative may hire at the expense of the estate professionals to assist in estate settlement.

IN TESTIMONY WHEREOF, I, [Name of Client], sign my name to this instrument this the _____ day of _____, [current year], and being first duly sworn, do hereby declare to the undersigned authority that I sign and execute this instrument as my last will and that I sign it willingly, that I execute it as my free and voluntary act for the purposes therein expressed, and that I am eighteen (18) years of age or older, of sound mind, and under no constraint or undue influence.

_____
[Name of Client]

We _____ and _____, the witnesses, sign our names to this instrument, being first duly sworn, and do hereby declare to the undersigned authority that [Name of Client] signs and executes this instrument as [his or her] Last Will and Testament dated _____, [current year], and that [he or she] signs it willingly and that each of us, in the presence and hearing of [Name of Client] and in the presence of the other subscribing witness, hereby signs this Last Will and Testament as witness to [Name of Client]'s signing, and that to the best of our knowledge, [Name of Client] is eighteen (18) years of age or older, of sound mind, and under no constraint or undue influence, all on this the _____ day of _____, [current year].

_____   _____
Witness   Address

_____   _____
Witness   Address

STATE OF KENTUCKY   )
) SCT.
COUNTY OF HOPKINS   )

Subscribed, sworn to, and acknowledged before me by [Name of Client], and subscribed and sworn to before me by _____ and _____, witnesses, this the _____ day of _____, [current year].

_____
Notary Public, State at Large
My Commission Expires: _____
Notary ID: _____

   Comment: The above provisions are in compliance with the writer's own state law to avoid the necessity of locating witnesses to the will at a later date. This provision should be modified to meet the requirements of the lawyer's own state law.

PREPARED BY:

_____
[Name of Attorney]
[Name of Law Firm]
Attorneys at Law
[Street Address]
[City], [State] [Zip Code]
[Telephone Number]

Notes

1. Cruzan v. Director, MO Dep't of Health, 497 U.S. 261 (1990).
2. *In re* Quinlan, 70 N.J. 20, 355 A.2d 647 (1976).
3. Matter of Conroy, 98 N.J. 321, 486 A.2d 1209 (1985).
4. 497 U.S. 261.
5. Based on KRS 311.625.
6. A helpful resource is HUNT, A LAWYER'S GUIDE TO ESTATE PLANNING (American Bar Association 4th ed. 2018).

CHAPTER 3

Social Security

   I. Overview 68
  II. Social Security Basics. 69
      A. Persons Eligible for Social Security 69
      B. Payment Procedures 70
      C. Rules for Representative Payee. 70
      D. Rules for Overpayments. 71
      E. Rules for Underpayments 71
      F. Lump Sum Death Benefit. 72
 III. Insured Status. 72
      A. Insured Individuals. 72
      B. Fully Insured Individuals. 72
      C. Currently Insured Individuals. 73
      D. Disability Insured Individuals. 73
      E. Earning Credits 73
 IV. Calculating Benefits 74
      A. Determining the Primary Insurance Amount (PIA) 74
      B. Determining the PIA by the Average Indexed
         Monthly Earnings Method. 75
      C. Alternate Methods of Calculating PIA. 75
      D. How the Family Maximum Rule Affects the Benefit
         Amount 75
      E. Grounds for Reduction of Benefits. 76
   V. Social Security Retirement (Old-Age Benefits) 76
      A. Background. 76
      B. How Excess Earnings May Reduce Social Security
         Retirement Benefit Amount. 78
 VI. Husband's and Wife's Benefits 78
      A. Introduction 78
      B. Deemed Valid Marriages 79
      C. How a Spouse Qualifies for Husband's and Wife's Benefits. . . . 79
      D. How a Divorced Spouse Qualifies for Husband's or
         Wife's Benefits 79
      E. When Husband's and Wife's Benefits Terminate. 80

VII. Widow's and Widower's Benefits 81
    A. Introduction 81
    B. How a Spouse Qualifies for Widow's or
       Widower's Benefits 81
    C. How a Divorced Spouse Qualifies for Widows or
       Widower's Benefits 82
    D. When Widow's or Widower's Benefits Terminate. 83
VIII. Mother's or Father's Benefits. 83
    A. Introduction 83
    B. How a Divorced Spouse Qualifies for Mother's or
       Father's Benefits. 83
    C. When Mother's or Father's Benefits Terminate 84
IX. Parent's Benefits 84
    A. Introduction 84
    B. How to Qualify for Parent's Benefits. 85
    C. When Parent's Benefits Terminate 85
X. Child's Benefits. 85
    A. Introduction 85
    B. How to Qualify for Child's Benefits 86
    C. How the Dependency Requirement is Satisfied 86
    D. Rules for Adopted Children 86
    E. Rules for Grandchildren and Step-Grandchildren. 87
    F. When a Child's Benefits Terminate 87
XI. Disability Insurance Benefits 88
    A. Introduction 88
    B. How an Individual Qualifies for Disability Benefits. 89
    C. Substantial Gainful Activity (SGA) 89
    D. What Constitutes SGA for Blind Individuals 89
    E. Drug Addiction and Alcoholism Are No Longer
       Basis for Disability. 90
    F. When Disability Benefits Terminate. 90
XII. Appeals Procedure. 90
    A. The Initial Determination Stage 90
    B. The Reconsideration Stage. 91
    C. The Administrative Law Judge (ALJ) Stage 91
    D. The Appeals Council Stage 91
    E. Judicial Review in Federal Court 92
    F. Expedited Appeals Process 92
    G. Attorney's Fees. 92
Appendix A: Social Security Retirement Checklist 93

I. Overview

Clients will have some questions concerning social security benefits. They will be interested in deciding whether or not to take early benefits, wait until full retirement age, or delay benefits until age 70 in order to receive a larger monthly benefit. The discussions at Sections IV and V will be of interest in that regard as will the reduction of benefits, discussed in Section V.B. Clients will also be interested in the issues around taxation of their benefits. The income tax issue is discussed in Chapter 9, Section XII.B.

The calculation of retirement benefits for your clients and their spouses is another area of interest. This is discussed in Section IV. Benefits for the surviving spouse are also of importance. Those discussions begin in Section VI. Note that benefits for a surviving spouse also apply to a divorced spouse, depending on the length of the marriage and a few other factors. Section VI.D will be helpful in that area.

Few elder clients have children young enough to be concerned about a child receiving benefits. But, for some elder clients, benefits that are payable to an adult disabled child are important. Those benefits may be payable prior to the parents retirement under the disability insurance benefits, which are discussed beginning at Section XI. Once the parent is retired, then benefits will be payable due to the parent's retirement (see the discussion at Section X).

It is easy to get bogged down in the details of the social security law. At its simplest, social security provides retirement benefits for your elder client and surviving spouse, as well as benefits for persons who may be dependent on a retired elder client, particularly a disabled adult child. The Social Security Administration (SSA) has an excellent web page that provides a significant amount of information (see www.ssa.gov), including a booklet entitled *Understanding the Benefits*. You may want to print it and give to your client. The chapter concludes with a checklist that may be of help to your client (see Appendix A).

II. Social Security Basics

A. Persons Eligible for Social Security

To advise the elder client, an understanding of the basics of social security eligibility and benefits is essential. The Social Security Act encompasses a number of programs designed to provide for the financial needs of the general population and especially for the elderly.[1] Programs especially pertinent to an elderly client include retirement insurance, survivors insurance, and disability insurance. Social security benefits can be paid to the following:

- A disabled insured worker under full retirement age.
- A retired insured worker at age 62 or older.
- The spouse of a retired or disabled worker entitled to benefits who:
  1. Is age 62 or older, or
  2. Cares for a child under age 16 or a child over age 16 who is disabled and entitled to benefits on the worker's social security record, and
  3. Has been married to the worker for a year, or is the parent of the worker's child.
- The unmarried divorced spouse of a retired or disabled worker entitled to benefits if age 62 or over and if married to the worker for at least ten years.

- The divorced spouse of a fully insured worker who has not yet filed a claim for benefits if both the divorced spouse and the worker are age 62 or older, were married for ten years, and have been finally divorced for at least two continuous years.
- The dependent, unmarried child of a retired or disabled worker who is entitled to benefits, or of a deceased insured worker if the child is:
  1. Under 18.
  2. 18 and a full time school student.
  3. 18 or older but has a disability which began before age 22.
- The surviving spouse, including a surviving divorced spouse who was married to the worker for ten years, of a deceased insured worker provided the widow(er) is age 60 or older.
- The disabled surviving spouse, including a disabled divorced surviving spouse who was married to the worker for ten years, of a deceased insured worker if the widow(er) is age 50 to 59 and becomes disabled:
  1. Within seven years after the month the insured worker died, or who becomes disabled.
  2. Within seven years after the last month the widow(er) was previously entitled to benefits based on the deceased insured worker's earnings record.
- The surviving spouse, including the surviving divorced spouse, of a deceased insured worker, regardless of age, if the surviving spouse or surviving divorced spouse is caring for a child who is either under age 16 or became disabled before age 22.
- The dependent parents of a deceased insured worker who are age 62 or older.

B. *Payment Procedures*

The question of when your elderly client will receive his or her monthly payment depends on a few factors. Generally, payments are dated and delivered on the second Wednesday of the month for individuals born on the 1st through the 10th of the month, on the third Wednesday of the month for individuals born on the 11th through the 20th of the month, on the fourth Wednesday of the month for individuals born on the 21st of the month or later. If the payment Wednesday falls on a federal holiday, payments are dated and delivered on the preceding day that is not a federal holiday.[2]

All federal benefits, including social security payments, are sent by direct deposit.[3] Beneficiaries who receive their social security through direct deposit still need to advise SSA of a change of address or residence to enable SSA to communicate with the beneficiary or send the beneficiary forms.

C. *Rules for Representative Payee*

Elder clients who can no longer manage their own financial affairs can have their benefits paid to a representative payee. The payee is determined by the SSA. It will pay benefits to a representative payee on behalf of a beneficiary in cases where the beneficiary is legally incompetent or physically incapable of managing his benefits.[4] The SSA considers different types of evidence in determining if a representative payee should be appointed, including the opinion of the beneficiary's physician, statements of relatives or friends of the beneficiary, as well as a court order of adjudication.[5] When selecting who should serve as payee, the SSA considers the relationship of the potential payee to the beneficiary, the amount of interest the potential payee takes in the beneficiary, any legal authority that the potential payee has to act on behalf of the payee, if the potential payee has custody of the beneficiary, and if the potential payee will be able to take care of the beneficiary's needs.[6] Preference is given by SSA to legal guardians, spouses, or relatives who have custody of the beneficiary or who demonstrate "strong concern for the personal welfare of the beneficiary."[7] Accordingly, an individual with a power of attorney from the beneficiary who does not meet this criteria may not be approved by SSA as payee. A representative payee is required to use the beneficiary's payments for food, shelter, clothing, medical care, and personal comfort items, and provide an annual accounting to SSA.[8] If the payee misuses the beneficiary's benefits, the beneficiary's only recourse is against the payee, as SSA considers its obligations to the beneficiary satisfied when correct payment is made to the payee.[9]

D. Rules for Overpayments

If an overpayment of benefits occurs, SSA will withhold the individual's benefits until the overpayment is satisfied. An individual may seek a waiver of the overpayment if the individual was without fault and recovery of the overpayment would be against equity and good conscience or defeat the purpose of social security.[10] If a waiver of the overpayment is not obtained, SSA may still provide some relief by reducing the amount withheld from the individual's benefits. Use Form SSA-632 for a waiver or reduced monthly payments. If the overpayment is caused by the individual's intentional false statements or representation, willful concealment of, or deliberate failure to furnish material information, adjustment of the overpayment to avoid a hardship on the recipient is not permitted.[11] If the individual is an enrollee in Part B Medicare, and the overpayment of benefits is not caused by the individual's intentional false statements, willful concealment of material information, and so on, SSA will continue to allow the required amount for payment of the Part B premium to be paid so that the individual will continue to qualify for Medicare Part B coverage.[12] If the individual is deceased, SSA may withhold any payment due the individual's estate or withhold benefits from persons such as the individual's widow(er) or children who are due benefits on the individual's earnings record unless a hardship adjustment is obtained.[13]

E. Rules for Underpayments

If an underpayment of benefits occurs, SSA will pay the underpayment either in a single lump sum payment if the individual is not entitled to monthly benefit payments, or by increasing the individual's monthly benefit payment if the individual is entitled to monthly benefit payments.[14] If the individual is deceased, social security will pay the underpayment to the individual's surviving spouse, provided he or she was residing in the deceased's household at the time of death or entitled to a monthly benefit on the basis of the deceased's earnings record. If there is no surviving spouse who meets this criteria, SSA will utilizes a priority list to determine who should receive the underpayment, commencing with the deceased's children who are entitled to receive benefits on the deceased's earnings record.[15]

F. Lump Sum Death Benefit

A rather odd benefit that used to be meaningful when funeral expenses were small remains in the law. A lump sum death benefit of $255 is available if an individual is either fully insured or currently insured at her death.[16] The benefit is payable to the insured's surviving spouse provided that the surviving spouse was living in the insured's household at the time of death. If the insured's surviving spouse was not living in the insured's household at the time of the insured's death, the surviving spouse remains entitled to the lump sum benefit if the surviving spouse is eligible for either widow's or widower's benefits or mother's or father's benefits. The lump sum benefit is not payable to a divorced spouse.[17] If there is no surviving spouse, the lump sum benefit may be paid to the insured's child provided the child was eligible for benefits on the insured's earnings records for the month the insured died. If the insured is survived by more than one child, each child receives an equal share.[18]

III. Insured Status
A. Insured Individuals

In order for benefits to be paid to an individual, the individual must meet insured status. An individual can be fully insured, currently insured, or insured for disability status. To determine the insured status of an individual, SSA uses the lifetime record of the individual's reported earnings and counts the number of quarters which are termed covered credits. These credits are also referred to as quarters of coverage. Earning records are no longer mailed annually except to workers age 60 and over who are not receiving benefits and do not have a "My Social Security Account." A person's earnings record can be obtained by a request to the SSA using Form SSA-7004 or by going to www.ssa.gov and creating a My Social Security Account. The practitioner should note that while attainment of insured status is necessary to qualify for payment of benefits, insured status has no bearing on the amount of benefits to be paid an individual. That is based on the person's earnings record.

B. Fully Insured Individuals

Individuals with fully insured status are eligible for old-age retirement benefits, or as it is more commonly termed social security retirement benefits.

Generally, fully insured status for this purpose is easily determined. A person born in 1929 or later is considered fully insured for life if they have at least 40 quarters of coverage. A person born before 1929 needs fewer credits to have fully insured status.[19]

Also, SSA will grant fully insured status to individuals who were at least 55 years of age on January 1, 1984, and employees of a nonprofit, noncovered employers, whose employers did not have a wavier certificate from the IRS in effect on January 1, 1984, provided that the employees, depending on their age on January 2, 1984, had the required quarters of coverage.[20] Obviously, this is an exception that applies to very few individuals.

C. Currently Insured Individuals

An individual who does not meet fully insured status may meet currently insured status which may qualify the individual for payment of certain benefits. A person meets currently insured status if she has at least six quarters of coverage during the entire 13-quarter period ending with the calendar quarter in which she either (1) dies, (2) most recently became entitled to disability benefits, or (3) became entitled to retirement insurance benefits. After the currently insured person's death, child's benefits, mother's benefits, father's benefits, and the lump sum death benefit are the only benefits that are payable if an individual only meets currently insured status.

D. Disability Insured Individuals

Although elder clients will not usually be concerned with receiving benefits due to disability, a brief review of disability insured status may be helpful. An individual will meet disability insured status if he has at least 20 quarters of coverage during a 40-quarter period ending with the quarter in which he is determined disabled and was fully insured in that quarter, that is, the individual has paid social security taxes the last five out of ten years before he became disabled. Individuals who become disabled before age 31 may qualify for disabled insured status if in the quarter that the disability is determined to have begun or in a later quarter, the individual is (1) 30 or younger, (2) has credits in at least one-half of the quarters during the period beginning with the quarter after the quarter in which he attained age 21 and ending with the quarter in which he became disabled, and (3) meets fully insured status. If a person becomes disabled before the quarter in which she reaches age 24, she need have only six quarters of coverage in the 12-quarter period ending with the quarter in which her disability began. Persons who are disabled due to blindness, regardless of age, do not have to meet the 20 credits in 40 quarters or special insured status tests as long as the person meets fully insured status.

E. Earning Credits

Beginning in 1978 and continuing to the present, the commissioner of the SSA uses a formula that reflects national percentage increases in average wages and determines the amount of earnings that will equal a credit for each year. Each year the amount of wages or self-employment income necessary to acquire a quarter of coverage is published in the Federal Register.[21] For 2019, the figure is $1,360.[22] A maximum of four quarters of coverage may be earned each year based on total earnings for the year. In addition, earnings may include both agricultural and non-agricultural wages, self-employment income, military wages, and railroad compensation. For example, Hilda is employed in the year 2019 from February 15 through June 15, earning $5,440. Hilda has earned four quarters of coverage for the year 2019 as $1,360 × 4 is $5,440, despite the fact that Hilda worked only in the first two quarters of the year. If Hilda had earned only $2,720 during 2019, she would have earned two quarters of coverage, as $1,360 × 2 is $2,720. In addition, federal law imposes a ceiling on the amount of an individual's earnings that are subject to withholding for payment of social security taxes. For 2019, the maximum annual amount of earnings on which OASDI taxes are paid is $132,900.[23]

Certain calendar quarters cannot be counted for determining social security credits. A quarter of coverage cannot be earned for a calendar quarter if the calendar quarter (1) begins after the quarter in which the worker died, (2) has not started yet, (3) is within a prior period of disability that is excluded in figuring benefits, with the exception of the beginning and ending quarters of a prior disability period either of which may be counted if the preceding earnings requirements were met for that quarter, or (4) has been counted as a covered quarter.[24]

Prior to 1978 earning credits were determined differently. For those requirements see the Code of Federal Regulations.[25]

IV. Calculating Benefits

A. Determining the Primary Insurance Amount (PIA)

Once an individual with the required number of quarters of coverage establishes eligibility for benefits, SSA first calculates the individual's primary insurance amount (PIA) to determine the individual's benefit amount. For most individuals, SSA utilizes two methods: (1) the average monthly earnings record for individuals retiring in 1978 and earlier and (2) the average indexed monthly earnings method for individuals who retired in 1979 or later. The reason for the post 1979 method is tied to the inflationary American economy of the 1970s. In 1972, Congress linked increases in social security benefits to increases in the Consumer Price Index. Consequently, the more prices increased, the more wages increased, and therefore the more benefits increased. In order to prevent workers from receiving benefits greater than the wages they earned while employed, Congress implemented a new method of calculating PIA in 1979. To reiterate, most workers' primary insurance amounts are calculated in one of two ways:[26]

- Pre-1979. If before 1979 the worker reaches age 62, or becomes disabled or dies before age 62, SSA calculates the primary insurance amount pursuant to the average monthly wage method.
- Post-1979. If during 1979 or later the worker reaches age 62, or becomes disabled or dies before age 62, SSA calculates the primary insurance amount by the average indexed monthly wage method.

B. Determining the PIA by the Average Indexed Monthly Earnings Method

The steps in computing an individual's primary insurance amount under the average indexed monthly earnings method are difficult. The simplest approach is to review SSA publication *Your Retirement Benefit: How It's Figured*. It can be found at www.ssa.gov/pubs/EN-05-10070.pdf. Then use the Retirement Estimator at www.ssa.gov/estimator.[27]

C. Alternate Methods of Calculating PIA

Various other formulas are used by SSA to calculate the PIA of certain individuals, such as the aforementioned Average Monthly Wage method for older beneficiaries, as well as special formulas for individuals disabled during an earlier time of their lives[28] or for individuals for whom the majority of their social security earnings were reported prior to 1951.[29] Obviously, there aren't many of those still with us. The practitioner should always consult with SSA to determine the appropriate formula for her client, or view its excellent web page at www.ssa.gov.

D. How the Family Maximum Rule Affects the Benefit Amount

The amount of benefits that can be paid for any month based on the earnings of an individual is limited by law. If the total benefits to which all persons are entitled to from any one individual's earnings record exceeds the maximum amount prescribed by law, then the benefits must be reduced so that they do not exceed the maximum.[30] Benefits payable to a divorced spouse or surviving divorced spouse are exempt from the family maximum requirement.[31] In addition, the individual's own retirement or disability insurance benefit is exempt from reduction due to the family maximum requirement. Adjustment for the family maximum is made by proportionately reducing all the monthly benefits that are subject to the family maximum to bring the total amount of payments within the family maximum limit.

For individuals who are entitled to disability insurance benefits, SSA uses a fixed formula to determine the family maximum. Generally the family maximum is between 150 percent to 180 percent of the full retirement benefit. The formula can be found at https://www.ssa.gov/oact/cola/familymax.html and a helpful article is found at www.ssa.gov/planners/retire/applying7.html.

E. Grounds for Reduction of Benefits

An individual's benefits may be reduced or eliminated if:

- The individual is deported.[32]
- The individual is an alien who is outside of the United States for more than six full consecutive calendar months.[33]
- The individual is an alien who resides in a country to which the mailing of U.S. government checks is prohibited.[34]
- The individual has failed to furnish her social security number or apply for a social security number.[35]
- The individual is convicted of a subversive offense and the court imposes the additional penalty of loss of benefits.[36]
- The individual has waived her rights to benefits as a member of a recognized religious group and was previously granted the exception from paying social security taxes.
- The individual is confined in jail or a penal institution as a result of a conviction of a felony offense. However, a dependent of the prisoner may continue to receive benefits.[37]
- The individual is receiving benefits based on a disability for which drug addiction or alcoholism is a contributing material factor and the individual has failed to comply with his required treatment program.[38]
- The individual is receiving benefits because she has the insured person's child in her care and the child leaves her care. However, if the individual is 62 to 64 years of age, and has made the election to receive a reduced spouse's benefit, this provision does not apply.[39]
- The individual is receiving benefits due to a disability and refuses to accept rehabilitation services. A spouse's or child's benefits may also be reduced because of an individual's refusal to accept rehabilitation services.[40]
- The individual is receiving benefits as a spouse, widow(er), or parent and is also entitled to a government pension from a job for which they did not pay social security taxes.[41]

V. Social Security Retirement (Old-Age Benefits)

A. Background

An individual is entitled to social security retirement benefits (old-age benefits) if the individual is at least 62 years old, meets fully insured status, and applies for the benefits.[42] An individual's entitlement to old-age benefits ends with the month before the month of his death.[43] The monthly benefit rate for an individual who retires at full retirement age is equal to her primary insurance amount.[44] Full retirement age is no longer 65 years of age, but an age between 65 and 67 depending on the year of the individual's birth.

Age to Receive Full Social Security Benefits

Year of Birth	Full Retirement Age
1937 or earlier	65
1938	65 and 2 months
1939	65 and 4 months
1940	65 and 6 months
1941	65 and 8 months
1942	65 and 10 months
1943–1954	66
1955	66 and 2 months
1956	66 and 4 months
1957	66 and 6 months
1958	66 and 8 months
1959	66 and 10 months
1960 and later	67

The monthly benefit rate for an individual who retires after full retirement age is equal to her primary insurance rate plus the increase for retiring after full retirement age. There is no further benefit increase after age 70. The following table shows the increase for delayed retirement benefits.

Year of Birth	12-Month Rate of Increase	Monthly Rate of Increase
1933–1934	5.5%	11/24 of 1%
1935–1936	6.0%	1/2 of 1%
1937–1938	6.5%	13/24 of 1%
1939–1940	7.0%	7/12 of 1%
1941–1942	7.5%	5/8 of 1%
1943 or later	8.0%	2/3 of 1%

The monthly benefit rate for an individual who retires before full retirement age is the primary insurance amount less reduction for each month the individual retires before full retirement age. This reduction may be about 20 percent to 30 percent, depending on the person's age when claiming benefits. A quick way to estimate the reduced benefits is to use the social security quick reference found at https://www.ssa.gov/oact/quickcalc/.

Retirement age is the age at which entitlement to full benefits begins and the age at which an individual may begin to earn delayed retirement credits. As stated, the retirement age has been increased for individuals born on or after January 2, 1938. For those individuals who elect to delay retirement, their primary insurance amount will increase for each month that they delay retirement. Social security retirement benefits terminate the month before the month in which the individual dies.[45]

B. How Excess Earnings May Reduce Social Security Retirement Benefit Amount

If an individual receiving social security retirement (old-age benefits) earns more income than is allowed by the exemptions, the individual is said to have "excess earnings" and his benefits are reduced proportionately depending upon his age. Historically, excess earnings did not affect beneficiaries age 70 and older while beneficiaries under age 70 who continued to work were subject to excess earnings. However, on April 7, 2000, President Clinton signed into law the Senior Citizens' Freedom to Work Act of 2000, which eliminates excess earnings for individuals at full retirement age, effective January 1, 2000. Excess earnings will still affect individuals who receive social security retirement (old-age benefits) who have not reached full retirement age, that is, those individuals who elect early retirement with decreased benefits. For beneficiaries under full retirement age, $1 in benefits is withheld for every $2 in earnings in excess of the annual exempt amount. The annual exempt amount is adjusted yearly and is $17,040 in 2019. In the year the individual reaches full retirement age the deduction is $1 in benefits for every $3 above the exempt amount. The exempt amount is $45,360 during the year the individual reaches full retirement age, but only earnings during that year before reaching full retirement age are counted. It should be noted a former's spouse's benefits are not reduced because of an individual's excess earnings if the divorce has been final for at least two years.[46]

VI. Husband's and Wife's Benefits
A. Introduction

When an insured individual becomes eligible for benefits either on the basis of age or disability, the insured individual's spouse may also qualify for benefits.[47] A husband's or wife's monthly benefit is equal to one-half of the insured individual's primary insurance amount.[48] A person is considered the spouse of an insured individual if the person and the insured individual were validly married under state law or if the person would have the right to inherit from the insured individual under state law.[49] To determine if a person is the legal spouse of the insured individual, SSA looks to the laws of the state where the insured individual had a permanent home at the time the person seeking husband's or wife's benefits makes an application for benefits.[50] If a person is seeking widow's or widower's benefits, SSA looks to the laws of the state where the insured individual had a permanent home when the insured individual died.[51] A common-law marriage will be recognized as a legal marriage by SSA if the common-law marriage took place in a state that recognizes common-law marriages.[52]

B. Deemed Valid Marriages

Furthermore, SSA will deem a person as validly married to an insured individual and entitled to husband's or wife's benefits if the person underwent the marriage ceremony in good faith with the insured individual but the marriage is rendered invalid due to a legal impediment such as the insured individual not being divorced from his prior spouse.[53] SSA refers to this as a "deemed valid marriage." But to obtain benefits pursuant to a deemed valid marriage, the person seeking husband's, wife's, or widow(er)'s benefits must have been living in the same household as the insured individual at the time the insured individual died or if the insured individual is still living, at the time the spouse applies for benefits.[54] This rule does not apply for obvious reasons for divorced spouses from a deemed valid marriage.

C. How a Spouse Qualifies for Husband's and Wife's Benefits

An insured individual's spouse will qualify for husband's or wife's benefits if they meet the following requirements:[55]

- The insured individual qualifies for benefits on the basis of age or disability.
- The person seeking benefits is the insured person's wife or husband and any one of the following is met:
  1. The spouse was married to the insured individual for at least one year, or
  2. The spouse and the insured individual are the natural parents of a child, or
  3. The spouse was entitled to social security benefits in their own right the month before the marriage, or
  4. The spouse was entitled to annuity payments under the Railroad Retirement Act.
- The spouse applies for husband's or wife's benefits.
- The spouse is either:
  1. Age 62 years or older, or
  2. Age 61 years or younger and has in their care a child entitled to child's benefits on the insured individual's earnings record and the child is either 15 or younger or disabled.
- The spouse is not entitled to old-age or disability insurance benefits in his or her own right based on a primary insurance amount that is equal to or larger than the full wife's or husband's benefits (one-half of the insured individual's primary insurance amount).

D. How a Divorced Spouse Qualifies for Husband's or Wife's Benefits

Even though an elder client is divorced, there still may be entitlement to benefits from the former spouse's earnings record. This is a significant benefit, as entitlement does not reduce the former spouse's benefits. A divorced spouse is entitled to husband's or wife's benefits if each of the following is met:[56]

- The divorced spouse is the insured individual's divorced wife or husband.
- The divorced spouse was validly married to the insured individual under state law or was deemed validly married by SSA.
- The divorced spouse was married to the insured individual for at least ten years immediately before the divorce became final.
- The divorced spouse makes an application for benefits.
- The divorced spouse has not remarried.
- The divorced spouse is age 62 years or older.
- The divorced spouse is not entitled to old age or disability insurance benefits in her own right based on a primary insurance amount that is equal to or larger than the full wife's or husband's benefits.
- The divorced spouse has been divorced from the insured person for at least two years.

E. When Husband's and Wife's Benefits Terminate

An individual remains entitled to receive husband's or wife's benefits until the month before the month one of the following events occurs:[57]

- The spouse or divorced spouse becomes eligible for social security retirement benefits (old-age benefits) or disability benefits based on a primary insurance amount that is equal to or larger than the full wife's or husband's benefit.
- The spouse divorces the insured individual unless the spouse is eligible as a divorced spouse above.
- The divorced spouse marries someone, other than the insured, who is entitled to old-age benefits unless the person the divorced spouse marries is entitled to husband's, wife's, widow(er)'s, parent's, or disabled child's benefits.
- The spouse or divorced spouse is age 61 or younger and the child in their care reaches age 16 years (unless disabled) or is no longer entitled to child's benefits.
- The insured person dies or is no longer disabled (the spouse may be eligible for survivor benefits).
- The spouse's benefits are based on a deemed valid marriage and the spouse marries another person without divorcing the insured individual.
- The divorced spouse dies.
- The divorced spouse became entitled to benefits before the insured individual became entitled and the insured individual is no longer insured.

VII. Widow's and Widower's Benefits

A. Introduction

Many, if not most, elder clients whose spouses die are eligible for widow(er)'s benefits. An individual is entitled to widow(er)'s benefits if the individual was married to a person who was fully insured when he or she died.[58] The widow(er)'s benefit is equal to the deceased fully insured spouse's primary insurance amount.[59] However, the widow(er)'s benefit may be reduced if the insured spouse began receiving benefits before full retirement age or the benefit may be increased if the insured spouse delayed retirement beyond full retirement age.[60] In addition, widow(er)'s benefits are subject to the excess earnings rule discussed at Section V.B.

B. How a Spouse Qualifies for Widow's or Widower's Benefits

The elder client who is a widow(er) may be entitled to benefits from the earnings record of the client's deceased spouse. The rules are tedious. An individual is entitled to widow(er)'s benefits if each of the following applies:[61]

- The individual was married to a fully insured spouse at least nine months immediately before the fully insured spouse died *or* if the individual was married to the fully insured spouse for less than nine months, the spouse was expected to live for nine months, and one of the following applies:
    1. The death of the insured spouse was accidental, or due to active duty military service, or
    2. The individual had been previously married to the insured spouse for a nine-month period, that is, the parties remarried after a previous divorce from a prior marriage that lasted at least nine months, or
    3. Though not married the insured spouse would have married but for the prior spouse being institutionalized for mental incompetence and a divorce could have been unlawful under state law.
- The individual seeking widow(er)'s benefits and the deceased insured spouse are the natural parents of a child, or adopted the other's child during their marriage, or adopted a child under 18 years of age.
- The individual was entitled to social security benefits in his own right the month before the marriage.
- The individual applies for benefits.
- The individual is at least 60 years of age; or is at least 50 years of age and has a disability that began no longer than seven years after the insured spouse's death or the disability began at least seven years after the surviving spouse was last entitled to mother's or father's benefits, or to widow's or widower's benefits based on a disability, whichever occurred last.

- The individual is not entitled to a social security retirement benefit (old-age benefit) that is equal to or larger than the deceased insured spouse's primary insurance amount.
- The individual is unmarried unless:
  1. The individual marries after he became 60 years of age, or
  2. The individual is 60 years of age, remarried between age 50 and 60 years, and at the time of remarriage the individual was entitled to widow(er)'s benefits as a disabled widow(er), or
  3. The individual is at least 50 to 59 years of age, remarried between age 50 and 60 years, and at the time of remarriage the individual met the required disability standards, that is, the surviving spouse's disability began within the required time and before remarriage.

C. How a Divorced Spouse Qualifies for Widow's or Widower's Benefits

Even though an elder client is divorced, the elder client may be entitled to benefits based on a deceased former ex-spouse's earning's record. Again, the rules are tedious. An individual is entitled to widow or widower's benefits as the surviving divorced spouse of a fully insured individual if each of the following is met:[62]

- The individual is the insured person's surviving divorced wife or husband.
- The individual was validly married to the fully insured individual or deemed to be validly married for at least ten years immediately before the divorce was final.
- The individual applies for benefits.
- The individual is at least 60 years of age; or is at least 50 years of age and has a disability, provided that the disability began no later than seven years after the insured former spouse died or the disability started at least seven years after the surviving spouse was entitled to mother's or father's benefits, or widow's or widower's benefits based on a disability, which ever occurred last.
- The individual is not entitled to a social security retirement benefit (old-age benefit) that is equal to or larger than the deceased fully insured's spouse's primary insurance amount.
- The individual is unmarried or if married:
  1. The individual marries after reaching 60 years of age, or
  2. The individual is 60 years of age, remarried between age 50 and 60 years, and at the time of remarriage the individual was entitled to widow(er)'s benefits as a disabled widow(er), or
  3. The individual is at least 50 to 59 years of age, remarried between age 50 and 60 years, and at the time of remarriage the individual met the required disability standards, that is, the surviving spouse's disability began within the required time and before remarriage.

D. When Widow's or Widower's Benefits Terminate

An individual remains entitled to receive widow(er)'s benefits until the month before the month one of the following occurs:[63]

- The individual becomes entitled to a social security retirement benefit (old-age benefit) that is equal to or larger than the deceased insured spouse's primary insurance amount.
- The individual's widow's or widower's benefit is based on disability and the disability ends. However, an individual's benefits may continue until completion of a vocational rehabilitation program if the individual meets certain criteria.[64]
- The individual dies, in which case the individual's benefits terminate the month before the month of death.

VIII. Mother's or Father's Benefit

A. Introduction

An individual is entitled to a mother's or father's benefit if he or she is the widow or widower of a fully insured or currently insured person.[65] While this is not a common benefit for an elder client, it does arise in some situations, such as, marriages later in life in which children are born or adopted and the older spouse dies survived by children who are disabled or under 16 years of age. This benefit, termed a mother's or father's benefit, is designed to provide financial assistance for an individual who has children who are deprived of support by the death of their fully or currently insured parent. The mother's or father's benefit is equal to 75 percent of the insured person's primary insurance amount.[66] An individual is entitled to a mother's or father's benefit if each of the following applies:[67]

- The individual is a widow or widower of a person who was either fully or currently insured when the insured died.
- The individual applies for the benefit or the individual was entitled to a wife's or husband's benefit for the month before the insured person died.
- The individual is unmarried.
- The individual is not entitled to a widow's or widower's benefit or to a social security retirement benefit (old-age benefit) that is equal to or greater than the full mother's or father's benefit.
- The individual has in her care the insured person's child who is entitled to child's benefits and the child is either 15 or younger or is 16 or older and disabled.

B. How a Divorced Spouse Qualifies for Mother's or Father's Benefit

A former spouse who has a child age 15 years or younger or who is 16 or older and disabled with a deceased fully or currently insured individual (the ex-spouse) may qualify as well for mother's or father's benefit. An individual who is the surviving divorced spouse of a deceased fully or currently insured person is entitled to mother's or father's benefits if each of the following applies:[68]

- The individual was validly married to the fully insured individual or deemed to be validly married but the marriage ended in a final divorce and:
  1. The individual is the mother or father of the insured's child, or
  2. The individual was married to the insured person when one of them adopted the other's child or when both of them adopted a child under 18 years of age.
- The individual is unmarried.
- The individual is not entitled to widow's or widower's benefits, or to a social security retirement benefit (old-age benefit) that is equal to or larger than the full mother's or father's benefit.
- The individual has in her care the insured's child who is 15 or younger *or* who is age 16 or older and disabled.

C. When Mother's or Father's Benefit Terminate

A mother's or father's benefit will end the month before the month one of the following events occurs:[69]

- The individual becomes entitled to a widow's or widower's benefit or to a social security retirement benefit (old-age benefit) that is equal to or greater than the full mother's or father's benefit.
- The child in the individual's care becomes age 16 and is not disabled or is no longer otherwise entitled to child's benefits.
- The individual remarries unless the individual marries someone who is entitled to old-age, disability, wife's, husband's, widow's, widower's, father's, mother's, parent's, or disabled child's benefits.
- The individual dies.

IX. Parent's Benefits
A. Introduction

In some cases, an elder parent must rely on an adult child to provide much needed support. Parent's benefits are designed to provide financial assistance to a parent who has been deprived of this support by the death of a child. Therefore, an elder client who was dependent upon an adult child for support may qualify for parent's benefits if the child dies. In order for the parent to qualify, the child must have died fully insured.[70] The parent's monthly benefit is equal to $82^1/_2$ percent of the insured child's primary insurance amount provided the parent is the only parent entitled to benefits on the insured child's earnings record.[71] If more than one parent is entitled to benefits on the insured child's earnings record, each parent's monthly benefit amount is equal to 75 percent of the insured child's primary insurance amount.[72]

B. How to Qualify for Parent's Benefits

An individual is entitled to parent's benefits if each of the following applies:[73]

- The individual is the biological mother or father of the insured deceased person, or the individual is the adoptive parent of the insured person who was adopted before age 16, or the individual is the step-parent of the insured and the individual married the insured's parent or adoptive parent before the insured became age 16.[74]
- The individual is at least 62 years of age.
- The individual has not married since the insured person died.
- The individual applies for benefits.
- The individual is not entitled to a social security retirement benefit (old-age benefit) equal to or greater than the parent's benefit amount.
- The individual was receiving at least one-half of his support from the insured at time she died *or* at the beginning of any period of disability she had that continued up to her death. Proof of the support must be furnished to SSA within two years of the insured person's death unless good cause can be shown or the Soldier's and Sailor's Civil Relief Act of 1940 applies.[75]

C. When Parent's Benefits Terminate

Parent's benefits terminate the month before the month when one of the following occurs:[76]

- The individual becomes entitled to an old-age benefit equal to or greater than the parent's benefit.
- The individual marries, unless the marriage is to someone entitled to wife's, husband's, widow's, widower's, mother's, father's, parent's, or disabled child's benefits.
- The individual dies.

X. Child's Benefits

A. Introduction

A child may be entitled to child's benefits on the earnings record of an insured person who is entitled to social security retirement benefits (old-age benefits), disability benefits, or who has died. Many elder clients have custody of their grandchildren. If so, an elder client may be entitled to additional social security benefits if she has a minor child in her care. The child's monthly benefit amount is equal to one-half of the insured person's primary insurance amount if that person is alive or three-fourths of the primary insurance amount if that person has died.[77]

B. How to Qualify for Child's Benefits

In order to qualify for child's benefits, the individual must meet the following conditions:[78]

- The individual is the insured person's child.
- The individual is a dependent of the insured person.
- The individual applies for benefits.
- The individual is unmarried.
- The individual is under age 18, or the individual is over 18 years of age and has a disability that began before age 22 years of age, or the individual is over 18 years of age and is a full-time elementary or secondary student.

C. How the Dependency Requirement Is Satisfied

The dependency requirement is satisfied if the individual is the legal child of the insured person.[79] A child who is the biological child of the insured also satisfies the dependency requirement provided that the child was not adopted during the insured's lifetime.[80] A child who is adopted by a third party may still qualify for benefits from the insured-biological parent if the child was either living with or receiving support from the insured-biological parent at the time the child applies for benefits, or at the time the insured-biological parent died, or at the time the insured-biological parent became disabled.[81] A stepchild will be considered a dependent of the insured if the stepchild was either living with or receiving one-half of his support from the insured at the time the stepchild applies for benefits, or at time the insured died, or at time the insured became disabled.[82]

D. Rules for Adopted Children

In addition, a child, including an elder client's grandchild, who is adopted may qualify for child's benefits as well. If a child is legally adopted by the insured **before** the insured became entitled to old-age benefits, the child is considered a dependent of the insured and entitled to child's benefits.[83] If the child is adopted by the insured **after** the insured became entitled to old-age or disability benefits, the child must meet certain dependency requirements to qualify for benefits. If the child was 17 or younger when the adoption was started, the child is considered a dependent and eligible for benefits. If the child is over 18 years of age when the adoption is started, the child is considered a dependent if the child was living with or receiving one-half of her support from the insured for the year immediately preceding the month in which the adoption was granted.[84] A child who is adopted by the insured's surviving spouse after the insured's death is treated as a dependent and is eligible for benefits if the child was either living with or receiving one-half of her support from the insured at the time of the insured's death and the insured had started adoption proceedings before he or she died or his or her surviving spouse began and completed adoption proceedings within two years of the insured's death.[85]

E. Rules for Grandchildren and Step-Grandchildren

A grandchild or step-grandchild may be eligible for child's benefits based on an insured grandparent's earnings record provided that the grandchild's or step-grandchild's natural or adoptive parents are either deceased or disabled.[86] Furthermore, in order to qualify for benefits, grandchildren or step-grandchildren must meet certain dependency requirements. A grandchild or step-grandchild is considered a dependent of the insured if the grandchild or step-grandchild began living with the insured before she reached 18 years of age, and one of the following applies:[87]

1. The grandchild/step-grandchild was living with the insured in the United States and was receiving one-half of her support from the insured in the year before the insured/grandparent became eligible for old-age or disability benefits, or
2. The grandchild/step-grandchild was living with the insured/grandparent in the year before the period of disability began for the insured if the insured had a period of disability that lasted until the insured's death or became eligible for disability benefits, or
3. If the grandchild/step-grandchild is less than one year of age, the grandchild/step-grandchild had been living with the insured/grandparent, and the insured provided one-half of the grandchild's/step-grandchild's support for substantially all of the period from birth.

If a grandchild or step-grandchild is adopted by the insured's surviving spouse after the insured's death, the grandchild/step-grandchild is considered a dependent of the insured and eligible for child's benefits if each of the following applies:[88]

1. The adoption took place in the United States.
2. At the time of the insured's death, the natural parent, adoptive parent, or stepparent of the child was not living in the insured's household and making contributions towards the grandchild's/step-grandchild's support.
3. The grandchild/step-grandchild meets the dependency requirements for a grandchild/step-grandchild as discussed above.

F. When a Child's Benefits Terminate

A child's benefits terminate upon the occurrence of one of the following events:[89]

- The child reaches 18 years of age, unless the child is disabled or a full-time student (with certain limitations).
- The child marries, unless the child is 18 or older, disabled, and marries an individual entitled to child's benefits based on disability, or an individual entitled to old-age, divorced wife's, divorced husband's, widow's, widower's, mother's, father's, parent's, or disability benefits.
- The insured's entitlement to old-age or disability benefits ends for a reason other than death or the attainment of full retirement age. However, a child's entitlement to benefits continues if the insured person's benefits are terminated due to a finding that drug addiction or alcoholism was a contributing factor to the insured's disability, *or* the insured's benefits are terminated after 36 months of payment, *or* after a 12-month suspension for noncompliance with treatment *and* the insured person remains disabled.
- The child dies.

XI. *Disability Insurance Benefits*
A. *Introduction*

Disability insurance benefits have limited applicability for elder clients. But a limited review of the law is helpful if the lawyer has an elder client who has not reached retirement age but who may be entitled to disability benefits if she is unable to work. Also, the client may have a disabled adult child who is entitled to benefits. An individual who has the required number of quarters of coverage may qualify for disability insurance benefits if she becomes disabled. See Section III.D. for a discussion of the quarters of coverage. A disabled individual's monthly benefit is equal to the individual's primary insurance amount as if she was seeking old-age benefits at age 62 years.[90]

The term *disability* is defined by SSA as the inability to do any substantial gainful activity by reason of any medically determinable physical or mental impairment that can be expected to result in death or that can be expected to last for a continuous period of not less than 12 months.[91] An individual must have a severe impairment that makes her unable to do her previous work or any substantial gainful activity that exists in the national economy.[92] The impairment must result from anatomical, physiological, or psychological abnormalities that can be shown by medically acceptable clinical and laboratory diagnostic techniques.[93] Evidence of an impairment includes objective medical evidence such as laboratory reports and observations, as well as the individual's and other's statements as to her impairment, daily activities, and restrictions.[94] In determining whether work exists in the national economy for an individual to perform, factors such as (1) the nonexistence of work in the individual's immediate area, (2) whether a specific job vacancy exists, and (3) whether the individual would be hired if she applied for work, are deemed irrelevant by SSA.[95]

B. *How an Individual Qualifies for Disability Benefits*

An individual will qualify for disability benefits if:[96]

- The individual is under a disability as defined by SSA. An individual who is no longer disabled but who had a previous disability that ended within the 12-month period before she applied is also eligible.
- The individual has filed an application for disabled worker's benefits.
- The individual meets disability insured status.
- The individual has been disabled for five consecutive months, beginning with the month that the individual was both disabled and insured for disability purposes. No waiting period is required if the individual was previously entitled to disability benefits within five years of the month the individual again became disabled. An individual is entitled to a retroactive payment of benefits for up to 12 months before the application for disability is filed provided the five-month waiting period is satisfied.[97]
- The individual has not yet reached full retirement age.

C. *Substantial Gainful Activity (SGA)*

If an individual is able to engage in substantial gainful activity (SGA), SSA will find the individual is not disabled.[98] SGA is defined as (1) work activity that is substantial, that is, work that involves doing significant physical or mental activities, and (2) work activity that is gainful, that is, the type of work that is usually performed for compensation.[99] For 2019, an individual who earned $1,220 or more per month is presumed by SSA as performing SGA and therefore not entitled to disability insurance benefits or Supplemental Security Income (SSI) payments.[100] An individual who earns more than $1,220 per month can refute the presumption of SGA by showing that he incurred certain impairment-related work expenses that he could deduct from any income earned through employment.[101]

D. *What Constitutes SGA for Blind Individuals*

An individual is considered by SSA as disabled due to blindness if the individual meets the definition of statutory blindness, which is defined as central visual acuity of 20/200 or less in the better eye with the use of corrective lens.[102] An eye that has a limitation in the field of vision so that the widest diameter of the visual field subtends an angle no greater than 20 degrees is considered to have a central visual acuity of 20/200 or less. Blind persons under age 55 who are able to do substantial gainful activity do not qualify to be paid disability insurance benefits, but SSA may establish a period of disability for these individuals to protect the individual's earnings record so that the individual may qualify in the future.[103] For example, Bob, who is 45 years of age meets the statutory definition of blindness in 2010. Bob worked construction and had significant earnings prior to becoming blind. Bob is no longer employable as a construction worker due to his blindness but finds work at a lesser paying job. Though Bob has worked sufficient quarters to qualify for disability insurance status, he is able to engage in SGA which disqualifies him from receiving cash benefits. SSA will freeze Bob in 2010 as eligible for disability insurance status though he will not receive cash benefits. If Bob in 2016, at age 51 years, becomes unable to perform SGA, Bob will qualify for disability cash benefits based on his higher earnings as frozen in 2010, rather than his lesser earnings following the onset of his blindness. For individuals 55 years of age and older, SSA uses a formula that reflects increases in the national wage index to determine SGA. For 2019, the SGA level for blind individuals over 55 years of age is $2,040.[104]

E. Drug Addiction and Alcoholism Are No Longer Basis for Disability

If either drug addiction or alcoholism is a contributing factor to an individual's disability, the individual is not entitled to disability benefits.[105] If an individual is disabled independent of his drug addiction or alcoholism, the individual is entitled to disability benefits.

F. When Disability Benefits Terminate

An individual remains entitled to disability insurance until one of the following occurs:[106]

- The month before the month the individual reaches full retirement age, at which time disability benefits are automatically converted to old-age benefits.
- The month immediately preceding the termination month. The termination month is the third month following the month in which an individual's impairments are no longer considered disabling by SSA. For example, Juanita's impairments are no longer considered disabling by SSA as of August. Juanita remains eligible for benefits for September and October but her benefits will cease in November. November is the termination month, the third month following August, the month in which Juanita's impairments are no longer disabling.

XII. Appeals Procedure
A. The Initial Determination Stage

Certain decisions made by SSA are subject to administrative and judicial review. These decisions are referred to as "initial determinations." Decisions such as an individual's entitlement to benefits, whether an individual's benefits should be terminated, the amount of benefits an individual is due, and whether an overpayment of benefits should be repaid are initial determinations.[107] Certain other decisions are not initial determinations and are not subject to administrative and judicial review. Decisions such as the denial of a request to be a person's payee, the assignment of a monthly payment date for benefits, and determining a representative's fee, are not subject to review.[108] An initial determination is binding unless the individual requests a reconsideration.[109]

B. *The Reconsideration Stage*

An individual who is dissatisfied with an initial determination has the right to request a reconsideration. In addition to the insured, any individual who shows in writing that her benefits may be adversely affected by the initial determination may request a reconsideration.[110] A reconsideration must be requested within 60 days after the date the individual received notice of the initial determination.[111] Good cause must be shown before the 60-day time period can be extended.[112] For most individuals, the reconsideration process consists of case review only, that is, the individual can submit additional evidence but there is no hearing. If the reconsideration involves the termination of disability benefits on the basis that the individual is no longer disabled, the individual may request a disability hearing, which is conducted by the state agency responsible for issuing disability determinations.[113] A reconsideration determination is binding unless the individual requests a hearing before an administrative law judge.[114]

C. *The Administrative Law Judge (ALJ) Stage*

An individual who is dissatisfied with a reconsideration decision may request a hearing before an administrative law judge (ALJ). A request for an ALJ hearing must be filed within 60 days of the date the individual received notice of the unfavorable reconsideration.[115] Again, good cause must be demonstrated if the deadline for requesting an ALJ hearing is missed.[116] An individual or his representative may appear before the ALJ to argue his case. Subpoenas may be issued for certain witnesses or documents by the SSA upon request by a party.[117] However, no hearing is necessary if the ALJ issues a decision wholly favorable to the appellant or the parties notify the SSA that they do not wish to appear.[118] The decision of the ALJ is binding unless the individual requests a review of the decision by the Appeals Council.[119]

D. *The Appeals Council Stage*

An individual who is dissatisfied with the AJJ's decision may request a review of the decision by the Appeals Council.[120] A request for a review by the Appeals Council must be filed within 60 days of the date the individual received notice of the unfavorable ALJ decision.[121] In addition, good cause must be demonstrated if the request is not filed timely.[122] The Appeals Council, itself, is permitted within 60 days of the ALJ decision to initiate a review of the ALJ decision even if no appeal is filed.[123] New evidence can be considered by the Appeals Council if the evidence relates back to the time before the ALJ's decision.[124] Briefs may be filed by the parties.[125] Oral argument is not permitted unless requested by a party and the request is approved by the Appeals Council.[126] The Appeals Council may either deny the request for review, grant the request for a review and issue a decision, or remand the case to an ALJ for further consideration.[127]

E. Judicial Review in Federal Court

An individual who is aggrieved by an adverse decision of the Appeals Council may file a complaint in the district court for the judicial district where the individual resides or has his principal place of business within 60 days of the date of the receipt of the adverse decision.[128] The scope of the court's review is limited to whether the Appeals Council's decision is supported by substantial evidence. The court may affirm, modify, or reverse the Appeals Council's decision and, in certain cases, the court may remand the case back to SSA.[129]

F. Expedited Appeals Process

An expedited appeals process is available if both the individual and SSA agree that the only factor preventing a favorable determination or decision is that a particular provision in the law is unconstitutional. The request must be made within 60 days after notice of the reconsideration is received, or at any time after a request for an ALJ hearing has been made, or within 60 days after the receipt of an adverse ALJ decision, or at any time after a request for a review of the Appeals Council decision has been made provided that no decision has been issued by the Appeals Council.[130] If all parties consent, an agreement is executed with SSA and the individual has 60 days to file an action in federal district court, bypassing any remaining administrative stages.[131] The 60-day time period commences upon receipt of the notice that the agreement has been signed by SSA along with a copy of the agreement.[132]

G. Attorney's Fees

A representative may charge a fee for his services for representing a client in a social security case.[133] The representative must file a written request with SSA before charging the fee for her services. The SSA will then decide the amount of fee the representative is permitted to charge for her services. If the representative is an attorney and the claimant is entitled to past-due benefits, SSA will pay the entire fee, or a portion thereof, from the claimant's back-due benefits. The size of the fee is limited to the smallest of (1) 25 percent of the back-due benefits, (2) the amount of fee set by SSA, or (3) the amount of fee agreed upon by the attorney and the claimant.[134] If the representative is a non-attorney, SSA will not withhold the claimant's proceeds for payment of the fee even if the fee is authorized by SSA.[135]

Appendix A: Social Security Retirement Checklist[136]

What's the best age to start receiving retirement benefits? The answer is that there isn't a "best" age that applies to everyone. It's a personal decision based on your situation and, ultimately, it's your choice. To help you make an informed choice, consider the following factors as you think about when to start receiving your social security benefits.

What you should know before you apply

- What does "retirement" mean?

For these purposes, retiring means getting your social security retirement benefit. It might mean that you've also stopped working. However, these two things don't need to happen at the same time. For example, you have the option of delaying your monthly benefit even after you stop working. Delaying your benefit will increase your monthly benefit amount (see below).

- Your benefits are based on your entire earnings history.

Do you know how your benefit is calculated? Your monthly benefit amount is based on your highest 35 years of earnings. If you don't have 35 years of earnings, your monthly benefit will be reduced, because years with no earnings will count as zeros. Learn your estimated monthly benefit amount by reading your social security statement at www.socialsecurity.gov /myaccount, or use the Retirement Estimator at www.SocialSecurity.gov /retire/estimator.html.

- Your monthly benefit is higher if you wait to start.

When should you start your retirement benefit? You can start receiving benefits as early as age 62. However, *the longer you wait (up to age 70), the higher your monthly benefit will be—for the rest of your life.* If you're married and you're the higher earner, delaying your benefit may also mean higher survivor benefits for your spouse when you pass away. You can see the impact of starting your monthly benefits at different ages by checking your social security statement or the retirement estimator. Both are available online at www .socialsecurity.gov/onlineservices. For more information on how delaying increases your monthly benefit, read Social Security publication *When to Start Receiving Retirement Benefits* (Publication No. 05-10147), at www.socialsecu rity.gov/pubs/EN-05-10147.pdf.

- Your full retirement age may be higher than you think.

Your "full retirement age" is determined by the year you were born. The retirement age used to be 65 for everyone, but is gradually increasing to 67. As the full retirement age goes up, benefits claimed at earlier ages go down. Find out your full retirement age at www.socialsecurity.gov/planners/retire /ageincrease.html.

■ Your benefits may be temporarily reduced if you work while receiving benefits.

Working after you start receiving retirement benefits may affect your monthly benefit amount, depending on your age and how much you earn. If you are younger than your full retirement age, and your earnings exceed certain dollar amounts, some of your monthly benefit may be withheld. The Social Security Administration will increase your monthly benefit *after you reach full retirement age* to account for the months of withheld benefits. When you reach your full retirement age, you can work and earn as much as you want and your benefit will not be affected. Find more information at www .socialsecurity.gov/planners/retire/whileworking.html.

■ Your benefits may be taxed.

Some people have to pay federal income taxes on part of their social security benefits. This usually happens only if you have other substantial income (e.g., wages, interest, or dividends) in addition to your benefits. Learn more at www.socialsecurity.gov/planners/taxes.html.

If you have a special claiming situation

■ You or your family members may be eligible for spousal and family benefits.

Are you eligible for benefits based on your spouse's, or ex-spouse's, earnings record? If you were married for ten years or more, you may be eligible for benefits on your ex-spouse's record. Do you have a spouse who is eligible based on your earnings record? Spouses and ex-spouses can generally receive up to half of the worker's full retirement age monthly benefit amount, and widow(er)s can receive more than that. However, if you are eligible for your own benefit and a spouse benefit, you will only receive the higher of the two benefit amounts. Learn more about benefits for your family at https:// www.ssa.gov/planners/retire/applying7.html, spouse's benefits at www .socialsecurity.gov/planners/retire/applying6.html, and survivors benefits at www.socialsecurity.gov/planners/survivors.

■ You have additional benefit choices if you are widowed and retired.

If you are eligible for both your own retirement benefit and a survivor benefit based on a deceased spouse's or deceased ex-spouse's record, you have additional options to consider. You may want to apply for one benefit and delay applying for the other benefit to let it grow. When you apply for benefits, ask the social security representative if you can receive one benefit and delay the other to increase its value.

■ You can receive benefits if you are a citizen or lawfully present.

As long as you are legally present in the country and you and your employers have contributed to social security during your working years, you may be eligible for benefits. The social security web page at www .socialsecurity.gov/planners/retire/applying5.html has more information.

- Your benefit may be reduced if you worked in jobs not covered by social security.

If you worked in a job where you didn't pay social security taxes, and you are now receiving a retirement or disability pension based on those earnings, your social security benefit may be affected. Learn more at www .socialsecurity.gov/planners/retire/gpo-wep.html.

Additional things you should think about

- Your longevity and health

Retirement may be longer than you think. As you consider when to begin receiving retirement benefits, take into account how long you might live. Today, more than one in three 65-year-olds will live to age 90. You can use the Life Expectancy Calculator at https://www.ssa.gov/oact/population /longevity.html to see the average life expectancy for someone your age—but keep in mind that many people live longer than "average." Social security benefits last as long as you live, providing valuable protection against outliving savings and other sources of retirement income. Delaying your benefit to let it grow is one way to increase your monthly social security protection.

- Retroactive benefits

If you are past your full retirement age when you start receiving benefits, you can choose to receive up to six months of retroactive monthly benefits. However, using this option changes the start of your benefit to an earlier date. Remember that by choosing to start your benefit earlier, your monthly benefit amount will be lower for the rest of your life, and your spouse's survivor benefits may also be lower.

- Signing up for Medicare

Consider whether you need to apply for Medicare at age 65, even if you aren't applying for monthly retirement benefits. If you have already started receiving your retirement benefits, you will be automatically enrolled in Medicare when you turn 65. Medicare Part A (Hospital Insurance) is free for most people, and Medicare Part B (Medical Insurance) requires a monthly premium. Generally, if you have not already started receiving retirement benefits, you will want to sign up for Medicare three months before turning 65, unless you have group health coverage through a current employer. **NOTE:** If you don't have group health coverage through a current employer and you don't sign up for Medicare Part B when first eligible, then you may have to pay a late enrollment penalty for as long as you have Part B. Also, you may have to wait to enroll, which will delay this coverage. If you have a Health Savings Account (HSA) when you sign up for Medicare, you can't contribute to your HSA once your Medicare coverage begins. If you contribute to your HSA after your Medicare coverage starts, you may have to pay a tax penalty. If you'd like to continue contributing to your HSA, you shouldn't apply for Medicare, social security, or Railroad Retirement Board (RRB) benefits.

- Applying for your benefits

Once you have decided when you want to start receiving your monthly social security benefit, you can apply up to four months before the date you want your benefits to start. Visit www.socialsecurity.gov/retire to apply.

For more information read the social security publication, *When to Start Receiving Retirement Benefits* (Publication No. 05-10147), at www.socialsecurity.gov/pubs/EN-05-10147.pdf, and visit the Retirement Planner at https://www.ssa.gov/planners/.

Notes

1. The Social Security Act is found in Title 42 of the United States Code. Title 20 of the Code of Federal Regulations contains the applicable regulations.
2. 20 C.F.R. § 404.1807.
3. 31 U.S.C. § 3332.
4. 20 C.F.R. § 404.2010.
5. *Id.* § 404.2015.
6. *Id.* § 404.2020.
7. *Id.* § 404.2021.
8. *Id.* § 404.2040.
9. *Id.* § 404.2041.
10. *Id.* § 404.506.
11. *Id.* § 404.502(c)(2).
12. *Id.* § 404.502(d).
13. *Id.* § 404.502(b).
14. *Id.* § 404.503(a).
15. *Id.* § 404.503(b).
16. *Id.* § 404.391.
17. Section 4313 of SSA Handbook.
18. 20 C.F.R. § 404.392.
19. *Id.* § 404.110(b).
20. *Id.* § 404.112.
21. 42 U.S.C. § 413(d)(1).
22. 64 Federal Register 53702 (Oct. 24, 2018).
23. *Id.*
24. 20 C.F.R. § 404.146.
25. *Id.* § 404.141.
26. *Id.* § 404.204.
27. *Id.* § 404.210(b).
28. *Id.* § 404.250.
29. *Id.* § 404.240.
30. *Id.* § 404.403.
31. *Id.* § 404.403(a)(3).
32. *Id.* § 404.464.

33. *Id*. § 404.460.
34. *Id*. § 404.460(c). List includes Cuba, North Korea, Democratic Kampuchea (Cambodia), and Vietnam.
35. *Id*. § 404.469.
36. *Id*. § 404.465.
37. *Id*. § 404.468.
38. *Id*. § 404.470.
39. *Id*. § 404.421.
40. *Id*. § 404.422.
41. *Id*. § 404.408a.
42. *Id*. § 404.310.
43. *Id*. § 404.311(c).
44. *Id*. § 404.312(a).
45. *Id*. § 404.311.
46. *Id*. § 404.415.
47. *Id*. § 404.344.
48. *Id*. § 404.333.
49. *Id*. § 404.345.
50. *Id*.
51. *Id*.
52. Section 307 of the Social Security Handbook.
53. 20 C.F.R. § 404.346.
54. *Id*. § 404.346(b).
55. *Id*. § 404.330.
56. *Id*. § 404.331.
57. *Id*. § 404.332.
58. *Id*. § 404.335.
59. *Id*. § 404.338.
60. *Id*. § 404.313.
61. *Id*. § 404.335.
62. *Id*. § 404.336.
63. *Id*. § 404.337.
64. *Id*. § 404.337(c)(1).
65. *Id*. § 404.339.
66. *Id*. § 404.342.
67. *Id*.
68. *Id*. § 404.340.
69. *Id*. § 404.341.
70. *Id*. § 404.370.
71. *Id*. § 404.373(a).
72. *Id*. § 404.373(b).
73. *Id*.
74. *Id*. § 404.374.
75. *Id*. § 404.370(f).
76. *Id*. § 404.371.
77. *Id*. § 404.353(a).
78. *Id*. § 404.350.
79. *Id*. § 404.360.
80. *Id*. § 404.361.
81. *Id*.
82. *Id*. § 404.363.

83. *Id.* § 404.362.
84. *Id.* § 404.362(b)(1)(ii).
85. *Id.* § 404.362(c)(1).
86. *Id.* § 404.358.
87. *Id.* § 404.364.
88. *Id.* § 404.362(c)(2).
89. *Id.* § 404.352.
90. *Id.* § 404.317.
91. *Id.* § 404.1505(a).
92. *Id.*
93. *Id.* § 404.1508.
94. *Id.* § 404.1512.
95. *Id.* § 404.1566(a).
96. *Id.* § 404.315.
97. *Id.* § 404.315(a)(4).
98. *Id.* § 404.1571.
99. *Id.* § 404.1572(a)(b).
100. *Id.* § 404.1574(b)(2)(vii).
101. *Id.* § 404.1576.
102. *Id.* § 404.1581.
103. *Id.* § 404.1582.
104. 65 Federal Register 53702 (Oct. 24, 2018).
105. 20 C.F.R. § 404.1535.
106. *Id.* § 404.316.
107. *Id.* § 404.902. See for complete list of various determinations subject to review.
108. *Id.* § 404.903. See for complete list of various actions which are not initial determinations.
109. *Id.* § 404.906.
110. *Id.* § 404.908(a).
111. *Id.* § 404.909.
112. *Id.* § 404.911.
113. *Id.* § 404.914.
114. *Id.* § 404.921.
115. *Id.* § 404.933(b).
116. *Id.* § 404.933(c).
117. *Id.* § 404.950(d).
118. *Id.* § 404.948(a)(b).
119. *Id.* § 404.955.
120. *Id.* § 404.967.
121. *Id.* § 404.968(a).
122. *Id.* § 404.968(b).
123. *Id.* § 404.969.
124. *Id.* § 404.970.
125. *Id.* § 404.975.
126. *Id.* § 404.976(c).
127. *Id.* § 404.967.
128. *Id.* § 405(g).
129. *Id.*
130. *Id.* § 404.924.
131. *Id.* § 404.927.

132. *Id.*
133. *Id.* § 404.1720.
134. *Id.* § 404.1730(b)(1).
135. *Id.* § 404.1730(b)(2).
136. Social Security Administration.

CHAPTER 4

Veterans Benefits

I. Overview 102
II. Introduction to Veterans Benefits 103
III. Disability Compensation Benefits 103
    A. Introduction 103
    B. Eligibility for Disability Compensation Benefits 103
    C. "Service Connected" and "Line of Duty" Defined 103
    D. Grades of Disability. 104
    E. Amount of Payments 104
IV. Pension Benefits 104
    A. Introduction 104
    B. Eligibility for Pension Benefits 105
    C. Wartime Service Defined 105
    D. Non-Service Connected Defined. 105
    E. Resource Limits 106
    F. Excluded Resources. 106
    G. Treatment of Income 106
    H. Exclusions from Income 107
    I. Amount of Payments 108
    J. Aid and Attendance (A&A) Benefits for Pension Recipients . 108
    K. Housebound Benefits for Pension Recipients. 108
    L. Election of Benefits 109
V. Dependency and Indemnity Compensation (DIC) Benefits. 109
    A. Introduction 109
    B. How a Surviving Spouse Qualifies for DIC Benefits 109
    C. How a Child Qualifies for DIC Benefits 110
    D. How a Parent Qualifies for DIC Benefits 110
    E. Eligibility Requirements for DIC Benefits. 110
    F. Amount of DIC Benefits for a Surviving Spouse 111
    G. Effect of Remarriage of Surviving Spouse 111
    H. Amount of DIC Benefits for Dependent Child or Children . . 111
    I. Amount of DIC Benefits for a Surviving Dependent Parent. . 112

   VI. Improved Survivors Pension Benefits (Death Pension) 112
       A. Introduction 112
       B. Eligibility for Survivors Pension Benefits 112
       C. How a Surviving Spouse Qualifies for Survivors
          Pension Benefits....................................... 113
       D. Amount of Survivors Pension Benefits for a Surviving
          Spouse 113
       E. Amount of Survivors Pension Benefits for Surviving Child.. 114
  VII. Aid and Assistance and Homebound Benefits................. 114
 VIII. Medical Benefits 114
       A. Introduction 114
       B. Enrollment Requirement................................ 114
       C. Medical Benefits for Dependents 115
   IX. Burial Benefits... 115
    X. Claims for Benefits....................................... 116
       A. Introduction 116
       B. The Board of Veterans' Appeals 117
       C. The Court of Veterans' Appeals 117
       D. U.S. Court of Appeals for the Federal Circuit 118
Appendix A: VA Benefits Checklist................................. 118

I. Overview

Most clients who are entitled to veterans benefits are already receiving those benefits. Nonetheless, it is helpful to have an overview of benefits available to clients who are veterans. This chapter discusses those benefits available to veterans other than retirement benefits. Your client will be fully aware of these benefits and will often be receiving those benefits at the time of your interview.

A veteran who became disabled while on active duty is entitled to a disability pension due to those service-connected or line-of-duty injuries (see Section III). The surviving spouse or other qualified dependent may also be entitled to benefits after the veteran's death under what are referred to as dependency and indemnity compensation (DIC) (see Section V). Further, veterans who have served in wartime and meet financial need requirements may receive a pension benefit that can be enhanced, depending on the veteran's health needs, by aid and assistance benefits (A&A) or homebound benefits (see Section IV). These benefits are also available for a qualified surviving spouse or dependent upon the death of the veteran (see Section VI). It is these benefits that your client may not be aware of for which you can provide invaluable assistance. For example, an elderly veteran client or his or her spouse who is in need of assisted living or other long-term care facilities may be entitled to a pension or the AIA or homebound benefits.

The Department of Veterans Affairs (DVA) web page, www.va.gov, is a helpful resource. It has a wealth of information. A helpful brochure to give your clients is the Summary of VA Benefits brochure found on the VA's web page

www.benefits.va.gov/Benefits/benefits-summary/SummaryofVABenefits
Flyer.pdf. Appendix A provides a checklist of information needed when
applying for VA benefits.

II. Introduction to Veterans Benefits

An individual who is a veteran or the spouse of a veteran may be eligible for
various benefits from the DVA.[1] As many elderly clients are veterans, a general understanding of these benefits is helpful. Benefits of particular rele-
vance to an elderly client are disability compensation benefits, pension
benefits, survivor's benefits, medical benefits, and burial benefits. The ensuing discussion will provide the practitioner with an overview of benefits to
which his or her client may be entitled.

III. Disability Compensation Benefits

A. Introduction

Disability compensation benefits are a form of tax-free disability benefits payable to veterans who have a disability as a result of their military service. Disability compensation benefits are payable both to veterans who are disabled
during wartime[2] and peacetime.[3] The benefit rate is the same for both.[4] Disability compensation benefits are payable to a veteran regardless of the veteran's income or financial resources. However, a veteran who earns a significant
wage may find it difficult to prove disability at the higher levels.

B. Eligibility for Disability Compensation Benefits

In order to be eligible for disability compensation benefits, a veteran must
show:

- The veteran is disabled as a result of a service-connected injury.
- The veteran was injured while in the line of duty.
- The veteran was discharged from service under conditions that were
  other than dishonorable.

C. "Service Connected" and "Line of Duty" Defined

The term *service connected* means that the disability was incurred or aggravated during active service in the line of duty.[5] The term *line of duty* means
that the injury or disease was incurred or aggravated during a period of
active military, naval, or air service unless such injury or disease was the
result of the veteran's own willful misconduct and, for claims filed after
October 31, 1990, was a result of the veteran's abuse of alcohol or drugs.[6] It is
not limited to wartime service. The requirements of line of duty are not met if
at the time the injury was incurred or the disease was contracted, the veteran

was avoiding duty by desertion or absent without leave, confined under a court-martial for an unremitted (still valid) dishonorable discharge or confined under sentence of a civil court for a felony-related offense.

D. *Grades of Disability*

The DVA utilizes a rating system that provides for ten grades of disability. A veteran may be rated from 0 percent, 10 percent, 20 percent, 30 percent, 40 percent, 50 percent, 60 percent, 70 percent, 80 percent, 90 percent, or 100 percent disabled. A 100 percent disability rating is also referred to as a "total disability" rating. The higher the rating of disability, the more the DVA will pay the veteran in benefits. A rating of 0 percent disability is referred to as "noncompensable" but may still qualify the veteran for certain benefits such as preference for federal or state jobs or health care. However, in order to receive any monetary compensation, the veteran must be rated at the minimal 10 percent disability.

E. *Amount of Payments*

For 2019, compensation payments for a veteran with no dependents range from $140.05 per month for a 10 percent disability rating to $3,057.13 per month for a 100 percent disability rating.[7] In addition, certain severe injuries, such as the loss of a limb or loss of a body organ, entitle a veteran to higher monthly benefits. These tax-free benefits are termed special monthly compensation (SMC) and are paid in addition to the monthly disability benefit. Payment amounts vary depending on the extent of the injury. In 2019, the payment for a veteran with no dependents range from $3,804.04 to $8,749.09. Each year new benefit amounts are published in the Federal Register and on the DVA web site. Veterans with dependents who have a disability rating of at least 30 percent are entitled to additional compensation as well.[8] For example, a veteran in 2019 with a total disability rating who has a spouse and no children is entitled to an additional $170.45 per month.[9] In 2019, a veteran rated totally disabled who has both a spouse and children is entitled to an additional $295.28 per month for the spouse and the first child, with an additional $84.69 per month for each additional child.[10] If the veteran has no spouse but has children, in 2019, the veteran is entitled to an additional $113.99 per month for the first child, and an additional $84.69 per month for each additional child.[11] If the veteran has a parent dependent upon her for support, for 2019, the veteran is entitled to an additional $136.79 for each parent who is dependent.[12]

IV. *Pension Benefits*

A. *Introduction*

Certain other veterans may be eligible for pension benefits. Unlike disability compensation benefits, eligibility for pension benefits is based on the veteran's income and financial resources. This pension is a tax-free monetary

benefit provided to help veterans with financial hardships by providing supplemental income. A veteran cannot receive both disability compensation
benefits and pension benefits.

B. Eligibility for Pension Benefits

In order to qualify for pension benefits, a veteran must show:

- The veteran served in active military service during a period of war
  (defined in the following section) for at least 90 days with at least one
  day during a wartime period, or was discharged prior to completing
  90 days of service because of a service-connected disability, except
  after September 7, 1980, the active military service is 24 months or the
  full period for which the veteran was called to active duty.
- The veteran is a patient in a nursing home receiving skilled nursing
  care.
- The veteran is permanently and totally disabled from a "non-service-
  connected" disability (defined in Section IV.D) or has reached the age
  of 65 years.
- The veteran is receiving either social security disability or supplemental security insurance benefits.
- The veteran's discharge from active service was under conditions
  other than dishonorable.
- The disability is not the result of the veteran's willful misconduct.
- The veteran's net worth is within the required limits (defined in Section IV.E).
- The veteran's annual income does not exceed the maximum pension
  rate, as explained more fully in Sections IV.G and H.

C. Wartime Service Defined

For purposes of eligibility for pension coverage, a veteran must have served
during a period of war, though not necessarily in the theater itself. For example, service exclusively in Kansas during World War II qualifies a veteran for
wartime service. Wartime service is defined as:[13]

- World War II: December 7, 1941, through December 31, 1946. The ending date is extended to July 25, 1947, for soldiers who were on continuous active duty on or before December 31, 1946, through July 25,
  1947.
- Korean War: June 27, 1950, through January 31, 1955.
- Vietnam War: August 6, 1964, through May 7, 1975.
- Persian Gulf War: August 2, 1990, through a date to be determined.

D. Non-Service Connected Defined

The term *non-service connected* means that the disability of the veteran was
not incurred or aggravated in the line of duty in active military service.[14]

E. Resource Limits

In order to qualify for pension benefits, a veteran's resources must be limited. A pension is denied a veteran or is discontinued when the net worth, in 2019, of the veteran and the veteran's spouse is $127,066, including as net worth the annual income of the veteran, the veteran's spouse, and the veteran's dependent children.[15] The term *net worth* is defined as the market value, less mortgages or other encumbrances, of all real and personal property owned by the veteran; except the veteran's dwelling, if a single family unit, including a reasonable lot area, household and personal effects, and family transportation vehicles are excluded.[16]

F. Excluded Resources

Certain other resources are excluded by the DVA from consideration in the veteran's net worth. A complete listing is in the Code of Federal Regulations. A partial listing follows:

- Agent Orange settlement payments[17]
- Resources belonging to a child that are set aside for the education of the child until age 23 years.[18]
- Restitution payments to individuals of Japanese ancestry who were interned during World War II[19]
- Payments made to veterans pursuant to the Radiation Exposure Compensation Act of 1990[20]
- Monetary allowance for a child of a Vietnam veteran suffering from spina bifida[21]

G. Treatment of Income

Unless otherwise excluded, payments to the veteran or her dependents of any kind from any source are to be counted as income.[22] The annual income of the veteran, her dependent spouse, and dependent children is deducted on a dollar-for-dollar basis from the pension amount to determine the actual amount the veteran will receive. The DVA recognizes three types of income:[23]

- Recurring income: income that is received or anticipated in equal amounts and at regular intervals.
- Irregular income: income that is received or anticipated during a 12-month annualization period, but which is receive in unequal amounts or at irregular times.
- Nonrecurring income: income that is received or anticipated on a one-time basis during a 12-month annualization period.

H. Exclusions from Income

Numerous types of income are excluded from consideration as income by the DVA. Among these exclusions are the following:

- Welfare, defined as donations from public or private relief, welfare, or charitable organizations.[24]
- Maintenance, defined as the value of maintenance received from a relative, friend, or a charitable organization. The expense of maintenance is not deductible if paid from the individual's income.[25]
- DVA pension benefits.[26]
- Reimbursement for casualty loss to the extent of the value of the destroyed property.[27]
- Profit from the sale of property other than in the ordinary course of business.[28]
- Monies in joint accounts acquired by the death of the joint owner.[29]
- Unreimbursed medical expenses paid within the past 12-month period regardless of when incurred provided that the expenses are in excess of 5 percent of the veteran's and her dependents' annual pension rates. Payments for housebound and aid and assistance (A&A) benefits are not included.[30]
- Expenses for the last illness, burial, and just debts of the veteran or dependents, paid within a 12-month period.[31]
- Education expenses.[32]
- Child's income to the extent that the child's income does not exceed the lowest amount of gross income for which a single individual must file a federal tax return *and* if the child is in post-secondary education or vocational rehabilitation, the amount paid by the child for tuition, books, fees, and materials.[33]
- Domestic Volunteer Service Act programs payments provided such payments do not exceed the minimum wage.[34]
- Distributions from the DVA's Special Therapeutic and Rehabilitation Activities Fund.[35]
- Hardship exclusion of a child's income.[36] A hardship exclusion may be available if claimed by the veteran in certain cases. A hardship exists when annual expenses for family maintenance exceed all income that can be counted along with the veteran's pension benefits. Expenses necessary for reasonable family maintenance include expenses for basic necessities, such as food, clothing, and shelter, and other expenses, to be determined on a case-by-case basis, which are necessary to support a reasonable quality of life.[37]
- Survivor benefit annuity.[38]
- Settlements exempt statutorily under 38 C.F.R. § 3.279.
- Cash surrender value of life insurance.[39]
- Income tax refunds.[40]
- Radiation Exposure Compensation Act payments.[41]

I. Amount of Payments

Each year new figures for pension benefit amounts are published in the Federal Register and on the DVA web site. A veteran who is not married or married but separated and not contributing support to his spouse is entitled, during 2019, to $13,537 per year in pension benefits, which amount is reduced by the veteran's annual income.[42] If the veteran is married and living with or reasonably contributing support to his spouse, during 2019, the veteran is entitled to $17,724 per year in pension benefits, which amount is reduced by the veteran's other annual income.[43] If the veteran is single but has a child in his custody or a child that he reasonably contributes support to, the veteran in 2019 is also entitled to $17,724 per year in pension benefits, which amount is reduced by the veteran's annual income.[44] If the veteran has both a spouse and a child or children, the veteran in 2019 is entitled to an additional annual $2,313 per child. The lawyer should note that benefit rates change annually. These amounts may be verified on the Veterans Administration website, www.va.gov.

J. Aid and Attendance (A&A) Benefits for Pension Recipients

A veteran who receives a basic pension and requires a high degree of care may also qualify for aid and attendance (A&A) benefits. Veterans who are either living in a nursing home or require personal health care services on a daily basis in their home because the veteran cannot perform daily functions, including bathing, eating, or dressing, are eligible for A&A benefits. These services at one's home must be performed by persons licensed to perform such services or by persons under the supervision of licensed persons.[45] In order to qualify for A&A benefits, the veteran must be certified as in need of A&A benefits by a DVA physician or private physician approved of by the DVA. If a veteran is single and eligible for pension and A&A benefits, during 2019, she is entitled to $22,577 per year in total benefits less a reduction for the veteran's annual income.[46] If a veteran qualifies for A&A benefits as well as pension benefits and the veteran has either a spouse or a child for whom the veteran reasonably contributes support, in 2019, the veteran is entitled to $26,766 per year in total benefits less the required income deduction. A veteran with more than one dependent is entitled to an additional $2,313 annually per child benefit for 2019. Again, benefit rates will change annually.

K. Housebound Benefits for Pension Recipients

A veteran who does not qualify for A&A benefits but who receives a pension may be eligible for housebound benefits. A veteran is automatically eligible for housebound benefits if the veteran has a single service-connected disability rating of 100 percent and an additional service-connected disability rating for a separate disability of 60 percent.[47] Another way a veteran can qualify for housebound benefits occurs when the veteran meets the required definition of housebound status. The status of "housebound" is met when the veteran is substantially confined to her immediate premises due to a service-connected disability and it is reasonably certain that the veteran will remain housebound for the remainder of her life.[48] The disability does not have to be service related. For 2019, a veteran with no dependents who is entitled to housebound benefits has an increased pension of $16,540 per year less any required deduction for the veteran's income.[49] For 2019, a veteran with a spouse or child who qualifies for housebound benefits is entitled to an increased pension of $20,731 per year less the required income deduction.[50] If a veteran has more than one dependent, each additional child entitles the veteran to an additional $2,313 per year in pension benefits for 2019. Of course, benefit rates will change annually.

L. Election of Benefits

A veteran who is entitled to both disability compensation benefits and pension benefits cannot receive both types of benefits.[51] The veteran must elect which to receive, but the veteran may reverse her decision at any time and receive the other form of benefits.[52]

V. Dependency and Indemnity Compensation (DIC) Benefits

A. Introduction

Dependency and indemnity compensation (DIC) benefits are available for dependents of deceased veterans. DIC is a tax-free monetary benefit generally payable to a surviving spouse, child, or parent of a veteran who died while on active duty, active duty for training, or inactive duty training, or to survivors of veterans who died from their service-connected disabilities.

B. How a Surviving Spouse Qualifies for DIC Benefits

A surviving spouse is defined as a person who was married to the veteran at the time of the veteran's death, who lived with the veteran from the time of marriage to the date of the veteran's death, and has not either (1) remarried since the death of the veteran or (2) cohabitated with another person since the death of the veteran. If the surviving spouse remarried after December 15, 2003, and was 57 years of age or older at the time of remarriage, the survivor is still entitled to continue to receive benefits, if one of the following applies:

- The spouse married the veteran before January 1, 1957.
- The veteran and the spouse were married before the expiration of 15 years after the termination of the period of service in which the injury or disease causing the death of the veteran was incurred or aggravated.
- The veteran and the spouse were married for one year or more.

- The veteran and the spouse were married for less than one year but a child was born of the marriage or was born to them before the marriage.
- The spouse had a child with the veteran and cohabitated continuously until the veteran's death or, if separated, was not at fault for the separation, and has not remarried.

C. How a Child Qualifies for DIC Benefits

An individual is considered a child of a veteran if:[53]

- The claimant is an unmarried person who is the natural child of the veteran under 18 years of age.
- The claimant is the adopted child of the veteran who was adopted before age 18.
- The claimant became the step-child of the veteran before age 18.
- The claimant is more than 18 years of age but became permanently incapable of self-support before reaching 18 years of age.
- The claimant is under age 23 and in school.

D. How a Parent Qualifies for DIC Benefits

An individual is considered the parent of a veteran if:[54]

- The claimant is the natural mother or father of the veteran.
- The claimant is the adopted mother or father of the veteran.
- The claimant was the veteran's de facto parent for at least one year before the veteran entered service.

E. Eligibility Requirements for DIC Benefits

In order for a dependent of a veteran to qualify for DIC payments, one of the following must apply:

- The veteran died while on active duty, active duty for training, or inactive duty training.
- The death of a veteran was due to a service-connected disability and the evidence establishes that such disability was either the principal or a contributory cause of the veteran's death, or if the death was not service-connected the veteran was eligible for disability compensation for a service-connected disability that would be rated at 100 percent disability.[55]
- The veteran at the time of death was either receiving compensation or entitled to receive compensation[56] for a service-connected disability that was rated at 100 percent disabling for at least a ten-year period prior to the veteran's death.[57]

- The veteran at the time of death was either receiving compensation or entitled to receive compensation for a service-connected disability rated at 100 percent disabling for at least a five-year period from the date of the veteran's discharge or release from active duty.[58]
- The veteran at the time of death was either receiving compensation or entitled to receive compensation for at least one-year before his or her death if the veteran was a former prisoner of war who died after September 30, 1999.

F. Amount of DIC Benefits for a Surviving Spouse

For veterans who died on or before December 31, 1992, the rate of DIC benefits to a surviving spouse is based on the highest pay grade of the deceased veteran, with an increasing scale for the higher ranks.[59] The current DIC benefits for a surviving spouse can be found at www.va.gov. For veterans who die on or after January 1, 1993, the basic rate of DIC benefits for 2019 is $1,319.04 per month.[60] If the surviving spouse has one or more children below the age of 18 of a deceased veteran, the dependency and indemnity compensation paid monthly to the surviving spouse is increased by $326.77 for each such child for 2019.[61] In addition, if the surviving spouse was married to the veteran for at least eight years while the veteran had a disability rated at 100 percent, the surviving spouse is entitled to an additional $280.09 per month in 2019.[62] A surviving spouse of a veteran who died on or before December 31, 1992, may elect to receive the post January 1, 1993, benefit rate if greater.

In addition, if the surviving spouse is a patient in a nursing home or in need of aid and attendance, the monthly benefit amount in 2019 is increased by $326.77.[63] If the surviving spouse does not qualify for A&A benefits, but does qualify for housebound benefits, the monthly benefit amount in 2019 is increased by $153.08.[64]

G. Effect of Remarriage of Surviving Spouse

A surviving spouse is not entitled to DIC benefits if the surviving spouse remarries or cohabitates with another person as if married. However, if the surviving spouse's subsequent marriage is terminated by death, divorce, or annulment, the surviving spouse may become eligible again for DIC benefits.[65] Likewise, if the surviving spouse ceases to cohabitate with another person, her entitlement to DIC benefits may be reinstated.[66] If the surviving spouse remarries after December 19, 2003, and is 57 years of age or older at the time of remarriage, the surviving spouse is entitled to continue receiving benefits.

H. Amount of DIC Benefits for Dependent Child or Children

DIC benefits may be paid to a surviving child or children of the veteran only when there is no surviving spouse unless a specific exception applies.[67] Each year benefit rates change. For 2019, the rates are $556.93 for one child, $801.19 for two children, $1,045.47 for three children, and $198.68 per additional child if more than three children.[68] DIC benefits are paid to children 18 years of age and older in the following cases:

- A child who is at present time 18 years of age or older but who was disabled before age 18 years is entitled to an additional benefit amount in 2019 of $326.77.[69]
- In cases where there is both a surviving spouse and a child who at the present time is 18 years of age or older who became disabled before reaching 18 years of age, the child is entitled to DIC benefits in 2019 of $556.93 per month.[70]
- A child age 18 through 23 years of age who is enrolled in an approved educational institution is entitled to DIC benefits in 2019 of $276.84 per month.[71]

I. Amount of DIC Benefits for a Surviving Dependent Parent

A surviving dependent parent may be entitled to DIC benefits if the parent meets the required need test.[72] A sole surviving dependent parent with annual income, in 2019, of more than $15,394 does not qualify for DIC benefits.[73] For every $1 in annual income from $800 to $15,394, the DIC monthly benefit amount to a sole surviving dependent parent is reduced by 8 cents per dollar to a minimum of $5 per month. The maximum benefit amount, in 2019, is $652 per month. Only a surviving dependent parent with annual income of $800 or less per year would be entitled to the full monthly benefit amount.

VI. Improved Survivors Pension Benefits (Death Pension)

A. Introduction

The survivors pension benefit, which is often referred to as a death pension, is a tax-free monetary benefit payable to a low-income, un-remarried surviving spouse and/or unmarried children of a deceased veteran with wartime service. There are three survivors pension benefit plans available: improved, section 306, and old-law pension. All claims filed since January 1, 1979, are under the improved pension program. Accordingly, this section discusses eligibility requirements for death pension benefits under the improved pension program.

B. Eligibility for Survivors Pension Benefits

A dependent of a veteran whose death is not service connected may qualify for death pension benefits if the veteran served in the active military, naval, or air service on or before September 7, 1980, for 90 days or more during a period of war, with at least one day during a wartime period, or was discharged with a service-connected disability; and the veteran was discharged for conditions other than dishonorable.[74] For dependents of veterans who entered service after September 7, 1980, the veteran must have completed 24 months of continuous active duty with at least one day during a wartime period for the veteran's dependents to be eligible for death pension benefits unless one of the stated exceptions applies.[75] In addition, an eligible dependent must meet the limited resource requirement as discussed in Section IV.E.

C. How a Surviving Spouse Qualifies for Survivors Pension Benefits

In order to qualify for survivors pension benefits, the surviving spouse must meet one of the following requirements:[76]

- The surviving spouse was married to the veteran for at least one year.
- The surviving spouse was married to the veteran for less than a year if a child was born to the parties before or after marriage.
- The surviving spouse married the veteran after the veteran's discharge, provided the marriage occurred before certain dates called "delimiting dates":[77]
  1. For veterans of World War II, the marriage took place before January 1, 1957.
  2. For veterans of the Korean War, the marriage took place before February 1, 1965.
  3. For veterans of the Vietnam War, the marriage took place before May 8, 1985.
  4. For veterans of the Persian Gulf War, the marriage took place before January 1, 2001.

D. Amount of Survivors Pension Benefits for a Surviving Spouse

Each year new figures are published in the Federal Register and on the DVA web site for the maximum death pension benefits available for surviving dependents. If the surviving spouse of veteran does not have a child of the veteran in her custody, for 2019 the annual rate for death pension benefits is $9,078, less the required deduction for the surviving spouse's other annual income.[78] If the surviving spouse of the veteran has a child of the veteran's in her custody, for 2019, the annual rate for death pension benefits is $11,881, plus $2,313 per year for each additional child less the reduction for other annual income of the surviving spouse and child(ren).[79] For 2019, a surviving spouse without a dependent who is in need of aid and attendance (A&A) is entitled to a total annual benefit of $14,509 before the deduction for other annual income.[80] If the surviving spouse has a child of the veteran's in her custody and is entitled to A&A, the total annual benefit for 2019 is $17,309 plus $2,313 for each additional child less the annual income deduction.[81] A surviving spouse who does not meet A&A criteria but does meet housebound status is entitled, during 2019, to a total annual benefit of $11,095 less the annual income deduction.[82] A surviving spouse who meets housebound status and has a child of the veteran's in her custody is entitled to a total annual benefit, during 2019, of $13,893 plus $2,313 for each additional child less the annual income deduction.[83] As benefit rates change annually, check the Federal Register and the DVA website for current rates.

E. Amount of Survivors Pension Benefits for Surviving Child

A child of a deceased veteran who is eligible to receive death pension benefits and who is not in the surviving spouse's custody is entitled to receive pension benefits for 2019 in the amount of $2,313 per year less the deduction for the child's other annual income.[84]

VII. Aid and Assistance and Homebound Benefits

The A&A and homebound benefits discussed in Sections IV.J and K. are also available for a surviving spouse of a deceased wartime veteran who has not remarried. The spouse can receive one but not both of these benefits.

VIII. Medical Benefits

A. Introduction

In addition to monetary benefits, a veteran and her dependents may be entitled to medical benefits. Medical benefits are divided into (1) basic care consisting of services such as hospital care, outpatient care, long-term care, home health care, mental health care, and dental care[85] and (2) preventative care, consisting of services such as periodic medical exams, health education, and eye examinations.[86]

B. Enrollment Requirement

Due to budgetary restraints, the DVA requires most veterans to enroll in the DVA health care system to receive hospital or outpatient care. A veteran may enroll in person at any VA medical facility, by mail, or by the Internet at www.va.gov/health-care/apply/application/introduction. Certain veterans are exempt from the requirement to enroll, including veterans who are rated at 50 percent or more for a service-connected disability.[87] The secretary of the DVA is required to follow a priority list in determining which veterans should receive hospital care and medical services. The priority list in order from highest to lowest priority is:[88]

- Veterans with service-connected disabilities rated 50 percent or greater.

- Veterans with service-connected disabilities rated at 30 percent or 40 percent.
- Veterans who are former prisoners of war or who were awarded the Purple Heart.
- Veterans with service-connected disabilities rated at 10 percent or 20 percent.
- Veterans who were discharged from active duty for a disability incurred in the line of duty.
- Veterans entitled to disability compensation pursuant to 38 U.S.C. § 1511.
- Veterans who are in receipt of increased pension benefits based on a need for either aid and attendance or housebound status.
- Veterans, otherwise not listed, who are not disabled but who are unable to defray the expenses of necessary care based on a means test threshold.
- All other veterans eligible for hospital care, medical services, and nursing home services who are not required to make co-payments for their care.
- All other veterans who agree to make specified co-payments for services.

C. Medical Benefits for Dependents

Certain dependents are eligible for medical care from the DVA through CHAMPVA. The medical care is equivalent to that provided dependents of the participants in TRICARE, the Department of Defense medical care program for active duty and retired personnel. Dependents who are eligible for medical benefits include:[89]

- The spouse or child of a veteran who is rated at 100 percent disabled with a service-connected disability.
- The surviving spouse or child of a veteran who either died as a result of a service-connected disability or at the time of death had a total disability that was permanent in nature.
- The surviving spouse or child of a soldier who died in active military service in the line of duty and not due to the soldier's own misconduct and the dependents are not eligible for TRICARE.

IX. Burial Benefits

A veteran may be entitled to various burial benefits including:

- Interment in a national cemetery.[90]
- A burial and funeral allowance of $780 and $780 for plot-interment allowance (if not buried in a national cemetery) when:[91]
  1. The veteran dies in a VA facility.

2. The veteran dies in a facility where the veteran was receiving hospital or nursing home care paid for in part by the DVA.

■ A burial and funeral allowance of $300 and $780 for a plot-interment allowance if not hospitalized by the VA at the time of death when:[92]

1. The veteran was receiving or was entitled to compensation or pension benefits at the time of death.
2. The veteran died while hospitalized by the VA, or while receiving care under VA contract at a non-VA facility.
3. The veteran died while a patient at a VA-approved state nursing home.
4. The veteran died because of a service-related disability.

■ An interment allowance of $780 if the veteran is not buried in a national cemetery.[93]

■ For veterans who die from service-connected disability, a burial allowance of $2,000 or the current burial benefit for federal employees whose death occurs in the performance of duty, whichever amount is greater, and which if elected is in lieu of other burial benefits.[94]

■ A headstone, marker, or medallion for a veteran who was eligible for burial in a national cemetery.

X. Claims for Benefits

A. Introduction

The forms necessary to file a claim for veteran's benefits are available from the DVA or on the internet at http://www.va.gov. The DVA web page has an excellent explanation of the claims process. The DVA is required to assist a veteran with her claim for benefits.[95] A claimant has the right to a hearing at any time in the process. The hearing should be held in the DVA office that has jurisdiction over the claim or the DVA office nearest the claimant's home that has adjudicative functions.[96] The purpose of a hearing is to enable the claimant to introduce material evidence into the record and to allow witnesses to testify on the claimant's behalf. The DVA must notify the claimant and her representative in writing of any decision that affects the payment of benefits or granting of relief.[97] Furthermore, all notifications must advise the claimant of the reason for the decision, the date the decision will be effective, the right to a hearing, the right to initiate an appeal by filing a notice of disagreement which will entitle the individual to a statement of the case for assistance in perfecting an appeal, and the periods in which an appeal must be initiated and perfected. In addition, any notice that the DVA has denied a benefit sought must include a summary of the evidence considered.[98]

B. *The Board of Veterans' Appeals*

The Board of Veterans' Appeals (BVA) is located in Washington, D.C. BVA members review benefit claims determinations made by local DVA offices and issue decisions. An individual who wishes to appeal an adverse decision from the DVA has a one-year period to file a notice of disagreement (NOD).[99] Decisions that can be appealed to the BVA include denials for claims for benefits and eligibility for medical treatment.[100] Decisions, such as the need for medical care or the type of medical treatment needed, are not appealable to the BVA.[101] A claimant has the right to request a hearing before the BVA, which is held either in Washington, D.C. or at a local DVA office. In addition, some regional DVA offices are equipped to hold hearings by video conference. Each decision of the BVA must include a written statement of the BVA's findings and conclusions, the reasons for those findings and conclusions, and an order granting or denying relief.[102]

C. *The Court of Veterans Appeals*

An individual who is dissatisfied with a decision from the BVA can appeal to the Court of Veterans' Appeals (CVA). The Notice of Appeal must be filed within 120 days from the date the BVA's decision was mailed.[103] The postmark date of the decision is considered the first day of the 120-day appeal period. If an individual files a motion to reconsider with the BVA within the required 120-day period and the motion to reconsider is denied by the BVA, the individual has an additional 120 days to file an appeal to the CVA.[104] The address for the CVA is Clerk of the Court, United States Court of Veterans Appeals, 625 Indiana Avenue, NW, Suite 900, Washington, DC 20004-2950.

Unless specifically granted, there is no oral argument before the CVA. The CVA has authority to decide questions of law; interpret constitutional, statutory, and regulatory provisions; and interpret DVA decisions.[105] The CVA cannot set aside findings of fact by the BVA unless said findings are clearly erroneous.[106]

D. *U.S. Court of Appeals for the Federal Circuit*

A party who receives an adverse decision from the CVA may file an appeal to the U.S. Court of Appeals for the Federal Circuit within 60 days of the final decision by the CVA.[107] The Court of Appeals for the Federal Circuit must decide all questions of law, including interpreting constitutional and statutory provisions, and hold unlawful any regulation or interpretation that is arbitrary, capricious, or an abuse of discretion, *or* contrary to a constitutional right, power, privilege or immunity, *or* in excess of statutory jurisdiction or authority, and so on, *or* without observance of procedure required by law.[108]

Appendix A: VA Benefits Checklist

Military Information

_____ Military discharge or separation papers (DD214) for all active duty, reserve service, and National Guard service (if available)

_____ Proof of name change, if name is different from that in military records

Personal Information

_____ Copies of all divorce papers or death certificates from previous marriages (for both veteran and spouse, if veteran is *currently* married)

_____ Copies of marriage licenses from all marriages of veteran and his/her current spouse

_____ Names, dates, and places of all previous marriages of veteran and his/her current spouse

_____ Veteran's last date of employment and job description (if employed within five years and if available)

Financial Information for Veteran and His/Her Dependents

_____ Proof of *all* household assets
    _____ Latest bank and financial statements (all pages of statements even if they are blank!)
    _____ Latest IRA and 401K statements (if applicable)
    _____ Trust fund and/or annuity statements
    _____ Latest CD statements
    _____ Statements from life insurance company
    _____ Latest mutual fund statements
    _____ Current value of all stocks and bonds
    _____ Value of any business interest
    _____ Value of any real estate (include copies of deeds to real estate)
    _____ Value of *all* other investments
    _____ Voided deposit slip for checking account

_____ Proof of *all* household GROSS income
    _____ Current monthly pension statements showing GROSS amount before taxes/insurance or other deductions
    _____ Proof of current monthly social security payment/award letter
    _____ Current year's annuity statements showing GROSS amount before any deductions
    _____ Statement showing expected current year's IRA distribution
    _____ Expected TOTAL interest/dividends for next 12 months
    _____ Statement showing NET income from rental property, including primary place of residence
    _____ SSI and SSDI payments

Medical Information for Veteran and His/Her Dependents

_____   Signed care provider report
_____   Print out from pharmacy showing last six month's out-of-pocket medical costs related to prescriptions for veteran and his/her dependents
_____   Proof of medical insurance premiums with name of company and frequency of payments
_____   Statement showing Medicare Part D premium amount (if applicable)
_____   Picture ID and health insurance cards
_____   Signed physician's statement

Notes

1. Veteran's benefits are codified in Title 38 of the United States Code and the applicable regulations are found in Title 38 of the Code of Federal Regulations.
2. 38 U.S.C. § 1110.
3. *Id.* § 1131.
4. *Id.* § 1134.
5. 38 C.F.R. § 3.1(k).
6. *Id.* § 3.1(m).
7. *Id.* § 1114; 84 Fed. Reg. 10392 (Mar. 20, 2019).
8. 38 U.S.C. § 1115.
9. *Id.* § 1115(1)(A); 84 Fed. Reg. 10392 (Mar. 20, 2019).
10. 38 U.S.C. § 1115(1)(B); 84 Fed. Reg. 10392 (Mar. 20, 2019).
11. 38 U.S.C. § 1115(1)(C); 84 Fed. Reg. 10392 (Mar. 20, 2019).
12. 38 U.S.C. § 1115(1)(D); 84 Fed. Reg. 10392 (Mar. 20, 2019).
13. 38 C.F.R. § 3.2.
14. *Id.* § 3.1(l).
15. 38 U.S.C. 1522; 38 C.F.R. § 3.274(a) as update on the DVA website, www.va.gov.
16. 38 C.F.R. § 3.275(b).
17. *Id.* § 3.275(f).
18. *Id.* § 3.275(e).
19. *Id.* § 3.275(g).
20. *Id.* § 3.275(h).
21. *Id.* § 3.275(i).
22. *Id.* § 3.271(a).
23. *Id.*
24. *Id.* § 3.272(a).
25. *Id.* § 3.272(b).
26. *Id.* § 3.272(c).
27. *Id.* § 3.272(d).
28. *Id.* § 3.272(e).
29. *Id.* § 3.272(f).
30. *Id.* § 3.272(g).
31. *Id.* § 3.272(h).
32. *Id.* § 3.272(i).
33. *Id.* § 3.272(j).
34. *Id.* § 3.272(k).

35. *Id.* § 3.272(l).
36. *Id.* § 3.272(m).
37. *Id.* § 3.23(d)(6).
38. *Id.* § 3.272(n).
39. *Id.* § 3.272(q).
40. *Id.* § 3.272 (r).
41. *Id.* § 3.272(s).
42. 38 U.S.C. § 1521(b) as updated on the DVA website, www.va.gov.
43. *Id.* § 1521(c) as updated on the DVA website, www.va.gov.
44. *Id.*
45. 38 U.S.C. § 1114(r)(2).
46. *Id.* § 1521(d) as updated on the DVA website, www.va.gov.
47. *Id.* § 1521(e) as updated on the DVA website, www.va.gov.
48. *Id.* § 1114(s).
49. *Id.* § 1521(e).
50. *Id.*
51. *Id.* § 5304(a); 38 C.F.R. § 3.700.
52. 38 C.F.R. § 3.701.
53. *Id.* § 3.101(4)(A).
54. *Id.* § 3.57.
55. *Id.* § 3.32(a).
56. Certain military retirees must elect to receive either military retirement pay or compensation pay. Dependents of those retirees who elect to receive military retirement pay still qualify for DIC pursuant to this language.
57. 38 U.S.C. § 1318(b)(1).
58. *Id.* § 1318(b)(2).
59. *Id.* § 1311(a)(3).
60. *Id.* § 1311(a)(1) as updated on the DVA website, www.va.gov.
61. *Id.* § 1311(b) as updated on the DVA website, www.va.gov.
62. *Id.* § 1311(a)(2) as updated on the DVA website, www.va.gov.
63. *Id.* § 1311(c) as updated on the DVA website, www.va.gov.
64. *Id.* § 1311(d) as updated on the DVA website, www.va.gov.
65. *Id.* § 103(d)(1)(2).
66. *Id.* § 103(d)(3).
67. *Id.* § 1313(a).
68. *Id.*
69. *Id.* § 1314(a) as updated on the DVA website, www.va.gov.
70. *Id.* § 1314(b) updated on the DVA website, www.va.gov.
71. *Id.* § 1314(c) updated on the DVA website, www.va.gov.
72. *Id.* § 1315.
73. *Id.* updated on the DVA website, www.va.gov.
74. 38 U.S.C. 1541(a).
75. *Id.* § 5303(A).
76. 38 C.F.R. § 3.54(a).
77. *Id.* § 3.54(a)(3).
78. 38 U.S.C. § 1541(b) as updated on the DVA website, www.va.gov.
79. *Id.* § 1541(c) as updated on the DVA website, www.va.gov.
80. *Id.* § 1541(d)(1) as updated on the DVA website, www.va.gov.
81. *Id.* § 1541(d)(2) as updated on the DVA website, www.va.gov.
82. *Id.* § 1541(e)(1) as updated on the DVA website, www.va.gov.

83. *Id*.
84. *Id*. § 1542 as updated on the DVA website, www.va.gov.
85. 38 C.F.R. § 17.38(a)(1).
86. *Id*. § 17.38(a)(2).
87. 38 U.S.C. § 1705(c)(2).
88. *Id*. § 1705(a).
89. *Id*. § 1713(a).
90. *Id*. § 2402.
91. *Id*. § 2303(a).
92. *Id*. § 2302(a).
93. *Id*. § 2303(b).
94. *Id*. § 2307.
95. *Id*. § 3.103(a).
96. *Id*. § 3.103(c).
97. 38 C.F.R. § 3.103(f).
98. *Id*.
99. *Id*. § 7105(b)(1).
100. *Id*. § 20.101(a).
101. *Id*. § 20.101(b).
102. *Id*. § 7104(d).
103. 38 U.S.C. § 7266(a).
104. Curtis v. West, 13 Vet. App. 114 (1999).
105. 38 U.S.C. § 7261(a).
106. *Id*. § 7261(a)(4).
107. *Id*. § 7292.
108. *Id*. § 7292(d)(1).

CHAPTER 5

Medicare

   I. Overview 124
  II. Introduction. 124
 III. Medicare Part A 124
     A. Introduction 124
     B. Hospital Services Covered by Medicare Part A. 125
     C. Skilled Nursing Facility Services Covered by
        Medicare Part A. 126
     D. Home Health Care Services Covered by Medicare Part A . . . 126
     E. Hospice Services Covered by Medicare Part A 127
  IV. Medicare Part B 128
     A. Introduction 128
     B. Services Covered by Medicare Part B 129
     C. Preventive Services Covered by Medicare Part B 129
     D. Additional Services Covered by Medicare Part B. 130
     E. Services Not Covered by Medicare Part B 130
   V. Assignment 130
     A. How Assignment Works. 130
     B. The Limiting Charge 131
     C. Private Contracts 131
  VI. Medigap Insurance 132
     A. Medigap Insurance for Original Medicare Participants. 132
     B. When Medigap Insurance Can Be Purchased 132
 VII. Medicare as Primary or Secondary Payer. 133
     A. Medicare as Primary Payer 133
     B. Medicare as Secondary Payer 133
     C. Medicare and Workers' Compensation and Federal Black
        Lung Program 134
     D. Medicare and No-Fault Insurance 134
VIII. Medicare Advantage Plans—Part C. 134
     A. Introduction 134
     B. Medicare Advantage Plans 134
  IX. Medicare Part D 135

    X. Appeals Procedures 136
        A. Appeals Procedures for Entitlement to Medicare Benefits . . . 136
        B. Appeals Procedures for Claims. 137
Appendix A: Overview of Medicare Benefits 138
Appendix B: Medicare Checklist for New Beneficiaries 140

I. Overview

This chapter provides an overview of the Medicare program. There is a wealth of information available in regard to Medicare. To learn more, visit www.medicare.gov. A quick summary of Medicare benefits is provided in Appendix A in this chapter, with more detail provided in the sections that follow. Also, Appendix B provides a checklist of steps to take prior to age 65 as your clients make decisions concerning Medicare coverage.

II. Introduction

Few benefits are as important to the elder client as is Medicare. Try to avoid it as one may, a knowledge of Medicare benefits is essential for the lawyer advising elder clients. So let's dig in. Medicare is a health insurance program that affects elder clients 65 years of age and older as well as persons under the age of 65 years who meet certain qualifications. Medicare is divided into four main components, Part A, which provides hospital insurance; Part B, which provides medical insurance; Part C, also referred to as Medicare Advantage, which provides alternate forms of coverage to Part A and Part B Medicare to qualified individuals; and Part D, which pays a portion of prescription drugs.

III. Medicare Part A

A. Introduction

Medicare Part A is primarily financed through a payroll tax. Part A helps pay for care in hospitals, skilled nursing facilities, and some home health care. Generally, Medicare Part A is available for persons age 65 or older, younger people with disabilities, and people with end-stage renal disease or ALS. A person is eligible for premium-free Part A if they are age 65 or older and they or their spouse worked and paid Medicare taxes for at least 40 quarters or about ten years of work. A person qualifies for Part A at age 65 without having to pay premiums if:

- The person is receiving retirement benefits from social security or the railroad retirement board.
- The person is eligible to receive social security or railroad retirement benefits but has not yet filed for them.
- The person or their spouse had Medicare-covered government employment.

For a quick reference go to https://www.medicare.gov/eligibility premiumcalc/.

Persons under the age of 65 years are eligible for Part A coverage provided they have been entitled to at least 24 months of benefits due to disability under either the Social Security Act or the Railroad Retirement System. Persons suffering from end-stage renal disease or ALS may qualify as well for Medicare.[1] An otherwise qualified person, that is, a person over 65 years of age who has Part B coverage, may purchase Part A coverage if she or her spouse did not pay Medicare taxes.[2] For 2019, the Part A premium is $437 per month for uninsured individuals and $240.66 per month for individuals with 30 or more quarters of social security covered earnings.[3]

B. Hospital Services Covered by Medicare Part A[4]

Medicare Part A covers inpatient services at a hospital or a critical access hospital (CAH), including bed and board, nursing services, use of facilities, medical social services, drugs, biologicals, supplies, appliances, equipment, diagnostic and therapeutic services, medical and surgical services by certain interns and residents-in-training, and transportation services, including transport by ambulance.[5] Medicare Part A will pay for blood given at a hospital or skilled nursing facility during a covered stay, but the beneficiary must pay for the first three pints of blood unless the blood comes from a blood bank at no charge, or the blood is donated by the beneficiary or someone else on her behalf. Medicare Part A does not cover private duty nursing, or provide for payment of a television or telephone in the beneficiary's room. Medicare Part A will only pay for a private room if medically necessary or if no other rooms are available.[6]

A stay in the hospital is defined as a benefit period. Each benefit period can last up to 90 days. For each benefit period in 2019 the beneficiary pays a total of $1,364 for a hospital stay of 1 to 60 days. Thereafter, the beneficiary must pay $341 per day for days 61 through 90 of a hospital stay. Each beneficiary has a nonrenewable reserve of 60 days of inpatient hospital services that he or she may only utilize after he or she has spent more than 90 days in the hospital.[7] If the beneficiary elects to use his or her lifetime reserve, the beneficiary must pay $682 per day for days 91 through 150 of a hospital stay.[8] The beneficiary must pay all costs for each day beyond 150 days, or each day beyond 90 days once the 60 day reserve is used. Current amounts can be found at www.medicare.gov/your-medicare-costs.

A benefit period starts the day the beneficiary enters the hospital or skilled nursing facility. The benefit period is terminated when the beneficiary has not received hospital or skilled nursing care for 60 consecutive days.[9] If a beneficiary enters the hospital after one benefit period has ended, a new benefit period begins. However, if a beneficiary enters the hospital before the expiration of the previous benefit period, then the patient is considered within the same benefit period. A beneficiary must pay the inpatient hospital deductible for each benefit period but there is no limit to the number of benefit periods a beneficiary may have.

C. Skilled Nursing Facility Services Covered by Medicare Part A

Medicare Part A also pays for the cost of a semi-private room, meals, skilled nursing and rehabilitative services, and other medically necessary services and supplies for a beneficiary who is hospitalized in a skilled nursing facility.[10] This is not to be confused with long-term custodial care in a nursing facility, which is only partly covered for 100 days as discussed later. Skilled nursing and skilled rehabilitation services are defined as services that:[11]

- Are ordered by a physician
- Require the skills of technical or professional personnel, such as registered nurses, licensed practical nurses, physical therapists, occupational therapists, and speech pathologists or audiologists
- Are furnished directly by, or under the supervision of, such personnel
- Are required on a daily basis
- Furnished because of a condition for which the beneficiary received inpatient hospital care or critical access hospital (CAH) services or arose while the beneficiary was receiving care in a skilled nursing facility or swing bed hospital for a condition for which the beneficiary (had earlier) received inpatient hospital or inpatient CAH services
- Services that could only be provided in a skilled nursing facility as a practical matter

While Medicare Part A does not cover long-term facility costs indefinitely, it does cover up to 100 days of care in a skilled nursing facility (SNF). A skilled nursing facility is defined as an institution that is primarily engaged in providing skilled nursing care and related services to residents who require either medical and nursing care *or* rehabilitation services.[12] In order to qualify for coverage, the beneficiary must have been hospitalized at least three consecutive days not counting the day of discharge before entering the skilled nursing facility.[13] It is not necessary that the beneficiary enter the SNF immediately after her discharge from the hospital to qualify, but the beneficiary must be admitted to the SNF within 30 days of her discharge from the hospital.[14] For certain injuries, hip fractures for example, mending at home may be required before rehabilitation can begin and the 30-day period may be extended.[15] Medicare pays all costs for a stay in a skilled nursing facility for the first 20 days. Thereafter, in 2019, the beneficiary must pay $170.50 per day for days 21 through 100.[16] The beneficiary must pay all costs beyond the 100th day in the benefit period. Medicare will *not* pay for custodial care in an SNF.

D. Home Health Care Services Covered by Medicare Part A[17]

Medicare Part A pays for home health care costs. Home health care is skilled nursing care and other health care services that the beneficiary receives at her home for treatment of an illness or injury. All Medicare beneficiaries can receive home health care benefits. In order to qualify, the beneficiary must meet a five-part test:[18]

1. The beneficiary must be confined to her home or an institution that is not a hospital, skilled nursing facility, or nursing facility.
2. The beneficiary's physician must certify that the beneficiary needs medical care in her home.
3. The beneficiary must need either intermittent (but not full time) skilled nursing care or physical therapy or speech language pathology services.[19]
4. The beneficiary must be under an appropriate plan of care.
5. The home health agency caring for the beneficiary must be approved by the Medicare program.

If all five conditions are met, Medicare will cover skilled nursing care, as defined in Section III.C, on a part-time or intermittent basis, that is provided at the beneficiary's residence. Medicare will also cover home health aide services on a part-time or intermittent basis, which includes help with personal care, such as bathing, using the toilet, or dressing.

Medicare will *not* cover home health aide services unless the beneficiary is receiving skilled care such as nursing care or therapy. Medicare also covers certain types of therapy, including physical therapy, which includes exercise to regain movement and to strengthen a body area and training on how to use special equipment and to perform daily activities such as getting out of a wheelchair or a bathtub. Speech language pathology services are also covered, which includes exercise to regain and strengthen speech skills. Medicare will also cover occupational therapy, which helps the beneficiary become able to perform daily activities such as eating, combing one's hair, and putting on one's clothes. Medicare will also pay for certain medical supplies and equipment.

Medicare will *not* pay for 24-hour-per-day care at the beneficiary's home, prescription drugs, or the delivery of meals to the beneficiary's home. Nor will Medicare pay for homemaker services or personal care such as bathing, using the toilet, or help when getting dressed when this is the only type of care the beneficiary needs.[20]

E. Hospice Services Covered by Medicare Part A[21]

Medicare Part A provides coverage of hospice costs as well. In order to qualify for hospice benefits, a beneficiary must meet a four-part test:[22]

1. The beneficiary is eligible for Medicare Part A benefits.
2. The beneficiary's physician and the hospice medical director must certify that the beneficiary is terminally ill and probably has less than six months to live.
3. The beneficiary signs a statement choosing hospice care instead of routine Medicare covered benefits for their terminal illness.[23]
4. The beneficiary receives care from a Medicare-approved hospice program.[24]

If the beneficiary meets the preceding qualifications then Medicare will pay for doctor services, nursing care, medical equipment such as wheelchairs and walkers, drugs for the control and relief of pain, home health aide and homemaker services, physical and occupational therapy, speech therapy, social worker services, dietary counseling, and counseling to help the beneficiary and his family with grief and loss.[25]

Medicare will also pay for respite care, which is care given to a hospice patient by another caregiver so that the usual caregiver can rest.[26] The beneficiary may be cared for in a Medicare-approved facility such as a hospice facility, hospital, or nursing home. A beneficiary can stay in a Medicare-approved hospital or nursing home for up to five days each time he receives respite care and there is no limit to the number of times the beneficiary may receive respite care. While receiving hospice care, the beneficiary will pay no more than $5 per each prescription drug and other similar products to treat pain relief and symptom control and the beneficiary will pay only 5 percent of the Medicare-approved inpatient respite care costs.[27]

A beneficiary who lives longer than six months still continues to receive hospice services if his or her physician re-certifies that he or she is terminally ill. A hospice patient can receive hospice care for two 90-day periods followed by an unlimited number of 60-day periods, provided that the beneficiary's physician certifies at the beginning of each period of care that the beneficiary is terminally ill.[28] If the beneficiary's health improves or his illness goes into remission, then hospice care will cease. In addition, a hospice patient always has the right to stop hospice care for whatever reason and receive regular Medicare benefits.[29]

In order to locate a hospice program, the practitioner may wish to contact her state hospice agency. In addition, more information can be obtained from The National Hospice and Palliative Care Organization, 1731 King Street, Arlington, VA 22314, www.nhpco.org, or The Hospice Association of America, 228 7th Street, SE, Washington, D.C. 20003, http://hospice.nahc.org.

IV. Medicare Part B

A. Introduction

Medicare Part B, also known as the Medicare Supplementary Medical Insurance program (SMI), helps pay for doctors, physical and occupational therapists, outpatient hospital care, and other types of medical services that Part A does not cover.[30] In order to qualify for Part B coverage the beneficiary must pay the premium, which for 2019 is a minimum of $135.50 per month.[31] However, the premium is graduated and can be as high as $460.50 depending on the beneficiary's income. See www.medicare.gov/your-medicare-costs/medicare -costs-at-a-glance for the income levels and premium costs. Enrolling in Part B is purely voluntarily. Usually the premium is deducted and paid from the beneficiary's monthly social security, railroad retirement, or civil service retirement. Beneficiaries who do not receive any of these payments may elect to have Medicare send them a bill every three months for payment of the premium.

B. Services Covered by Medicare Part B[32]

Medicare Part B pays for the following types of services:[33]

- Medical services, including physicians' services; outpatient medical and surgical services and supplies; diagnostic tests; ambulatory surgery center facility fees for approved procedures; and durable medical equipment such as wheelchairs, hospital beds, oxygen, and walkers.
- Clinical laboratory services, such as blood tests and urinalysis.
- Home health care, including part-time skilled care, home health aide service, durable medical equipment when supplied by the home health agency while the beneficiary receives Medicare-covered home health care, and other supplies and services associated with home health care.
- Outpatient hospital services, including services for the diagnosis and treatment of an illness or injury, including any needed pints of blood, but the beneficiary must pay for the first three pints of blood.[34] If the blood is from a blood bank at no charge, or the beneficiary or someone on his or her behalf donates the blood, the only charge is for the blood processing and handling service.

C. Preventive Services Covered by Medicare Part B

In addition, Medicare Part B pays for certain preventive services as follows:

- Bone mass measurements for certain individuals who are at risk for losing bone mass.[35]
- Colorectal cancer screening, including fecal occult blood test once per year, flexible sigmoidoscopy, once every four years, colonoscopy, once every ten years, or every two years if the beneficiary is at high risk for cancer of the colon, and a barium enema which the doctor can substitute for the sigmoidoscopy or colonoscopy for all people with Medicare age 50 and older.[36]
- Diabetes monitoring, including coverage for glucose monitors, test strips, lancets, and self-management training for all persons with Medicare who have diabetes, including non-users of insulin.
- Mammogram screening once every year for all women with Medicare age 40 and older.[37]
- Pap smear and pelvic examination, including a clinical breast exam once every three years but once per year if the beneficiary is at high risk for cervical or vaginal cancer.[38]
- Prostate cancer screening, including a digital rectal examination once every year and a prostate specific antigen (PSA) test once every year for all men age 50 and older.
- Vaccinations, including a flu shot once per year, pneumonia shot, and a Hepatitis B shot if the beneficiary is in a medium to high risk group.
- Annual wellness exam.

A complete listing and explanation of these services is available at www
.medicare.gov/what-medicare-covers.

D. Additional Services Covered by Medicare Part B

In addition to the preventive services just outlined, Medicare Part B helps
pay for ambulance services on a limited basis; artificial limbs and eyes; braces
for the arms, legs, back, and neck; chiropractic services on a limited basis;
emergency care; eyeglasses (one pair) for a beneficiary who has had cataract
surgery; kidney dialysis and kidney transplants; medical supplies, such as
colostomy bags, surgical dressings, splints, casts, and some diabetic supplies;
outpatient prescription drugs on a very limited basis; prosthetic devices,
including breast prosthesis after mastectomy; services of practitioners such as
clinical psychologists, social workers, and nurse practitioners; heart, lung,
and liver transplants under certain conditions; and x-rays and other diagnostic tests.[39]

E. Services Not Covered by Medicare Part B

Services and supplies not covered by Medicare Part B include most outpatient prescription drugs; routine or yearly physical exams (other than annual
wellness exams); vaccinations besides those just listed; orthopedic shoes; custodial care such as help with bathing, dressing, using the toilet, and eating at
home or at a nursing home; most dental care and dentures; routine foot care;
hearing aids; routine eye care; and cosmetic surgery.[40] In addition, except in
limited circumstances, Medicare Part B will not pay for health care received
outside of the United States.

V. Assignment

A. How Assignment Works

The beneficiary in 2019 must pay a yearly $185 deductible before Medicare
Part B will begin coverage.[41] After the deductible is met, Medicare Part B will
pay all but 20 percent of the approved amount.[42] The 20 percent of the
approved amount that Medicare will not pay is called the coinsurance payment. The beneficiary is responsible for the coinsurance payment. If the beneficiary's physician or provider accepts assignment (participating provider)
then the amount Medicare approves for the service or supply is considered
payment in full by the physician or provider and the beneficiary does not
pay except for the coinsurance amount. About 96 percent of all providers are
participating providers.

   For example, if the beneficiary is billed $250 by her doctor for a service,
and Medicare approves $185 of the bill, then the beneficiary will pay 20 per-
cent of the approved amount, or $37, assuming that the beneficiary has
already met her yearly $185 deductible. If this was the first bill of the year for

the beneficiary, she would have to pay the entire $185 to meet her yearly deductible of $185.

If the beneficiary's doctor only accepts assignments on a case-by-case basis, then the outcome changes. The provider is termed a non-participating provider. These are providers who still choose to accept Medicare assignment but have not signed an agreement to accept Medicare. These account for about 4 percent of providers and the result is different. The Medicare-approved amount for physicians who accept assignment only on a case-by-case basis is reduced by 5 percent. If the beneficiary is billed $150 by her doctor, and Medicare would normally approve $100 of the charge, then the Medicare-approved amount drops to $95 due to the 5 percent penalty assessed against physicians who only accept assignment on a case-by-case basis. Medicare pays the physician 80 percent of the approved amount of $95, which means Medicare pays the beneficiary's physician $76. The beneficiary pays $19, which is 20 percent of the approved amount of $95. Thus Medicare penalizes physicians who accept assignment only on a case-by-case basis.

B. *The Limiting Charge*

If the beneficiary's doctor is a "non-participating" doctor (has not entirely opted out of Medicare) then the doctor is allowed to charge up to 15 percent more than the Medicare-approved amount.[43] This is called the limiting charge. Medicare applies the same 5 percent penalty for the approved amount for the doctor's services. The beneficiary may have to pay the entire bill to the physician at the time the service is provided and be reimbursed by Medicare.

For example, assume the amount charged by the physician who doesn't accept assignment is $150. Medicare approves $100, which is reduced by the 5 percent penalty for a total Medicare-approved amount of $95. Medicare allows the physician to bill the beneficiary an additional 15 percent more than the Medicare-approved amount if the physician doesn't accept assignment. Assuming the physician chooses to bill the beneficiary up to the limit, the beneficiary is billed $109.25 (which is 15 percent more than $95). As the physician does not accept assignment, the beneficiary must pay the entire $109.25 to the physician. Medicare will then pay the beneficiary $76, which is 80 percent of the approved amount of $95. The net cost to the beneficiary is $23.25.

If a physician or provider has opted out of Medicare, there is no limit on what can be charged. Only about 1 percent or less of physicians have opted out of Medicare. The beneficiary will have to pay the entire bill. This is discussed next.

C. *Private Contracts*

Federal law requires a physician who has opted out of Medicare to execute an agreement with the patient in which both the patient and the physician agree that the service provided by the physician will not be covered by

Medicare. This agreement is called a private contract.[44] Medicare will pay nothing for the services of a physician when a private contract is executed by the beneficiary. The beneficiary's Medigap policy will pay nothing as well. In addition, Medicare will not limit the amount that the physician can charge for the service, that is, there is no limiting charge.

For example, the beneficiary executes a private contract for the provision of services by a physician. The bill is $150. The beneficiary must pay the entire $150, as Medicare does not pay for services rendered through a private contract. If the beneficiary is covered by Medigap insurance, this insurance also pays nothing.

A private contract may not be executed if the beneficiary is faced with an emergency or urgent health care situation.[45] Federal law requires that certain providers must always accept assignment.[46] These providers include hospitals, skilled nursing facilities, home health agencies, comprehensive outpatient rehabilitation facilities, and providers of outpatient physical and occupational therapy or speech pathology services.

VI. Medigap Insurance

A. Medigap Insurance for Original Medicare Participants[47]

Beneficiaries who choose coverage under original Medicare are entitled to purchase supplemental insurance policies, often referred to as Medigap policies.[48] A beneficiary who has employer or union health care coverage or other private health insurance coverage will have little need to purchase a Medigap policy. In all but three states (Minnesota, Massachusetts, and Wisconsin) there are ten standardized Medigap plans, labeled A through J.[49] Medigap policies pay most, if not all, of the original Medicare coinsurance costs. Medigap plans may also cover the original Medicare plan deductibles. The three states mentioned have different standardized plans.

Basic benefits that must be included in all Medigap plans include coverage for all Part A coinsurance costs as well an additional 365 days of hospital care, which can be used during the lifetime of the beneficiary. In addition, each Medigap plan must provide coverage for the Part B coinsurance (20 percent of the Medicare-approved amount) and pay for the first three pints of blood each year. Plans A through J may differ on other areas of coverage, including payment of Part B deductibles, payment for at-home recovery, and payment for preventive care. Certain Medigap plans are allowed to charge greater deductibles than others. For more information on Medigap policies, the practitioner should go to www.medicare.gov/find-a-plan to find out what Medigap plans are available in the practitioner's state and the terms of these plans.

B. When Medigap Insurance Can Be Purchased

A beneficiary may purchase a Medigap policy during the open enrollment period. The insurance company cannot deny the beneficiary coverage or modify the price of the policy due to the beneficiary's past or current health problems.[50] The open enrollment period commences when a beneficiary is both 65 years of age *and* is enrolled in Medicare Part B. If either one of these two conditions are not met, then the open enrollment period does not commence until both requirements are fulfilled. A beneficiary who waits until after the expiration of the open enrollment period to purchase Medigap policy coverage may be denied coverage or charged more for the policy than a beneficiary who acts within the six-month enrollment period.

As would be expected, there are recognized exceptions to this rule. If a beneficiary's health care coverage through an employer is terminated, then the beneficiary may purchase a Medigap policy after the expiration of his open enrollment period. Likewise, a beneficiary may purchase a Medigap policy whose Medicare managed care plan is terminated after the expiration of his open enrollment period. If a beneficiary's Medigap policy is terminated after his open enrollment period has terminated, then he may purchase another Medigap policy.

VII. *Medicare as Primary or Secondary Payer*

A. *Medicare as Primary Payer*[51]

For many Medicare beneficiaries with health insurance policies, Medicare acts as the primary payer, that is, Medicare pays first on all claims. This group includes retired individuals who are covered by retiree health plans, individuals who are covered by their employer's or their spouse's employer's health insurance but the employer has few employees, and individuals who choose not to be covered by a group health plan. However, for certain Medicare beneficiaries who have other health insurance benefits, Medicare may be the secondary payer rather than the primary payer.

B. *Medicare as Secondary Payer*

For those individuals who are over 65 years of age, Medicare will act as the secondary payer if all of the following are met:[52]

- The individual is over 65 years of age.
- The individual is covered by Part A Medicare.
- The individual is covered under a group health plan because of his or her employment or his or her spouse's employment (regardless of the spouse's age),[53] and the employer has 20 or more employees.[54]

For those individuals who are under 65 years of age and disabled, Medicare will act as the secondary payer if all of the following are met:[55]

- The individual is under 65 years of age.
- The individual is covered by Part A Medicare.
- The individual is covered under a group health plan because of her employment or employment of a family member (regardless of the family member's age), and the employer has 100 or more employees.

C. Medicare and Workers' Compensation and Federal Black Lung Program

Medicare will not pay for any item or service if payment has been made pursuant to an individual's workers' compensation award or if payment for a service or item can reasonably be expected to be made later by the individual's workers' compensation award.[56] If the individual's workers' compensation does not pay within 120 days, the individual is allowed to file a claim with Medicare.[57] Medicare will make a conditional payment that must be refunded by the provider after the provider is paid by the individual's workers' compensation. In cases where an individual has a preexisting condition, workers' compensation may not pay the individual's entire claim. Medicare will cover those services that were provided for the preexisting condition. Medicare will also act as a secondary payer after payment by the individual's workers' compensation award.[58]

For those individuals who are covered by the federal Black Lung program, Medicare will not pay for medical services that are related to the individual's lung disease. If the federal Black Lung program denies coverage for medical services related to the individual's lung disease, then the individual's medical provider may submit a claim to Medicare along with the denial notice from the federal Black Lung program. For medical services unrelated to the individual's lung disease, Medicare will pay according to the normal rules.

D. Medicare and No-Fault Insurance

Medicare acts as the secondary payer where no-fault insurance or liability insurance is available as the primary payer.[59] A provider is required to collect from an insurer before billing Medicare if the services are covered by the no-fault or liability insurer carrier. Medicare can make a conditional payment if claims will not be paid for within 120 days.

When the no-fault or liability insurer pays, then Medicare will recover its conditional payment. The beneficiary is responsible for ensuring Medicare is reimbursed for its conditional payment.

VIII. Medicare Advantage Plans—Part C

A. Introduction

Congress created Medicare Advantage plans, which allows private insurance companies to offer alternate plans of health care coverage to Medicare beneficiaries. These alternate plans include health maintenance organizations, preferred provider organizations, private fee-for-service plans, special needs plans, and medical savings accounts. These plans bundle Part A, Part B, and usually Part D coverage into one plan. Each offers additional services and coverage to a Medicare beneficiary but with additional costs.

B. Medicare Advantage Plans[60]

A beneficiary may elect to receive Medicare coverage through a Medicare Advantage plan.[61] Medicare beneficiaries are eligible to join a Medicare Advantage plan if each of the following is met:

- The beneficiary has both Part A (hospital insurance) and Part B (medical insurance) coverage.
- The beneficiary does not have end-stage renal disease, in other words, the beneficiary does not have permanent kidney failure and is being treated with dialysis or a transplant.
- The beneficiary resides in the service area of the applicable plan. Participants who move out of the coverage area cannot remain covered by the plan. They must dis-enroll from the plan and revert to original Medicare coverage or choose to join another Medicare-managed care plan that offers coverage in their new area.

In most Medicare Advantage plans, participants may only utilize physicians and hospitals that have agreed to treat members of the plan. In addition, a participant in a plan may only see a specialist if he or she obtains a referral from the plan physician. The plan may charge a premium in addition to the monthly Part B premium, as well as a fee, referred to as a copayment, such as $5 or $10, each time the participant sees the plan physician. However this copayment is substituted for the regular 20 percent coinsurance payment charged in regular Medicare. The participant must continue to pay the monthly Part B premium even after he or she enrolls in a plan.

One advantage of a beneficiary enrolling in a Medicare Advantage plan is that the plan participant may be entitled to extra services and supplies not normally available to beneficiaries in regular Medicare, such as outpatient prescription drugs. Another advantage, as mentioned previously, is that the participant forgoes the normal 20 percent coinsurance payment for a set copayment fee for a certain service or item. The practitioner may go to www.medicare.gov/find-a-plan for a list of all plans offered in the beneficiary's area as well as information about what extra benefits and costs may be associated with each plan.

IX. *Medicare Part D*

Medicare Part D is a federal program administered through private insurance companies. These companies provide retail prescription drug coverage to Medicare recipients. This program began in 2006. Individuals can enroll in a separate, stand-alone Part D drug plan, or, if they choose, their Part D drug plan can be part of their Part C Medicare Advantage plan.

Upon enrollment, the person pays a monthly premium to the insurance company for the Part D coverage, or if they so elect the premium cost can be deducted from their monthly social security. There are a number of insurance carriers offering Part D coverage. Thus, there are multiple options among the various providers, as well as various options offered by each insurance company.

The Part D drug plans vary, but generally they have the following features. Most plans have an annual deductible that must first be met, which in 2019 can be no more than $415. After meeting the deductible, the individual will pay a copay for medications. Typically, the amount of the copay will vary depending on whether the medications are generic or preferred brand medications. For example, the copay might be $10 for a generic drug and $50 for a preferred brand name. Once the individual has spent $3,820, in 2019, then the third phase of charges for medications applies, in which the individual will pay only 25 percent for brand name medications and 37 percent for generic medications. Once the total payments by the individual have reached $5,100, in 2019, a fourth and final stage, termed catastrophic coverage, kicks in, in which the individual will only pay 5 percent of medication costs for the rest of the year. These amounts are modified annually. Companies are free to have lower thresholds, as these amounts are the cap amounts that a company can have in its Part D plan. Current information as to income levels and premiums is available at https://www.medicare.gov/your-medicare-costs /medicare-costs-at-a-glance.

Persons may enroll in a Part D plan at the same time they apply for Medicare benefits. A person may change plans annually during the annual enrollment period, which is from mid-October through early December of each year. However, failure to elect Part D coverage when first eligible triggers an enrollment penalty of a 1 percent increase in the insurance premium for each month of delayed enrollment. This is a permanent penalty that is added to the monthly premiums paid by the individual. An exception exists for persons who had creditable coverage during the period of non-enrollment. It should also be noted that persons at higher income levels, currently above $85,000 for single taxpayers and $170,000 for married taxpayers will pay a higher Part D premium.

X. Appeals Procedures

A. Appeals Procedures for Entitlement to Medicare Benefits

An individual may appeal a decision by Medicare that he is not eligible for Medicare. For example, Medicare determines that Joseph does not qualify for Medicare benefits because he does not meet the residency requirement. Joseph may appeal this decision. The steps in the appeal decision are:[62]

- Initial determination: a decision is rendered denying Medicare coverage can be appealed within 60 days of the date of the initial denial.
- Reconsideration: an aggrieved party has 60 days to request a reconsideration of the initial determination.
- Administrative law judge hearing: an aggrieved party has 60 days after an adverse reconsideration determination is rendered to request a hearing before an administrative law judge.
- Appeals council review: an aggrieved party has 60 days to file an appeal with the appeals council seeking a review of an unfavorable administrative law judge's ruling.
- Federal district court: an aggrieved party has 60 days to file an action in federal district court to obtain judicial review of the appeals council's decision denying benefits.

B. *Appeals Procedures for Claims*

For claims involving payment of Part A and Part B benefits, a similar appeals procedure is used, with a few exceptions. The first exception is that an administrative hearing is not available if the amount in controversy is less than $160 (2019) and judicial review is not available if the amount in controversy is less than $1,630 (2019).[63] The second exception involves whether the appeal involves original Medicare, that is, Part A or Part B, Part C Medicare Advantage or other Medicare health plan, or Part D prescription drug coverage.

If the appeal involves either Part A or Part B Medicare the appeal process starts upon receipt of the Medicare summary notice (MSN). The MSN provides notice of the items, services, and supplies that have been billed; what amount Medicare will pay; and what amount the individual is to pay. A request for a redetermination must be made within 120 days of receipt of the initial determination. This is termed a Level 1 appeal. Upon receipt of a redetermination there is a 180-day limitation for filing a request for a reconsideration. This is termed a Level 2 appeal and is handled by a qualified independent contractor who did not take part in the Level 1 decision. The third level of appeal involves an appeal within 60 days of the decision from the qualified independent contractor. This appeal is before an administrative law judge who will conduct a hearing. If this decision is appealed, the appeal must be filed within 60 days after receipt of notice of the administrative law judge's decision. This appeal is before the appeals council. Finally if a decision of the appeals council is appealed that appeal must be filed within 60 days and is in the U.S. district court.

If the appeal of a denial of benefits is from a Part C Medicare Advantage plan, or other Medicare health plan, the process is similar. The first level is requesting a reconsideration. The second level involves a review by an independent review entity. The third level of appeal is to an administrative law judge, and then to the appeal's council and finally the U.S. district court. When appealing a decision on a Part C Medicare health plan, the time limit for filing a Level 1 appeal is 60 days. If the decision is adverse, it is automatically sent to an independent review entity for reconsideration. If the Medicare beneficiary has additional information it must be provided within ten days after the date of receipt of the notice that the case file has been forwarded to the independent review entity. An appeal from the Level 2 determination is to an administrative law judge. Thereafter, the appeal process involves the fourth level of the appeals council and the fifth level of the U.S. district court. In each instance, the time for filing an appeal is 60 days from receipt of notice.

If the appeal involves Part D prescription drugs, the appeal process is similar to the one for Part C coverage. The 60-day time limit is applied at each of the five levels of appeal.

Appendix A: Overview of Medicare Benefits

What Is Medicare?

Medicare is health insurance for people age 65 or older, people under age 65 with certain disabilities, and people of any age with end-stage renal disease (permanent kidney failure requiring dialysis or a kidney transplant) or ALS.

What Are the Different Parts of Medicare?

MEDICARE PART A (HOSPITAL INSURANCE) HELPS COVER:

- Inpatient hospital care
- Skilled nursing facility care (limited duration)
- Hospice care
- Home health care

MEDICARE PART B (MEDICAL INSURANCE) HELPS COVER:

- Services from doctors and other health care providers
- Outpatient care
- Home health care
- Durable medical equipment
- Some preventive services, including certain vaccines and cancer screenings

MEDICARE PART C (ALSO CALLED MEDICARE ADVANTAGE):

- Includes all benefits and services covered under Part A and Part B provided by Medicare-approved private insurance companies
- May include extra benefits and services for an extra cost
- Usually includes Medicare prescription drug coverage (Part D) as part of the plan

MEDICARE PART D (MEDICARE PRESCRIPTION DRUG COVERAGE):

- Helps cover prescription drug costs
- Is run by Medicare-approved private insurance companies
- May help lower prescription drug costs and help protect against higher costs in the future

Other Medicare Terms

Some other terms you might need to know include:

- **Original Medicare**. Original Medicare is sometimes called traditional Medicare. Original Medicare coverage is managed by the federal government. If you don't choose a Medicare Advantage Plan (such as Medicare HMO or PPO), you will have original Medicare.
- **Medicare Supplement Insurance** (also called **Medigap**). Medigap helps pay some of the costs that original Medicare does not cover, such as copayments and deductibles. You need both Part A and Part B to purchase a Medigap policy.

Appendix B: Medicare Checklist for New Beneficiaries

If you're approaching your 65th birthday, you're probably already experiencing a Medicare information overload. A stack of mail and constant phone calls may only serve to muddy the Medicare waters. This Medicare checklist outlines steps you will take when deciding what best fits your health care needs.

1. GATHER ALL OF YOUR PERSONAL HEALTH INFORMATION. As you navigate through your Medicare options, you'll want this information close at hand. This will help avoid any potential delays in obtaining full coverage. Be sure to gather the following items:

- Social security number
- Other insurance plans and policy numbers
- Contact information for health care providers
- List of current prescriptions
- List of current and previous health conditions
- Financial and legal information

2. SPEND SOME TIME RESEARCHING THE BASICS OF MEDICARE AND ITS VARIOUS PARTS. A great starting place is the Medicare Resource Center and blog. Here are some quick basic facts.

- Part A is hospital insurance.
- Part B is doctor's office insurance.
- Part C is Medicare Advantage plans.
- Part D is prescription drug coverage.
- Medicare supplemental plans, or Medigap plans, help cover the gaps in coverage beyond Part A and Part B. These federally standardized plans help cover expenses such as coinsurance.
- Most people will automatically enroll in Medicare Part A and Part B the first day of the month in which they turn 65.
- People under 65 receiving social security disability benefits must receive these benefits for 24 months prior to enrolling in Medicare.
- If you need further assistance identifying this period, contact your local social security office.

3. ASSESS YOUR CURRENT EMPLOYER BENEFITS OR YOUR SPOUSE'S CURRENT EMPLOYER COVERAGE IF EITHER OF YOU PLAN TO WORK PAST AGE 65.

- Depending on the associated costs of your employer-based group health plan, you may or may not want to begin Medicare at age 65. When in doubt about your current coverage, contact your employer's HR department.
- Understand how working past age 65 may affect you and how Medicare and employer health coverage work together.

4. CHECK TO SEE IF YOUR DOCTOR ACCEPTS MEDICARE.

- If they do, they have to accept whatever Medicare supplement plan you choose. Remember that all Medicare supplemental plans are standardized by the federal government, so there is no difference in the eyes of your doctor or specialist.
- With Medicare Advantage plans, you will likely have a provider network. Simply ask your doctor if they accept the insurance carrier you are considering.

5. CALCULATE COSTS PER MONTH AND PER YEAR YOU CAN AFFORD TO SPEND ON PREMIUMS, COPAYS, AND DEDUCTIBLES.

- Identifying this cost will help you better understand what plans and rates will best suit your health needs and budget.

Notes

1. 42 U.S.C. § 1395(c).
2. *Id*. § 1395i-(2)(a).
3. 83 Fed. Reg. 52455 (Oct. 17, 2018).
4. Information for this section has been obtained from *Medicare & You 2019*, published by the Department of Health and Human Services, Publication No. 10050-51.
5. 42 U.S.C. § 1395x(b).
6. 42 C.F.R. § 409.11(b)(1).
7. *Id*. § 409.61(a)(2).
8. 83 Fed. Reg. 52459 (Oct. 17, 2018).
9. 42 C.F.R. § 409.60.
10. *Id*. § 409.20.
11. *Id*. § 409.31.
12. 42 U.S.C. § 1395i-3(a).
13. 42 C.F.R. § 409.30(a).
14. *Id*. § 409.30(b).
15. *Id*. § 409.30(b)(2).
16. 83 Fed. Reg. 52459 (Oct. 17, 2018).
17. Information for this section has been obtained from *Medicare and Home Health Care,* published by the Department of Health and Human Services, Publication No. 10969.
18. 42 C.F.R. § 409.42.
19. *Id*. § 409.44.
20. *Id*. § 409.49.
21. Information for this section has been obtained from *Medicare Hospice Benefits,* published by the Department of Health and Human Services, Publication No. 02154.
22. 42 C.F.R. § 418.20.
23. *Id*. § 418.24.
24. *Id*. § 418.100.
25. *Id*. § 418.202.
26. *Id*. § 418.204.
27. *Id*. § 418.400.

28. 42 U.S.C § 1395d(a)(4).

29. 42 C.F.R. § 418.28.

30. 42 U.S.C. § 1395j *et seq.*

31. 83 Fed. Reg. 52462 (Oct. 17, 2018).

32. Information for this section has been obtained from *Medicare & You 2019*, published by the Department of Health and Human Services, Publication No. 10050-51.

33. 42 U.S.C. § 1395(k)(a); 42 C.F.R. § 410.10.

34. 42 C.F.R. § 410.161.

35. *Id.* § 410.31.

36. *Id.* § 410.37.

37. *Id.* § 410.34.

38. *Id.* § 410.56.

39. See generally *id.* § 410 *et seq.*

40. 42 U.S.C. § 1395y(a), 42 C.F.R. § 411.

41. 42 U.S.C. § 1395l(b).

42. *Id.* § 1395l(a).

43. 42 C.F.R. § 414.48(b).

44. 42 U.S.C. § 1395a.

45. *Id.* § 1395a(2)(A)(iii).

46. *Id.* § 1395a(a).

47. Information for this section has been taken from *Medicare Choosing a Medigap Policy*, published by the Department of Health and Human Services, Publication No. 02110.

48. 42 U.S.C. § 1395ss.

49. See Choosing a Medigap Policy for these options: https://www.medicare.gov /pubs/pdf/02110-medicare-medigap-guide.pdf.

50. 42 U.S.C. § 1395ss(s).

51. Information for this section was obtained from *Medicare and Other Benefits: Who Pays First*, Department of Health and Human Services, Publication No. 02179.

52. 42 U.S.C. § 1395y(b)(1)(A)(ii) and 42 C.F.R. § 411.172.

53. The term *spouse* includes divorced spouse and common-law spouse.

54. 42 C.F.R. § 411.172(b) requires Medicare to act as primary payer rather than secondary payer for individuals who are enrolled in a multi-employer plan through their employer, provided the employer has fewer than 20 employees and the plan identifies these individuals as excluded from coverage.

55. 42 U.S.C. § 1395y(b)(1)(B)(I) and 42 C.F.R. § 411.100(a)(iii).

56. 42 U.S.C. § 1395y(b)(2)(A).

57. 42 C.F.R. § 411.21 defines prompt payment as payment within 120 days after receipt of the claim.

58. 42 C.F.R. § 411.40(b)(3).

59. 42 U.S.C. § 1395y(b)(2)(A).

60. Information for this section has been obtained from *Medicare & You 2019*, published by the Department of Health and Human Services, Publication No. 10050-51.

61. 42 U.S.C. § 1395w-21.

62. *Id.* § 139ff.

63. *Id.* § 1395ff(b)(2)(A).

CHAPTER 6

Supplemental Security Income

  I. Overview 144
 II. Introduction to Supplemental Security Income 144
III. Eligibility Requirements 145
    A. How an Individual Qualifies for SSI on the Basis of Age 145
    B. How an Individual Qualifies for SSI on the Basis of
       Disability 145
    C. How an Individual Qualifies for SSI on the Basis
       of Blindness 146
    D. Persons Who Are Ineligible for SSI Benefits 146
 IV. Treatment of Income 146
    A. Introduction 146
    B. What Constitutes Earned Income 147
    C. Earned Income That Does Not Count 147
    D. What Constitutes Unearned Income 148
    E. Unearned Income That Does Not Count 148
    F. In-Kind Support and Maintenance 150
    G. The One-Third Reduction Rule 150
    H. Presumed Value Rule 151
    I. Deeming of Income 151
    J. Types of Income That SSA Does Not Deem 152
    K. Other Rules for Deeming Income 153
    L. Rules for Changes in the Status of a Spouse 154
    M. What Is Not Considered Income 154
  V. Treatment of Resources 156
    A. Introduction 156
    B. Resources Defined 156
    C. When Resources Are Counted 157
    D. Rules for Jointly Held Assets 157
    E. Assets That Are Not Considered Resources 158
    F. Disposition of Resources 160
    G. Transfer of Resources 161
 VI. The Application Procedure 162
VII. Underpayment of Benefits 163

VIII. Overpayment of Benefits 163
  IX. The Appeals Procedure...................................... 164
    A. The Initial Determination................................ 164
    B. The Reconsideration Stage............................... 164
    C. The Administrative Law Judge Stage 165
    D. The Appeals Council Stage 165
    E. Federal District Court 165
Appendix A: Overview of Social Security Disability Programs:
    SSI and SSDI 166
Appendix B: Supplemental Security Income Checklist................. 168

I. Overview

Since Supplemental Security Income (SSI) is a welfare program intended for low income individuals, it is not a benefit that will normally be considered when a lawyer is working with an elder client. Yet, some clients will become SSI eligible as they qualify for Medicaid benefits to pay nursing home costs. Thus understanding SSI will be an aid in advising a client about Medicaid. Where SSI becomes important is when advising an elder client who has a disabled or incompetent adult child. Often a child with disabilities or an incompetency will be receiving SSI benefits and Medicaid benefits. The lawyer needs to have some general understanding of this benefit in determining how that adult child should inherit from their parents. This typically involves either disinheriting an adult disabled child in order for the child to continue to receive those important benefits, or supplementing those benefits by drafting a special needs or supplemental care trust in order to care for their child without the loss of the benefit. With these types of trusts, a question arises as to what benefits the trust can pay without reducing or losing the SSI and Medicaid benefits. It is for this reason that the discussions in Section III.B and the discussions throughout Section IV will be helpful. The discussion on trusts in Chapter 7, Section X will also be helpful. You will find the special needs trust forms at Chapter 7, Appendices A, B, and C. In some situations, the first party special needs trust form will be needed.

As a client sometimes has difficulty distinguishing between SSI and social security disability, a helpful overview is provided in Appendix A. Appendix B provides a checklist of items needed when applying for SSI benefits.

II. Introduction to Supplemental Security Income

Supplemental Security Income (SSI) is a government assistance program administered by the Social Security Administration (SSA) that provides a modest income for aged, blind, and disabled persons who have limited income and assets.[1] SSI will seldom be a consideration when working with elder clients. An understanding of SSI will most often be needed when the elder client has a child who qualifies (or may qualify) for these benefits and the estate plan is considering how best to care for the child after the elder client's death. The estate plan usually will need to be structured so as to maintain these benefits.

SSI went into effect on January 1, 1974, and replaced former programs such as Old Age Assistance, Aid to the Blind, and Aid to the Permanently and Totally Disabled.[2] Every aged, blind, or disabled U.S. citizen or lawful resident who is eligible on the basis of income and resources is entitled to receive government assistance in the form of cash benefits and Medicaid with the exception of residents of the section 209(b) states who must meet the state's own stricter standard of disability in order to receive Medicaid.[3] In addition, states may supplement the SSI cash subsidy with an additional payment of funds. The 2019 SSI benefit amount is $771 for an individual, $1,157 for an eligible couple, and $386 for an essential person.[4] See Section IV.I for the definition of an "essential person."

III. Eligibility Requirements

A. How an Individual Qualifies for SSI on the Basis of Age

To qualify on the basis of age, an individual must be 65 years of age or older.[5] If an applicant is seeking SSI benefits on the basis of her age, the applicant must file supporting evidence with the Social Security Administration (SSA) demonstrating the applicant's date of birth.[6] If an applicant is 68 years of age or older, the person need only present documentary evidence regarding her age that is at least three years old.[7] Proof of age can be a public record of birth, religious record of birth, or the record of a baptism established or recorded before the individual's fifth birthday.[8] While SSA is to give birth records and baptism records the highest probative value in determining an applicant's age, other documents, including school records, census records, Bible records, marriage records, life insurance policies, and military records can also be used to prove an applicant's age.[9]

B. How an Individual Qualifies for SSI on the Basis of Disability

To be considered disabled, an adult individual must meet the social security definition of disability, which is the person must be unable to engage in any substantial gainful activity by reason of any medically determinable physical or mental impairment that can be expected to result in death or that has lasted or can be expected to last for a continuous period of not less than 12 months.[10] In addition, in order to be found disabled, an individual must be determined to be under a physical or mental impairment or impairments that are so severe as to prevent the individual from doing his previous work and considering the individual's age, education, and work experience, the individual is unable to engage in substantial gainful work that exists in the national economy.[11] Substantial gainful activity is defined as work that involves doing significant and productive physical or mental duties that are done or intended to be done for pay or profit.[12] In determining if an individual's physical or mental impairment or impairments is of a sufficient medical severity, SSA will consider the combined effects of all of the individual's impairments without regard to the fact that any one of these impairments would not be sufficient to constitute a severe impairment.[13] If the individual is under 18 years of age, disability is defined as a medically determinable physical or mental impairment that results in marked and severe functional limitations and can be expected to result in death, or has lasted or can be expected to last 12 or more months.

C. How an Individual Qualifies for SSI on the Basis of Blindness

An individual who has central visual acuity of 20/200 or less in the better eye with the use of corrective lens is considered blind.[14] An eye that has a limitation in the field of vision so that the widest diameter of the visual field subtends to an angle no greater than 20 degrees is considered by SSA to have a central visual acuity of 20/200 or less.[15] A problem with an applicant's vision that does not meet the statutory definition of blindness may still be considered along with the other impairments of the applicant in determining if the applicant is eligible for benefits.[16] Persons who are blind need not be unable to perform substantial gainful activity but for those blind individuals who do work, SSA will consider their income and resources in determining their eligibility for benefits.[17]

D. Persons Who Are Ineligible for SSI Benefits

Certain individuals are ineligible for SSI benefits. These persons include:

- Individuals who do not apply for all other benefits to which they may be entitled.[18]
- Individuals who reside in a public institution such as a hospital or jail.[19] However, certain individuals who are hospitalized may remain eligible for benefits for a two-month period while others may remain eligible for benefits up to three months.[20]
- Individuals who have received 36 months of benefits and are disabled due to a drug or alcohol addiction.[21]
- Individuals who leave the United States for 30 consecutive days or more.[22]

IV. Treatment of Income

A. Introduction

Eligibility for SSI is subject to some very strict income criteria. The following discussion provides more detail than many will need, but familiarity with these exacting rules may prove helpful. But you are warned Section IV may put you to sleep. It is tedious. SSA counts any income an individual receives in determining the individual's eligibility for benefits. Income is defined as anything an individual receives in cash or in kind that the individual can use to meet her needs for food, clothing, and shelter.[23]

B. What Constitutes Earned Income

SSA divides income into two classifications, earned income and unearned income. Earned income may be received by the individual in cash or in kind.[24] Earned income consists of the following types of payments:[25]

- Wages, including salaries, commissions, bonuses, severance pay. Also included is the value of food, shelter, or clothing, as well as other items that are paid instead of cash, which SSA refers to as in-kind earned income. For domestic and agricultural workers, in-kind pay is treated as unearned income.[26]
- Net earnings from self-employment.
- Payments for services performed in a sheltered workshop or work activities center.
- Certain royalties and honoraria.

C. Earned Income That Does Not Count[27]

Certain types of earned income are not counted by SSA. These include:

- Income that is not counted pursuant to federal law.
- Refunds of federal income taxes pursuant to section 32 of the Internal Revenue Code (relating to the earned income tax credit) and payments received from an employer pursuant to section 3507 of the Internal Revenue Code (relating to advance payment of the earned income tax credit).
- Up to $30 of earned income in a month provided it is infrequent and irregular, which is defined by SSA as once in a calendar quarter received from a single source or if the individual cannot reasonably expect it.
- Student earnings for students under age 22 up to $1,870 per month but no more than $7,550 in a calendar year if the individual is regularly attending school.
- Any portion of the $20 monthly exclusion that has not been excluded from an individual's unearned income in that same month.
- Sixty-five dollars of earned income in a month.
- Earned income the individual uses to pay impairment work-related expenses if the individual is disabled and under 65 years of age and for an individual over 65 years of age, if the individual is disabled and received SSI or state disability for the month before the individual reached 65 years of age.
- One-half of remaining earned income in a month.
- Earned income used to meet any expenses reasonably attributable to the earning of income if the individual is blind and under age 65 and

for individuals over 65 years of age, if the individual received SSI as a blind person for the month before he reached age 65.

- Any earned income an individual receives and uses to fulfill an approved plan to achieve self-support if the individual is blind or disabled and under age 65 and for individuals over 65 years of age, for those individuals who were blind or disabled and received SSI for either disability for the month before they reached 65.

- Income compensation provided to volunteers by AmeriCorps State and National and AmeriCorps NCCC.

D. What Constitutes Unearned Income

Unearned income is all income that is not classified as earned income.[28] That's not much help. Fortunately, unearned income is defined in 20 C.F.R. § 416.1121 and includes:[29]

- Annuities, pensions, and other periodic payments.
- Alimony and support payments, including both cash and in-kind contributions.
- Dividends, interest, and certain royalties.
- Rental income from the lease of real or personal property. SSA will deduct an individual's ordinary and necessary expenses, such as interest and taxes, but does not allow depreciation or depletion of property as a deductible expense.[30]
- Death benefits. SSA will allow an individual to deduct hospital and medical expenses, funeral and burial costs, and other expenses paid for by the individual who received the death benefits.
- Prizes and awards. The term *award* includes funds received as a result of a court decision or arbitration.[31]
- Gifts and inheritances. As with death benefits, the individual who receives an inheritance may deduct any expenses of the deceased paid with the inheritance.
- Support and maintenance in kind. SSA considers this food, clothing, or shelter furnished to an individual. This is explained more fully in Section IV.F. SSA evaluates this type of unearned income by either the one-third reduction rule or the presumed value rule.[32]

E. Unearned Income That Does Not Count

SSI rules also exclude many items of unearned income from countable income. For the typical recipient, perhaps, the most frequently used exclusion is the general $20 exclusion that applies first against an individual's total unearned income (other than income based on need, such as payments in which the recipient's income is a factor). Any part of this $20 exclusion that is not used against unearned income applies to earned income, as mentioned in the preceding section.

Other exclusions from unearned income are found in 20 C.F.R. § 416.1124 and include the following: (1) the value of most benefits provided under a number of federal programs, such as the Food Stamp Act, the National Housing Act, a public agency's refund of taxes on real property or food; (2) assistance based on need and funded by a state and/or one of its political subdivisions; (3) any part of a grant, scholarship, fellowship, or gift used for paying tuition, fees, or other necessary educational expenses; (4) food raised by an individual or his spouse if consumed by their household; (5) assistance under the Disaster Relief and Emergency Assistance Act or under a federal statute because of a catastrophe declared by the president to be a major disaster; (6) the first $60 per calendar quarter of unearned income received infrequently or irregularly; (7) payments to an individual for providing foster care to a child placed in the individual's home by a qualified agency; (8) interest earned on excluded burial funds and appreciation in the value of an excluded burial arrangement left to accumulate and become part of the separately identifiable burial fund; (9) certain home energy and other needs-based support and maintenance assistance; (10) and one-third of support payments made by an absent parent to or for an eligible child.[33]

To see how countable income is calculated and applied against the federal benefit rates (FBR) in a simple example, assume that Sue is eligible for SSI. In 2019, she receives monthly wages of $195 and a social security check for $400. Her countable income and monthly benefit will be calculated as follows:

Earned income:
    $195 (wages)
    −65 (exclusion of first $65)
    $130
    −$65 (exclusion of one-half of the month's remaining earned income)
    $ 65 total countable earned income.

Unearned income:
    $400 (social security benefits)
    −20 (exclusion of first $20)
    $380 total countable unearned income

Total countable income:
    $ 65 countable earned income
    +380 countable unearned income
    $445

Sue's monthly SSI benefit:
    $771 federal benefit rate (2019)
    −445 countable income
    $326

As the example shows, an individual's countable income counts against the maximum monthly SSI federal benefit rate (FBR) dollar for dollar.

F. In-Kind Support and Maintenance

SSA treats in-kind support as unearned income and values in-kind items received by an individual at their current market value.[34] However, SSA utilizes special rules to evaluate food, clothing, and shelter. The rules are tedious. In-kind support and maintenance is defined as food, clothing, or shelter that is given to an individual or that an individual receives because another person pays for it.[35] Shelter includes room rent, mortgage payments, real property taxes, heating fuel, gas, electricity, water, sewerage, and garbage collection services.[36] SSA does not consider an individual to be receiving in-kind support and maintenance in the form of room or rent if the individual lives with other people and is paying his or her own share for the room or rent pursuant to a business arrangement.[37] A business arrangement is found to exist when the amount paid equals the current market rental value.

G. The One-Third Reduction Rule

SSA utilizes two approaches to valuing in-kind support and maintenance. One method is the one-third reduction rule. The one-third reduction rule is applied if the individual resides in another person's household for a full calendar month and the individual receives both food and shelter from the person with whom she is living.[38] If the one-third reduction rule applies, no income exclusions are applied to the reduction amount, that is, the one-third reduction is absolute.[39] In addition, if the one-third reduction rule is applied by SSA, SSA does not count any other in-kind support and maintenance received by the individual.[40] For an individual receiving the full $771 SSI benefit amount, the reduction is $257 (one-third of $771).

The one-third reduction rule does not apply if the individual is residing in another's household on a temporary basis. A temporary absence may constitute a hospital stay or a stay with another person for a maximum of two calendar months if the individual intends to return home and does so by the end of the second month.[41] For example, Faye, on March 5, moves in with her daughter, Shelly, but she intends to return to her own residence on April 21 and does in fact do so. The one-third reduction rule will not apply to Faye. An individual is considered by SSA to be living in another person's household unless the other person with whom the individual is living is a spouse, minor child, or ineligible person whose income may be deemed to the individual.[42] An individual is considered by SSA to be living in his own household if:[43]

- The individual or his spouse has an ownership interest in the property, including a life estate.
- The individual or his spouse is liable to a landlord for rent.
- The individual pays a pro rata share of household operating expenses. A pro rata share of expenses is the average monthly household operating expenses divided by the number of people in the household, regardless of their age.[44] SSA will average household operating

expenses over the previous 12 months to determine the individual's pro rata share. Household expenses include expenditures for food, rent, mortgage, property taxes, heating fuel, gas, electricity, water, sewerage, and garbage collection services.[45]
- The individual lives in certain non-institutional care situations.
- All members of the individual's household receive government assistance payments, such as welfare benefits, SSI payments, disaster relief payments, and veterans benefits based on need.[46]

H. Presumed Value Rule

The second method utilized by SSA in determining evaluating in-kind support and maintenance is the presumed value rule. SSA will only apply the presumed value rule when the one-third reduction rule does not apply.[47] The presumed value rule applies if:[48]

- The individual resides in another person's household but does not receive food and shelter from that person.
- The individual resides in her own household.
- The individual resides in a non-medical institution such as a nonprofit education or vocational training institution, nonprofit retirement home, or for-profit institution where a third party pays for the individual's support and maintenance.

SSA does not determine the actual value of food, clothing, and shelter received by the individual. Rather SSA presumes that the food, clothing, and shelter is worth a maximum value. The maximum value is one-third of the individual's benefit rate plus the amount of the general income exclusion of $20. For example, Teresa receives the full $771 per month in SSI benefits. Teresa's son, William, pays her rent of $300 per month. Teresa lives alone so the one-third reduction rule does not apply so instead the presumed value rule applies. SSA will reduce Teresa's monthly benefits by $257 (one-third of $771) plus an additional $20 for a total reduction of $277 per month. An individual may rebut the presumption that her in-kind support and maintenance is not equal to the presumed value if the individual can demonstrate the current market value of any food, clothing, and shelter she receives less any payment made for her is less than the presumed value or the actual amount that a third party pays for food, clothing, and shelter is lower than the presumed value.[49]

I. Deeming of Income

The term *deeming of income* refers to when SSA counts a third party's income as income to the beneficiary.[50] This is done simply in recognition of the fact that members of a family unit are financially responsible for one another when they live in the same household. Income may be deemed in four situations: (1) an ineligible spouse, (2) an ineligible parent, (3) an eligible alien's sponsor, or (4) an essential person.[51] An essential person is a category of persons based on person(s) living with and providing essential care for an individual receiving state benefits.[52] SSA will consider the income of an ineligible spouse, parent, sponsor, or essential person in the current month to determine if the individual is eligible for benefits in that month.[53] Generally, SSA will consider the income of the ineligible spouse, parent, sponsor, or essential person in the second month prior to the current month to determine the individual's benefit amount for the current month.[54]

J. Types of Income That SSA Does Not Deem

However, SSA does not include the following types of income of an ineligible spouse or parent:[55]

- Income excluded by federal law other than the Social Security Act.
- Public income-maintenance the ineligible spouse or parent receives and any income that was either counted or excluded in determining the amount of that payment.
- Any income of the ineligible spouse or parent that was used by the public income-maintenance program to determine the amount of the program's benefit to someone else.
- Any portion of a grant, scholarship, or fellowship used to pay tuition or fees.
- Money received for providing foster care to an ineligible child.
- The value of food stamps and Department of Agriculture donated foods.
- Food raised by the parent or spouse and consumed by the household's members.
- Tax refunds on income, real property, or food purchased by the family.
- Income used to fulfill a plan for achieving self-support.
- Income used to pay court-ordered support, or support payments under Title IV-D of the Social Security Act.
- Income used to comply with the terms of court-ordered support, or support payments enforced under Title IV-D of the Social Security Act.
- The value of in-kind support and maintenance.
- Alaska Longevity Bonus payments to an individual who is a resident of the state of Alaska, and who prior to October 25, 1985, met the 25-year residency requirement for receipt of this payment in effect prior to January 1, 1983, and who was eligible for SSI.
- Disaster assistance.
- Income received infrequently or irregularly.
- Work expenses if the ineligible spouse or parent is blind or disabled.
- Income of the ineligible spouse or parent that was paid under a federal, state, or local government program to provide chore, attendant, or homemaker services.
- Certain support and maintenance assistance.

- Housing assistance.
- The value of a commercial transportation ticket.
- Refunds of federal income taxes and advances made by an employer relating to the earned income tax credit.
- Payments from a fund established by a state to aid victims of crime.
- Relocation assistance.
- Hostile fire pay received from one of the uniformed services.
- Impairment-related work expenses incurred and paid by an ineligible spouse or parent if the ineligible spouse or parent receives disability benefits under Title II of the Social Security Act.
- Interest earned on excluded burial funds and appreciation in value of excluded burial arrangements.

K. Other Rules for Deeming Income

For an essential person or for a sponsor of an alien (a person lawfully admitted to the United States), SSA will deem all income as defined by 20 C.F.R. § 416.1102, except for support and maintenance assistance as well as income excluded by federal law outside of the Social Security Act.[56] For an ineligible child, SSA does not deem any income to the beneficiary from the ineligible child, but SSA does reduce the ineligible child's allocation under 20 C.F.R. § 416.1163 if the ineligible child has income.[57]

In deeming income from an ineligible spouse who resides in the same household as the SSI beneficiary, SSA first determines how much earned and unearned income the ineligible spouse has using the exclusions just listed.[58] SSA then deducts an allowance for ineligible children in the household to help meet the children's needs. However, SSA does not allocate for ineligible children who are receiving public income-maintenance payments.[59] The allocation for each ineligible child is the difference between the federal benefit rate for an eligible couple and the federal benefit rate for an eligible individual.[60] Each ineligible child's allocation is reduced by the amount of the ineligible child's own income as discussed in the preceding paragraph.[61] SSA first deducts the allocations from the ineligible spouse's unearned income and if the ineligible spouse's unearned income is insufficient to cover the allocations, SSA deducts the remaining balance from the ineligible spouse's earned income.[62] If the amount of the ineligible spouse's income that remains after the allocations is not more than the difference between the federal benefit rate for an eligible couple and the federal benefit rate for an eligible individual, SSA will not deem income from an ineligible spouse.[63] SSA will subtract only the eligible individual's own countable income to determine if they are eligible for benefits.[64] If the amount of the ineligible spouse's income that remains after the allocations is more than the difference between the federal benefit rate for an eligible couple and the federal benefit rate for an eligible individual, SSA will treat the individual and her spouse as an eligible couple, by combining the remainder of the ineligible spouse's unearned income with the eligible spouse's own unearned income, and the remainder of the ineligible spouse's earned income with the eligible spouse's earned income, applying all appropriate exclusions and subtracting the couples' countable income from the federal benefit rate for an eligible couple.[65]

L. Rules for Changes in the Status of a Spouse

SSA uses special rules if a change in the status of couples occurs. If an ineligible spouse becomes eligible for SSI benefits, both spouses are treated as newly eligible. The couple's eligibility and benefit amount for the first month they are eligible as a couple will be based on their income for that month. In the second month, their benefit amount will be based on their income in the first month.[66] If spouses separate or divorce, SSA will no longer deem the ineligible spouse's income to the eligible spouse to determine the eligible spouse's eligibility for benefits beginning with the first month following the separation or divorce.[67] If an ineligible spouse begins living with an ineligible spouse, SSA will deem the ineligible spouse's income to the eligible spouse in the first month thereafter to determine if the eligible spouse remains qualified to receive benefits.[68] If an ineligible spouse dies, SSA will no longer deem income from the ineligible spouse in the first month thereafter to determine the surviving eligible spouse's eligibility to receive benefits.[69] If an eligible spouse becomes institutionalized in a medical facility and the $30 federal benefit rate applies for personal care items, SSA will no longer deem the ineligible spouse's income to the institutionalized eligible spouse beginning with the first month in which the $30 federal benefit rate applies.[70]

M. What Is Not Considered Income

SSA does not consider the following as income:[71]

- Medical care and services given to the individual free of charge or paid directly by a third party.
- Room and board received by the individual during their medical confinement.
- Assistance provided in cash and in kind by a federal, state, or local government program whose purpose is to provide medical care, including vocational rehabilitation.
- In-kind assistance (except food, clothing, and or shelter) provided under a nongovernment program whose purpose is to provide medical care or medical services.
- Cash provided by any nongovernmental medical care or medical services program or under a health insurance policy (except cash to cover food, clothing, or shelter) if the cash is either repayment for program-approved services that the individual has already paid for or a payment that is restricted to the future purchase of a program-approved service. For example, Marvin pays $33 to purchase medicine. Marvin's insurance company reimburses him for this expenditure. The reimbursement is not counted by SSA as income.

- Direct payment of an individual's medical insurance premiums by a third party.
- Payments from the Department of Veterans Affairs resulting from unusual medical expenses.
- Social services consisting of
  - Assistance provided in cash or in kind under a federal, state, or local government program whose purpose is to provide social services including vocational rehabilitation. SSA considers cash given to an individual by the Department of Veterans Affairs to purchase aid and attendance as exempt under this provision.
  - In-kind assistance (except for food, clothing, or shelter) provided under a nongovernment program whose purpose is to provide social services.
  - Cash provided by a nongovernment social services program (except cash to cover food, clothing, and shelter) if the cash is either repayment for program-approved services the individual has already paid for or a payment restricted to the future purchase of a program-approved service. For example, Julia is unable to do her own household chores and a private social security agency gives her cash to pay for a homemaker, SSA does not consider the cash as income.
- Receipts from the sale, exchange, or replacement of a resource. SSA considers these as resources that have changed their form. For example, George sells his automobile for $500. The $500 in proceeds is not income but rather another form of a resource.
- Income tax refunds. However, the earned income tax credit payment may be treated as earned income.[72]
- Payments by credit life or credit disability insurance. For example, Henry becomes disabled and the credit disability policy he has on his residence makes the mortgage payments. SSA does not consider these payments as income.
- Loan proceeds. Money borrowed by an individual is not income nor is money repaid an individual for a loan. However, interest received by an individual on money loaned is treated as income by SSA.
- Certain bills paid for the individual. Payments by a third party directly to the supplier of services is not considered income by SSA. However, if the payments are made for food, shelter, and clothing, the payments are treated as in-kind income and dealt with under the in-kind income provisions. If payments are made for services other than for the provision of food, clothing, or shelter, the payments are not considered as in-kind income by SSA. For example, Wanda's daughter pays her grocery bill. SSA will treat this payment as in-kind income because the payments are made by a third party (daughter) to a provider of food, clothing, or shelter. However, if Wanda's daughter paid her monthly cable television bill instead, SSA would not consider the payments as in-kind income because cable television cannot be used to provide food, clothing, or shelter.

- Replacement of income that an individual has already received. For example, Jasper loses his paycheck and a replacement check is issued. The paycheck is treated by SSA as income but the replacement check is not.
- Weatherization assistance.
- Receipt of certain non-cash items (except for food, shelter, or clothing) that would constitute nonliquid resources if kept is not income. For example, Darla inherits a house that she uses as her principal place of residence. SSA considers the value of the inheritance as income because the house provides shelter but the house is valued under the presumed value rule instead.[73]

V. Treatment of Resources

A. Introduction

In order to qualify for SSI benefits, an individual must have limited resources. An individual without an eligible spouse may have no more than $2,000 in non-excludable resources.[74] An individual with an eligible spouse may have no more than $3,000 in non-excludable resources.[75] If an individual is married to a person who is not eligible to receive benefits, and the individual resides with his ineligible spouse, SSA will deem the eligible spouse's resources to include any otherwise non-excluded resources owned by the ineligible spouse regardless of whether the resources are actually available to the eligible spouse.[76] Pension funds held by the ineligible spouse are excluded. SSA defines pension funds as funds held in individual retirement accounts (IRA), as described by the Internal Revenue Code, or in work-related pension plans, including plans for self-employed individuals.[77]

B. Resources Defined

Resources are defined as cash or other liquid assets or any real or personal property that an individual or her spouse owns and could convert to cash to be used for her support and maintenance.[78] If the individual has the legal authority to liquidate the property or her interest in the property, said property is considered a resource.[79] If the property cannot be liquidated, the property is to be excluded by SSA as a resource.[80] Liquid resources are defined as cash or other property that can be converted to cash within 20 days, excluding certain non-work days, for example, Saturdays, Sundays, and legal holidays.[81] Examples of liquid resources according to SSA are stocks, bonds, mutual fund shares, promissory notes, mortgages, life insurance policies, savings accounts, checking accounts, certificates of deposit, and other such items.[82] Nonliquid resources are property that is not cash and that cannot be converted to cash within 20 working days.[83] Examples of nonliquid resources according to SSA are loan agreements, household goods, automobiles, trucks, tractors, boats, machinery, livestock, buildings, and land.[84] With the exception of automobiles, non-liquid assets are to be evaluated based on their equity value. Equity is defined as the price that an item can reasonably be expected to sell for on the open market in the individual's particular area less any encumbrances.[85] If an individual has more resources than permitted, SSA may allow the individual to continue receiving benefits in certain limited situations.[86]

C. When Resources Are Counted

Resource determinations are made at the first of the month.[87] If a resource increases in value during the month, or an individual acquires an additional resource or replaces an excluded resource with a non-excluded resource, SSA will count the increase in the value of resources at the first moment of the next month.[88] If a resource decreases in value during the month, or an individual spends a resource or replaces a non-excluded resource with a resource that is excluded, SSA will count the decrease in the value of resources at the first moment of the next month.[89] Items that are received in cash or in kind during a month are evaluated first under the income counting rules by SSA, and if kept these items are evaluated as resources at the first moment of the next month.[90] If an individual sells, exchanges, or replaces a resource, SSA still considers the proceeds, exchange, or replacement as a resource, including resources that were never counted by SSA because they were sold, exchanged, or replaced the same month they were received.[91]

D. Rules for Jointly Held Assets

If an individual holds an account such as a checking account, savings account, or certificate of deposit with a financial institution, SSA will consider the account the sole property of the individual and a resource to be counted, if the account is held in the individual's name alone and the individual can withdraw the funds from the account at will.[92] If an account is held in joint ownership with others who are not SSI recipients, SSA considers the account the sole property of the eligible individual and the non-recipients are viewed as having no ownership interest.[93] For example, Bob receives SSI and has a joint checking account with his wife, Carol, who is not eligible for SSI. SSA considers all of the checking account's funds as Bob's resource. If the account is held in joint ownership with other SSI recipients, SSA considers that the funds in the account belong in equal shares to the SSI recipients.[94] If the account is held by a "deemor," for example a non-eligible spouse, then SSA considers the funds in any joint held account to be owned by the "deemor."[95] For example, Mary receives SSI but her husband, Joe, does not. Joe's name is on a certificate of deposit along with his brother. SSA considers the entire value of the certificate of deposit to be Joe's property. SSA allows a claimant, recipient, or deemor to rebut ownership of a joint account. To rebut ownership of an account, the individual must:[96]

- Submit her statement, along with the corroborating statements from the other account holders, regarding who really owns the account, the purpose of the joint account, who has made deposits and withdrawals from the account, and how the withdrawals were spent.

- Submit account records showing deposits, withdrawals, and interest, if any, in the months for which ownership of the account is at issue.
- Correct the account title to show that the individual is no longer a co-owner if the individual does not own any of the funds; or if the individual only owns a portion of the funds, separate the funds owned by the other account holder(s) from her own funds and correct the account title to show that the account funds are solely owned only by the individual.

E. Assets That Are Not Considered Resources

Certain resources are excluded by SSA in determining the eligibility of an individual to receive benefits. SSA excludes the following:[97]

- The home and any land that appertains thereto. A home is any property in which the individual (and spouse if applicable) has an ownership interest and that serves as the individual's principal place of residence, including the shelter in which the individual resides, the land on which the shelter is located, and related outbuildings.[98] An individual's home is not counted regardless of value.[99] If an individual moves out of her home with the intent not to return, the home becomes a countable resource because the home is no longer the individual's principal place of residence.[100] The home will be counted as a resource effective with the first day of the month following the month the home is no longer the individual's principal place of residence. If an individual moves out of her home and into an institution, SSA will still consider the home as the individual's principal place of residence, regardless of the individual's intent to return home, if the individual's spouse or dependent relatives continue to live there. If an individual sells her home, SSA will not count the proceeds as a resource if they are used to purchase another home within three months from the date that the individual received the proceeds.[101] In addition, there are specific regulations concerning the sale of an individual's home by installment contract.[102]
- Household goods and personal effects regardless of value.[103] Household goods are defined as household furniture, furnishings, and equipment commonly found in or about a house that are used in the connection with the operation, maintenance, and occupancy of the home, including items such as furniture, furnishings, and equipment used in the functions and activities of home and family life, as well as those items that are for comfort and accommodation.[104] In addition, an individual's wedding ring and engagement ring, as well his spouse's wedding and engagement rings are exempt, along with prosthetic devices, dialysis machines, hospital beds, wheel chairs, and other similar items required because of an individual's physical condition,

unless those items are used primarily by other members of the household.[105]

- An automobile regardless of value.[106] Automobile is defined as a passenger car or other vehicle used to provide necessary transportation.[107]
- Property of a trade or business that is essential to self-support without regard to value or rate of return. Up to $6,000 of an individual's equity in non-business income-producing property will be excluded if it produces a net annual income to the individual of at least 6 percent of the excluded equity. If the individual's equity is greater than $6,000 and the net annual income requirement of 6 percent is met, SSA will count only the amount that exceeds $6,000 toward the allowable resource limit.[108] If an individual owns more than one piece of property, and each produces income, SSA looks at each piece of property to see if the 6 percent rule is met and SSA calculates the equity in each item of property producing a 6 percent return to determine if the total equity is $6,000 or less. If the individual's total equity in the properties that produce a 6 percent return is over $6,000, all equity over $6,000 is counted towards the allowable resource limit.[109]
- Nonbusiness property that is essential to the means of self-support. Nonbusiness property is considered to be essential for an individual's or her spouse's self-support if the property is used to produce goods or services necessary for her daily activities.[110] Up to $6,000 in equity of nonbusiness property is excluded if it produces a 6 percent or greater rate of return. Nonbusiness property can include land that is used to produce vegetables or raise livestock for personal consumption.[111]
- Resources of a blind or disabled individual that are necessary to fulfill an approved plan for achieving self-support. The plan must be tailored specifically for the individual, be in writing, and be approved by SSA.[112] A total of 48 months may be allowed by SSA to complete the plan.
- Stock in a regional or village corporation held by Alaskan natives during the 20-year period in which the stock is inalienable pursuant to the Alaska Native Claims Settlement Act.[113]
- Life insurance owned by the individual and spouse. Life insurance is considered to the extent of its cash surrender value, but if the face value of life insurance does not exceed $1,500, SSA will not count any part of the cash surrender value as a resource.[114] SSA does not consider term insurance a resource.[115]
- Restricted allotted Native American lands.[116]
- Payments or benefits provided under federal statute other than Title XVI of the Social Security Act when the exclusion of these payments as income or a resource is required by law. For example, VA Aid and Attendance payments are exempt from consideration as a resource.
- Disaster relief payments, including any interest earned on the payments.[117]

- A burial space and burial funds. The term *burial space* includes burial plot, gravesite, crypt, mausoleum, urn, niche, and so on.[118] The entire value of the burial space is exempt from consideration as a resource for the individual as well as their spouse.[119] The term *burial funds* includes revocable burial contracts; burial trusts; installment sales contract for the burial spaces; and cash, accounts, or other financial instruments clearly designated for the individual's or her spouse's burial expenses that is kept separate from other resources.[120] Up to $1,500 for an individual and $1,500 for her spouse in burial funds is excluded by SSA as a resource.[121] If the individual owns a life insurance policy with a cash surrender value that is excluded under the life insurance exception, the $1,500 burial funds exclusion is reduced accordingly by the cash surrender value of the life insurance policy.[122] For example, Janet has a life insurance policy with a cash surrender value of $800. Janet can only claim $700 in burial funds as an exempt resource. In addition, the $1,500 in burial funds must be reduced proportionately by any funds that the individual holds in an irrevocable burial trust.[123]
- Title XVI or Title II (SSI and SSD) retroactive payments are excluded for six months following their receipt.[124] However, items purchased with retroactive payments are not exempt from exclusion as resources even if purchased before the expiration of the six-month period.[125] For example, Carlos receives $8,000 in retroactive SSI payments on January 1. Carlos purchases a boat for $8,000 on March 1. SSA will view the boat as a non-exempt resource on April 1. If the $8,000 in funds remained unspent by Carlos, SSA would not view the funds as a resource on April 1. Of course if Carlos lived on an island and needed the boat for transportation to and from the grocery, he could argue that the boat should be exempt under 416 C.F.R. § 1218(b)(iv) as a vehicle that is necessary in order to perform transportation for essential daily activities.
- Housing assistance paid pursuant to the U.S. Housing Act of 1937, the National Housing Act; section 101 of the Housing and Urban Development Act of 1965, Title V of the Housing Act of 1949, or section 202(h) of the Housing Act of 1959.[126]
- Federal income tax refunds and earned income tax credit funds.[127]
- Crime compensation payments paid to victims for a period of nine months beginning the month after the payments are received.[128]
- Relocation assistance funds provided by state or local government.[129]
- Funds placed in dedicated assistance accounts for children 17 years of age and younger to be used for certain purposes such as the child's medical treatment and education.[130]

F. Disposition of Resources

If an individual's resources exceed the limitations allowed by SSA, the individual and her spouse are ineligible for benefits.[131] However, SSA will permit an individual to continue receiving benefits even if that individual is over-resourced, if the individual's total includable liquid resources do not exceed the statutory limit, *and* the individual agrees in writing to (1) dispose of her excess non-liquid resources within the required time period and (2) to repay any overpayment with the proceeds from the disposal of the excess non-liquid resources.[132] The individual must agree in writing to dispose of real property in nine months and personal property in three months.[133] If an over-resourced individual has been unable to sell real estate within the nine-month period, SSA will not count the real estate as a resource if the over-resourced individual has made reasonable efforts to sell.[134] Reasonable efforts to sell consist of an individual taking all necessary steps to sell the property in the geographical area covered by the media serving the area where the property is located, specifically, by either listing the property with a realtor or making efforts to sell the property themselves, such as placing a "For Sale" sign on the property and the showing of the property to interested buyers.[135] SSA may allow an additional three-month period for an individual to dispose of personal property if the individual can demonstrate good cause.[136] If excess non-liquid property includes real property that is utilized as housing for a joint owner, SSA will not require the sale of said property if the sale would cause the joint owner undue hardship due to the loss of housing to the other owner.[137]

G. *Transfer of Resources*

If an individual or his spouse disposes of assets at less than fair market value on or after the look-back period, the individual is ineligible for benefits for a specified period.[138] The look-back date is a date that is 36 months either before the individual applies for benefits or, if later, the date on which the individual or his spouse transfers resources for less than fair market value. The penalty is calculated by adding the total value of all resources disposed of by the individual or his spouse on or after the look-back date divided by the maximum monthly SSI benefit plus the amount of the maximum state supplementary payment payable to the individual in question for the month in which the individual applies for benefits or transfers resources for less than fair market value, whichever is later. For example, a $7,500 transfer by an SSI applicant within 36 months is divided by $771, resulting in 9.72 months rounded down to nine months beginning the month following applying for SSI benefits. The penalty period cannot exceed 36 months.[139] Certain transfers are exempt from consideration.[140] These exempt transfers include:

- The transfer of an individual's home to his spouse, child under 21 years of age, disabled or blind child over 21 years of age, sibling who has an equity interest in the home and has resided in the home for at least one year before the individual became institutionalized, or adult child who resided in the home for at least two years before the individual became institutionalized and provided care that helped the individual to remain at home.

- The transfer of resources by an individual to his spouse or to another for the sole benefit of the individual's spouse or the transfer of resources by the individual's spouse to another for the individual's spouse's sole benefit.
- The transfer of resources to a trust established solely for the benefit of the transferor's child who is either blind or disabled.
- The transfer of resources to a trust established solely for the benefit of an individual who is not 65 years of age and who is disabled.
- The transfer of resources was intended to be at fair market value or for valuable consideration.
- The transfer of resources was for a purpose exclusively other than to qualify for benefits.
- An undue hardship under procedures to be established by SSA would result if benefits were denied.

VI. The Application Procedure

In order to receive benefits, an individual must file an application.[141] In order to file an application, an application form prescribed by SSA must be filled out, filed at a social security office or authorized federal or state office, and the application must be signed by the claimant or a third party.[142] The claimant must be living at the time the application is filed.[143] If an applicant is 18 years of age or older, mentally competent and physically able, the claimant must sign her own application.[144] If the claimant is under age 18, mentally incompetent, or physically unable to sign the application, a court-appointed representative or a person who is responsible for the care of the claimant may sign the application.[145] If the claimant is institutionalized, the manager or principal officer of the institution may sign the application on the claimant's behalf.[146] SSA may accept a third party's signature on an application in order to prevent a claimant from losing benefits if there is a good reason why the claimant cannot sign the application, such as the claimant's unexpected hospitalization.[147] An application for benefits is considered filed if SSA receives a written inquiry regarding benefits, such as a letter at the appropriate office and the claimant or their representative follows up with a signed application form within 60 days of the receipt of the notice from SSA of the need to file a signed application.[148] Furthermore, an application for benefits is considered filed if an oral inquiry regarding SSI benefits such as a telephone call is made to the appropriate office and followed up with a signed application within 60 days of the receipt of the notice from SSA of the need to file a signed application.[149] When an individual files an application for Title II benefits, SSA is required to explain to that person the requirements for receiving SSI benefits and give the individual the opportunity to file an application for SSI benefits if it appears that the individual is within two months of age 65 years or older or it appears that the individual may qualify as a blind or disabled person and it is not certain if the individual's Title II benefits would render him ineligible for SSI benefits.[150] If the individual applying for Title II benefits does not file an application for SSI benefits on the appropriate form after their right to file for SSI benefits is explained to them, SSA is required to treat the filing of the claim for Title II benefits as an oral inquiry for SSI benefits and provide the claimant with written notice of their right to file for SSI benefits.[151]

VII. Underpayment of Benefits

An underpayment can only occur for a period in which the individual had filed an application for benefits and met all conditions for eligibility for benefits.[152] An underpayment is defined as nonpayment when payment is due or payment of less than the amount due. Installment payments must be made if the underpayment equals or exceeds 12 times the monthly federal benefit rate plus any federally administered state supplemental payments. However, installment payments are not required if the individual is no longer eligible for benefits or is expected to die within 12 months.[153] The installments are paid in not more than three installment payments. The first and second installment payments cannot exceed 12 times the maximum monthly federal benefit rate unless the individual due the underpayment (1) has outstanding debt for food, clothing, shelter, medicine, or medically necessary services, supplies, and equipment, or (2) the individual is either incurring at the current time or will incur in the near future expenses for medicine or medically necessary services, supplies, and equipment, or (3) the individual is purchasing a home.[154] If the beneficiary due the underpayment is under age 18, and is owed an amount that exceeds six times the monthly federal benefit rate plus any federally administered state supplemental payments, the representative payee of the individual must establish a dedicated account and the funds used for only certain expenditures, such as medical treatment and education.[155]

VIII. Overpayment of Benefits

An overpayment is defined by SSA as payment of more than the amount due for any period, including any state supplementary payments administered by SSA.[156] An overpayment may be waived by SSA if the overpaid individual was without fault in connection with the overpayment and the recovery of the overpayment would (1) defeat the purpose of Title XVI, or (2) be against equity and good conscience, or (3) impede efficient administration of Title XVI due to the small amount involved.[157] Whether an individual is "without fault" depends on all the pertinent circumstances regarding the overpayment in the particular case. SSA is required to consider the individual's understanding of the reporting requirements, the agreement to report events affecting payments, knowledge of the occurrence of events that should have been reported, efforts to comply with the reporting requirements, opportunities to comply with the reporting requirements, understanding of the obligation to return checks which were not due, and the ability of the individual to comply with reporting requirements (e.g., the individual's age, comprehension, memory, and physical and mental condition).[158] SSA is required to take into account the individual's physical, mental, educational, and linguistic limitations, including, if applicable, their inability to speak English. SSA is required to find an individual at fault if the overpayment was caused when (1) the individual failed to furnish information that they knew or should have known was material, (2) the individual made an incorrect statement, that the individual knew or should have known was incorrect, or (3) the individual failed to return a payment that he knew or should have known was incorrect.[159]

If the overpayment is not waived by SSA, the individual must repay the overpayment. If an individual is still receiving their benefits, SSA will require the individual to pay the lesser of either (1) the amount of the individual's benefit payment for that month or (2) an amount equal to 10 percent of the individual's total income, which includes the individual's SSI and state supplementary payments.[160] The 10 percent limitation does not apply if SSA determines that the overpayment occurred because of fraud, willful misrepresentation, or concealment of material information committed by the individual or their spouse or if the recovery of the overpayment is made pursuant to an agreement to dispose of excess resources. For individuals who are no longer receiving SSI benefits, SSA can refer the overpayment case to the Internal Revenue Service for attachment of their income tax refund.[161]

IX. The Appeals Procedure

A. The Initial Determination

An initial determination is defined as any decision by SSA that is subject to administrative and judicial review.[162] Decisions that are viewed by SSA as initial determinations include:[163]

- Eligibility for benefits
- Amount of benefits
- Suspension or termination of benefits
- Whether payments should be made to a payee

Certain decisions made by SSA are not initial determinations and are therefore not subject to administrative and judicial review. Examples of decisions that are not initial determinations include the denial of a request to be an individual's payee and the denial of a request to utilize the expedited appeals process.[164]

B. The Reconsideration Stage

The individual has 60 days after receipt of the initial determination to request a reconsideration of an adverse initial determination.[165] If an individual files an appeal within ten days after the receipt of a notice to reduce or terminate benefits, the individual may continue receiving benefits.[166] A notice to terminate or reduce benefits is considered received five days after the mailing date unless there is a reasonable showing to the contrary. Good cause must be demonstrated in order to keep receiving benefits if the individual does not file their appeal within the ten-day limit. A claimant may submit new evidence during the reconsideration stage, but there is no hearing.

C. *The Administrative Law Judge Stage*

The individual has 60 days after receipt of an adverse reconsideration to request a hearing before an administrative law judge.[167] SSA is required to give the claimant at least 20 days' notice of the time and place of the hearing. The claimant may submit new evidence, testify, and present witnesses and subpoena witnesses. In addition, the claimant is entitled to cross examine, if present, the medical expert and vocational expert.

D. *The Appeals Council Stage*

The claimant must request a review by the appeals council within 60 days of the receipt of an adverse decision by the administrative law judge.[168] The claimant may submit new evidence and file a brief, but there is no testimony. The appeals council may reverse or uphold the administrative law judge's decision if it so chooses, or remand the case for another hearing before the administrative law judge.

E. *Federal District Court*

The claimant has 60 days after receipt of an adverse decision by the appeals council to file an original action in federal district court.[169] An expedited appeals process to proceed immediately to federal district court is available at certain stages in the administrative process if a written request is submitted by the claimant and both the claimant and SSA agree that the only factor preventing a decision in the claimant's favor is a provision of the law that the claimant believes is unconstitutional.[170]

Appendix A: Overview of Social Security Disability Programs: SSI and SSDI

The Social Security Administration has two disability programs that are federally funded. They are often confused because they have many similarities and some important differences. This appendix describes the differences between Supplemental Security Income (SSI) and Social Security Disability Insurance (SSDI).

Similarities

MEDICAL AND FUNCTIONAL DISABILITY CRITERIA

- Both programs have the same criteria for determining disability based on medical evidence and functional abilities.

APPLICATION PROCESS

- Both programs utilize the same application process, although they have different application forms, and share one disability determination.

HEALTH INSURANCE

- Each program has an associated health insurance program.

Key Difference: Non-Medical Criteria

- SSI is based on need.
- SSDI is based on contributions by employees and employers to the social security trust fund as authorized by the Federal Insurance Contributions Act (FICA).

Other Differences

- Benefit amount
- Eligibility dates
- Health insurance
- Work incentives

COMPARISON OF SSI AND SSDI

Supplemental Security Income (SSI)	Social Security Disability Insurance (SSDI)
Benefits to:	Benefits to:
• Low income • Disabled, blind, or elderly individuals • The monthly benefit amount is set each year by Congress; some states provide additional financial support	• Insured • Disabled or blind individuals and some eligible family members
Based on need:	Based on earnings:
• Need is a complete picture of income, living arrangements, and personal resources	• Employees & employers pay into Social Security • Amount based on FICA contributions
Documentation:	Documentation:
• Income • Living arrangement • Personal resources and assets (limits on)	• Recent wage information (e.g., W-2, pay-check stubs) • Work and earnings history

Disabled Adult Child (DAC)

An adult who becomes disabled before age 22 may be eligible for "child's" benefits if a parent is deceased or starts receiving retirement or disability benefits. Social security considers this a child's benefit because it is paid on a parent's social security earnings record.

- Applicants must meet the SSA disability criteria for adults and must be unmarried.
- Since benefits are paid based on the parent's earnings record, it is not necessary for the adult child to have ever worked.
- A disabled adult child already receiving SSI benefits should still check to see if benefits may be payable on a parent's earnings record. Circumstances may have changed (e.g., parent's death, retirement, or disability status) since the initial application. Higher benefits might be payable, and entitlement to Medicare may be possible.
- SSDI benefits continue as long as the child remains disabled.

Appendix B: Supplemental Security Income Checklist

You may not need all of the following documents. Sometimes one document can substitute for another. The lists are not all-inclusive.

Social Security Card or Number

You will need to apply for a social security number if you do not have one. If you need one, a number will be assigned at the time social security entitles you to SSI benefits.

Proof of Age

- A public birth record recorded before age five; or
- A religious birth record recorded before age five; or
- Other documents showing your age or date of birth.

If you already proved your age when you applied for social security benefits, you do not need to prove it again for SSI.

Citizenship or Alien Status Record

If you are a citizen, examples of documents you may need are:

- Birth certificate showing you were born in the United States; or
- Religious record of birth or baptism showing your place of birth in the United States; or
- Naturalization certification; or
- U.S. passport or passport card; or
- Certificate of citizenship.
- If you are an alien, examples of documents you may need are:
- A current immigration document; for example, an I-551 (Permanent Resident Card); or
- I-94 (Arrival/Departure Record).

If you are an alien who has served in the U.S. Armed Forces, you may need your military discharge paper (form DD-214).

Proof of Income

If you have income, you may need to provide the following:

- Earned income: payroll stubs, or if self-employed, a tax return for the last tax year.
- Unearned income: any records you have (for example, award letters, bank statements, court orders, receipts) showing how much you receive, how often, and the source of the payment.

- Work expenses: income that is not counted if it qualifies as SSI WORK INCENTIVES. See www.ssa.gov/disabilityresearch/workincentives .htm for more information.

Proof of Resources

- Bank statements for all checking and savings accounts
- Deed or tax appraisal statements for all property you own besides the house you live in
- Life or disability insurance policies
- Burial contracts, burial plots, and so on
- Certificates of deposit, stocks, or bonds
- Titles or registrations for vehicles like cars, trucks, motorcycles, boats, campers, and so on.

Proof of Living Arrangements

- Lease or rent receipt
- Names, dates of births, medical assistance cards, or social security numbers for all household members
- Deed or property tax bill
- Information about household costs for rent, mortgage, food, and utilities

Medical Sources (if You Are Filing as Blind or Disabled)

- Medical records, if you have them
- Names, addresses, and telephone numbers of doctors and other providers of medical services to you and the approximate dates you were treated
- Names of the prescription and non-prescription medications that you take

Work History

- Job titles
- Type of business
- Names of employers
- Dates worked
- Hours worked per day and hours worked per week
- Days worked per week and rates of pay for work you did in the 15 years before you became unable to work because of your illnesses, injuries, or conditions
- Description of job duties for the type of work you performed

Other Sources

If you are applying as a disabled child, or on behalf of a disabled child, you will need to provide the names, addresses, and telephone numbers of people (for example, teachers or caregivers) who can provide information about how the child's medical condition affects his or her daily activities. Also, if the child has an individualized education plan (IEP) at his or her school, it is helpful to submit a copy of the plan.

Things to Remember

- **Do not wait to apply.** If you think you may be eligible for SSI, you should contact the Social Security Administration right away. The earliest the Social Security Administration (SSA) will pay SSI is the month after the filling date of your application, or the month after you first meet all the eligibility requirements, whichever is later. The SSA may use the date you contact us as the filing date. If you do not have all of the things the SSA needs, it will give you time to provide them.
- **SSA needs to see the original documents.** If you do not have the original document, the SSA can accept a certified copy from the office that issued the original document. The SSA does not accept photocopies. It will return the original documents to you.
- **Keep a copy of things you send to Social Security Administration.** Keep track of the dates you send information to SSA, or talk to SSA, as well as the name of the social security employee with whom you spoke.

Notes

1. Supplemental Security Income is found in Title 42 of the United States Code. The applicable regulations are found in Title 42 of the Code of Federal Regulations.

2. Enactment of 42 U.S.C. § 1601 of the Social Security Act by Pub. L. No. 92-603 creating SSI did not apply to Puerto Rico, Guam, or the Virgin Islands. Disabled residents in these jurisdictions continue to receive benefits under prior law.

3. 42 U.S.C. § 1396(a); 20 C.F.R. § 435.541(a),(b).

4.. 83 Fed. Reg. 53702 (Oct. 24, 2018).

5. 42 U.S.C. § 1382c(a)(1)(a).

6. 20 C.F.R. § 416.801.

7. *Id.*

8. 20 C.F.R. § 416.802

9. *Id.* § 416.803.

10. 42 U.S.C. § 1382c(a)(3)(a).

11. *Id.* § 1382c(a)(3)(B).

12. 20 C.F.R. § 416.910.

13. 42 U.S.C. § 1382c(a)(3)(g).

14. *Id.* § 1382c(a)(2).

15. 20 C.F.R. § 416.981.

16. *Id*. § 416.985.
17. *Id*. §§ 416.983, 416.984.
18. *Id*. § 416.210.
19. *Id*. § 416.211.
20. *Id*. § 416.212.
21. *Id*. § 416.214.
22. *Id*. § 416.215.
23. *Id*. § 416.1102.
24. *Id*. § 416.1110.
25. *Id*.
26. *Id*. § 416.1110(a).
27. *Id*. § 416.1112
28. *Id*. § 416.1120.
29. *Id*. § 416.1121.
30. *Id*. § 416.1121(d).
31. *Id*. § 416.1121(e).
32. See Sections IV.F and G.
33. 20 C.F.R. § 416.1124.
34. *Id*. § 416.1130(a).
35. *Id*. § 416.1130(b).
36. *Id*.
37. *Id*.
38. *Id*. § 416.1131.
39. *Id*. § 416.1131(a)(2)(b).
40. *Id*. § 416.1131(2)(c).
41. *Id*. § 416.1149.
42. *Id*. § 416.1132(b).
43. *Id*. § 416.1132(c).
44. *Id*. § 416.1133.
45. *Id*. § 416.1133(c).
46. *Id*. § 416.1142.
47. *Id*. § 416.1140(a)(1).
48. *Id*. § 416.1141.
49. *Id*. § 416.1140(a)(2).
50. *Id*. § 416.1160(a).
51. *Id*.
52. *Id*. § 416.222(a).
53. *Id*. § 416.1160(b)(1).
54. *Id*. § 416.1160(b)(2).
55. *Id*. § 416.1161(a).
56. *Id*. § 416.1161(b).
57. *Id*. § 416.1161(c).
58. *Id*. § 416.1163(a).
59. *Id*. § 416.1163(b).
60. *Id*. § 416.1163(b)(1).
61. *Id*. § 416.1163(b)(2).
62. *Id*. § 416.1163(b)(3).
63. *Id*. § 416.1163(d)(1).
64. *Id*.
65. *Id*. § 416.1163(d)(2).

66. *Id.* § 416.1163(f)(1).
67. *Id.* § 416.1163(f)(2).
68. *Id.* § 416.1163(f)(3).
69. *Id.* § 416.1163(f)(4).
70. *Id.* § 416.1163(f)(5).
71. *Id.* § 416.1103.
72. *Id.* § 416.1110(c).
73. See Section IV.H on presumed value rule.
74. 20 C.F.R. § 416.1205(c).
75. *Id.*
76. *Id.* § 416.1202(a).
77. *Id.*
78. *Id.* § 416.1201.
79. *Id.* § 416.1201(a)(1).
80. *Id.*
81. *Id.* § 416.1201(b).
82. *Id.*
83. *Id.* § 416.1201(c)(1).
84. *Id.*
85. *Id.* § 416.1201(c)(2)(i).
86. See Section V.F on disposition of resources.
87. 20 C.F.R. § 416.1207(a).
88. *Id.* § 416.1207(b).
89. *Id.* § 416.1207(c).
90. *Id.* § 416.1207(d).
91. *Id.* § 416.1207(e). The example given in the Code of Federal Regulations is: Miss L., a disabled individual, receives a $350.00 unemployment insurance benefit on January 10, 1986. The benefit is unearned income to Miss L. when she receives it. On January 14, Miss L. uses the $350.00 payment to purchase shares of stock. Miss L. has exchanged one item (cash) for another item (stock). The $350.00 payment is never counted as a resource to Miss L. because she exchanged it in the same month she received it. The stock is not income, it is a different form of a resource exchanged for cash. Since a resource is not countable until the first moment of the month following its receipt, the stock is not a countable resource to Miss L. until February 1.
92. 20 C.F.R. § 416.1208(b).
93. *Id.* § 416.1208.
94. *Id.*
95. *Id.* § 416.1208(c)(2).
96. *Id.* § 416.1208(c)(4).
97. 42 U.S.C. § 1382b(a).
98. 20 C.F.R. § 416.1212(a).
99. *Id.* § 416.1212(b).
100. *Id.*
101. *Id.* § 416.1212(d).
102. *Id.* § 416.1212(d), (d), (f) & (g).
103. *Id.* 416.1216(b).
104. *Id.* § 416.1216(a).
105. *Id.* § 416.1216(b).

106. *Id*. § 416.1218(b)(2).
107. *Id*. § 416.1218(a).
108. *Id*. § 416.1222(a).
109. *Id*.
110. *Id*. § 416.1224.
111. *Id*.
112. *Id*. § 416.1226.
113. *Id*. § 416.1228.
114. *Id*. § 416.1230.
115. *Id*.
116. *Id*. § 416.1234.
117. *Id*. § 416.1237.
118. *Id*. § 416.1231(a)(2).
119. *Id*. § 416.1231(a)(1).
120. *Id*. § 416.1231(b)(3).
121. *Id*. § 416.1231(b)(1).
122. *Id*. § 416.1231(b)(5).
123. *Id*.
124. *Id*. § 416.1233.
125. *Id*. § 416.1233(c).
126. *Id*. § 416.1238.
127. *Id*. § 416.1235.
128. *Id*. § 416.1229.
129. *Id*. § 416.1239.
130. *Id*. § 416.1247.
131. *Id*. § 416.1240(a).
132. *Id*. § 416.1240(a)(1).
133. *Id*. § 416.1242.
134. *Id*. § 416.1245(b).
135. *Id*. § 416.1245(b)(3).
136. *Id*. § 416.1242(c).
137. *Id*. § 416.1245(a).
138. 42 U.S.C. § 1382b(c).
139. *Id*. § 1382b(c)(1)(A)(iv)(II).
140. *Id*. § 1382b(c)(1)(C).
141. 20 C.F.R. § 416.305.
142. *Id*. § 416.310.
143. *Id*. § 416.310(d).
144. *Id*. § 416.315(a).
145. *Id*. § 416.315(b).
146. *Id*.
147. *Id*. § 416.315(c).
148. *Id*. § 416.340.
149. *Id*. § 416.345.
150. *Id*. § 416.350(a).
151. *Id*. § 416.350(b).
152. *Id*. § 416.536.
153. *Id*. § 416.545(c).
154. *Id*. § 416.545(d).
155. *Id*. § 416.546.

156. *Id.* § 416.537.
157. *Id.* § 416.550.
158. *Id.*
159. *Id.*
160. *Id.* § 416.571.
161. *Id.* § 416.580.
162. *Id.* § 416.1402.
163. *Id.*
164. *Id.* § 416.1403.
165. *Id.* § 416.1409.
166. *Id.* § 416.1336(b).
167. *Id.* § 416.1433(b).
168. *Id.* § 416.1468(a).
169. 42 U.S.C. § 1383(c)(3).
170. 20 C.F.R. §§ 416.1423–.1428.

CHAPTER 7

Medicaid

I. Overview 176
II. Introduction to Medicaid Eligibility 176
    A. Individuals Who Are Covered by Medicaid. 177
III. Services Covered by Medicaid. 177
    A. Mandatory Covered Services. 177
    B. Optional Services Covered by Medicaid 178
IV. Eligibility for Long-Term Care Benefits 179
V. Financial Qualifications. 179
    A. Definition of Income 179
    B. Income Capped States. 180
    C. Non-Income Capped States 180
VI. Resources 181
    A. Resource Exemptions 181
VII. Spousal Impoverishment Rules 182
    A. The Fair Hearing Procedure 184
VIII. Five-Year Look-Back Rule. 184
IX. Planning for a Married Couple 186
    A. Spend Down. 186
    B. Promissory Note or Purchase of Annuity 187
X. Transfers to Trusts 188
    A. Introduction 188
    B. Medicaid Exemption for Transfers to Trusts. 188
XI. Estate Recovery. 190
XII. Appeals Procedures for Medicaid. 192
Appendix A: Will with Testamentary Third Party Special Needs Trust
    for Couple with Handicapped Child/Person. 195
Appendix B: Third Party Special Needs Inter Vivos Trust 209
Appendix C: First Party Special Needs Inter Vivos Trust. 220
Appendix D: Qualifying Income Trust. 229
Appendix E: Income Only Trust 235

I. Overview

Your elder clients will have little concern about qualifying for Medicaid unless they anticipate or fear residing in a nursing home facility. About the only other situation in which the clients will be concerned about Medicaid eligibility, short of being in a nursing home themselves, is if they have an adult disabled child who is eligible for Medicaid, or may become eligible in the future, to pay for nursing home or other long-term care. If the child is entitled to benefits, or may be entitled to benefits, it is important that the child not receive an inheritance from the parents that will cause the child to lose Medicaid eligibility. For this reason, if the parent intends to pass any of her estate to the adult disabled child, a third party special needs trust must be prepared. This type of trust is sometimes referred to as a supplemental care trust. It will have provisions that make it clear that the child is not inheriting outright from the parents, and that the child's inheritance will be held in trust with the trust having limitations that preclude trust distributions for any services that could be paid for by Medicaid or other government programs. The text at Section X discusses these trusts. The trust forms in the Appendices will also be helpful.

Another situation that may arise is if the child's parents did not prepare a special needs trust, the child's parents are now deceased and the child is entitled to receive either an inheritance or the child is entitled to a personal injury award, either of which will result in the child receiving an amount of money that would otherwise disqualify the child from Medicaid benefits. The Medicaid law specifically allows a first party special needs trust for a disabled individual under 65 years of age. This is discussed in Section X.B. A first party special needs trust form is found in Appendix C.

Some clients will need to know how to become eligible for Medicaid in order to pay for nursing home expenses. For information on Medicaid eligibility, Sections IV, V, and VI are essential. Additionally, the spousal impoverishment rules in Section VII and the spend-down rules in Section IX are extremely important. The review of the permissible trusts in Section X is also essential information for your client. Finally, a basic understanding of estate recovery will round out our basic treatment of Medicaid benefits in Section XI.

II. Introduction to Medicaid Eligibility

Medicaid is a joint federal and state program that provides medical assistance for persons with limited incomes and limited resources.[1] There are variances of Medicaid benefits among the states. Thus, this discussion is broad. The reader must be aware of the regulations and nuances of her own state. Although the focus of this text is on Medicaid benefits for elder clients in nursing homes an understanding of the general rules of Medicaid eligibility and the services provided by Medicaid is helpful. A useful website is www.medicaid.gov. Several ABA publications are also excellent; they include *Don't Let Dementia Steal Everything, The Law of Later-Life Healthcare and Decision Making* and *Elder Law and Later-Life Legal Planning*.

A. Individuals Who Are Covered by Medicaid

To participate in Medicaid, federal law requires states to cover certain groups of individuals. Low-income families, qualified women and children, and individuals receiving Supplemental Security Income (SSI) are examples of mandatory eligible groups. States have the option of providing additional coverage to cover other groups, such as individuals receiving home- and community-based services and children in foster care who are not otherwise eligible.[2]

The Affordable Care Act of 2011 creates an opportunity for states to elect to expand Medicaid to cover nearly all low-income Americans under age 65. Eligibility for children was extended to at least 138 percent of the federal poverty level in every state and states were given the option to extend the eligibility to adults with income at or below 138 percent of the federal poverty level. Most states have chosen to expand coverage; however, because the Affordable Care Act is such a political "hot potato," it is not clear at this writing what coverage will be available long term for those who have been made newly eligible.

III. Services Covered by Medicaid

A. Mandatory Covered Services

Each state's Medicaid program is authorized to cover a variety of services in that particular state's plan. A state's plan must cover the following types of services if the state chooses to extend coverage to what are termed categorically needy persons:[3]

- Inpatient hospital services, other than services in an institution for mental disease
- Outpatient hospital services
- Rural health clinic services
- Federally qualified health center services
- Laboratory and X-ray services
- Nursing facility services, other than services for in an institution for mental diseases, for individuals 21 years of age or older
- Early and periodic screening, diagnostic, and treatment services for persons under 21
- Family planning services and supplies furnished to individuals of child-bearing age
- Physician's services furnished in the office, the patient's home, hospital, or nursing facility
- Services performed by a nurse-midwife that the nurse-midwife is legally authorized to perform
- Services performed by a certified pediatric nurse practitioner or certified family nurse practitioner

B. Optional Services Covered by Medicaid

States are also permitted to extend Medicaid coverage for the following types of services:[4]

- Medical and surgical services furnished by a dentist
- Medical care, or remedial care, furnished by licensed practitioners within the scope of their practice as defined by state law
- Home health care services
- Private duty nursing services
- Clinic services furnished under the direction of a physician, including services furnished by clinic personnel to eligible homeless individuals
- Dental services
- Physical therapy and related services
- Prescription drugs, dentures, prosthetic devices, and prescribed eyeglasses
- Diagnostic, screening, preventive, and rehabilitative services, including any medical or remedial services recommended by a physician or licensed practitioner in the healing arts within the scope of her practice under state law which are provided in a facility, the patient's home, or other setting
- Inpatient hospital services and nursing facility services for individuals 65 years of age or older in an institution for mental disease
- Services in an intermediate care facility for persons with intellectual disabilities
- Inpatient psychiatric hospital services for individuals under 21 years of age
- Hospice care
- Respiratory care service
- Home and community care for functionally disabled elderly individuals
- Community-supported living arrangements
- Personal care services furnished to an individual who is not an inpatient or resident of a hospital, nursing facility, intermediate care facility of the mentally disabled, or institution for mental disease that are (1) authorized by a physician, (2) provided by an individual who is qualified to provide such services and who is not a member of the individual's family, and (3) furnished in a home or other location
- Primary care case management services
- Any other medical care, and other type of remedial care recognized under state law, specified by the Secretary of the Department for Health and Human Services, but not including payments for care or services furnished to inmates of a public institution, except as a patient in a medical institution, or payments for care or services for an individual who is less than 65 years of age and who is a patient in an institution for mental disease

IV. Eligibility for Long-Term Care Benefits

The primary reason your client will be interested in the Medicaid program is to pay for their own long-term care expenses or those of an aging parent or other relative. Typically, the aged person is reaching a point of medical necessity where they cannot continue to live in their personal residence and need to transition to a nursing home or other long-term care facility. If the client has resources that are below certain limitations, then the Medicaid program will pay for the person's long-term care expenses.

A person may be eligible for Medicaid long-term care benefits if the person:[5]

- Is a U.S. citizen or certain qualified alien;
- Is aged 65 or over, blind, or disabled;
- Resides in a facility that participates in the Medicaid program and is placed in a Medicaid-certified bed;
- Requires and meets the nursing facility level of care criteria giving consideration to the medical diagnosis, age-related dependencies, care needs, services and health personnel required to meet these needs and the feasibility of meeting the needs through alternative institutional or non-institutional services; and
- Is income and resource eligible.

Obviously, most nursing home residents will meet the level of care requirements, otherwise they would not be in the nursing facility. The nursing homes will assess the six activities of daily living, which include eating, walking, bathing, dressing, toileting, and transferring from a bed to a chair. If the person is unable to perform two or more of these activities without assistance, they are typically nursing home eligible and may be eligible for Medicaid benefits. Then financial qualifications involving income and resource requirements must be met. Not all states have the same income and resource or asset requirements. A knowledge of the lawyer's own state requirements is essential.

V. Financial Qualifications

When determining eligibility for Medicaid payments for long-term care, the states generally consider a person's finances in one of two ways. Although all states look both to income and resources (assets) in determining eligibility, the states differ on how they treat income. Some states are income-capped states and others are non-income-capped states. These concepts are discussed in Sections V.B and C.

A. Definition of Income[6]

Most states define income by using the income definitions under the SSI program (see Chapter 6, Section IV). This definition is broad and includes both earned and unearned income. Of significance is that income of the non-institutionalized spouse is not deemed to be the income of the nursing home spouse. There is a difference among the states as to whether a qualified retirement account or an IRA is income or a resource. Some states consider only the distribution received from these retirement accounts to be income. Others consider the entire value of the retirement account or IRA to be a resource. Be sure of your state's definition.

B. Income-Capped States[7]

Income-capped states have an income limit of three times the Supplemental Security Income (SSI) payment amount, which is also termed the Federal Benefit Rate (FBR). In income-capped states, an individual is not entitled to Medicaid benefits if her income exceeds three times the FBR. In 2019, this amount is $2,313 a month.

If an individual's income exceeds this limit, they do not qualify for Medicaid even though they have no resources from which to pay for their long-term care. This problem is solved by the use of a Qualifying Income Trust (QIT), or as it is sometimes termed a Miller Trust.[8] Some states use other names such as an Income Only Trust or an Income Diversion Trust. For our purposes, we will refer to these trusts as a QIT. To become eligible, the individual must establish a QIT and transfer to it the monthly income they receive that is in excess of the $2,313 limit. There are specific requirements for these trusts. Generally, the trust must be irrevocable, the money in the trust can only be used for restricted needs as required by the state Medicaid office, and upon the individual's death, the balance in the trust must be paid to the state Medicaid office. When the individual is a nursing home resident they are required to write two checks each month from their own income for their long-term care. One check is from their primary checking account and the other check is from the QIT. The state then pays the balance owed to the nursing home. A QIT is discussed in Section X, and a trust form is found in Appendix D. Be sure to know your own state's requirements.

C. Non-Income-Capped States[9]

Non-income-capped states take a simpler approach. These states are sometimes referred to as medically needy states or spend-down states. These states have an income limit for Medicaid qualification just as the income-capped states do. The difference is these states allow the individual to spend down their excess income for their medical needs, which in most situations simply means paying their nursing home bill. The spend down will take the individual below the state's income limit, thus the income standard does not result in denied eligibility. At its simplest, it means that in these states it is not necessary to go through the process of paying nursing home bills from two accounts; and it avoids the necessity of preparing a QIT.

VI. *Resources*

The second financial qualification concerns the resources (assets) that may be owned by the individual seeking Medicaid payments for nursing home expenses. Generally, most states limit the resources for single individual to $2,000, although in some states the amount is somewhat less and in others it is as high as $15,000. Obviously, the attorney must know the requirements of his own state. Generally, all resources are accounted. If the institutionalized spouse is married, the resources of both spouses are totaled to determine the total countable resources.

Most annuities are considered a resource, but an annuity is considered income rather than a resource if it meets the requirements of the Deficit Reduction Act of 2005. An annuity meets the requirements of this act if it is irrevocable, non-assignable, is actuarially sound, and provides for payments in equal amounts during the term of the annuity. There can be no deferred or balloon payments. The annuity is deemed actuarially sound if it is payable over the life expectancy of the annuitant based on social security life expectancy tables. If the annuity does not meet these criteria then it is a resource.

In many states qualified retirement accounts and IRAs are treated as income, rather than a resource. In those states, the minimum distributions required under the Internal Revenue Code must be taken, usually beginning at age 59 $^1/_2$ rather than 70 $^1/_2$. This amount is treated as income. In other states the retirement account or IRA is deemed a resource. Know your state law.

When determining the total countable resources of a couple it does not matter in whose name the resource (asset) is titled. This should be contrasted with income items, which are only countable when made payable to the institutionalized spouse. This is an important distinction. The spouse who is not institutionalized (termed the community spouse) can retain all of his income because only the income of the institutionalized spouse is considered.

A. *Resource Exemptions*[10]

There are a few exemptions. One vehicle, at any value,[11] jewelry, clothing, and furniture are considered exempt or noncountable resources.[12] The home is considered an exempt source if its equity value is below $585,000 though some states use the higher maximum limit of $878,000.[13] The limit does not apply if the community spouse lives in the house, or it is occupied by a child under 21, or a child of any age who is blind or permanently and totally disabled. These are 2019 values, which are adjusted annually.

For a single person, the home is exempt under the theory that it may be needed for the institutionalized individual should his or her condition improve and be able to return to the home. In some states, after six months of residing in a nursing home the state will begin to assess whether or not the individual is unable to return home at which point the state deems the residence no longer a "home." This will then require the personal residence to be sold with the proceeds being used to privately pay until the proceeds are spent, at which time the Medicaid program will again pay for the individual's long-term care. In those states that do not require the home to be sold, there are several problems to consider. The nursing home resident will not have funds with which to pay taxes, insurance, maintenance, and repairs on the residence. This will require the family members to pay those expenses. Then upon the death of the nursing home resident, the state will seek to recoup the amount it has paid for the person by placing a claim against the residence. As can be seen, this creates complications in deciding how best to treat the home.

There are a couple of other exceptions that may save the residence from being sold to pay nursing home costs. The residence can be transferred to a disabled adult child without penalty. Similarly, the residence can be transferred to a caregiver child. A caregiver child includes a natural child or a stepchild who has lived with the parent or in the parent's home for at least two years prior to the parent being institutionalized and has provided such care that without that care the parent would have been in a nursing home at least two years earlier. A final exception is rare but is available for a sibling who has lived in the residence for at least one year prior to the other sibling going to the nursing home and has an equity ownership in the residence. In this situation the home can be transferred to the sibling.[14]

Business property essential to the means of self-support is an exclusion. Life insurance up to the face value of $1,500[15] and burial expenses subject to the cap the state places on these expenses are exempt.[16] Generally, pre-paid funeral expenses are also exempt regardless of value.[17] An additional small exemption is up to $6,000 of non-business income-producing property if it produces a net annual return of at least 6 percent.[18] Some states limit this exclusion to $6,000 of equity, though other states do not impose a dollar limit. In these more lenient states, the purchase of rental property in the name of the community spouse may provide a planning opportunity.[19]

With these few exceptions, the institutionalized spouse can retain virtually nothing. The situation is not quite as austere if there is a spouse. The spousal impoverishment rules that are discussed in Section VIII provide some relief for the spouse who is not a nursing home resident. In Medicaid-speak this spouse is referred to as the community spouse.

VII. Spousal Impoverishment Rules

These are clear rules that are designed to allow the community spouse to live in the marital residence and with some resources to provide for that spouse. The first consideration is the income of the community spouse. The community spouse can always keep her own income. If that spouse's separate income is below what is termed the minimum monthly maintenance needs allowance (MMMNA) then some of the nursing home spouse's income can be given to the community spouse.[20]

In 2019, this amount is $2,057.50 with a maximum amount used in some states that is as high as $3,160.50. For purposes of illustration, using the lower allowance and assuming the nursing home spouse has $2,500 per month of social security or other income and the community spouse only has $1,000 of income, then $1,057.50 of the nursing home spouse's income will be given to the community spouse.

The home at an equity value of $585,000 or $878,000 at the option of the state is deemed an exempt resource and can be transferred to the community spouse without running afoul of the resource requirements. The treatment of the home does vary among the states. Some states treat the home as exempt but seek repayment for Medicaid payments from the proceeds of the sale of the home following the death of the community spouse. Some states will cap the value of an exempt home for the community spouse at the equity values in Section VI.A with the excess being a countable resource of the institutionalized spouse. It is necessary to know the law of your particular state and know how it treats the home.

Since the home is considered an exempt resource, then the title should be placed in the sole name of the community spouse, who then should execute a will passing the house to the ultimate estate beneficiaries. Even this may be a problem as the institutionalized spouse's statutory share under state law should be asserted if the community spouse dies first. For example, if that statutory share is one-third of all real estate, then only two-thirds of the value of the personal residence will be available for the ultimate estate beneficiaries. One-third of the personal residence must reimburse the state for its Medicaid payments. Some states will allow the home after being deeded to the community spouse to then be given by the community spouse to third parties, such as the children. This avoids the statutory share problem. But other states will treat such a gift as a transfer disqualifying the institutionalized spouse from Medicaid benefits. It should not be so confusing, but the states vary on treatment of the home. Be certain of your state law.

Even though the resources of both spouses are considered countable resources, states treat retirement accounts differently. In some states, IRAs, 401(k)s, profit-sharing plans, or other qualified retirement accounts that are owned by the community spouse are not considered a countable resource. The retirement account is only considered as income to the community spouse based on the minimum distribution rules. This amount is deemed the income of the community spouse. It is the sole property of the community spouse. Not all states follow this approach.

After determining the value of all countable resources the community spouse (in 2019) is allowed to keep between $25,284 and up to as much as $126,420 of those resources. The total of countable resources is divided by two with the community spouse receiving the minimum amount if the resources are small or the maximum amount if the resources are large. If the resources are such that one-half of that value lies between the maximum and minimum then there are two possible results. In some states, the community spouse simply receives that one-half amount. In other states, the spouse can receive the full amount and is not relegated to the 50 percent calculation. This calculation is best understood by the following illustration.

MEDICAID COMMUNITY SPOUSE RESOURCE ALLOWANCE

Couples' combined assets	$50,000	$100,000	$150,000	$250,000	$500,000
Amount the community spouse keeps in a 50% state	$25,000	$50,000	$75,000	$125,000	$126,420
Amount the community spouse keeps in a 100% state	$50,000	$100,000	$126,420	$126,420	$126,420

In order to determine the countable resources and those resources that are exempt, it is necessary to go to the local Medicaid office to have a resource assessment, or as it is sometimes informally referred to as a "snapshot" taken of all available resources to determine those resources that are exempt and those that are non-exempt.[21] This can be done even though an application has not been made for Medicaid payment. Simply schedule a conference with the local Medicaid office after the nursing home spouse has been institutionalized. Normally, the state office will not do this evaluation prior to the spouse being in a nursing home. Get a copy of the "snapshot."

A. The Fair Hearing Procedure

An individual may request a "fair hearing" from his state Medicaid agency with the hope of persuading the agency to permit the community spouse to keep a greater amount of income or resources than is allowed by state law. Each state's hearing system must provide for a hearing before the Medicaid agency or an evidentiary hearing at the local level with the right to an appeal to a state agency hearing. In addition, the state hearing system must meet the due process standards set forth in *Goldberg v. Kelly*, 397 U.S. 254 (1970), and any additional standards required by federal law.[22] Either the institutionalized spouse or the community spouse may request the fair hearing. Either spouse must demonstrate "exceptional circumstances resulting in significant financial distress"[23] at the fair hearing before the minimum monthly needs allowance for the community spouse may be exceeded. In order to exceed the permitted community spouse resource allowance, either spouse must prove that the community spouse resource allowance (including any income generated from resources) "is inadequate to raise the community spouse's income to the minimum monthly maintenance needs allowance."[24]

VIII. Five-Year Look-Back Rule[25]

In all states other than California, there is a 60-month look-back rule that is designed to find if any transfers without consideration have been made prior to applying for Medicaid benefits. In California it is 30 months. When applying for Medicaid benefits, the applicant is required to disclose all transfers to a third party for less than fair market value prior to applying for benefits that were made in the past 60 months. This is referred to as a look-back provision, which is designed to keep individuals from qualifying for benefits even though they had the ability to privately pay but for the gifted assets. Once the five-year term has been met, any gifts prior to that time are not considered nor do they have to be disclosed.

If transfers were made within that 60-month time frame, then the Medicaid office determines the period of time for which the Medicaid applicant is ineligible for Medicaid benefits. The amount of the gifts during the 60 months are divided by the average cost of nursing home care in the person's home state to determine the length of ineligibility. Each state will set this amount yearly. Assuming, for illustration purposes, the gift was valued at $120,000 and the average monthly nursing home cost is $6,000 there will be 20 months of ineligibility due to the gift. The period of ineligibility begins to run from the date of the application for benefits and not the earlier date of the gift.

Uncompensated transfers also fall within the look-back period. For example, a disclaimer of an inheritance that the institutionalized spouse receives that is made within 60 months is subject to the penalty, as is the failure to claim an inheritance. For example, if the community spouse predeceases the institutionalized spouse and wills all property to other estate beneficiaries, the institutionalized spouse's statutory share from the estate of the deceased spouse is considered a transfer for purposes of the look back.

Certain transfers are exempt and will not result in a penalty of ineligibility. A transfer of an individual's home to the following persons is exempt:[26]

- The spouse
- A disabled child or a child under 21 years of age
- A caregiver child over 21 years of age who resided in the home for at least two years before the transfer and provided care that permitted the parent to reside at home
- A brother or sister who has an equity interest in the home and who resided in the home at least one year before the individual was institutionalized

In addition to transfers of an individual's residence, certain transfers of an individual's assets, such as monies, are exempt:[27]

- Transfers made to the individual's spouse
- Transfers made to a third party for the benefit of the individual's spouse
- Transfers made by the individual's spouse to a third party for the benefit of the individual's spouse
- Transfers made to a trust for the individual's child under 21 years of age
- Transfers made to a trust for the individual's blind or disabled child over 21 years of age
- Transfers made to a trust created for the individual described in 42 U.S.C. § 1396p(d)(4), provided the individual is less than 65 years of age and disabled
- Transfers to certain trusts that are exempted by law from considerations

If an individual can demonstrate that she attempted to dispose of assets for fair market value or the assets were disposed of for another reason other than to qualify for Medicaid or the assets that were transferred for less than fair market value have been returned, the individual remains eligible for Medicaid.[28] Further, if an individual can demonstrate that denial of eligibility would create an undue hardship, the individual remains eligible for Medicaid.[29]

In some situations, transfers to a relative in compensation for personal care services provided for the elderly client may be deemed transfers for fair consideration. For example, this situation could arise when an adult child provides significant personal care for her elderly parent that enables the parent to remain in her personal residence. The contract should be in writing. The charges for services must be reasonable. It must be clear what services are provided, including services that will be provided should the parent require nursing home care. The more detailed and specific the contract the better. A lump sum payment is possible for such a contract provided that the contract contains provisions for repayment should the elderly parent die before all services are performed.[30]

A gift of the personal residence to those individuals specified in Section VI.A is permissible. The more difficult question is whether or not the community spouse can then gift the personal residence to third parties, such as the children, without that transfer being deemed a disqualifying transfer. There is a variance among the states as to the extent to which the community spouse can transfer the residence, which was discussed in Section VII. Be sure of your state laws.

IX. Planning for a Married Couple

When a spouse is about to enter a nursing home, the community spouse is faced with the concern of how to maximize the couple's assets to better ensure his or her own financial security. Earlier, as explained in Section V.A, in most all states the spouse's own income remains their separate income. If their income is less than the minimum monthly maintenance needs allowance, the community spouse's income is increased to that minimum amount (see Section VII). There are several things that can be done concerning the couple's resources (assets).

A. Spend Down

After the resource assessment "snapshot," the institutionalized spouse can spend the amount designated as non-exempt resources to pay any debts the couple owe. In addition, the institutionalized spouse can purchase exempt resources. The most obvious one is for the institutionalized spouse's funds to be used to purchase prepaid funerals for both spouses. Additionally, a new or late model car can be purchased, repairs can be made to the home, and any needed appliances can be purchased. These are the most obvious and simplest steps that can be taken.

B. *Promissory Note or Purchase of Annuity*

A planning option available in some states is to give about one-half of the individual's resources to a third party and then loan the other one-half to the third party. The promissory note must meet Medicaid requirements. The note must be irrevocable, non-assignable, not self-cancelling, and bear appropriate interest. The loan term should be less than the life expectancy of the individual, based on social security life expectancy tables, though for practical purposes the term will be set at the penalty period. To illustrate, assume resources of $240,000, pension income of $1,500 monthly, $8,000 monthly nursing home expenses, and a transferred resource factor of $6,000 (average nursing home cost per state). The individual gives his child $120,000, loans his child $120,000, and receives a note paying $6,200 for 20 months. The penalty period is 20 months ($120,000 ÷ $6,000). The loan payment plus pension income pays $7,700 of the nursing home cost with the child paying $300 per month from this gift for a total of $6,000. After 20 months the individual qualifies for Medicaid and the child has $114,000. Know your state law before using this technique. The same can be done with a Medicaid compliant annuity, which is discussed below.

The Deficit Reduction Act of 2005 authorizes a particular type of annuity that can be utilized.[31] There are specific requirements for this type of annuity. It must be irrevocable, non-assignable, actuarially sound in that it pays out its interest and principal over the life expectancy of the annuitant based on social security life expectancy tables, and in the event the annuitant (nursing home resident) dies, the state must be named as the beneficiary of the remaining balance of the contract. These type of annuities can be funded with any liquid asset of the institutionalized spouse.

Assume a couple had $300,000 in resources, plus their home. Following the resource assessment, the community spouse is entitled to $126,400 and the institutionalized spouse only $2,000. That leaves $171,600 in excess resources. The community spouse now buys a Medicaid compliant annuity for the community spouse with the approximate $170,000 in excess resources, which pays the community spouse $3,000 monthly for five years. The state is the primary beneficiary with the children a secondary beneficiary. The institutionalized spouse now qualifies for Medicaid. There is no penalty for transfers between spouses. And the annuity is considered income of the community spouse and not a countable resource. You have to find a company that sells Medicaid compliant annuities. A variation of this approach involves purchasing the annuity before the resource assessment. This will lessen the resources for the community spouse and create some resources that must be spent down by the other spouse.

Some attorneys use a promissory note in much the same way as the annuity.[32] This was illustrated in the first paragraph above. The community spouse loans to one of the children the $171,600 and the child executes a Medicaid compliant promissory note. Remember the note cannot be a self-canceling note. It must be non-assignable and irrevocable. Interest should be paid consistent with IRS federal tax rates and monthly payments are made on the loan for a period of time that is less than the community spouse's life expectancy as determined under social security tables.

Both of these approaches require a clear understanding of Medicaid regulations in the lawyer's home state. But when properly executed, the annuity or earlier discussed promissory note can be quite beneficial.

X. Transfers to Trusts

A. Introduction

The Omnibus Budget Reconciliation Act of 1993 (OBRA 93) introduced rules to restrict the ability of persons who transfer assets into a trust to qualify for Medicaid. Prior to the enactment of OBRA 93, certain trusts known as Medicaid Qualifying Trusts were recognized as a valid means of sheltering one's assets while maintaining eligibility for Medicaid. A Medicaid Qualifying Trust, simply defined, was a grantor trust in which assets placed in the trust were only counted as resources available to the grantor if the trustee had discretion to disburse the assets to the grantor. If the trustee had no discretion to disburse the assets to the grantor, then those assets were not counted in determining the Medicaid eligibility of the grantor. Thus individuals with significant financial holdings could make themselves eligible for Medicaid by placing their non-exempt assets into a Medicaid Qualifying Trust. OBRA 93 eliminated the Medicaid Qualifying Trust as a planning tool. Section 1917(d) of the Social Security Act now requires that a state count a trust established with an individual's assets as a resource in determining the individual's eligibility for Medicaid with the exception of those trusts discussed in Section X.B.

B. Medicaid Exemption for Transfers to Trusts

Federal law recognizes certain trusts as exempt from the resource rules. One such trust is based on 42 U.S.C. § 1396p(d)(4)(A) and is useful when a disabled individual under 65 years of age receives a personal injury award or an inheritance.[33] This trust is sometimes termed a Payback Trust or a First Party Special Needs Trust. A sample trust form is in Appendix C. The trust can only be funded with assets of the individual; and the trust must be created for the individual's benefit by a parent, grandparent, a legal guardian of the individual, or a court. The trust must be for the sole benefit of the disabled person. Further, the trust must contain a payback provision to the state for Medicaid payments that have been paid by the state for the individual. This type of special needs trust exempts those trust assets from being considered resources for purposes of Medicaid eligibility. The trust will remain exempt throughout the person's lifetime, even beyond age 65; however, no assets should be added to the trust after the individual reaches age 65, nor should the assets be co-mingling with any other assets for the child. The trust can then be used to supplement the persons needs while still retaining the benefit of Medicaid or other government benefits. The trust assets will supplement the SSI and Medicaid benefits. The assets should not be used to provide for those basic necessities that are covered by the SSI program. Be certain of the requirements of your state Medicaid office.

A second type of trust authorized in 42 U.S.C. § 1396p(d)(4)(C) may hold the assets of an individual who is disabled as defined in section 1614(a)(3) and are exempt as a resource if each of the following is met:[34]

- The trust is established and managed by a nonprofit association.
- A separate account is maintained for each beneficiary of the trust, but, for purposes of investment and management of the trust's funds, the trust pools these accounts.
- The accounts in the trust are established for the sole benefit of individuals who are disabled as defined in section 1614(a)(3) by the individual, individual's parent, grandparent, legal guardian, or by a court.
- The trust is required to pay any remaining benefits left in the trust after the individual's death to the state up to the amount equal to the total amount of medical assistance paid on behalf of the individual by the state.

These trusts are referred to as "pooled trusts." A pooled trust that does not have the 65-year age limit of the prior trust allows an individual to qualify for Medicaid by transferring excess resources to the trust. The trust offers the benefit of pooling funds for investment purpose and management. The trust then can make distributions for permissible purposes much the same as the earlier discussed Payback Trust.

A third exemption is an irrevocable trust that pays income only to the individual. This trust, authorized in 42 U.S.C. § 1396p(d)(3)(B), will not be counted as a resource for Medicaid eligibility after the 60-month look-back period, but the income will be paid to the nursing home with Medicaid paying any balance owed. No principal can be expended. These trusts are referred to as Income Only Trusts or Medicaid Asset Protection Trusts A sample trust form is in Appendix E. The key to this type of trust is that no possibility must exist for the individual to receive any principal from this trust. For this reason its utility is limited, but in some situations this limitation is not that significant. For example, assume an individual owns a home with acreage, and two rental properties and $200,000 in various investments. The home, acreage, and rental properties could be placed in this type of trust with the elderly client receiving income only from the trust assets. There is a difference of opinion among attorneys as to whether or not the individual can act as trustee of their own trust. One view is that since the grantor has no discretion to make distributions of principal, then there is no reason the grantor cannot act as his or her own trustee. A more conservative approach is to name one of the children as the trustee to avoid any arguments from the state seeking to disallow the trust. Once the 60-month look-back period has been satisfied, then the transfer of these properties to the trust meets those requirements. The assets are no longer considered a resource. Since the individual receives income from the trust property, then the income is available for payment to the nursing home. The remaining assets could be placed in the trust, but since most individuals want to maintain the ability to access liquid assets for possible future needs, those assets could remain a resource available for the individual who may never need to be in nursing home care. If nursing home care becomes essential, then the earlier discussions concerning spend down and the use of Medicaid-compliant annuities or promissory notes are still possible options.

A fourth trust is used in those states that do not extend coverage to medically needy institutionalized persons who have income over certain levels. In those states a section 1396p(d)(4)(B) trust may be created to allow qualification for Medicaid benefits. In this situation, the individual has resources within the state's limits, usually $2,000, but has income in excess of three times the federal benefit rate discussed in Section V.B, which in 2019, is $2,313 monthly. The trusts will be composed of the individual's pension, social security, and other income, including any accumulated income from the trust. The trust must provide that the state will receive all amounts remaining in the trust upon the death of the individual up to an amount equal to the total medical assistance furnished to the individuals by the state.[35] These trusts are often referred to as Miller Trusts or Qualifying Income Trusts (QIT).[36]

The individual must first receive the income, then place it in the trust. If the individual transfers the right to receive the income to the trust, the transfer may be penalized under the transfer of assets provision. Payments from a QIT are limited to a personal needs allowance, spousal and dependent allowances, medical and remedial expenses not covered by a third party, including nursing facility services and home- and community-based services provided under the waiver programs.

After eligibility has been established through a QIT, an institutionalized individual may have to pay some, if not most, of her income to the nursing facility less the permitted payments. After these payments are withheld, all remaining income of the individual is classified as the patient pay amount and must be paid to the nursing facility. A sample trust is shown in Appendix D.

XI. *Estate Recovery*

States are required to seek recovery of expenditures made on behalf of Medicaid recipients who meet certain conditions. The term *estate* is defined as all real and personal property and other assets included within the individual's estate, as defined for purposes of state probate law . . . and . . . may include, at the option of the state . . . any other real and personal property and other assets in which the individual had any legal title or interest at the time of death . . . including such assets conveyed to a survivor, heir, or assign of the deceased individual through joint tenancy, tenancy in common, survivorship, life estate, living trust, or other arrangement.[37]

A state is required to seek recovery against the following classes of persons:[38]

- ▪ An individual who becomes an inpatient in a nursing facility, intermediate care facility for the mentally disabled, or other medical institution, when the individual is required to turn over all of his income but a personal needs allowance *and* it is determined after notice and opportunity for a hearing that the individual cannot be expected to be discharged to return home;

- An individual who was 55 years of age or older when she received medical assistance, provided that the state may only seek recovery for nursing facility services, home- and community-based services, related hospital services, and prescription drug services. A state may at its option seek recovery for other items and services paid for under the state's plan; or
- An individual who received benefits under a long-term care insurance policy issued pursuant to a state plan in which assets or resources were to be disregarded by those who purchased the policy and Medicaid pays for the individual's nursing facility costs and other long-term care services for said individual. This applies only to state long-term care insurance plans that were approved after May 14, 1993. An individual who purchased a long-term policy in a state with an approved plan as of May 14, 1993, is exempt.[39]

A lien may not be imposed against the property, either real or personal, of the Medicaid recipient until the death of the recipient. However, there are two exceptions to this rule.[40]

- If a court judgment is obtained against an individual for benefits that were incorrectly paid the individual.
- If in the case of real estate, the Medicaid recipient is institutionalized in a nursing facility, intermediate care facility for the mentally disabled or other medical institution that requires him to spend all of his income for medical care but a personal needs allowance as a condition of receiving the services *and* it is determined that he cannot be expected to be discharged and to return home.

However, a lien may not be imposed against the residence of a Medicaid recipient if any one of the following applies:[41]

- The spouse of the individual resides in the home;
- A child under 21 years of age resides in the home;
- A child over 21 years of age resides in the home who is disabled or blind; or,
- A brother or sister of the individual resides in the home who holds an equity interest in the home and who has resided there at least one year before the individual was admitted to the medical institution.

Recovery cannot be made against the estate of the institutionalized individual until after his spouse's death. Recovery cannot be made against the estate after the surviving spouse's death if any one of the following applies:[42]

- The institutionalized individual is survived by a child under 21 years of age.
- The institutionalized individual is survived by a child over 21 years of age who is disabled or blind.

Furthermore, no recovery is permitted against a deceased institutionalized individual's former residence if any of the following applies:[43]

- A brother or sister of the institutionalized individual resided in the home for at least one year prior to the date of the individual's admission to the medical facility and the sibling continues to reside in the home.
- A son or daughter resided in the institutionalized individual's home for at least two years prior to the date of the individual's admission to the medical facility and said child proves to the state that they provided care which allowed the institutionalized individual to remain in the home and the child continues to reside in the home.

In addition to the preceding, states are required to establish procedures under which the state Medicaid agency must waive estate recovery if estate recovery would create an *undue hardship*.[44]

XII. *Appeals Procedure for Medicaid*

Generally, the state Medicaid agency must afford a hearing to any of the following individuals:[45]

- Any applicant who requests a hearing because his claim for services is denied or is not acted upon with reasonable promptness
- Any recipient who requests a hearing because she believes the agency has taken an action erroneously
- Any resident of a skilled nursing facility (SNF) or nursing facility (NF) who requests a hearing because he believes that the SNF or NF has erroneously determined that he must be transferred or discharged

The state's Medicaid agency must provide for either a hearing before the agency or an evidentiary hearing at the local level with the right to appeal to a state agency hearing.[46] The state may offer local hearings in some areas but not in others.[47] The hearing system must meet the due process standards set forth in *Goldberg v. Kelly*, 397 U.S. 254 (1970).[48]

The state or local Medicaid agency must mail the notice to the individual at least ten days before for the date of the action.[49] However, an advance notice of ten days is not required if:[50]

- The agency has factual information confirming the death of the Medicaid recipient.
- The agency receives a clear written statement signed by the recipient that the recipient no longer wishes to receive Medicaid services or gives information that requires either termination or reduction of services and the recipient indicates his understanding of this fact.
- The recipient has been admitted to an institution where he is ineligible for Medicaid services.
- The recipient's whereabouts are unknown and the post office returns the recipient's mail indicating that the recipient left no forwarding address.

- The recipient has been accepted for Medicaid services in another jurisdiction, including another jurisdiction within the same state.
- The recipient's physician prescribes a change in the recipient's level of medical care.
- The date of action will occur in less than ten days in cases involving a resident of nursing facility who is a threat to the health or safety of the other residents of the facility.

A state Medicaid agency may require that the request for a hearing be in writing and the state must allow the applicant or recipient a reasonable time, not to exceed 90 days from the date that the notice of action was mailed, to request a hearing.[51] The state is not permitted to limit or interfere with the applicant or recipient's freedom to make a request for a hearing and the state is permitted to assist the applicant or recipient in submitting and processing her request for a hearing.[52] In cases involving a recipient of Medicaid services, if the recipient requests a hearing before the date of action, the state cannot terminate or reduce services until a decision is rendered after the hearing unless:[53]

- The sole issue is one of federal or state law or policy.
- The agency promptly informs the recipient in writing that services are to be terminated or reduced pending the hearing decision.

If an applicant or recipient requests a hearing before the date of the action and services are provided by the state Medicaid agency, the agency is permitted to institute recovery procedures against the applicant or recipient for the cost of those services if the agency prevails at the hearing.[54]

If a recipient requests a hearing no more than ten days after the date of the action, a state may, if it wishes, reinstate services, and if the state chooses to reinstate services, the services must continue until a hearing decision is issued, unless at the hearing it is determined that the sole issue is one of federal or state law or policy.[55] The state Medicaid agency must reinstate and continue services until a decision is rendered following a hearing if action is taken by the state agency without the required advance notice, the recipient requests a hearing within ten days of the mailing date of the notice of action, and the agency determines that the action resulted from other than the application of federal or state law or policy.[56]

If a hearing is requested, the applicant or the recipient, or his representative, must be afforded the opportunity to:[57]

- Examine at a reasonable time before the date of the hearing and during the hearing the content of the applicant/recipient's case file and all documents and records to be used by the state, local agency, skilled nursing facility, or nursing facility (whichever may be the case) at the hearing.
- Produce witnesses.
- Establish all pertinent facts and circumstances.
- Present an argument without undue interference.
- Question or refute any testimony or evidence, including an opportunity to confront and cross-examine adverse witnesses. The hearing

must be conducted at a reasonable time, date, and place and only after adequate written notice of the hearing has been given.[58] In addition, the hearing must be conducted by an impartial official or individual who has not been directly involved in the initial determination of the action in question.[59]

If the hearing involves medical issues such as those concerning a diagnosis, an examining physician's report, or a medical review team's decision, and if the hearing officer considers it necessary to have a medical assessment other than that of the individual involved in making the original decision, such a medical assessment must be obtained at the state Medicaid agency's expense and be made part of the record.[60]

A hearing recommendation or decision must be based exclusively on evidence introduced at the hearing.[61] The record must consist only of:[62]

- The transcript or recording of testimony and exhibits, or an official report containing the substance of what transpired at the hearing
- All papers and requests filed in the proceeding
- The recommendation or decision of the hearing officer

The decision that follows an evidentiary hearing must be in writing and it must summarize the facts and identify the regulations that support the hearing officer's decision.[63] The state Medicaid agency must take final administrative action within 90 days from the date of the request for a hearing.[64] If a local evidentiary hearing is held and an adverse decision is rendered against the applicant or recipient, the agency must:[65]

- Inform the applicant or recipient of the decision;
- Inform the applicant or recipient that they have a right to appeal the decision to the state agency, in writing, within 15 days of the mailing of the notice of the adverse decision;
- Inform the applicant or recipient of their right to request that their appeal be a de novo hearing; and,
- Discontinue services after the adverse decision.

Unless the applicant or recipient specifically requests a de novo hearing after a local evidentiary hearing, the state agency hearing may consist of a review by the agency hearing officer of the record of the local evidentiary hearing to determine whether the decision of the local hearing officer was supported by substantial evidence in the record.[66] A person who participated in the local decision that is being appealed is not permitted to participate in the state agency decision-making process.[67] And, finally, the state agency must notify the applicant or recipient in writing of the decision and inform her of her right to request a state Medicaid agency hearing or to seek judicial review, if available.[68]

Appendix A: Will with Testamentary Third Party Special Needs Trust for Couple with Handicapped Child/Person

This will is similar to the inter vivos trust for a handicapped person. It contains the same trust provisions as the inter vivos trust to ensure eligibility for SSI and Medicaid. Unlike the inter vivos trust, this will has traditional provisions for a will and creates a testamentary trust for the handicapped person. The will is drafted for a handicapped child, but the word "child" may be changed to the appropriate relationship or the word "individual" can be inserted. An excellent ABA resource is Clifton B. Kruse, Jr., *Third Party and Self-Created Trusts*, 3rd edition, American Bar Association (Chicago, 2002).

LAST WILL AND TESTAMENT

OF

[FULL NAME OF CLIENT]

I, [full name of client], currently of [client's city], [client's state], make this my last will and testament, hereby revoking all wills and codicils previously made by me.

1. Family Information. My [husband or wife]'s name is [husband or wife's full name], and all references in this will to "my [husband or wife]" are only to [him or her].

My [son or daughter], [handicapped child's full name], is handicapped to such a degree as to require special care and due to [his or her] condition, no outright distribution is made to my [son or daughter]. My other [child is or children are], [full names of children], and all references in this will to "my [child is or children are]" only to [him her or them].

COMMENT: The full name of the spouse should be inserted, then the full name of each of the children is also inserted. As can be seen, the handicapped child is treated differently than the other children to make it clear that the handicapped child has no outright distribution under the will. If there are step-children or the concern to include after-born children, adopted or illegitimately born children, or the disinheritance of a child, then reference should be made to paragraph 1 in the Simple Will in Chapter 2, Section XIV.

---

2. Payment of Debts, Death Taxes and Funeral Expenses. I direct that all of my just debts, my funeral expenses, costs of estate administration, and death taxes, if any, be paid from the residue of my estate as soon as possible after my death. I further direct that any real property that is subject to a

mortgage or lien shall pass under my will subject to such mortgage or lien, rather than such indebtedness being paid from my estate. Death taxes means any estate or inheritance taxes, but not generation-skipping transfer taxes, imposed under the laws of any jurisdiction due to my death on any property passing by reason of my death whether or not such property passes under this will. Any generation-skipping transfer taxes resulting from a transfer occurring under my will shall be paid from the property that incurred such tax and shall not be paid from my other estate assets.

COMMENT: This is a standard paragraph requiring payment of final expenses. If there is real estate subject to a mortgage, the second sentence of the paragraph makes the distribution of that real estate subject to the mortgage rather than the mortgage being paid from the residue of the estate. If there is no such encumbered real estate, the sentence can be deleted. Of course, if the mortgage is to be paid from the residue, then the sentence should be deleted; or to avoid any confusion, the sentence should be redrafted to clarify that mortgage indebtednesses on real estate are to be paid from the estate. Any state or federal death taxes are to be paid from the residue. If any part of those taxes are to be paid otherwise, then specific provisions should be made for those payments.

---

3. Disposition of Tangible Personal Property. I give to my [husband or wife], all of my personal and household effects, including but not limited to furniture, furnishings, appliances, clothing, jewelry, automobiles and any other similar tangible personal property. If my [husband or wife] does not survive me, I give all such tangible personal property to my [child or children], in as nearly equal shares as is possible.

OPTION 1: If no agreement personal representative decides If my children cannot agree upon this division within ninety (90) days after the appointment of my personal representative, then the division made by my personal representative shall be final and binding upon my children and shall not be subject to question by anyone or in any court.

OPTION 2: If no agreement sell and pass to residue If my children cannot agree upon this division within ninety (90) days after the appointment of my personal representative, then my personal representative shall sell all property with respect to which my children have not reached an agreement and the net sales proceeds shall be distributed as part of the residue of my estate.

COMMENT: Gifts of personal property can be the source of family disagreements and even litigation. While the initial gift of such property to the surviving spouse is not a problem, the problem arises when the personal property passes to the children. Options 1 and 2 provide two different approaches for handling distribution in the event of a disagreement. The lawyer may choose either of those options, write his/her own method of resolving the conflict, or leave out these options and hope for the best. This writer has found that going to court over grandmother's clock is something most clients don't want. Thus, Option 1, Option 2, or some variation may be helpful.

I may leave with my will or among my papers a handwritten letter or handwritten memorandum concerning the distribution of certain items of my tangible personal property. If so, I direct my personal representative to distribute those items of my tangible personal property as I have provided in that letter or memorandum.

COMMENT: Some clients have items of personal property that they want to give to particular family members or friends. Rather than having a lengthy will naming these items and then having to document their transfer to the court, some lawyers prefer the use of a handwritten letter that is dated and signed at the bottom of the page by the testator as a preferable option. This approach allows the ease of changing the document over the years. It has the disadvantage of possibly not being an enforceable document depending on state law. If the document qualifies under state law as a holographic codicil or due to enactment of Section 2-513 of the Uniform Probate Code, then it is enforceable and the personal representative is required to account for those items named in the letter and to ensure their distribution to the correct beneficiary. A problem with the handwritten letter is that it is unlikely that it will be written in a way to address the lapse of a gift if a beneficiary predeceases the testator or the applicability of the rule of ademption in the event the gift is no longer in existence at the testator's death. The lawyer must refer to his or her own state law as to these two issues.

---

4. Residuary Estate. I give the residue of my estate to my [husband or wife], if [he or she] survives me. If my [husband or wife] does not survive me, I give the residue of my estate one-half (^{1}/2) to my children, [full names of children who receive outright], in equal shares. If a child is deceased, such child's share shall be distributed to [describe alternate distribution plan]. I give the remaining one-half (^{1}/2) of the residue of my estate to my trustee for [full name of handicapped child] to be held in trust for [him or her] to be administered and distributed according to the following terms:

COMMENT: This residuary clause gives the entire residue to the surviving spouse. Obviously, if there is no surviving spouse then appropriate changes must be made. The estate then passes outright to those children other than the handicapped child. The handicapped child's share then passes into the testamentary trust in the will. If a child who is to receive a distribution outright is deceased, the will must address the alternate distribution, such as per stirpes among that child's own descendants, or whatever other plan of distribution is desired. Also, a decision must be made as to what percentage of the estate is to be distributed to each child and then appropriate changes must be made to this paragraph.

---

a. Throughout the lifetime of my [son or daughter], [full name of handicapped child], unless this trust is sooner terminated, the trustee shall pay or use all, part, or none of the income and principal of the trust to or for the benefit of my [son or daughter], [full name of handicapped child], to provide for [his or her] extra and supplemental care, maintenance, support and education, in addition to the benefits [he or she] otherwise receives as a result of [his or her] handicap or disability from any local, state or federal government, or from any public or private agencies, any of which provide services or benefits to persons who are handicapped.

COMMENT: This is a typical wording for a special needs trust. The intent is to give the trustee sole discretion in making distributions and to clarify that all distributions are supplemental to other benefits the beneficiary receives.

---

b. It is the express purpose of this trust to supplement other benefits which my [son or daughter] is entitled to receive. This trust is not intended to provide basic support, but rather is to be a discretionary trust to provide for supplemental needs of my [son or daughter] which are not otherwise provided for by various public and private assistance. To this end, the trustee may provide benefits for my [son or daughter] which the trustee considers necessary for [his or her] care, maintenance, support and education that cannot, in the trustee's opinion, be provided by the aforementioned public and private assistance programs. This includes but is not limited to such items as vacation, entertainment and recreational trips and the expenses of a traveling companion to accompany my [son or daughter] on such trips; personal items such as radios, televisions and other electronic entertainment devices; healthcare services, supplies, and special equipment; training programs; and rehabilitation supplemental to those my [son or daughter] is entitled to receive under any public or private assistance program. The trustee's obligation to make such payments is entirely discretionary; provided, however, the trustee may not exercise any discretion in making distributions from this trust that would make my [son or daughter] ineligible for any public or private benefits otherwise available to my [son or daughter] from any agency, private or public, including state or federal social service agencies.

COMMENT: This paragraph continues to clarify that the trust is supplemental to basic needs that are provided by state or federal programs, such as SSI or Medicaid. The third and fourth sentences are not essential and may be omitted. The final sentence in the paragraph makes it clear that the trustee is not permitted to make any distributions that would cause ineligibility for assistance benefits, such as SSI and Medicaid.

c. Any payments from this trust shall be paid directly to the person or business which supplies such services or benefits.

COMMENT: This paragraph may not be essential in some states. It is inserted to avoid the result of a distribution being treated as a resource for the beneficiary if it is paid to an account such as a guardianship account held for the benefit of the beneficiary from which payments are made for services or benefits received by the beneficiary. Some states take the position that such a distribution is a resource, which will then create partial or total ineligibility for government benefits. Making direct distributions to the provider of the services or benefits should avoid this unintended result.

d. This trust shall terminate upon the death of my [son or daughter] and shall be distributed to [describe distribution plan]. In the event of a determination by any agency or court of competent jurisdiction that the income or principal of this trust is liable for the basic maintenance, support and medical care of my [son or daughter] which would otherwise be provided for [him or her] by local, state, or federal government agencies or programs, or from any public or private agencies, then and in such event this trust shall terminate and the then remaining trust assets shall be distributed to [describe distribution plan].

COMMENT: Provisions must be added to state the recipient of trust assets upon the death of the beneficiary. The second sentence in the paragraph is not essential, but in most situations it is desirable. As can be seen, this sentence requires the trust to terminate and be distributed in the event a court or government agency treats the trust as a resource for the beneficiary. Obviously, the recipient of the trust assets must be someone the grantor believes will maintain the trust assets for the benefit of the beneficiary even though those assets will then be owned by that person.

5. Protection from Creditors. The trust beneficiary shall not have the right to sell, transfer, assign, alienate, pledge, or in any way encumber trust

assets, including income and principal, nor shall trust assets be subject to execution, levy, sale, garnishment, attachment, bankruptcy, or other legal proceedings. Any such actions by the trust beneficiary or a third party seeking to enforce a claim against the trust assets shall not be recognized under any circumstances by the trustee. These provisions do not prevent the trustee from making distributions for the benefit of the trust beneficiary in such amounts and at such times as the trustee determines necessary for the trust beneficiary as required in paragraph 4 above.

COMMENT: This is a standard paragraph that precludes the trust assets from being attached by claims of creditors, including government agencies seeking reimbursement for payments made by them under a Medicaid or other government program.

---

6. Trustee Powers. In the administration of the trusts, the trustee shall have the following powers and rights and all others granted by law:

a. To sell publicly or privately any trust property, for cash or on time, without an order of court and upon such terms and conditions as my trustee deems proper; and no person dealing with my trustee shall have any obligation to look to the application of the purchase money.

b. To invest and reinvest all or any part of the principal of the trust in any stocks, bonds, mortgages, shares or interests in common trust funds, mutual funds, or other securities or property, real, personal, or mixed, and of any kind or nature whatsoever, as the trustee deems proper, and without diversification if the trustee deems it advisable, irrespective of whether or not such securities or property are eligible for trust investment under state or any other law, and may change any investment received or made by the trustee, and may hold cash if the trustee deems it advisable.

c. To exercise broad discretion as to diversification of trust property, and shall not be required to reduce any concentrated holdings merely because of such concentration, and shall have full discretion as to the percentage to be invested in fixed income securities, and is specifically relieved from any requirements, legal or otherwise, as to the percentage of the trust assets to be invested in fixed income securities, and may invest or retain invested any trust estates wholly in common stocks.

d. To sell, convey, lease or mortgage, repair and improve, and take any and all other steps with regard to any real estate that may at any time be a part of the principal of the trust; and any lease of such real property or contract with regard thereto made by the trustee shall be binding for the full period of the lease or contract, even though the period shall extend beyond the termination of the trust.

e. To vote shares of stock held in the trust at stockholders' meetings in person or by special, limited, or general proxy, with or without power of substitution, as seems best to the trustee.

f. To participate in the liquidation, reorganization, consolidation, incorporation and reincorporation, or any other financial readjustment of any corporation, limited liability company or business in which the trust is, or shall be financially interested.

g. To borrow money from any source for any purpose connected with the protection, preservation, improvement or development of the trust hereunder, whenever in the trustee's judgment the trustee deems it advisable, and as security to mortgage or pledge any real estate or personal property forming a part of the trust upon such terms and conditions as the trustee may deem advisable.

h. To hold any and all securities in bearer form, in the trustee's own name, or the name of some other person, partnership, or corporation, or in the name of a duly appointed nominee, with or without disclosing the fiduciary ownership.

i. To divide the principal of the trust property into parts or shares and to distribute or allot same, and to make such division in cash or in kind or both. For the purpose of such division or allotment, the judgment of the trustee concerning the propriety thereof and relative value of property so distributed or allotted shall be binding and conclusive with respect to all interested persons.

j. To merge and consolidate the trust property of any separate trust held hereunder with other trusts and then to administer such trust property as a single trust provided the separate trust is for the benefit of the same persons with substantially the same terms, conditions and federal tax consequences.

k. To pay such income and principal during the minority or incapacity of any beneficiary for whose benefit income and principal may be expended, in any one or more of the following ways: (1) directly to the beneficiary; (2) to the legal guardian or committee of the beneficiary; (3) to a relative of the beneficiary to be expended by the relative for the beneficiary; or (4) by expending the same directly for the beneficiary. Any distribution is subject to provisions in paragraph 4. The trustee shall not be obliged to see to the application of the funds so expended, but the receipt of such person shall be full acquittance to the trustee.

l. To continue and operate any business owned by me at my death and to do any and all things deemed appropriate by the trustee, including the power to form a limited liability company or incorporate the business and to put additional capital into the business, for such time as the trustee deems advisable, without liability for loss resulting from the continuance or operation of the business except for the trustee's own negligence; and to close out, liquidate, or sell the business at such time and upon such terms as the trustee deems proper, and in this connection a sale may be made (pursuant to an agreement entered into by me during my lifetime, or otherwise) to a partner, officer, member, employee or beneficiary under this trust. I am aware of the fact that certain risks are inherent in the operation of any business and, therefore, my trustee shall not be liable for any loss resulting from the retention and operation of any business unless such loss results directly from my trustee's gross negligence or willful misconduct.

m. To have the same powers, authorities, and discretions in the management of the trust as I would have in the management and control of my own personal assets. The trustee may continue to exercise any powers and discretions granted in this instrument for a reasonable period after the termination of any trust under this instrument.

COMMENT: The preceding powers are a set of standard powers that appear throughout this book. The powers should be reviewed to be certain that you the lawyer understand each power, the client is in agreement with each of the powers granted, and that the powers granted are needed. Because this is a generic and broad statement of powers, some of these powers may not be necessary. For example, powers to sell or lease real estate are not needed if the grantor knows the trust will consist only of cash and other intangible investments.

---

7. Limitation on Powers of Individual Trustee. Notwithstanding any other powers granted to my trustee in this instrument, an individual trustee (a) shall have no power to make payments or distributions that would discharge the trustee's legal obligation to support the trust beneficiary, (b) shall not exercise any power or discretion in any manner that would be deemed to be a general power of appointment under Internal Revenue Code Section 2041, (c) shall be limited by the ascertainable standard of "maintenance, support, health and education" when making payments or distributions to the trustee personally or to anyone for whom the trustee has a beneficial interest, and (d) shall possess no incidence of ownership or powers with respect to life insurance in which the trustee is the insured and has fiduciary power over such life insurance.

COMMENT: There are some situations in which an individual trustee may have adverse estate or income tax consequences when given broad powers as trustee. If a corporate trustee is used, then this paragraph is not needed. But an individual trustee must be certain that acting as trustee does not result in any adverse estate or income tax consequences. This paragraph is intended to ensure that adverse tax consequences are avoided if overly broad powers are granted in the trust instrument. The lawyer is urged to exercise caution when using individual trustees coupled with broad discretionary powers of income and principal distribution to a trust beneficiary because of possible adverse tax consequences. An ABA resource to acquaint oneself with these issues is L. Rush Hunt and Lara Rae Hunt, A Lawyer's Guide to Estate Planning, American Bar Association (Chicago: 2018) § 14.4.

---

8. Trustee Resignation. My trustee may resign at any time by giving written notice to my successor trustee named below, if any, and if none, then

written notice shall be given to each current adult income beneficiary who is then living.

COMMENT: If a trustee resigns, there must be some method of notice and appointment of a successor trustee. This paragraph provides a method of notification. It is not an essential trust provision, but is a helpful one.

---

9. Trustee Succession and Appointment. The initial trustee shall be [name of trustee]. If my initial trustee ceases to act as trustee due to death, incompetency, resignation or any other reason, then [name of successor trustee] shall be successor trustee. My successor trustee may name [his or her] own successor trustee by a written instrument delivered to the successor trustee, or by will. The successor trustee shall be an individual or a financial institution possessing trust powers under state or federal law. Any further vacancy in the office of trustee shall be filled by decision of the probate court where I resided at the time of my death. No trustee or successor trustee shall be required to post a surety bond for serving as trustee or successor trustee.

COMMENT: A decision must be made as to succession of trustees and the method of appointing a successor trustee if all of those named successor trustees are unable to serve. It is also essential to clarify whether successor trustees must only be financial institutions or if individuals may also be considered. Once a decision is made as to the succession of trustees, then the last three sentences should be reviewed to be certain to what extent each of those are needed.

---

10. Powers of Successor Trustee. Each successor trustee shall have the same rights, titles, powers, duties, discretions, and immunities and otherwise be in the same position as if originally named trustee. No successor trustee shall be personally liable for any act or failure to act of a predecessor trustee. Further, a successor trustee may accept the account furnished and the property delivered by or for a predecessor trustee without liability for so doing, and such acceptance shall be a full and complete discharge to the predecessor trustee.

COMMENT: This paragraph clarifies that a successor trustee has the same powers as the initial trustee. Further, the paragraph relieves the successor trustee from liability for the prior acts of the resigning trustee and waives any requirements of audit or inquiry into the activities of the prior trustee. This is essential for any successor trustee.

---

11. Compensation of Trustee. **OPTION 1: Corporate trustee compensation** A corporate trustee shall receive compensation in accordance with its regular schedule of fees in effect at the time such services are rendered.

OPTION 2: Individual does not receive compensation An individual trustee shall not be paid any compensation, but shall be reimbursed for out-of-pocket expenses.

OPTION 3: Individual does receive compensation An individual trustee shall be paid [insert amount of compensation] as compensation for such services and shall be reimbursed for out-of-pocket expenses.

COMMENT: Three options are provided, but the actual drafting of this paragraph may be different than each of these options. If the only trustee to be used is a corporate trustee, then Option 1 is a standard trust provision. If there is a possibility of individual trustees, then care should be given to the method for setting this fee. If no fee is to be paid because the trustee is a close family member, then it is suggested that Option 2 be used. If the grantor expects a fee to be charged, then an amount or a formula, such as a percentage of income or principal, must be set. It is unwise to simply provide for compensation to be a reasonable fee, as that leaves an individual trustee with great uncertainty as to the fee to be charged. Without the grantor clarifying compensation, the trustee could find him or herself in litigation with the beneficiary or the beneficiary's guardian.

---

12. Appointment of Personal Representative. My [husband or wife], shall be the personal representative of my estate. If my [husband or wife] fails to qualify as personal representative, or having qualified, dies, becomes incompetent, resigns, or declines to continue to serve, then my [relationship of successor PR] [name of successor PR] shall serve as my successor personal representative. Neither my [husband or wife] nor my successor personal representative shall be required to furnish any surety bond for serving as my personal representative.

COMMENT: The full names of the personal representative and successor personal representative are required as is a decision concerning the waiver of a surety bond. The form, as drafted, assumes the intent to waive such bond.

---

13. Powers of Personal Representative. I hereby grant to my personal representative (including my successor personal representative) the absolute power to deal with any property, real or personal, held in my estate, as freely as I might in the handling of my own affairs. This power may be exercised independently and without the approval of any court, and no person dealing

with my personal representative shall be required to inquire into the propriety of the actions of my personal representative. Without in any way limiting the generality of the foregoing provisions, I grant to my personal representative in addition to those powers specified under state law the following powers:

a. To sell, exchange, assign, transfer and convey any security or property, real or personal, held in my estate at public or private sale, at such time and at such reasonable price and upon such reasonable terms and conditions (including credit) as my personal representative may determine; and without regard to whether or not such sale is necessary in order to settle my estate.

b. To lease any real estate for such term, or terms, and upon such reasonable conditions and rentals and in such manner as my personal representative deems proper, and any lease so made shall be valid and binding for its full term even though such lease term extends beyond the duration of the administration of my estate; to make repairs, replacements and improvements, structural or otherwise, to any such real estate; to subdivide real estate, dedicate real estate to public use and grant easements as my personal representative deems proper.

c. To employ accountants, attorneys and such other agents as my personal representative deems necessary; to pay reasonable compensation for such services and to charge same to (or apportion same between) income and principal as my personal representative deems proper.

d. To join with my [husband or wife] on my behalf in filing income tax returns, or to consent for gift tax purposes to having gifts made by either of us during my life considered as made one-half by each of us, and any resulting tax liability shall be paid by my estate, except such portion as my personal representative and my [husband or wife] agree should be paid by my [husband or wife].

COMMENT: A statement of the powers of the personal representative is not essential, as those powers are specified by state law; however, those state laws may not be sufficiently broad. Often state laws do not include power over real estate. Paragraph 13.c may not be essential, but this writer prefers to clarify that the personal representative may hire at the expense of the estate professionals to assist in estate settlement. Paragraph 13.d deals with the signing of tax returns and, while not essential, still is appropriate in most situations.

---

14. Certification of Incompetency. **OPTION 1: Decided by treating physician** Any person acting or named to act in a fiduciary capacity in this will is considered to be unable to serve or to continue serving when a physician whom such person has consulted within the prior three years has certified as to such consultation and the certification states that the person is incapable of managing the affairs of my estate or any trust I have established, regardless

of cause and regardless of whether there is an adjudication of incompetency. No person is liable to anyone for actions taken in reliance on the physician's certification or for dealing with a personal representative or trustee other than the one removed for incompetency based on these certifications.

OPTION 2: Decided by two physicians Any person acting or named to act in a fiduciary capacity in this will is considered to be unable to serve or to continue serving when a written certification is received from two (2) physicians, both of whom have personally examined the person and at least one (1) of whom is board-certified in the specialty most closely associated with the health condition alleged to cause such incompetency. The certification must state that the person is incapable of managing his or her own finances, regardless of cause and regardless of whether there is an adjudication of incompetence, or need for a conservator, guardian, or other personal representative. No person is liable to anyone for actions taken in reliance on these certifications, or for dealing with a personal representative or trustee other than the one removed for incompetency based on these certifications.

COMMENT: This provision relates both to paragraph 9 concerning the succession of trustees, paragraph 12 regarding the successor personal representative, and paragraph 15 concerning the appointment of an alternate guardian. It defines incompetency, which is one of those events requiring a successor trustee, personal representative or an alternate guardian. The first option involves consultation with the person's personal physician, whereas Option 2 involves a panel of two physicians, one of whom is board certified in the speciality most closely associated with the health condition of the person acting in a fiduciary capacity. Clients differ as to which provision they prefer. Absent a strong preference by the testator, Option 1 is the provision most frequently used.

---

15. Appointment of Guardian. If my [husband or wife] does not survive me, my [relationship to guardian], [name of guardian], shall be guardian of each child for whom it is necessary to appoint a guardian. If [name of guardian] does not act as guardian, or having qualified dies, becomes incompetent, resigns, or declines to continue to serve, then my [relationship to alternate guardian], [name of alternate guardian] shall be guardian of each child for whom it is necessary to appoint a guardian. No surety bond shall be required of my guardians.

COMMENT: This is a standard paragraph naming a guardian for any children for whom a guardian is necessary, which includes the handicapped child in this drafting situation and may include other children. Some drafting changes may be needed due to state law requirements if the handicapped child is an adult child for whom the testator is the court-appointed guardian.

If there is only one possible guardian and no alternate guardian, then the second sentence can be omitted. This paragraph omits the requirement of a surety bond.

---

16. Employment of Attorney. I request but do not require that my personal representative employ the law firm of [insert name of law firm], [city], [state] to be my estate's attorney as the attorneys in that law firm are the most familiar with my intentions expressed in this will.

COMMENT: This paragraph may be appropriate when the client is expecting the lawyer who drafted the will to be available to settle the estate. Often the children do not know the parent's preference for a lawyer, thus the provision is inserted. The employment of the testator's lawyer is made permissive to avoid any appearance of self-dealing by the lawyer preparing the will. There will be situations in which the client insists the wording be made mandatory. If so, the lawyer may wish to document this fact by memo to the file, signed by the client.

IN TESTIMONY WHEREOF, I, [full name of client], sign my name to this instrument this _____ day of _____, [current year], and being first duly sworn, do hereby declare to the undersigned authority that I sign and execute this instrument as my last will and that I sign it willingly, that I execute it as my free and voluntary act for the purposes therein expressed, and that I am 18 years of age or older, of sound mind, and under no constraint or undue influence.

_____
[full name of client]

We _____ and _____, the witnesses, sign our names to this instrument, being first duly sworn, and do hereby declare to the undersigned authority that [full name of client] signs and executes this instrument as [his or her Last Will and Testament dated _____, [current year], and that [he or she] signs it willingly and that each of us, in the presence and hearing of [full name of client] and in the presence of the other subscribing witness, hereby signs this Last Will and Testament as witness to [full name of client]'s signing, and that to the best of their knowledge, [full name of client] is eighteen (18) years of age or older, of sound mind and under no constraint or undue influence, all on this _____ day of _____, [current year].

_____   _____
Witness   Address

_____   _____
Witness   Address

STATE OF [State of Notary]   )
) SCT.
COUNTY OF [County of Notary])
    Subscribed, sworn to, and acknowledged before me by [full name of client], and subscribed and sworn to before me by _____ and _____, witnesses, this the _____ day of _____, [current year].

                              _____
                              Notary Public, State at Large
                              My Commission Expires:_____

COMMENT: The preceding provisions are in compliance with the writer's own state law to avoid the necessity of locating witnesses to the will at a later date. This provision should be modified to meet the requirement of the lawyer's own state law.

PREPARED BY:

_____
[Name of Attorney]
[Name of Law Firm]
Attorneys at Law
[Street Address]
[City], [State] [Zip Code]
[Telephone Number]

Appendix B: Third Party Special Needs Inter Vivos Trust

This trust is one that may be used when provisions need to be made for a child or other person who has a disability that is severe enough for the person to qualify for Medicaid and SSI benefits. These types of trusts have several different common names, but the essence of the trust is that its benefits are paid only after state Medicaid and any other state or federal benefits. Thus, the trust operates as a supplement to those governmental benefits. This trust is typically used by third parties who desire to set aside funds for a person who qualifies for Medicaid benefits without the trust assets being considered resources that would disqualify the trust beneficiaries from that Medicaid benefit. An excellent ABA resource is Clifton B. Kruse, Jr., *Third Party and Self-Created Trusts*, 3rd edition, American Bar Association (Chicago, 2002).

TRUST AGREEMENT

I, [grantor's name], currently of [grantor's city], [grantor's state], as grantor and [trustee's name], currently of [trustee's city], [trustee's state], as trustee hereby enter into this trust agreement, and I transfer to my trustee the property described in Schedule A. This property and all investments, reinvestments and additions which may sometimes be referred to in this instrument as the "trust property" or "trust assets" are to be held subject to the following provisions:

COMMENT: This trust provides for a separate trustee from the grantor. If the grantor and trustee are to be the same person, then a minor modification should be made to this paragraph to reflect this person is acting as grantor and trustee.

---

1. Name of Trust. This instrument and the initial trust hereby established may be named the "[full name of handicapped child] Trust."

COMMENT: It is not essential that a trust have a name, but it has become common practice in recent years. Thus, the beneficiary's name or some abbreviation of it may be used. If the lawyer prefers, some other name may be used.

---

2. Beneficiary Information. My child, [full name of handicapped child] whose date of birth is [insert date of birth], is the beneficiary of this trust and references to "my child" or "the beneficiary" are only to [him or her].

COMMENT: This paragraph is drafted for a handicapped beneficiary who is the child of the grantor. If the beneficiary is not a child, then the relationship should be inserted in lieu of the word "child" followed by the full name of the person who is the beneficiary. If the beneficiary is someone other than a child, then appropriate changes should be made to change the reference to "my child" to the appropriate relationship or to delete the phrase entirely. It is not essential to include the beneficiary's date of birth. This can be retained or deleted as deemed appropriate.

3. Trust Provisions for Beneficiary. The trustee shall hold and administer the trust property, including property which the trustee receives under my will or from any other source as follows:

a. Throughout the lifetime of the beneficiary, unless this trust is sooner terminated, the trustee shall pay or use all, part, or none of the income and principal of the trust to or for the benefit of the beneficiary, to provide for [his or her] extra and supplemental care, maintenance, support and education, in addition to the benefits my child otherwise receives as a result of [his or her] handicap or disability from any local, state or federal government, or from any public or private agencies, any of which provide services or benefits to persons who are handicapped.

COMMENT: This is a typical wording for a special needs trust. The intent is to give the trustee sole discretion in making distributions and to clarify that all distributions are supplemental to other benefits the beneficiary receives.

b. It is the express purpose of this trust to supplement other benefits which the beneficiary is entitled to receive. This trust is not intended to provide basic support, but rather is to be a discretionary trust to provide for supplemental needs of the beneficiary which are not otherwise provided for by various public and private assistance. To this end, the trustee may provide benefits for the beneficiary which the trustee considers necessary for [his or her] care, maintenance, support and education that cannot, in the trustee's opinion, be provided by the aforementioned public and private assistance programs. This includes but is not limited to such items as vacation, entertainment and recreational trips and the expenses of a traveling companion to accompany the beneficiary on such trips; personal items such as radios, televisions and other electronic entertainment devices; healthcare services, supplies, and special equipment; training programs; and rehabilitation supplemental to those the beneficiary is entitled to receive under any public or private assistance program. The trustee's obligation to make such payments is entirely discretionary; provided, however, the trustee may not exercise any discretion in making distributions from this trust that would make the beneficiary ineligible for any public or private benefits otherwise available to the beneficiary from any agency, private or public, including state or federal social service agencies.

COMMENT: This paragraph continues to clarify that the trust is supplemental to basic needs that are provided by state or federal programs, such as SSI or Medicaid. The third and fourth sentences are not essential and may be omitted. The final sentence in the paragraph makes it clear that the trustee is not permitted to make any distributions that would cause ineligibility for assistance benefits, such as SSI and Medicaid.

---

c. Any payments from this trust shall be paid directly to the person or business which supplies such services or benefits.

COMMENT: This paragraph may not be essential in some states. It is inserted to avoid the result of a distribution being treated as a resource for the beneficiary if it is paid to an account such as a guardianship account held for the benefit of the beneficiary, from which payments are made for services or benefits received by the beneficiary. Some states take the position that such a distribution is a resource, which will then create partial or total ineligibility for government benefits. Making direct distributions to the provider of the services or benefits should avoid this unintended result.

---

d. This trust shall terminate upon the death of the beneficiary and shall be distributed to [describe distribution plan]. In the event of a determination by any agency or court of competent jurisdiction that the income or principal of this trust is liable for the basic maintenance, support and medical care of the beneficiary which would otherwise be provided for the beneficiary by local, state, or federal government agencies or programs, or from any public or private agencies, then and in such event this trust shall terminate and the then remaining trust assets shall be distributed to [describe distribution plan].

COMMENT: Provisions must be added to state the recipient of trust assets upon the death of the beneficiary. The second sentence in the paragraph is not essential, but in most situations it is desirable. As can be seen, this sentence requires the trust to terminate and be distributed in the event a court or government agency treats the trust as a resource for the beneficiary. Obviously, the recipient of the trust assets must be someone the grantor believes will maintain the trust assets for the benefit of the beneficiary even though those assets will then be owned by that person.

---

4. Protection from Creditors. The trust beneficiary shall not have the right to sell, transfer, assign, alienate, pledge, or in any way encumber trust assets, including income and principal, nor shall trust assets be subject to execution, levy, sale, garnishment, attachment, bankruptcy, or other legal proceedings. Any such actions by the trust beneficiary or a third party seeking to enforce a claim against the trust assets shall not be recognized under any circumstances by the trustee. These provisions do not prevent the trustee from making distributions for the benefit of the trust beneficiary in such amounts and at such times as the trustee determines necessary for the trust beneficiary subject to the provisions in paragraph 3.

COMMENT: This is a standard paragraph that precludes the trust assets from being attached by claims of creditors, including government agencies seeking reimbursement for payments made by them under a Medicaid or other government program.

---

5. Trustee Powers. In the administration of the trusts, the trustee shall have the following powers and rights and all others granted by law:

a. To sell publicly or privately any trust property, for cash or on time, without an order of court, upon such terms and conditions as shall seem best to the trustee; and no person dealing with the trustee shall have any obligation to look to the application of the purchase money therefor.

b. To invest and reinvest all or any part of the principal of the trust assets in any stocks, bonds, mortgages, shares, or interests in common trust funds, mutual funds, or other securities or property, real, personal, or mixed, and of any kind or nature whatsoever, as the trustee deems advisable, and without diversification if the trustee deems it advisable, irrespective of whether or not such securities or property are eligible for trust investment under state or any other law, and may change any investment received or made by the trustee, and may hold cash if the trustee deems it advisable.

c. To exercise broad discretion as to diversification of trust property, and shall not be required to reduce any concentrated holdings merely because of such concentration, and shall have full discretion as to the percentage to be invested in fixed income securities, and is specifically relieved from any requirements, legal or otherwise, as to the percentage of the trust assets to be invested in fixed income securities, and may invest and retain invested any trust estate wholly in common stocks.

d. To sell, convey, lease or mortgage, repair and improve, and take any and all other steps with regard to any real estate that may at any time be a part of the principal of the trust; and any lease of such real property or contract with regard thereto made by the trustee shall be binding for the full period of the lease or contract, though said period shall extend beyond the termination of the trust.

e. To vote shares of stock held in the trust at stockholders' meetings in person or by special, limited, or general proxy, with or without power of substitution, as to the trustee seems best.

f. To participate in the liquidation, reorganization, consolidation, incorporation and reincorporation, or any other financial readjustment of any limited liability company, corporation or business in which the trust is or shall be financially interested.

g. To borrow money from any source for any purpose connected with the protection, preservation, improvement or development of the trust hereunder, whenever in the trustee's judgment the trustee deems it advisable, and as security to mortgage or pledge any real estate or personal property forming a part of the trust upon such terms and conditions as the trustee may deem advisable.

h. To hold any and all securities in bearer form, in the trustee's own name, or the name of some other person, partnership, or corporation, or in the name of a duly appointed nominee, with or without disclosing the fiduciary ownership thereof.

i. To divide the principal of the trust property into parts or shares and to distribute or allot same, the trustee is authorized to make such division in cash or in kind or both; and for the purpose of such division or allotment, the judgment of the trustee concerning the propriety thereof and relative value of property so distributed or allotted shall be binding and conclusive with respect to all persons interested herein.

j. To merge and consolidate the trust property of any separate trust held hereunder with other trusts and then to administer such trust property as a single trust provided the separate trust is for the benefit of the same persons with substantially the same terms, conditions and federal tax consequences.

k. To pay such income and principal during the minority or incapacity of any beneficiary to whom income is herein directed to be paid, or for whose benefit income and principal may be expended, in any one or more of the following ways: (1) directly to the beneficiary; (2) to the legal guardian or committee of the beneficiary; (3) to a relative of the beneficiary to be expended for the beneficiary; or (4) by expending the same directly for the beneficiary. Any distribution is subject to the provisions in paragraph 3. The trustee shall not be obliged to see to the application of the funds so paid, but the receipt of such person shall be full acquittance to the trustee.

l. To continue and operate any business owned by me at my death and to do any and all things deemed appropriate by the trustee, including the power to form a limited liability company or incorporate the business and to put additional capital into the business, for such time as the trustee deems advisable, without liability for loss resulting from the continuance or operation of the business except for the trustee's own negligence; and to close out, liquidate, or sell the business at such time and upon such terms as the trustee deems proper, and in this connection a sale may be made (pursuant to an agreement entered into by me during my lifetime, or otherwise) to a partner, officer, member, employee or beneficiary under this trust. I am aware of the fact that certain risks are inherent in the operation of any business and, therefore, my trustee shall not be liable for any loss resulting from the retention and operation of any business unless such loss results directly from my trustee's gross negligence or willful misconduct.

m. To have the same powers, authorities, and discretions in the management of the trust as I would have in the management and control of my own personal assets. The trustee may continue to exercise any powers and discretions hereunder for a reasonable period after the termination of any trust under this instrument.

COMMENT: The preceding powers are a set of standard powers that appear throughout this book. The powers should be reviewed to be certain that you the lawyer understand each power, the client is in agreement with each of the powers granted, and that the powers granted are needed. Because this is a generic and broad statement of powers, some of these powers may not be necessary. For example, powers to sell or lease real estate are not needed if the grantor knows the trust will consist only of cash and other intangible investments.

---

6. Limitation on Powers of Individual Trustee. Notwithstanding any other powers granted to my trustee in this instrument, an individual trustee (a) shall have no power to make payments or distributions that would discharge the trustee's legal obligation to support the trust beneficiary, (b) shall not exercise any power or discretion in any manner that would be deemed to be a general power of appointment under Internal Revenue Code Section 2041, (c) shall be limited by the ascertainable standard of "maintenance, support, health and education" when making payments or distributions to the trustee personally or to anyone for whom the trustee has a beneficial interest, and (d) shall possess no incidence of ownership or powers with respect to life insurance in which the trustee is the insured and has fiduciary power over such life insurance.

COMMENT: There are some situations in which an individual trustee may have adverse estate or income tax consequences when given broad powers as trustee. If a corporate trustee is used, then this paragraph is not needed. But an individual trustee must be certain that acting as trustee does not result in any adverse estate or income tax consequences. This paragraph is intended to ensure that adverse tax consequences are avoided if overly broad powers are granted in the trust instrument. The lawyer is urged to exercise caution when using individual trustees coupled with broad discretionary powers of income and principal distribution to a trust beneficiary because of possible adverse tax consequences. An ABA resource to acquaint oneself with these issues is L. Rush Hunt and Lara Rae Hunt, A Lawyer's Guide to Estate Planning, American Bar Association (Chicago: 2018) § 14.4.

7. Trustee Resignation. My trustee may resign at any time by giving written notice to my successor trustee named below, if any, and if none, then written notice shall be given to each current adult income beneficiary who is then living.

COMMENT: If a trustee resigns, there must be some method of notice and appointment of a successor trustee. This paragraph provides a method of notification. It is not an essential trust provision, but is a helpful one.

8. Trustee Succession and Appointment. If [trustee's name] dies, becomes incompetent, resigns or ceases to serve for any reason, then [insert name of first successor trustee] shall serve as successor trustee. If [insert name of first successor trustee] dies, becomes incompetent, resigns or ceases to serve for any reason, then [insert name of second successor trustee] shall serve as successor trustee. The last serving successor trustee may name [his or her] own successor trustee by a written instrument delivered to the successor trustee or by will. The successor trustee may be an individual or a financial institution possessing trust powers under state or federal law. Any further vacancy in the office of trustee shall be filled by decision of the probate court where I resided at the time of my death.

COMMENT: A decision must be made as to succession of trustees and the method of appointing a successor trustee if all of those named successor trustees are unable to serve. It is also essential to clarify whether successor trustees must only be financial institutions or if individuals may also be considered. Once a decision is made as to the succession of trustees, then the last three sentences should be reviewed to be certain to what extent each of those are needed.

9. Powers of Successor Trustee. Each successor trustee shall have the same rights, titles, powers, duties, discretions, and immunities and otherwise be in the same position as if originally named trustee. No successor trustee shall be personally liable for any act or failure to act of a predecessor trustee. Further, a successor trustee may accept the account furnished and the property delivered by or for a predecessor trustee without liability for so doing, and such acceptance shall be a full and complete discharge to the predecessor trustee.

COMMENT: This paragraph clarifies that a successor trustee has the same powers as the initial trustee. Further, the paragraph relieves the successor trustee from liability for the prior acts of the resigning trustee and waives any requirements of audit or inquiry into the activities of the prior trustee. This is essential for any successor trustee.

10. Compensation of Trustee. **OPTION 1: Corporate trustee compensation** A corporate trustee shall receive compensation in accordance with its regular schedule of fees in effect at the time such services are rendered.

OPTION 2: Individual does not receive compensation An individual trustee shall not be paid any compensation, but shall be reimbursed for out-of-pocket expenses.

OPTION 3: Individual does receive compensation An individual trustee shall be paid [insert amount of compensation] as compensation for such services and shall be reimbursed for out-of-pocket expenses.

COMMENT: Three options are provided, but the actual drafting of this paragraph may be different than each of these options. If the only trustee to be used is a corporate trustee, then Option 1 is a standard trust provision. If there is a possibility of individual trustees, then care should be given to the method for setting this fee. If no fee is to be paid because it is a close family member, then it is suggested that Option 2 be used. If the grantor expects a fee to be charged, then an amount or a formula, such as a percentage of income or principal, must be set. It is unwise to simply provide for compensation to be a reasonable fee, as that leaves an individual trustee with great uncertainty as to the fee to be charged. Without the grantor clarifying compensation, the trustee could find him or herself in litigation with the beneficiary or the beneficiary's guardian.

11. Court Accountings. To the extent such requirements can be waived, the trustee shall not be required (a) to file any inventory of trust property or accounts or reports of the administration of the trusts, or to register the trusts, in any court, (b) to furnish any bond or other security for the proper performance of the trustee's duties or (c) to obtain authority from a court for the exercise of any power conferred on the trustee by this instrument. This waiver does not preclude the trustee from registering any trust created in this instrument and petitioning a court having jurisdiction over registered trusts for a judicial ruling on any matter relating to administration of any trust created by this instrument.

COMMENT: The first sentence is to clarify the normal situation that an inter vivos trust is not subject to judicial oversight. The second sentence may be omitted, but is suggested as a potential benefit in some states. In a state in which a trust can be registered, it may be possible to have minor trust matters resolved by the court in which the trust is registered. This creates a simplified process for dealing with minor administrative matters. Without this provision, a court might be reluctant to decide matters for a trust that is not required to be registered under state law.

---

12. Severability. If any provisions of this trust shall be unenforceable, the remaining provisions shall nevertheless be carried into effect.

COMMENT: This is the same type of standard provision often seen in contracts that is intended to save the document if a particular provision is found to be invalid or void. It is doubtful this provision will have any practical effect in most trust situations, but it is a "boilerplate" provision that is frequently found in trust instruments and for which there is no disadvantage.

---

13. Certification of Incompetency. **OPTION 1: Decided by treating physician** Any person acting or named to act as a trustee in this instrument is considered to be unable to serve or to continue serving when a physician whom such person has consulted within the prior three years has certified as to such consultation and the certification states that the person is incapable of managing the affairs of the trusts I have established in this instrument, regardless of cause and regardless of whether there is an adjudication of incompetency. No person shall be liable to anyone for actions taken in reliance on the physician's certification, or for dealing with a trustee other than the one removed for incompetency based on such certification.

OPTION 2: Decided by two physicians Any person acting or named to act as a trustee in this instrument is considered to be unable to serve or to continue serving when a written certification is received from two (2) physicians, both of whom have personally examined the person and at least one (1) of whom is board-certified in the specialty most closely associated with the health condition alleged to cause such incompetency. The certification must state that the person is incapable of managing the affairs of this trust, regardless of cause and regardless of whether there is an adjudication of incompetence. No person is liable to anyone for actions taken in reliance on these physician's certifications, or for dealing with a trustee other than the one removed for incompetency based on these certifications.

COMMENT: This provision relates back to paragraph 8 concerning the succession of trustees. It defines incompetency, which is one of those events requiring a successor trustee. The first option involves consultation with the trustee's personal physician, whereas Option 2 involves a panel of two physicians, one of whom is board certified in the speciality most closely associated with the health condition of the trustee. Clients differ as to which provision they prefer and are more concerned about the provision when the grantor is also the initial trustee. Absent a strong preference by the grantor, Option 1 is the provision most frequently used.

14. Titles and References. The underscored titles of paragraphs in this instrument are for information purposes only and shall be given no legal effect.

COMMENT: This is another common "boilerplate" provision that is perhaps not essential, but for which there is no disadvantage.

15. Choice and Effect of Law. This trust agreement is entered into and executed in the [State or Commonwealth] of [name of state]. It shall be administered in accordance with the laws of that state.

COMMENT: It is a standard provision in both trust instruments and in contracts to specify the state law that applies in interpretation of the instrument. This will usually be the grantor's state of residency, but also should be the state in which the lawyer is licensed to practice.

16. Power to Amend or Revoke. I reserve the right from time to time by written instrument delivered to the trustee to amend or revoke this instrument and the trusts hereby evidenced, in whole or in part.

COMMENT: The trust instrument should specify whether it is revocable or irrevocable. This particular trust is a revocable trust that becomes irrevocable upon the death of the grantor. This is because the trust will be an unfunded trust and will only receive assets after the grantor's death. In some situations, the lawyer or client will want the trust to be irrevocable, such as, situations in which the grantor will currently transfer assets to the trust. This is not as easy as it seems. Such a transfer will raise gift tax considerations that must be addressed before making the trust irrevocable and transferring assets to the trust. The general recommendation is that the trust remain revocable.

The undersigned have signed this instrument and have established the foregoing trust on this the _____ day of _____, [Current Year].
GRANTOR:

_____

[grantor's name]

TRUSTEE:

_____

[trustee's name]

STATE OF [State of Notary]   )
) SCT.
COUNTY OF [County of Notary])

The undersigned, a Notary Public within and for the state and county aforesaid, does hereby certify that the foregoing trust agreement executed by [grantor's name], as grantor, was on this day produced to me in my county by [grantor's name], who executed, acknowledged and swore the same before me to be [his or her] act and deed in due form of law.

Given under my hand and notarial seal on this the ___ day of _____, [Current Year].

_____

Notary Public, State at Large
My commission expires:_____

STATE OF [State of Notary]   )
) SCT.
COUNTY OF [County of Notary])

The undersigned, a Notary Public within and for the state and county aforesaid, does hereby certify that the foregoing trust agreement executed by [trustee's name], as trustee, was on this day produced to me in my county by [trustee's name], who executed, acknowledged and swore the same before me to be [his or her] act and deed in due form of law.

Given under my hand and notarial seal on this the ___ day of _____, [Current Year].

_____

Notary Public, State at Large
My commission expires:_____

PREPARED BY:

_____

[Name of Attorney]
[Name of Law Firm]
Attorneys at Law
[Street Address]
[City], [State] [Zip Code]
[Telephone Number]

Appendix C: First Party Special Needs Inter Vivos Trust

This is one of the types of trust discussed in Section X.B. It is one of the trusts that is specifically permitted under Medicaid law. Its use is limited to situations in which the special needs beneficiary has received a large sum of money, typically from a personal injury settlement, and establishes the trust to continue receiving Medicaid benefits with the trust functioning essentially as a supplemental trust to the Medicaid payments. The trade-off is that the state is reimbursed for its payments from the trust when the special needs beneficiary dies. The trust has very specific rules that must be met for it to be used. The trust is referred to as a First Party Special Needs Trust in this text because the source of funds from the trust are from the First Party, that is, the disabled individual. The disabled individual must be under 65 years of age with the trust providing that any monies left in the trust upon the death of the disabled individual are paid to the state to reimburse it for medical assistance paid on behalf of the disabled individual. Any balance can then be distributed as the disabled individual may direct in their last will and testament. The trust can only be established by the disabled individual's parent, grandparent, legal guardian, or by a court. It is essential that the monies be distributed directly to the trust and not first to the disabled individual and then from them to the trust.

TRUST AGREEMENT

THIS DECLARATION OF TRUST is made and entered this the _____ day of _____, [current year], by order of the [name of Court] District Court, [name of Judge], Judge, (hereinafter referred to as "Grantor") and [name of Trustee]. (hereinafter referred to as "Trustee") itself. This Trust is for the benefit of [name of disabled individual], who is handicapped and disabled (hereinafter referred to as "[first name of disabled individual]").

COMMENT: This form anticipates the trust being established by the court. Obviously there are drafting changes that need to be made if the trust is being established by the parent, grandparent, or legal guardian.

---

1. *Identifying the Trust.* The trust may be referred to as "The [name of disabled individual] Special Needs Trust, dated _____, [current year], and any amendments thereto."

2. *Transfers to the [name of disabled individual] Special Needs Trust.* The initial property of this Trust shall consist of $[amount distributed to trust] which shall be distributable to the Trustee pursuant to a personal injury settlement to be held, administered and distributed pursuant to the terms of this Trust by Order of the [name of Court] District Court in that certain action entitled: In Re: [legal caption of court case, where applicable], [name of Court] District Civil Action Number [file number for court case, where applicable].

Additional property may be transferred to this Trust from time to time which, upon acceptance by Trustee, shall be held by Trustee subject to all the terms and conditions of this Trust Agreement, provided, however, that Trustee shall not accept additions to this Trust which, when combined with the existing assets of the Trust, will cause the total assets of this Trust to exceed the amount that appears reasonably necessary to meet the special needs of [first name of disabled individual].

3. *Statement of Purpose.* The principal purpose of all parties of this trust agreement is to provide a system for fiscal management, administration and disbursement, advocacy and care for [first name of disabled individual]. The Trustee shall interpret all provisions of this trust to best effectuate these purposes and intentions.

4. *Irrevocability of this Trust.* The [name of disabled individual] Special Needs Trust shall be irrevocable.

5. *Reformation or Amendment.* The Trustee shall have the power, in its sole and absolute discretion, to amend or reform this agreement in any manner that is required for the sole purpose of ensuring that it qualifies and complies with applicable law that governs exclusion of resources for Federal or State (including any subdivision thereof) benefits.

Under no circumstances shall [first name of disabled individual] be able to amend, modify or revoke this trust through court order, even if allowed to do so under state law, if the result is that he/she gains direct access to the trust principal or income. [First name of disabled individual] does not have the power to assign, encumber, direct, distribute or authorize distributions from this trust.

6. *Primary Intent.* This Special Needs Trust contains instructions for providing for the supplemental special needs of [first name of disabled individual]. In carrying out this purpose, the intent is to supplement any benefits received (or for which [first name of disabled individual] may be eligible) through or from various governmental assistance programs and not to supplant any such benefits, unless the Trustee, in its sole and absolute discretion, determines that the government assistance is inadequate.

COMMENT: The provisions throughout this paragraph are designed to clarify that this trust is available to supplement those benefits provided by various government assistance programs. The primary ones of which are SSI and Medicaid.

Further, the purpose of this Trust is to provide extra, supplemental and emergency care, maintenance, and education in addition to and over and above the funds and/or benefits [first name of disabled individual] otherwise receives or is entitled to as a result of his/her disability, from any local, state, or federal government or any other private agencies, any of which provide services of benefits to handicapped and/or disabled persons. It is the express purpose of this Trust to use the Trust Estate only to supplement other benefits received by [first name of disabled individual] and no part of the Trust Estate shall be used to supplant or replace private health insurance benefits and public assistance benefits of any state or federal agency which has a legal responsibility to serve persons with disabilities which are the same or similar to the impairments suffered by [first name of disabled individual] herein.

This Trust is established in recognition of the fact that [first name of disabled individual] has a disability that may substantially impair his/her ability to provide for his/her own care or custody and which may constitute a substantial handicap. In making distributions to [first name of disabled individual] for his/her special needs, as herein defined, the Trustee shall take into consideration the applicable resource limitations of the public assistance programs for which [first name of disabled individual] is eligible.

7. *Disposition of Principal and Income.* The trustee shall pay or apply for the benefit of [first name of disabled individual] during his/her lifetime such amounts from the principal or income, or both, of the Trust for the satisfaction of [first name of disabled individual]'s supplemental care, as the Trustee, in the Trustee's sole and absolute discretion, may from time to time deem reasonable or necessary subject to the strict limitations set out in this instrument.

COMMENT: This paragraph and the subparagraphs following are designed to clarify the type of distributions permitted under this type of trust.

---

a. *Types of Distribution.* The following enumerates the kinds of supplemental, nonsupport disbursements that are appropriate for the Trustee to make from this Trust to or for the benefit of [first name of disabled individual]. Such examples are not exclusive: medical, dental, and diagnostic work and treatment for which there are no private or public funds otherwise available; medical procedures that are desirable in the Trustee's discretion, even though they may not be necessary or life-saving; supplemental nursing care and rehabilitative services; differentials in the cost between shelter for shared and private rooms in institutional settings; care appropriate for [first name of disabled individual] that assistance programs may not or do not otherwise provide; expenditures for travel, companionship, educational and cultural expenses.

b. *Prohibited Distributions.* The Trustee is prohibited from expending any of the Trust income or principal for any property, services, benefits, or medical care otherwise available to [first name of disabled individual] from any governmental source or from any private insurance carrier required to cover [first name of disabled individual]. The Trustee may pay any deductible amounts for [first name of disabled individual] on any insurance policies covering her/him. The Trustee should cooperate with [first name of disabled individual]'s conservator, guardian, or legal representative to seek support and maintenance for [first name of disabled individual] from all available resources, including but not limited to the Supplemental Security Income Program (SSI); the Old Age Survivor and Disability Insurance Program (OASDI); the Medicaid Program; Social Security Disability Income (SSDI), and any additional, similar, or successor programs; and from any private support sources.

8. *Trust Termination: Payment and Distributions on Death of [first name of disabled individual].* Unless sooner terminated by exhaustion of principal, this trust shall terminate upon the death of [first name of disabled individual]. The trust assets remaining at his/her death shall be paid to the (Department of Human Services or its successor agency) as reimbursement to the Medicaid Assistance Program of the State of [State in which disabled individual resides] for benefits provided by them to [first name of disabled individual] during the [first name of disabled individual]'s lifetime.

COMMENT: This paragraph is essential as it is the one that provides any remaining trust properties to be distributed to reimburse the state for its medical assistance payments.

---

9. *Excess Trust Property.* In the event that any Trust assets are remaining after payment for reimbursement to the Medical Assistance Program of the State of [State in which disabled individual resides] as set forth above, then the remainder of the trust property after reasonable expenses and costs for the trust shall be distributed, in whole or in part, to [first name of disabled individual]. Upon the death of [first name of disabled individual], the then remaining principal and accrued and undistributed income of this trust, not otherwise distributed to such individuals, corporations, or other appointees, as [first name of disabled individual] shall appoint by his/her will and testament, provided that his/her will and testament contains a reference to this specific power of appointment. To the extent that [first name of disabled individual] fails effectively to exercise this power of appointment, the remaining trust principal shall be distributed to [first name of disabled individual]'s estate.

COMMENT: In the event funds remain in the trust after reimbursement to the state, this paragraph establishes a power of appointment that may be exercised by the beneficiary by writing a will directing who receives these funds. Otherwise the funds are distributed to the disabled person's estate. There are no government restriction on the drafting of this paragraph, thus any pertinent drafting distribution can be included.

---

10. *Trust Administration and Protective Provisions.* This is a purely Discretionary Nonsupport Spendthrift Trust. None of the principal or income of the

Trust Estate or any interest therein shall be anticipated, assigned, encumbered, or be subject to any creditors' claims or to any legal process. This Trust and its principal are to be used only for the supplemental care of [first name of disabled individual]. No part of the trust estate shall be construed as part of his/her estate, or be subject to the claims of voluntary or involuntary creditors of [first name of disabled individual]. No part of the Trust Estate shall be liable nor available to [first name of disabled individual]'s creditors during his/her life or after his/her death. Further, [first name of disabled individual] and any creditor of his/hers may not compel a distribution from this trust.

COMMENT: This paragraph and the subparagraphs following are designed to reinforce the fact that these assets are not available until after SSI, Medicaid, or any other government benefits are paid.

---

a. *Restrictions.* This trust shall not replace public or private assistance benefits of any public or private entity that has a legal obligation to provide for [first name of disabled individual].

b. *Denial of Claims.* The Trustee shall deny any request by any public or private entity to disburse trust funds for support or other care that such entity has the obligation to provide [first name of disabled individual].

c. *Costs of Defending Trust.* All reasonable expenses in establishing, maintaining, administering, and defending this Trust, including but not limited to reasonable attorney's fees, accounting fees, Trustee's fees, and costs shall be proper charges to the Trust.

d. *Choice of Laws.* The validity of this Trust shall be determined by the laws, including valid regulations, of the United States and the State of [State in which disabled individual resides].

11. *Protection from Creditors.* No trust beneficiary shall have the right to sell, transfer, assign, alienate, pledge, or in any way encumber trust assets, including income and principal, nor shall trust assets be subject to execution, levy, sale, garnishment, attachment, bankruptcy, or other legal proceedings. Any such actions by a trust beneficiary or a third party seeking to enforce a claim against the trust assets shall not be recognized under any circumstances by the trustee. These provisions do not prevent the trustee from making distributions for the benefit of a trust beneficiary in such amounts and at such times as the trustee determines necessary that are consistent with the prior provisions of this trust instrument.

12. *Trustee Powers.* In the administration of the trusts, the trustee shall have the following powers and rights and all others granted by law:

a. To sell publicly or privately any trust property, for cash or on t i m e , without an order of court and upon such terms and conditions as my trustee deems proper; and no person dealing with my trustee shall have any obligation to look to the application of the purchase money.

b. To invest and reinvest all or any part of the principal of the trust in any stocks, bonds, mortgages, shares or interests in common trust funds, mutual funds, or other securities or property, real, personal, or mixed, and of any kind or nature whatsoever, as the trustee deems proper, and without diversification if the trustee deems it advisable, irrespective of whether or not such securities or property are eligible for trust investment under state or any other law, and may change any investment received or made by the trustee, and may hold cash if the trustee deems it advisable.

c. To exercise broad discretion as to diversification of trust property, and shall not be required to reduce any concentrated holdings merely because of such concentration, and shall have full discretion as to the percentage to be invested in fixed income securities, and is specifically relieved from any requirements, legal or otherwise, as to the percentage of the trust assets to be invested in fixed income securities, and may invest or retain invested any trust estates wholly in common stocks.

d. To sell, convey, lease or mortgage, repair and improve, and take any and all other steps with regard to any real estate that may at any time be a part of the principal of the trust; and any lease of such real property or contract with regard thereto made by the trustee shall be binding for the full period of the lease or contract, even though the period shall extend beyond the termination of the trust.

e. To vote shares of stock held in the trust at stockholders' meetings in person or by special, limited, or general proxy, with or without power of substitution, as seems best to the trustee.

f. To participate in the liquidation, reorganization, consolidation, incorporation and reincorporation, or any other financial readjustment of any corporation, limited liability company or business in which the trust is, or shall be financially interested.

g. To borrow money from any source for any purpose connected with the protection, preservation, improvement or development of the trust hereunder, whenever in the trustee's judgment the trustee deems it advisable, and as security to mortgage or pledge any real estate or personal property forming a part of the trust upon such terms and conditions as the trustee may deem advisable.

h. To hold any and all securities in bearer form, in the trustee's own name, or the name of some other person, partnership, or corporation, or in the name of a duly appointed nominee, with or without disclosing the fiduciary ownership.

i. To divide the principal of the trust property into parts or shares and to distribute or allot same, and to make such division in cash or in kind or both. For the purpose of such division or allotment, the judgment of the trustee concerning the propriety thereof and relative value of property so distributed or allotted shall be binding and conclusive with respect to all interested persons.

j. To merge and consolidate the trust property of any separate trust held hereunder with other trusts and then to administer such trust property as a single trust provided the separate trust is for the benefit of the same persons with substantially the same terms, conditions and federal tax consequences.

k. To pay such income and principal during the incapacity of any beneficiary for whose benefit income and principal may be expended, in any one or more of the following ways: (1) directly to the beneficiary; (2) to the legal guardian or conservator of the beneficiary; (3) to a relative of the beneficiary to be expended by the relative for the beneficiary; or (4) by expending the same directly for the beneficiary. Any distributions are subject to the prior provisions of this trust instrument. The trustee shall not be obliged to see to the application of the funds so expended, but the receipt of such person shall be full acquittance to the trustee.

l. To have the same powers, authorities, and discretions in the management of the trust as I would have in the management and control of my own personal assets. The trustee may continue to exercise any powers and discretions granted in this instrument for a reasonable period after the termination of any trust under this instrument.

13. *Limitation on Powers of Individual Trustee.* Notwithstanding any other powers granted to my trustee in this instrument, an individual trustee (a) shall have no power to make payments or distributions that would discharge the trustee's legal obligation to support the trust beneficiary, (b) shall not exercise any power or discretion in any manner that would be deemed to be a general power of appointment under Internal Revenue Code Section 2041, and (c) shall possess no incidence of ownership or powers with respect to life insurance in which the trustee is the insured and has fiduciary power over such life insurance.

14. *Trustee Resignation.* My trustee may resign at any time by giving written notice to my successor trustee named below, if any, and if none, then written notice shall be given to each current adult income beneficiary who is then living.

15. *Trustee Succession and Appointment.* If [name of Trustee] ceases to act as trustee due to death, incompetency, resignation or cease to serve for any reason, then [name of successor trustee] shall serve as successor trustee. The last serving successor trustee may name his or her own successor trustee by a written instrument delivered to the successor trustee or by will. The successor trustee may be an individual or a financial institution possessing trust powers under state or federal law. Any further vacancy in the office of trustee shall be filled by decision of the probate court where I resided at the time of my death.

16. *Powers of Successor Trustee.* Each successor trustee shall have the same rights, titles, powers, duties, discretions, and immunities and otherwise be in the same position as if originally named trustee. No successor trustee shall be personally liable for any act or failure to act of a predecessor trustee. Further, a successor trustee may accept the account furnished and the property delivered by or for a predecessor trustee without liability for so doing, and such acceptance shall be a full and complete discharge to the predecessor trustee.

17. *Compensation of Trustee.* [OPTION 1: Corporate trustee compensation] A corporate trustee shall receive compensation in accordance with its regular schedule of fees in effect at the time such services are rendered. An individual trustee shall receive compensation not to exceed the compensation paid to a corporate trustee.

[OPTION 2: Individual does not receive compensation] An individual trustee shall not be paid any compensation, but shall be reimbursed for out-of-pocket expenses

[OPTION 3: Individual does receive compensation] An individual trustee shall be

paid [amount of compensation] as compensation for such services and shall be reimbursed for out-of-pocket expenses.

18. *Court Accountings.* To the extent such requirements can be waived, the trustee shall not be required (a) to file any inventory of trust property or accounts or reports of the administration of the trusts, or to register the trusts, in any court, (b) to furnish any bond or other security for the proper performance of the trustee's duties or (c) to obtain authority from a court for the exercise of any power conferred on the trustee by this instrument. This waiver does not preclude the trustee from registering any trust created in this instrument and petitioning a court having jurisdiction over registered trusts for a judicial ruling on any matter relating to administration of any trust created in this instrument.

19. *Severability.* If any provisions of this trust shall be unenforceable, the remaining provisions shall nevertheless be carried into effect.

20. *Certification of Incompetency.* [OPTION 1: Decided by treating physician] Any person acting or named to act as a trustee in this instrument is considered to be unable to serve or to continue serving when a physician whom such person has consulted within the prior three years has certified as to such consultation and the certification states that the person is incapable of managing the affairs of the trusts I have established in this instrument, regardless of cause and regardless of whether there is an adjudication of incompetency. No person shall be liable to anyone for actions taken in reliance on the physician's certification or for dealing with a trustee other than the one removed for incompetency based on such certification.

[OPTION 2: Decided by two physicians] Any person acting or named to act as a trustee in this instrument is considered to be unable to serve or to continue serving   when a written certification is received from two (2) physicians, both of whom have personally examined the person and at least one (1) of whom is board-certified in the specialty most closely associated with the health condition alleged to cause such incompetency. The certification must state that the person is incapable of managing the affairs of this trust, regardless of cause and regardless of whether there is an adjudication of incompetence. No person is liable to anyone for actions taken in reliance on these certifications, or for dealing with a trustee other than the one removed for incompetency based on these certifications.

21. *Titles and References.* The underscored titles of paragraphs in this instrument are for information purposes only and shall be given no legal effect.

22. *Governing Law.* The laws of the State of [State in which disabled individual resides] shall govern the interpretation and validity of the provisions of this instrument and all questions relating to the management, administration, investment, and distribution of the trusts hereby created.

Notwithstanding the foregoing, the trustee shall have the power, exercisable in the trustee's sole and absolute discretion, to declare, by written instrument that the forum for this trust and all trusts established herein shall be another state in which event the laws of that state shall govern the interpretation and validity of the provisions of this instrument and all questions relating to the management, administration, investment, and distribution of the trusts hereby created.

We certify that we have read the foregoing Declaration of Trust and it correctly states the terms and conditions under which the Trust Estate is to be held, managed, and disposed of by Trustee in accordance with that certain Court Order in the matter of [legal caption of Court case, where applicable], [name of Court] District Civil Action Number [file number for Court case, where applicable].

GRANTOR:

_____

[name of Judge], Judge
[name of Court] District Court
TRUSTEE:
[name of Trustee]
BY: _____

STATE OF _____
COUNTY OF _____

Before me, the undersigned authority, came [name of Judge], Judge, [name of Court] District Court, Grantor, who is of sound mind and eighteen (18) years of age, or older, and acknowledged that he/she acting in his/her official capacity as [name of Court] District Judge, voluntarily dated and signed this writing or directed it to be signed and dated as above.

WITNESS my hand this the _____ day of _____, [current year].

_____

Notary Public, State at Large
My Commission Expires: _____

Notary ID: _____

Appendix D: Qualifying Income Trust

On occasion, a Qualifying Income Trust (QIT) is needed for a person in nursing home care who seeks to be Medicaid eligible but whose income is greater than the income cap under that particular state's Medicaid laws. The person otherwise qualifies for Medicaid, as they do not have sufficient resources to be disqualified, but under Medicaid law, the person is still deemed ineligible due to the amount of their income, such as social security and other pension income. This was discussed in Sections V.B and X.B. To become Medicaid eligible, a QIT or Miller trust (as it is sometimes termed) is required. The basics of the trust are that the income above the cap is distributed to the QIT. Then the person's remaining income is within the amount of the income cap and by a legal fiction, the excess income held in the QIT is not considered income in excess of the cap. This typically results in two checking accounts from which distribution is made to the nursing home. For those who have interest in understanding these trusts more fully, see Clifton B. Kruse, Jr., *Third Party and Self-Created Trusts*, 3rd edition, American Bar Association (Chicago, 2002). Also, the reader is cautioned that state law should be considered. The trust provided may need to be modified to meet the requirements of the lawyer's own state Medicaid office.

TRUST AGREEMENT

I, [grantor's name], by and through my attorney-in-fact, [attorney-in-fact's name], currently of [grantor's city], [grantor's state], acting as grantor and [trustee's name], currently of [trustee's city], [trustee's state], as trustee hereby enter into this trust agreement, which shall be held subject to the following provisions:

COMMENT: If the nursing home patient is mentally competent, he or she can act as the grantor of the trust. Otherwise, the person acting as the grantor's power of attorney may sign. Some states do not allow a third party to act as grantor, creating the oddity of an incompetent person signing a trust document if they do not have a person acting as their power of attorney. Hopefully, the lawyer drafting one of these trusts lives in a state whose Medicaid office is more reasonable than the one in the writer's own state.

---

1. Name of Trust. This instrument and the initial trust hereby established may be named the "[name of beneficiary] Qualifying Income Trust."

COMMENT: The trust is typically named after the beneficiary followed by the phrase "Qualifying Income Trust."

---

2. Beneficiary Information. The beneficiary of this trust is [name of beneficiary] and any references to "the beneficiary" are only to [him or her].

COMMENT: The beneficiary's name is inserted in this paragraph.

---

3. Trust Purpose. The grantor establishes this trust for the benefit of [name of beneficiary] in strict accordance with the limitations imposed by this instrument.

a. This trust is created pursuant to §1917(d)(4)(B) of the Social Security Act [42USC 1396p] and [insert applicable state statute or regulation]; and is created in order to enable the beneficiary to qualify for Medicaid benefits and to provide for the administration and disposition of the trust estate during and after the lifetime of the beneficiary, in accordance with the terms and conditions of this trust.

b. No distributions of income or principal may be made by the trustee to the beneficiary except in accordance with the terms set out in this agreement.

c. All interpretations and actions taken by the trustee pursuant to this trust shall be done for and with the purpose of creating, establishing, and maintaining the beneficiary's eligibility for Medicaid benefits. Any provisions of this trust which are deemed to be inconsistent or contrary to such purpose shall be deemed to be void and of no force or effect.

COMMENT: The essence of this trust is that distributions can only be made as permitted by state and federal Medicaid laws. The applicable state statute or regulation should be inserted in 3.a and any modifications required by the lawyer's own state should be made.

---

4. Trust Assets. The trust assets held in this trust shall be subject to the following restrictions.

a. The grantor shall transfer to the trustee by deposit to the bank account which has been established solely for receiving funds under this trust, the monthly income the beneficiary receives from pensions, social security, and other income permitted an individual under Section 1917(d)(4)(B) of the Social Security Act.

b. All such assets when transferred to the trust shall be registered or titled in the name of the trustee.

c. The trustee shall hold, invest, administer, and distribute the trust assets in accordance with the terms of this agreement and as required to maintain Medicaid eligibility for the beneficiary.

d. No assets may be transferred to the trust other than the beneficiary's income as defined above.

COMMENT: These are requirements from the writer's own state imposed by state regulation. The lawyer should consult his/her own state Medicaid regulations to be certain of any provisions that need to be added or any modifications that need to be made to these provisions.

5. Distribution of Income and Principal. The trustee shall make distributions of income and principal from the trust as follows:

a. During the lifetime of the beneficiary, the trustee shall distribute to the beneficiary or for the beneficiary's benefit all income, no less often than monthly as permitted by the [name of state agency handling Medicaid services], or other appropriate state or federal agency.

b. Currently it is anticipated that permissible trustee distributions include the beneficiary's personal needs allowance, a monthly maintenance needs allowance for the beneficiary's spouse and any dependent family members, the beneficiary's health insurance premiums, the amount the beneficiary is required to pay for nursing home or community-based health care, and such other expenses that may be determined by the [name of state agency handling Medicaid services] to be permissible.

c. The trustee shall have no discretion concerning distributions to the beneficiary or for the beneficiary's benefit. No payments from the trust may be made to any other person during the beneficiary's lifetime.

COMMENT: The Medicaid regulations are very specific regarding distributions from the trust. Those regulations require compliance. While these provisions are generally standard, there may be some variation from state to state; therefore some modifications may be necessary. Paragraph 5.b should be modified if the grantor is not married.

6. Termination of Trust. At the death of the beneficiary, the trust shall terminate and the remaining trust assets shall be distributed in an amount sufficient to pay the [State or Commonwealth] of [name of state] the amount of medical assistance paid by it on behalf of the beneficiary under the Medicaid program. The balance of the trust assets, if any, shall be distributed to the beneficiary's estate.

COMMENT: Any amounts held in the trust will be paid to the state Medicaid office after the death of the beneficiary to offset payments made by the Medicaid program for that person. Any excess funds can be distributed to that person's estate, but as a practical matter, there will be none.

7. Non-assignability of Interest. This is a spendthrift trust. None of the principal or income of the trust estate or any interest in the trust shall be anticipated, assigned, encumbered, or be subject to any creditors' claims or to any legal process.

COMMENT: This is a standard provision required by the writer's state Medicaid office.

---

8. Trustee Succession. In the event the initial trustee ceases to act due to death, incompetency, resignation or otherwise ceases to serve for any reason, then [name of successor trustee] shall serve as successor trustee. The last serving successor trustee may name his or her own successor trustee by a written instrument delivered to the successor trustee or by will. The successor trustee may be an individual or a financial institution possessing trust powers under state or federal law. If no successor trustee is named, then a successor trustee shall be named by the [name of court]. No trustee shall be required to post surety or personal bond while serving as trustee.

COMMENT: The method of trustee succession should be determined as in any trust.

---

9. Trustee Powers. In the administration of this trust, the trustee shall have all powers granted to trustees under state law, except as limited by the terms of this trust and as specifically limited by the following provisions.

a. If any trust funds remain after the required monthly distributions provided for hereinabove, such funds shall remain in the trust and cannot be sold or reserved.

b. No powers may be exercised that are inconsistent with regulations of the [name of state agency handling Medicaid services].

c. The trustee shall have the power to open bank accounts, to issue checks on, and make withdrawals from such account. Any and all bank accounts, including checking, certificates of deposit, and savings accounts, established in the name of the trust by the trustee shall be subject to withdrawal, and all checks, drafts and other obligations of the trust shall be honored by said depositories upon the signature of the trustee.

d. The trustee shall report to the [name of state agency handling Medicaid services] and any court of competent jurisdiction as required by regulation or court order.

e. The trustee may invest in non-income producing property.

f. The trustee shall take whatever legal steps may be necessary to initiate or continue any public assistance program for which the beneficiary is or may become eligible.

COMMENT: A broad statement of powers may result in the trust failing to meet Medicaid eligibility standards. Therefore, the powers contained in this trust are limited to those approved by the writer's own state Medicaid office.

10. Grantor Trust. This trust is a grantor trust; and pursuant to IRC Section 672(e) the trust income is taxed to the beneficiary.

COMMENT: This provision is inserted to clarify that the income is still taxed to the Medicaid eligible beneficiary.

11. Irrevocability. This trust is irrevocable and the grantor has no right to alter, amend, or revoke any provision of this agreement; however, the trustee is granted the limited right to amend this trust in order to comply with any provisions now or in the future required of the [name of state agency handling Medicaid services] in order for this trust to be treated as a qualifying income trust.

COMMENT: This trust must be irrevocable to meet Medicaid requirements.

12. Choice and Effect of Law. This trust agreement is entered into and executed in the [State or Commonwealth] of [name of state]. It shall be administered in accordance with the laws of that state.

COMMENT: It is a standard provision in both trust instruments and in contracts to specify the state law that applies in interpretation of the instrument. This will be the grantor's home state.

The undersigned have signed this instrument and have established the foregoing trust on this the _____ day of _____, [Current Year].

GRANTOR:

_____
[grantor's name]
TRUSTEE:

_____
[trustee's name]

STATE OF [State of Notary]   )
) SCT.
COUNTY OF [County of Notary]   )

The undersigned, a Notary Public within and for the state and county aforesaid, does hereby certify that the foregoing trust agreement executed by [attorney in fact's name], on behalf of the grantor and in [his or her] capacity as trustee, was on this day produced to me in my county by [attorney in fact's name], who executed, acknowledged and swore the same before me to be [his or her] act and deed in due form of law.

Given under my hand and notarial seal on this the ___ day of _____, [Current Year].

_____
Notary Public, State at Large
My commission expires:_____

PREPARED BY:

_____
[Name of Attorney]
[Name of Law Firm]
Attorneys at Law
[Street Address]
[City], [State] [Zip Code]
[Telephone Number]

Appendix E: Income Only Trust

This is one of the types of trust referred to in Section X.B. It is sometimes referred to as a Medicaid Compliant Trust or a Medicaid Asset Protection Trust. The trust qualifies under Medicaid law that permits a trust that distributes only income to the trust beneficiary that was established with property transferred into the trust in excess of 60 months to qualify the trust assets as excluded resources. This is obviously because the 60-month rule on transfers has been met. The trust income does provide an income source for the trust beneficiary that will be spent for the nursing home or the long-term care needs of the trust beneficiary, as is the case with any other income resources the individual owns. The state then is left paying the balance of any nursing home or long-term care expenses. When using this form be aware of the requirements of state law as there are variations among the states on the administration and interpretation of the Medicaid law.

TRUST AGREEMENT

We, [name of Grantor #1] and [name of Grantor #2], currently of [Grantors' City], Kentucky, acting as grantors hereby transfer to [name of Trustee], currently of [Trustee's City], Kentucky, acting as trustee, the sum of Ten Dollars ($10.00). This amount and all investments, reinvestments and additions which may sometimes be referred to in this instrument as the "trust property" or "trust assets" are to be held subject to the following provisions:

COMMENT: It is necessary to insert the names of the grantors who are also the income beneficiaries as well as the name of the trustee. Some writers are cautious and suggest that the trustee should be other than the grantors. For example, one or more of the children could act as the trustee. Others believe that the grantors may act as their own trustee since they have no discretion under the trust instrument.

---

1. *Name of Trust.* This instrument and the initial trust hereby established may be named the "[Name of Trust] Income Only Trust."

COMMENT: Typically the name of the trust is simply the name of the grantors followed by the phrase "Income Only Trust" if that is the terminology most common in the attorney's state. Technically, trusts do not need to have names, but it has become more common in recent years to see trusts that are named.

---

2. *Family Information.* Our children are [name of Child #1], [name of Child #2] and [name of Child #3], and all references in this trust to "our children" are only to them.

COMMENT: Typically the names of the children are inserted as they will be the ultimate beneficiaries of the trust. Again this is not essential as the names can be inserted later in the instrument.

---

3. *Provisions During Our Lifetime.* During the lifetime of both of us and during the lifetime of the survivor of us, the trustee shall pay to us, or to the survivor of us, all of the net trust income in quarterly or more frequent installments. The principal of this trust shall not be available under any circumstances for payment to either of us or to any future spouse of either of us. Under no circumstances may our trustee at any time make any such distribution of principal to either of us or to any future spouse. The term "principal" as defined in this instrument shall mean any real estate, money or other asset except for interest, dividends, rental income, or other ordinary income that does not qualify for capital gains treatment. Finally, the trustee shall make distributions of income only and shall not distribute principal, adjust between principal and income, convert principal to income, or convert principal or income to a new trust amount.

COMMENT: This is the essential provision in the trust. This provision makes it clear that only income can be distributed to the grantors. This trust is drafted for a husband and wife but can be easily modified for a single grantor.

---

4. *Payment of Debts and Funeral Expenses.* No portion of the assets of this trust shall be used for the payment of our debts or funeral expenses as the payment of those expenses is provided for in each of our last wills and testament.

COMMENT: This provision is inserted as a caution to remain consistent with the requirement that no principal can be distributed for the benefit of the grantor. Paragraph 3 is focused on lifetime distributions, whereas paragraph 4 is intended to preclude any distributions of principal at death due to any remaining expenses of the grantor at the time of death.

---

5. *Allocations at Our Deaths.* Following the death of the last of us to die, the trust shall terminate and the trust property shall be distributed in equal

shares to our children. If a child is deceased that deceased child's share shall be distributed to his or her then living descendants per stirpes.

COMMENT: This paragraph provides for the ultimate distribution of the trust assets to the trust remainderman after the death of the grantor or grantors. This distribution can be an outright distribution to the children as in this draft or in any other manner of distribution. For example, if there is a need to restrict the distribution for the remainderman beneficiaries, the trust could continue throughout the lifetime of those beneficiaries with appropriate trust provisions to provide for those beneficiaries.

---

6. *Special Provisions.* In addition to the other provisions of this trust agreement:

a. *Method of Payment.* If a person entitled to receive income or principal distributions is unable to manage his or her financial affairs due to any type of mental or physical incapacity, then distributions may be made to or for such person's benefit, including making distributions to such person's guardian, conservator or committee.

COMMENT: This provision is not essential, but is only provided for administrative convenience. It is not necessary.

---

7. *Protection from Creditors.* No trust beneficiary shall have the right to sell, transfer, assign, alienate, pledge, or in any way encumber trust assets, including income and principal, nor shall trust assets be subject to execution, levy, sale, garnishment, attachment, bankruptcy, or other legal proceedings. Any such actions by a trust beneficiary or a third party seeking to enforce a claim against the trust assets shall not be recognized under any circumstances by the trustee.

COMMENT: This is a typical asset protection provision. If the reader has other provisions they prefer to use for asset protection that is fine.

---

8. *Definitions.* For all purposes of this instrument, the following shall apply:

a. The words "child," "children," "descendant" or "descendants" shall exclude adopted persons unless they are adopted prior to eighteen (18) years; and shall include only persons legitimately born unless a decree of adoption terminates the parental rights of the natural mother during her lifetime, or the natural father signs a written notarized instrument during his lifetime in which he irrevocably states that the child is to be considered legitimately born for purposes of inheriting under this trust.

COMMENT: This paragraph is not essential. The writer often finds it helpful to define the terms children and descendants to be certain that an adopted person inherits under the instrument and to deal with the issue of illegitimacy of a descendant.

---

b. Whenever assets are to be divided and allocated "per stirpes," the assets to be divided or allocated shall be divided into as many equal shares as are necessary to divide or allocate one share to each then living child of such person and to provide one share collectively for the then living descendants of each child of such person who then is deceased leaving one or more descendants then living. Any collective share shall be divided and allocated per stirpes among the descendants of such deceased person in accordance with the preceding sentence.

COMMENT: Paragraph 8.b. seeks to define that ancient phrase "per stirpes," which is such a part of will and trust law. The use of that paragraph and definition is entirely discretionary with the lawyer.

---

9. *Trustee Powers.* In the administration of the trusts, the trustee shall have the following powers and rights and all others granted by law:

a. To sell publicly or privately any trust property, for cash or on time, without an order of court and upon such terms and conditions as our trustee deems proper; and no person dealing with our trustee shall have any obligation to look to the application of the purchase money.

b. To invest and reinvest all or any part of the principal of the trust in any stocks, bonds, mortgages, shares or interests in common trust funds, mutual funds, or other securities or property, real, personal, or mixed, and of any kind or nature whatsoever, as the trustee deems proper, and without diversification if the trustee deems it advisable, irrespective of whether or not such securities or property are eligible for trust investment under state or any other law, and may change any investment received or made by the trustee, and may hold cash if the trustee deems it advisable.

c. To exercise broad discretion as to diversification of trust property, and shall not be required to reduce any concentrated holdings merely because of such concentration, and shall have full discretion as to the percentage to be invested in fixed income securities, and is specifically relieved from any requirements, legal or otherwise, as to the percentage of the trust assets to be invested in fixed income securities, and may invest or retain invested any trust estates wholly in common stocks.

d. To sell, convey, lease or mortgage, repair and improve, and take any and all other steps with regard to any real estate that may at any time be a part of the principal of the trust; and any lease of such real property or contract with regard thereto made by the trustee shall be binding for the full period of the lease or contract, even though the period shall extend beyond the termination of the trust.

e. To vote shares of stock held in the trust at stockholders' meetings in person or by special, limited, or general proxy, with or without power of substitution, as seems best to the trustee.

f. To participate in the liquidation, reorganization, consolidation, incorporation and reincorporation, or any other financial readjustment of any corporation, limited liability company or business in which the trust is, or shall be financially interested.

g. To borrow money from any source for any purpose connected with the protection, preservation, improvement or development of the trust hereunder, whenever in the trustee's judgment the trustee deems it advisable, and as security to mortgage or pledge any real estate or personal property forming a part of the trust upon such terms and conditions as the trustee may deem advisable.

h. To hold any and all securities in bearer form, in the trustee's own name, or the name of some other person, partnership, or corporation, or in the name of a duly appointed nominee, with or without disclosing the fiduciary ownership.

i. To pay such income during the incapacity of any beneficiary for whose benefit income may be expended, in any one or more of the following ways: (1) directly to the beneficiary; (2) to the legal guardian, conservator, or committee of the beneficiary; (3) to a relative of the beneficiary to be expended by the relative for the beneficiary; or (4) by expending the same directly for the beneficiary. The trustee shall not be obliged to see to the application of the funds so expended, but the receipt of such person shall be full acquittance to the trustee.

j. To have the same powers, authorities, and discretions in the management of the trust as we would have in the management and control of our own personal assets. The trustee may continue to exercise any powers and discretions granted in this instrument for a reasonable period after the termination of any trust under this instrument.

10. *Trustee Resignation.* Our trustee may resign at any time by giving written notice to our successor trustee named below, if any, and if none, then written notice shall be given to each current adult income beneficiary who is then living.

11. *Trustee Succession and Appointment.* If [name of Trustee] ceases to act as trustee due to death, incompetency, resignation or ceases to serve for any reason, then [name of successor Trustee] shall serve as successor trustee. Our last serving trustee or successor trustees shall have the right to name his or her own successor trustee who may be an individual or a financial institution possessing trust powers under state or federal law.

COMMENT: The succession of trustees should be considered in the trust instrument. The writer may choose to have a series of successor trustees. The form provided simply has one successor trustee. This is entirely discretionary with the lawyer.

14. *Powers of Successor Trustee.* Each successor trustee shall have the same rights, titles, powers, duties, discretions, and immunities and otherwise be in the same position as if originally named trustee. No successor trustee shall be personally liable for any act or failure to act of a predecessor trustee. Further, a successor trustee may accept the account furnished and the property delivered by or for a predecessor trustee without liability for so doing, and such acceptance shall be a full and complete discharge to the predecessor trustee.

15. *Compensation of Trustee.* An individual trustee shall not be paid any compensation, but shall be reimbursed for out-of-pocket expenses.

COMMENT: The issue of trustee compensation should be addressed. The form assumes family members are acting as trustee and are charging no trustee fee. If a fee is to be charged then that should be addressed in this paragraph.

16. *Court Accountings.* To the extent such requirements can be waived, the trustee shall not be required (a) to file any inventory of trust property or accounts or reports of the administration of the trusts, or to register the trusts, in any court, (b) to furnish any bond or other security for the proper performance of the trustee's duties or (c) to obtain authority from a court for the exercise of any power conferred on the trustee by this instrument. This waiver does not preclude the trustee from registering any trust created in this instrument and petitioning a court having jurisdiction over registered trusts for a judicial ruling on any matter relating to administration of any trust created in this instrument.

17. *Severability.* If any provisions of this trust shall be unenforceable, the remaining provisions shall nevertheless be carried into effect.

18. *Certification of Incompetency.* Any person acting or named to act as a trustee in this instrument is considered to be unable to serve or to continue serving when a physician whom such person has consulted within the prior three (3) years has certified as to such consultation and the certification states that the person is incapable of managing the affairs of the trusts we have established in this instrument, regardless of cause and regardless of whether there is an adjudication of incompetency. No person shall be liable to anyone for actions taken in reliance on the physician's certification or for dealing with a trustee other than the one removed for incompetency based on such certification.

COMMENT: If individual trustees are used then the issue of incompetency should be addressed.

---

19. *Titles and References.* The underscored titles of paragraphs in this instrument are for information purposes only and shall be given no legal effect.

20. Governing Law. The laws of the State of [State] shall govern the interpretation and validity of the provisions of this instrument and all questions relating to the management, administration, investment, and distribution of the trusts hereby created.

Notwithstanding the foregoing, our trustee shall have the power, exercisable in the trustee's sole and absolute discretion, to declare, by written instrument that the forum for this trust and all trusts established herein shall be another state in which event the laws of that state shall govern the interpretation and validity of the provisions of this instrument and all questions relating to the management, administration, investment, and distribution of the trusts hereby created.

21. *Irrevocability.* We declare that this trust is irrevocable and may not be altered, amended, revoke or in any way modified, in whole or in part. It is our expressed intent by this trust instrument to preclude any right to modify this instrument upon execution by both of us.

COMMENT: It is essential that this trust be irrevocable. Further, the assets that are to comprise the trust must be transferred at or close in time to the execution of the trust instrument, as the 60-month requirement is based on the date of transfer of the assets not the date the trust instrument is executed.

The undersigned have signed this instrument and have established the foregoing trusts on this the _____ day of _____, [current year].

GRANTORS:

_____
[Name of Grantor #1]

_____
[Name of Grantor #2]
TRUSTEE:

_____
[Name of Trustee]

STATE OF _____)
) SCT.
COUNTY OF _____)

The undersigned, a Notary Public within and for the state and county aforesaid, does hereby certify that the foregoing trust agreement executed by [name of Grantor #1] and [name of Grantor #2], as grantors, was on this day produced to me in our county by [name of Grantor #1] and [name of Grantor #2], both of whom executed, acknowledged and swore the same before me to be their act and deed in due form of law.

Given under my hand and notarial seal on this the _____ day of _____, [current year].

                                                _____
Notary Public, State at Large
My Commission Expires: _____
Notary ID: _____

STATE OF _____   )
) SCT.
COUNTY OF _____   )

The undersigned, a Notary Public within and for the state and county aforesaid, does hereby certify that the foregoing trust agreement executed by [name of Trustee], as trustee, was on this day produced to me in our county by [name of Trustee], who executed, acknowledged and swore the same before me to be his/her act and deed in due form of law.

Given under my hand and notarial seal on this the _____ day of _____, [current year].

                                                _____
Notary Public, State at Large
My Commission Expires: _____
Notary ID: _____

PREPARED BY:

_____
[Name of Attorney]
[Name of Law Firm]
Attorneys at Law
[Street Address]
[City], [State] [Zip Code]
[Telephone number]

Notes

1. Medicaid is found in Title XIX of the Social Security Act, codified in Title 42, section 1396 *et seq.* of the United States Code.

2. 42 U.S.C. § 1396a(a)(10)(A)(ii)(V).

3. *Id.* § 1396a(a)(10)(A).

4. *Id.* § 1396(a)(10)(C).

5. *Id.* § 1396–1396r.

6. 20 C.F.R. §§ 416.1102, 416.1103, 416.1123.

7. 42 U.S.C. § 1396a(a)(10)(A)(ii)(V).

8. *Id.* § 1396p(d)(4)(B).

9. *Id.* § 1396a(a)(10)(c)(I).

10. 20 C.F.R. § 1201.

11. *Id.* § 416.1218.

12. *Id.* § 416.1216.

13. *Id.* § 416.1212.

14. 42 U.S.C. § 1396p(c)(2)(A).

15. 20 C.F.R. § 416.1230.

16. *Id.* § 416.1231.

17. *Id.*

18. Social Security POMS 51 01130.500.

19. 20 C.F.R. § 416.1222.

20. 42 U.S.C. § 1396r–5(d)(3).

21. 20 C.F.R. § 416.1207(d).

22. 397 U.S. 254 (1970).

23. 42 U.S.C. § 1396r–5(e)(2)(B).

24. *Id.* § 1396r–5(e)(2)(C).

25. *Id.* §§ 1396p(c), 1396p(c)(1)(B).

26. *Id.* § 1396p(c)(2)(A).

27. *Id.* § 1396p(c)(2)(B).

28. *Id.* § 1396p(c)(2)(C).

29. *Id.* § 1396p(c)(2)(D).

30. Reed v. Mo. Dep't Soc. Servs, 193 S.W.2d 839 (Mo. App. 2006).

31. 42 U.S.C. § 1396p(c)(1)(G).

32. *Id.* § 1396p(c)(i)(I).

33. *Id.* § 1396p(d)(4)(A).

34. *Id.* § 1396p(d)(4)(C).

35. *Id.* § 1396p(d)(4)(B).

36. Miller v. Ibarra, 746 F. Supp. 19 (D. Colo. 1991).

37. 42 U.S.C. § 1396p(b)(4).

38. *Id.* § 1396p(b).

39. According to HCFA, these states are California, Connecticut, Indiana, Iowa, and New York.

40. 42 U.S.C. § 1396p(a)(1).

41. *Id.* § 1396p(a)(2).

42. *Id.* § 1396p(b)(2)(A).

43. *Id.* § 1396p(b)(2)(B).

44. *Id.* § 1396p(b)(3).

45. *Id.* § 431.220.

46. *Id.* § 431.205.

47. *Id.*

48. *Id.* § 431.205.
49. *Id.* § 431.211.
50. *Id.* § 431.213.
51. *Id.* § 431.221.
52. *Id.*
53. *Id.* § 431.230.
54. *Id.* § 431.230(2)(b).
55. *Id.* § 431.231.
56. *Id.*
57. *Id.* § 431.242.
58. *Id.* § 431.240.
59. *Id.*
60. *Id.*
61. *Id.* § 431.244.
62. *Id.*
63. *Id.*
64. *Id.*
65. *Id.* § 431.232.
66. *Id.* § 431.233.
67. *Id.*
68. *Id.* § 431.245.

CHAPTER 8

Retirement Plans and Benefits

I. Overview 245
II. Background 246
III. Types of Retirement Plans 247
    A. Pension Plans 247
    B. Profit-Sharing Plans. 247
    C. Money-Purchase Plans 247
    D. 401(k) Plans. 248
    E. 401(k) SIMPLE Plans. 249
    F. Keogh or HR-10 Plans 249
    G. SEP 250
    H. IRA 250
    I. Simple IRA 251
    J. Roth IRA 251
IV. Participation, Vesting, and Nondiscrimination. 252
V. Top-Heavy Plans 253
VI. Penalty Taxes. 253
    A. Premature Distributions 253
    B. Minimum Distributions 254
VII. Taxation of Distributions. 256
    A. Income Taxation Distributions during Lifetime. 256
    B. Estate Taxation of Distributions at Death 257
VIII. Creditor Protection. 257
Appendix A: Comparison of Plans 259

I. Overview

The elder lawyer will not usually be involved in the client's selection of retirement plans and contributions to those plans. Typically those are benefits through the client's place of employment, or if the client is self-employed the client has established plans for the client and his or her employees. The attorney's involvement with retirement accounts involves advising the client of how to pass those assets to the ultimate estate beneficiaries as part of the client's estate plan. Therefore, the attorney needs to be aware of the restrictions on beneficiary designations of the various types of retirement accounts. Many retirement accounts require that the surviving spouse be the beneficiary of these accounts. Others have no restrictions. Also, the discussions about minimum distributions Section VI.B will be of particular importance.

An excellent opportunity to assist one's client in the estate planning process is the conversion of retirement accounts to Roth accounts in order to generate an income tax free asset for the client's elder years as well as to pass an income tax free retirement account to the client's ultimate estate beneficiaries. This is a costly option that will work best for higher income clients (see Section III.J).

Some clients will want to roll their retirement accounts into IRAs to avoid the restriction on designating someone other than a spouse as the beneficiary. This may be an important issue in a second marriage when the client intends for the retirement account to be available for the surviving spouse with the balance of it passing to children from a prior marriage. While nothing can be done with the typical pension plan, profit sharing plan or 401(k) plan without the spouse's consent, at retirement most of these accounts permit them to be transferred to an IRA owned by the participant. At this point there is greater flexibility in the estate plan.

Some clients who have large retirement accounts are concerned about possible creditor claims should the beneficiary of the retirement account have creditor problems. Retirement accounts are protected by creditor claims for the participant, as are IRA plans. These protections do not apply to the beneficiary. This creates a difficult problem. The best solution is for the retirement account to be made payable to a trust for the beneficiary that contains asset protection provisions. The trust is not considered a permissible beneficiary of a retirement account, but the IRS has ruled that the minimum distribution rules can be met through the trust beneficiary's life expectancy if several criteria are met. Those are discussed Sections VI.B and VIII.

A helpful chart of the various retirement accounts and their varying requirements is provided in Appendix A. An excellent ABA resource is Louis A. Mezzullo, *An Estate Planner's Guide to Qualified Retirement Plans* (ABA 2016).

II. Background

The area of pension law and retirement planning is quite complex. Nonetheless, the practitioner needs a general knowledge of this area of the tax law to advise elder clients. The ensuing discussion will review the basic features of retirement plans followed by a discussion of the issues to be considered when an elder client elects to begin receiving benefits. A helpful resource is found at www.irs.gov, entering "Types of Retirement Plans" in the search box in the top right-hand corner of the IRS website.

III. *Types of Retirement Plans*[1]

A. *Pension Plans*

A pension plan, which in the tax law is termed a *defined benefit plan*,[2] is a retirement plan that provides the participant with a fixed benefit. It is usually based on a combination of years of service and wages. For example, participants may receive an annual retirement benefit equal to 3 percent of the participant's average annual salary based on the five years of the highest salary times the participant's years of service. The annual benefit in 2019 cannot exceed the lesser of $225,000 per year or 100 percent of the three consecutive years of the highest salary. The maximum compensation in 2019 that can be taken into account when determining the preceding limit on benefits of an employee is $280,000. The benefit cap and compensation limits are both indexed annually for cost of living increases. The maximum annual benefit is actuarially reduced when benefits are paid before age 62 and increased when benefits are not paid until after age 65. The benefits are also reduced when individuals have less than ten years of service.

B. *Profit-Sharing Plans*

A profit-sharing plan, which in the tax law is one of several types of plans termed defined contribution plans,[3] is a plan in which the employer's contribution to the plan is fixed. The benefit to be received by a participant is not fixed. For example, each year after the employer has reviewed year-end profits, a dollar amount is contributed to the plan that is then earmarked to each participant's account on a pro rata basis. Another approach is for the employer to annually contribute a fixed percentage of salary to each participant's account in the plan. The annual contribution limit to a participants account is the lesser of 100 percent of the participant's compensation, or $56,000.[4] This limit of $56,000 is for 2019 and is adjusted annually for cost of living increases. The maximum compensation that can be taken into account when determining the limit on compensation in 2019 is $280,000, which is adjusted annually. The employer's income tax deduction is limited to 25 percent of total employee compensation.[5]

Unlike a pension plan, the participant's retirement benefit in a profit-sharing plan is uncertain. It is simply the amount contributed to his or her account plus the growth from the investment of those contributions. Another difference is that annual contributions are not required to be made to a profit-sharing plan. Thus, in years in which profitability is poor, a small or even no contribution may be made.

C. *Money-Purchase Plans*

A money-purchase plan is a defined contribution plan; however, the employer's contribution is fixed at a percentage of the participant's salary. Thus, it becomes a hybrid of a pension and a profit-sharing plan. Just as in a pension plan, the employer must make annual contributions, but as in a profit-sharing plan, the participant's benefit is uncertain because it depends on the investment experience. For example, in a money-purchase plan the employer sets an ongoing contribution commitment at a fixed percentage of salary, such as 10 percent of annual salary. The contribution limit (in 2019) for a money-purchase plan is the lesser of 25 percent of compensation or $56,000. This amount is adjusted annually for increases in the cost of living. The employer's income tax deduction is limited to 25 percent of total employee compensation.

D. 401(k) Plans

There are two types of employer-provided 401(k) plans: (1) a cash or deferred plan and (2) a salary reduction plan. In the cash or deferred plan, the employer's contribution may be received in cash by the employee and income tax paid on it, or the employee may elect to defer paying income tax on the contribution by having it credited to his or her 401(k) account.[6] The salary reduction plan allows an employee to elect to reduce his or her salary by a set percentage, which amount is deferred from income tax and is credited to the employee's 401(k) plan. The amount deferred is capped (in 2019) at an annual amount of $19,000. This amount is indexed for annual cost of living adjustments. An individual at least 50 years of age may defer an additional $6,000. This amount is also adjusted annually for cost of living increases. Once a deferral is made, it is treated just as is an employer contribution to any other qualified retirement plan; thus, the deferral cannot be withdrawn without tax penalties until retirement. However, a 401(k) plan does allow withdrawals before retirement in the case of some hardships.[7]

A 401(k) plan is not a separate plan, but must be offered in conjunction with a profit-sharing or stock bonus plan.[8] 401(k) plans are sometimes difficult to implement in businesses owing to the nondiscrimination rules. These rules require a reasonable balance in participation between the highly paid and the non-highly paid employees. If this requirement is not met, then a 401(k) plan is not available for any of the employees.[9] An alternative to these requirements is a "safe harbor 401(k)" which is a plan that fully vests contributions when made and has an accelerated vesting schedule. A helpful resource is found at www.irs.gov, entering "Operating a 401(k) Plan" in the search box in the top right-hand corner of the IRS website.

A recent addition to the 401(k) plan is a Roth 401(k) plan. Like the Roth IRA, the individual's contributions do not reduce taxable income. The advantages are the earnings from the investments are tax free and there is no tax when distributions are taken from the Roth IRA at retirement. Generally the same rules that apply to a 401(k) plan apply to the Roth 401(k). This includes the maximum contribution, which is set at $19,000 in 2019 with an additional $6,000 possible for those who are over age 50. Further, if the plan so permits, the traditional 401(k) plan can be converted to a Roth 401(k). Conversion requires the payment of income taxes on the value of the 401(k) account.

Obviously, to convert to a Roth the individual needs a high income or a substantial amount in savings with which to pay these taxes. Yet, for the right individual this is a significant savings for they and their ultimate estate beneficiaries.

E. 401(k) SIMPLE Plans

Another type of 401(k) plan is the SIMPLE 401(k) plan. Basically, a SIMPLE 401(k) plan relaxes some of the nondiscrimination requirements of a 401(k) plan. The deferred amount (in 2019) is limited to $13,000 (indexed annually for inflation), rather than the higher amount permissible under a traditional 401(k) plan. An additional deferral of $3,000 is allowed for employees age 50 or over. These plans are limited to an "eligible employer" who is one who: (1) employs 100 or fewer employees, each of whom receives at least $5,000 of compensation from the employer the preceding year; and (2) does not maintain another employer-sponsored retirement plan. A SIMPLE 401(k) requires the employer to make either (1) a matching contribution up to 3 percent of each employee's pay or (2) a non-elective contribution of 2 percent of each eligible employee's pay.

F. Keogh or HR-10 Plans

The retirement planning options available for the self-employed, including partnerships, were limited for many years. Changes in this area of the tax law, which became effective in 1985, have, with only a few restrictions, created parity between corporate and self-employed retirement plans.[10] Today the same rules that apply to corporate plans, including contribution limits, apply to the self-employed when they seek to adopt a pension, profit-sharing, money-purchase, 401(k), or SEP retirement plan for their business. Therefore, the explanations throughout this chapter generally also apply to Keogh plans.

One important difference between corporate and self-employed plans is in the determination of the contribution limit. The contribution limit for the self-employed's account is based on the "earned income" of the self-employed. Earned income is defined as net self-employment income less (1) the contribution made by the self-employed person to his or her own account and (2) 50 percent of the person's self-employed social security tax.[11] In some situations, this can create some difficult interrelated mathematical computations. The example that follows demonstrates how this rule reduces the contribution actually available for the self-employed.

EXAMPLE: A self-employed businessman wants to make the maximum 25 percent of compensation contribution to his money-purchase plan. Because he is self-employed, his contribution to the plan is deducted from his compensation to determine his earned income, on which the contribution percentage must then be applied. This rather circular problem is solved by dividing the contribution percentage by 1.0 plus the contribution percentage. The self-employed businessman can contribute only 20 percent of compensation (0.25 ÷ 1.25 = 20 percent). If the plan's maximum contribution is 25 percent, only 20 percent applies to the self-employed businessman, but 25 percent applies to all other employees.

G. SEP

The SEP is a simplified employee pension plan,[12] or, as it is sometimes referred to, a Super IRA, or SEP-IRA. The SEP is an employer-provided retirement plan, but record keeping and tax reporting are simplified. As in a profit-sharing plan, annual contributions are not required. The contributions, when made, are placed in each employee's own individual retirement account, and the contributions immediately become the employee's property. A salary deferral feature similar to a 401(k) can be offered as a part of the SEP.[13] The contribution limit in 2019 to a SEP is the lesser of 25 percent of compensation (not to exceed $280,000 as adjusted for inflation) or $56,000.[14] The higher limit makes the SEP just as attractive as a profit-sharing plan, but easier and less costly to administer. The only disadvantage is that the employee immediately owns the contribution in his or her account. Thus, there are no forfeitures of contributions to be redistributed to the other participants' accounts, as there are when an employee terminates employment and has unvested benefits.[15] A helpful resource is found at www.irs.gov, entering "Operating a SEP" in the search box in the top right-hand corner of the IRS website, or see IRS publication 4333.

H. IRA

An IRA is an individual retirement account[16] that can be established by any individual, whether participating in an employer-provided retirement plan or not. The maximum annual contribution to an IRA in 2019 is $6,000.[17] A married couple can each contribute up to $6,000 annually to his or her own IRA even if one of the spouses is not employed.[18] Individuals at least 50 years of age may make an additional $1,000 annual contribution.

As with other retirement plans, the earnings from an IRA are not currently subject to income tax but are taxed on receipt at withdrawal.[19] Generally, an individual who contributes to an IRA can deduct the annual IRA contribution from gross income on his or her personal income tax return, provided neither the individual nor his or her spouse is an active participant in an employer-sponsored qualified retirement plan. However, the right to make a tax deductible contribution on behalf of the nonparticipant spouse when the other spouse participates in an employer-provided retirement plan is phased out for couples who have an adjusted gross income between $193,000 and $203,000 (2019 amounts). Further, when an individual is an active participant in a qualified plan, the income tax deduction for a married couple begins phasing out at adjusted gross income levels between $103,000 and $123,000 (2019 amounts).

I. Simple IRA[20]

A significant modification to existing retirement plan law is the addition of the Savings Incentive Match Plan for Employees, which is known as a SIMPLE-IRA. Generally, elective employer contributions are made to an IRA on behalf of employees, and the employer makes either a matching contribution or a non-elective contribution. The nondiscrimination rules generally applicable to qualified plans do not apply. The top-heavy plan rules do not apply. There is a simplified reporting procedure. These simple plans are limited to employers with no more than 100 employees, each of whom receives at least $5,000 in compensation, if the employer does not maintain another qualified employee retirement plan. The employee may elect to have reduced from compensation (in 2019) up to $13,000 per year (to be adjusted annually for inflation). The employers' matching contribution can be either a non-elective contribution of 2 percent of compensation or an elective contribution up to 3 percent of compensation. A helpful resource is found at www.irs.gov, entering "Operating a SIMPLE IRA Plan" in the search box in the top right-hand corner of the IRS website.

J. Roth IRA[21]

A newer savings vehicle, the Roth IRA, offers a different type of IRA savings. The contributions are nondeductible but qualified distributions are received income tax free. Qualified distributions are those made after age 59 $^1/_2$, due to death or disability, or for a first-time home buyer expenses up to a $10,000 lifetime limit. A first-time home buyer is one who has not owned a principal residence for two years, but the distribution may be not only to the taxpayer and his or her spouse but also to children, grandchildren, or ancestors. The regular IRA-required minimum distribution rules do not apply. Contributions in 2019 are limited to $6,000 per year for each spouse. An additional $1,000 may be contributed by individuals 55 years of age or older. The contribution limits are adjusted annually. The contribution limit is reduced for joint income tax filers with adjusted gross income above $193,000 and then eliminated when adjusted gross income exceeds $203,000. The limitations are $122,600 to $137,000 for single taxpayers.

A Roth IRA is of limited benefit due to the compensation limits and the small annual contribution limit. The real benefit of the Roth IRA is that you can rollover amounts from other retirement accounts to an additional IRA, then convert that IRA to a Roth IRA. Income tax must be paid on the amount converted, but thereafter investment growth is tax free as are later distributions. The minimum distributions do not apply, allowing the account to grow tax free and later be distributed to the ultimate heirs as a large income tax free investment. This is the income tax code so nothing is simple. To learn more, a helpful resource is found at www.irs.gov, entering "Rollover of Retirement Plans and IRA Distributions" in the search box in the top right-hand corner of the IRS website. Also, you should work with the client's CPA or financial planner to be certain this rollover and conversion is handled properly.

IV. Participation, Vesting, and Nondiscrimination

The attorney needs to be aware of the concepts of participation, vesting, and nondiscrimination as used in the tax law even though you will not be designing the client's retirement plans. Each of these concepts involves specific statutory requirements that must be met before a retirement plan is qualified for the favorable income tax treatment that is essential under the tax law. Participation refers to the time that an employee becomes eligible to participate in the employer's retirement plan. Any employee age 21 with one year of service must be a participant in the plan.[22] To avoid including temporary or part-time employees, anyone who works 1,000 hours or less per year is not required to be a participant in the plan.[23] Participation can be extended to two years if desired, but to do so requires an immediate 100 percent vesting schedule for all participants.[24]

Even though an employee is a participant in a plan, the employee does not actually own anything until the contributions of the employer have "vested." Vesting occurs under one of three schedules:[25]

1. "Cliff" vesting, which requires 100 percent vesting after three years of service;
2. "Graded" vesting, which requires 20 percent vesting after two years and 20 percent each year thereafter; or
3. 100 percent immediate vesting if two years of service for eligibility is required.

Once a vesting schedule is selected for a retirement plan, that schedule will determine when an employee is considered to own the benefits in his or her account. If an employee terminates employment before being 100 percent vested, the portion of the account that is not vested is forfeited. The forfeitures will either reduce future employer contributions or be an extra allocation for the remaining employees.

Nondiscrimination rules are intended to ensure that the retirement plan is for all employees, not just a few of the highly compensated employees. Retirement plans are not intended to discriminate in coverage, contributions, or benefits in favor of the highly compensated.[26] The retirement plan will qualify as nondiscriminatory if (1) the percentage of non-highly compensated employees is at least 70 percent of the percentage of covered highly compensated employees (ratio test)[27] or (2) the plan must benefit a classification of employees that does not discriminate in favor of highly compensated employees and the average benefit percentage of the non-highly compensated employees must be at least 70 percent of the average benefit percentage of the highly compensated employees (average benefit percentage test). The "highly compensated" employees are those who are (1) 5 percent or more owners or (2) earning more than $125,000 per year (in 2019), and are in the top-paid group of employees.[28] A top-paid employee is one who ranks in the top 20 percent of compensation. The 2019 income level of $125,000 for "highly compensated" employees is adjusted for cost of living increases.

V. Top-Heavy Plans

Even though a plan meets all of the requirements to be qualified under the Internal Revenue Code, it may still be termed top-heavy, which brings to bear another set of rules. A top-heavy plan is one in which more than 60 percent of the aggregated accumulated benefits or account balances of the plan participants accrue to the benefit of the "key employees." A key employee is one who during the current plan year and the four prior years is (1) an officer of the employer with over $180,000 in compensation in 2019, (2) a 5 percent or greater owner, or (3) a 1 percent or greater owner having a compensation in excess of $150,000.[29]

For any year in which a plan is top-heavy, it must use an accelerated vesting schedule and modify its contribution requirements for the non-key employees.[30] The vesting schedule must be either a three year "cliff" vesting schedule, or a "graded" vesting requiring 20 percent vesting after two years and 20 percent each year thereafter.[31] The contributions in a defined contribution plan must be at least 3 percent of compensation for the non-key employee, or if less than 3 percent, then the same percentage for the key employees. If the plan is a defined benefit plan (pension plan), the fixed benefit for the non-key employees must be at least 2 percent of the employee's highest five-year average compensation for each year in which the plan is top-heavy.[32]

VI. Penalty Taxes

There are two tax penalties that can have an effect on a participant in a retirement plan. The practitioner must be aware of these penalties because they must be considered in making decisions about the distribution of benefits during lifetime or at death. The taxes are a penalty (1) on premature distributions and (2) due to the failure to make required minimum withdrawals from the plan.

A. Premature Distributions

Any distribution from a qualified retirement plan, 401(k), IRA, or SEP before the participant reaches 59 $1/2$ years of age is subject to a 10 percent premature distribution penalty.[33] The distribution also is subject to income tax. The tax does not apply if the distribution is made owing to the participant's death, disability, or divorce, if pursuant to a qualified domestic relations order.[34] The distribution also is not subject to the 10 percent penalty if made to the participant after age 55 pursuant to early retirement, or earlier if made in equal periodic payments over the life expectancy of the participant or the participant and his or her beneficiary. Payments for medical expenses also are excluded.[35] Further, most distributions from qualified retirement plans that are rolled over into an IRA within 60 days from distribution are not taxed as premature distributions.[36] But a 20 percent mandatory income tax withholding is required, even though the 60-day rollover requirement is met, unless the transfer is directly from trustee to trustee.[37]

B. Minimum Distributions

Distributions from all qualified retirement plans and IRAs must begin no later than April 1 following the year in which the participant reaches 70 $1/2$ years of age. This date is termed the *required beginning date*. IRS tables provide the life expectancy factor to be used by the participant in determining the minimum distribution to be received from the retirement plan.[38] This is a critical determination and care must be taken in making it. If distribution is not made in the minimum amount required, a penalty of 50 percent is imposed on the difference between the minimum required and the actual distribution. The penalty can be waived by the IRS if reasonable cause is established for the error and if steps are taken to ensure the error will be remedied.[39]

The IRS has simplified the required minimum distribution rules. Basically, the December 31 value of a retirement account for the previous year is divided by the life expectancy factor from the MDIB table.

TABLE FOR DETERMINING APPLICABLE DIVISOR FOR MDIB
(MINIMUM DISTRIBUTION)

Age and applicable divisor (life expectancy)	Age and applicable divisor (life expectancy)
70 27.4	93 9.6
71 26.5	94 9.1
72 25.6	95 8.6
73 24.7	96 8.1
74 23.8	97 7.6
75 22.9	98 7.1
76 22.0	99 6.7
77 21.2	100 6.3
78 20.3	101 5.9
79 19.5	102 5.5
80 18.7	103 5.2
81 17.9	104 4.9
82 17.1	105 4.5
83 16.3	106 4.2
84 15.5	107 3.9
85 14.8	108 3.7
86 14.1	109 3.4
87 13.4	110 3.1
88 12.7	111 2.9
89 12.0	112 2.6
90 11.4	113 2.4
91 10.8	114 2.1
92 10.2	115 and older 1.9

The life expectancy factor from this table is used in all cases except when the participant's spouse is the sole beneficiary and is more than 10 years younger than the participant. For these tables, see www.irs.gov Publication 590-B, Appendix B-Table II. A helpful resource is found at www.irs.gov. Insert "Retirement Topics—Required Minimum Distributions and Required Minimum Distributions for IRA Beneficiaries" in the search box in the top right-hand corner of the IRS website. This life expectancy table is used without regard to who the beneficiary is, or even if there is a beneficiary.

If a participant dies before the required beginning date, distribution is based on the single life expectancy factor tables for the beneficiary's own life expectancy determined for the beneficiary's age in the year following the year of death. If there is no named beneficiary, distribution must be made within five years. If the participant dies after the required beginning date, the required minimum distribution for the year of death must be distributed, then in the years following the year of death the minimum distribution is based on the longer of the participant's or the beneficiary's life expectancy. If there is no named beneficiary, distribution must be made over the remaining years of the participant's life expectancy based on the participant's age on his or her birthday in the year of death. These are the minimum amounts that must be distributed. Greater amounts can always be distributed.

There are exceptions to these rules for a surviving spouse. A surviving spouse may rollover the retirement account into the surviving spouse's own IRA and then treat the retirement account as the survivor's own IRA for purposes of distribution. If the surviving spouse prefers, distributions can begin based on his or her life expectancy or distributions can be delayed until the year in which the participant would have attained the age of 70 $\frac{1}{2}$. These exceptions apply if the participant died before the required beginning date. If the participant died after the required beginning date, the options are either a rollover or beginning distributions based on the survivor's life expectancy in the year following the year of the participant's death.

If a trust is named as the beneficiary, the minimum distributions are based on the life expectancy of the trust beneficiary, or if there is more than one trust beneficiary then the minimum distributions are based on the age of the oldest beneficiary. The naming of a trust as the beneficiary requires caution, as the general rule is that a beneficiary must be an individual. To qualify a trust as a beneficiary the following requirements must be met. The trust must be valid under state law. The trust is irrevocable, or by its terms becomes irrevocable upon the death of the owner. The beneficiaries of the trust are identifiable. A copy of the trust documents are provided to the IRA custodian by October 31 of the year following the year in which the participant dies. Upon meeting these requirements the trust will qualify as a beneficiary.

There are no required minimum distributions for a Roth IRA or Roth 401(k) for the owner of the account. If the beneficiary is the spouse, the Roth account can be rolled over to the surviving spouse's account ownership and then new beneficiaries designated. The surviving spouse does not have to receive minimum distributions. A beneficiary of a Roth account other than the surviving spouse has two options. The beneficiary must take the entire account balance by December 31 of the year containing the fifth anniversary of the owner's death. The second option is more complex. The beneficiary must start taking distributions over the beneficiary's life expectancy starting no later than December 31 of the year following the year of the owner's death. This second option is certainly more advantageous as the funds will continue to grow and compound tax free and distributions will of course be tax free as well.

For a helpful resource go to www.irs.gov and in the search box in the upper right-hand corner insert "Retirement Topics—Required Minimum Distributions," "Retirement Topics—Beneficiary," or "Publication 590-B."

VII. *Taxation of Distributions*

A. *Income Taxation of Distributions during Lifetime*

The income tax consequences of a distribution from a qualified retirement plan, an IRA, or a SEP depend on when it is made and whether it is distributed in installments or in a lump sum. A lump-sum distribution to a participant other than a self-employed person must be owing to the participant's death, disability, divorce, separation from service, deductible medical expenses or having reached age 59 $1/2$.[40] A lump-sum distribution to a self-employed person follows the same rules except for the separation from service exception. A lump-sum distribution for any other reason is subject to both income tax and the 10 percent premature distribution penalty.

A lump-sum distribution from a qualified plan that is not made for one of these reasons can be rolled into an IRA within 60 days of the distribution.[41] When this is done, the income tax continues to be deferred and the premature distribution penalty is avoided. However, the distribution must be a trustee-to-trustee transfer to avoid the imposition of a 20 percent income tax withholding.[42]

A distribution payable in periodic installments is subject to income tax under the annuity rules of Internal Revenue Code section 72. Basically, these rules prorate the annual payment between the employer's and the employee's contribution. The employee's contribution is returned tax free if it was made with after-tax contributions, whereas the remainder of the annuity payment is taxable. Many retirement plans do not permit after-tax employee contributions; thus, for those plans the entire annuity payment will be subject to income tax.

Distributions received in a lump sum after a participant reached age 59 $1/2$ previously received favorable income tax treatment. These "tax breaks" are not available after 1999.[43] An individual who reached 50 before January 1, 1986, is still entitled to some of these "tax breaks." The rules get complicated owing to numerous amendments in the distribution rules. Basically, some participants have options for capital gain treatment of pre-1974 contributions; and ten-year or five-year averaging.[44] Also, five-year averaging is still

available for those who were not 50 or older before January 1, 1986, if distribution was received after age 59 $^1/_2$. These special tax breaks have never
applied to IRAs and SEPs.[45] Few people will currently meet these age requirements. If in doubt, let the accountant do the advising.

The spouse of the participant has certain guaranteed rights that must be
considered. In a pension or money-purchase plan, the retirement benefit
must be payable in a joint and survivor's annuity, unless this option is
waived by the spouse. Generally, this is not required in profit-sharing plans;
however, the spouse must be designated as the beneficiary of the benefits in
the event of death, unless the spouse waives this right in writing.[46] This
restriction does not apply to IRAs.

B. Estate Taxation of Distributions at Death

Distributions following the death of the participant are subject to estate tax.[47]
They are included in the gross estate if (1) before death the annuity was payable to the decedent or to the decedent and another and (2) after death any
payment is made to a beneficiary who has survived the decedent. In other
words if, because of a contractual obligation owed to the decedent, payment
is made to a beneficiary who survived the decedent, the payment is included
in the gross estate. This includes not only commercial annuities and private
annuities but also the various types of qualified employee benefit plans, such
as pension plans, profit-sharing plans, 401(k) plans, SEPs, and IRAs. Due to
the current large estate tax exemptions, most clients will not owe an estate
tax.

Frequently, the beneficiary of an annuity has the payment option of
receiving a lump sum, in which event the lump-sum payment is included in
the gross estate. If payment is receivable as a periodic payment instead, then
the present value of the income right of the beneficiary is included in the
gross estate of the decedent. This computation is made according to the IRS
valuation tables in Treasury Regulation 20.2031-11. In those rare situations in
which someone other than the decedent and his or her employer contributed
to the annuity, a proportionate reduction is allowed for those third-party contributions to the purchase of the annuity when valuing the annuity.

VIII. Creditor Protection

Federal law provides protection for what are termed *qualified retirement plans*.
Qualified retirement plans are those protected by the Employee Retirement
Income Security Act of 1974 (ERISA) for claims by creditors.[48] This protection
covers most employer plans, such as 401(k)s, defined benefit plans (pension
plans), and profit-sharing plans. Other retirement plans, such as 403(b), 457,
traditional IRA, Roth IRA, SEP, and Simple IRA have more limited protection. First, a rollover from a qualified plan to an IRA retains its protection
from creditors under ERISA. Traditional and Roth IRAs and the other types
of retirement plans just mentioned are protected under federal bankruptcy

law. As long as the retirement account owner has filed for bankruptcy protection the protection exists with one exception. Traditional and Roth IRAs protection is limited to $1,000,000 which is the amount indexed for inflation and currently is $1,283,025.[49] This limit is not a problem in most situations as traditional IRAs and Roth IRAs have such low annual contribution amounts that any such account will seldom have ever reached the $1,000,000 threshold.

This protection is only available if there is a federal bankruptcy proceeding. There is no protection from non-bankruptcy creditor claims unless that protection is provided by state law. Many states do provide total asset protection from creditor claims even outside of federal bankruptcy protection. The attorney must be aware of her own state law. These federal law protections do not exist when the claim is for federal taxes or the claims of an ex-spouse. A final point is that an inherited IRA has no creditor protection. If creditor protection is important, then the IRA should be made payable to a trust that provides for creditor protection for the trust beneficiary. When drafting a trust for asset protection for retirement assets, be certain to comply with the trust requirements for it being a beneficiary of a retirement account as discussed in Section VI.B.

Appendix A: Comparison of Plans

Plan Type	Employer Eligibility	Contribution/Benefit Limits	
SIMPLE IRA	Sole Proprietorships Partnerships S and C Corporations L.L.C. Tax-Exempt Organizations State and Local Governmental Entities **All businesses with fewer than 100 employees who earn $5,000 or more in compensation**	Under age 50: $13,000 in 2019	Catch-up: age 50 and up $3,000 in 2019
		Salary deferral contributions cannot exceed the lesser of the dollar limit above or 100% of compensation. Employers are required to offer a dollar-for-dollar match up to 3% of compensation or make a mandatory contribution of 2% of compensation to all eligible employees.	
SEP IRA	Sole Proprietorships Partnerships S and C Corporations L.L.C. Tax-Exempt Organizations State and Local Governmental entities	Contributions cannot exceed the lesser of 25% of compensation or: $56,000 in 2019	
401(k)	Sole Proprietorships Partnerships S and C Corporations L.L.C. Tax-Exempt Organizations	Under age 50: $19,000 in 2019	Catch-up: age 50 and up $6,000 in 2019
		Total additional employer contributions such as matching and profit sharing cannot exceed 25% of all eligible employees' compensation. Total salary deferrals, matching, profit sharing, and any after-tax contributions (if allowed) for any individual cannot exceed $55,000 ($62,000 if age 50 and older) or 100% of compensation in 2019. Plans may allow participants to designate part or all of their deferrals as Roth contributions.	

Plan Type	Employer Eligibility	Contribution/Benefit Limits	
Safe Harbor 401(k)	Sole Proprietorships	Same as 401(k)	Same as 401(k)
	Partnerships S and C Corporations L.L.C. Tax-Exempt Organizations	Total additional employer contributions such as matching and profit sharing cannot exceed 25% of all eligible employee's compensation. Employers are required to offer eligible employees a match (dollar-for-dollar up to 3% of compensation, plus 50% of next 2% of compensation. The equivalent of dollar-for-dollar up to 4% is common) or make a mandatory contribution of 3% of compensation to all eligible employees. Total salary deferrals matching profit sharing, and any after-tax contributions (if allowed) cannot exceed $55,000 ($62,000) if age 50 and older or 100% of compensation in 2019. Plans may allow participants to designate part or all of their deferrals as Roth contributions.	
Profit Sharing	Sole Proprietorship Partnerships S and C Corporations L.L.C. State and Local Governmental Entities	Generally the lesser of 25% of compensation or: $56,000 in 2019	
Defined Benefit	Sole Proprietorships Partnerships S and C Corporations L.L.C. Tax-Exempt Organizations State and Local Governmental Entities Highly Profitable Businesses	Contributions are determined by an actuary based on the funding needed to pay the benefits provided under the plan. Benefit formulas may include several factors, including age, years of service, and compensation. Plans can provide an annual benefit in retirement up to 100% of an amount equal to the three consecutive years that produces the highest average compensation or $225,000 in 2019 whichever is less. An older employee population will generally result in higher contributions.	

Plan Type	Maximum Employee Eligibility Requirements	Set-up Deadline	Contribution Deadline
SIMPLE IRA	An employer can require an employee: 1) Earn $5,000 in each of any two prior calendar years, and 2) Be reasonably expected to earn $5,000 in the current year. There are no age or number of hour requirements.	October 1 of the current year	Salary deferral contributions must be deposited as soon as administratively possible, but no later than the 30 day following the month of deferral. Matching and non-elective contributions are due by the business's tax filing deadline, including extensions.
SEP IRA	An employer can require that an employee: 1) Be 21, 2) Work during any three of the immediately preceding five years, and 3) Currently earn at least $600 in 2019. There is no number of hour requirements.	Business's tax filing deadline, including extensions.	Business's tax filing deadline, including extensions.
401(k)	An employer can require than an employee: 1) Be age 21, and 2) Complete 1 year of service in which they work at least 1,000 hours.	Must be established prior to commencement of salary deferrals; must be established prior to business's year and to make employer contributions.	Salary deferral contributions must be deposited as soon as administratively possible, but no later than the 15th business day of the month following the deferral. Matching and profit sharing are due by the business's tax filing deadline, including extensions.
Safe Harbor 401(k)	Same as 401(k)	In general, a new plan must be established three months before the business's year-end (generally October 1 for calendar year plans).	Same as 401(k)

Plan Type	Maximum Employee Eligibility Requirements	Set-up Deadline	Contribution Deadline
Profit Sharing	An employer can require that an employee: 1) Be age 21, and 2) Work 1,000 hours in two preceding years. If a vesting schedule is used, only one year can be required.	Business's year-end.	Business's tax filing deadline, including extensions.
Defined Benefit	An employer can require that an employee: 1) Be age 21, and 2) Work 1,000 hours in two preceding years. If a vesting schedule is used, only one year can be required.	Business's year-end.	Earlier of business's tax filing deadline, including extensions, or minimum funding deadline (Sept. 15 for calendar year plans).

Notes

1. This discussion includes only the more common types of plans.
2. I.R.C. § 414(j).
3. *Id.* § 414(i).
4. *Id.* § 415(c)(1).
5. *Id.* § 404(a)(3).
6. *Id.* § 401(k)(2).
7. *Id.* § 401(k)(2)(B).
8. *Id.* § 401(k)(2).
9. *Id.* § 401(k)(3).
10. *Id.* § 401(c).
11. *Id.* § 401(c)(2).
12. *Id.* § 408(k).
13. *Id.* § 408(k)(6).
14. *Id.* § 402(h).
15. See Section IV in this chapter.
16. I.R.C. § 408.
17. *Id.* § 219(b).
18. *Id.* § 219(c).
19. *Id.* § 408(e).
20. *Id.* § 408(p).
21. *Id.* § 408(A).
22. *Id.* § 410(a)(1).
23. *Id.* § 410(a)(3).
24. *Id.* § 410(a)(1)(B).
25. *Id.* § 411(a)(2).
26. *Id.* § 401(a)(4), (5).

27. *Id.* § 410(b)(1).
28. *Id.* § 414(q).
29. *Id.* § 416(g), (i).
30. *Id.* § 416(a).
31. *Id.* § 416(b).
32. *Id.* § 416(c)(1)(2).
33. *Id.* § 72(t).
34. I.R.C. 402(a)(9), 414(p). An IRA transferred incident to a divorce is governed by I.R.C. 408(d)(6).
35. I.R.C. § 72(t)(2).
36. *Id.* §§ 402(a)(5), 408(d)(3).
37. *Id.* § 3405(c).
38. *Id.* § 401(a)(9).
39. *Id.* § 4974.
40. *Id.* § 4029(e)(4)(A).
41. *Id.* § 402(a)(5).
42. *Id.* § 3405(c).
43. *Id.* § 402(e).
44. *Id.* See irs.gov/taxtopics/tc412.
45. IRS Form 4972 and the accompanying general instruction booklet are helpful.
46. I.R.C. § 401(a)(11).
47. *Id.* § 2039
48. 29 U.S.C. § 1056(d).
49. 11 U.S.C. § 522(n).

CHAPTER 9

Income, Estate, Gift, and Generation-Skipping Taxes

I.	Overview	266
II.	Introduction to Federal Income Tax	267
III.	Filing Status	268
IV.	Gross Income Exclusions	269
V.	Gross Income Inclusions	270
VI.	Adjusted Gross Income	271
VII.	Standard Deduction	271
VIII.	Itemized Deductions	272
IX.	Tax Rate Schedules	272
X.	Tax Credits	273
XI.	Alternative Minimum Tax	273
XII.	Common Tax Issues for Elder Clients	274
	A. Tax Credit for the Elderly or Disabled	274
	B. Social Security Exclusion	275
	C. Sale of Personal Residence	275
	D. Medical Expense Deduction	275
	E. Retirement Plan Distributions	276
	F. Cost Basis	276
XIII.	Introduction to Federal Estate Tax	276
XIV.	Gross Estate	277
	A. Gifts	277
	B. Transfers with Control Retained by Decedent	279
	C. Annuities and Retirement Benefits	281
	D. Joint Interests	281
	E. Powers of Appointment	282
	F. Life Insurance	283
XV.	Adjusted Gross Estate	284
XVI.	Taxable Estate	284
XVII.	Net Estate Tax	285
XVIII.	Filing and Payment	286
XIX.	Introduction to Federal Gift Tax	287

      A. Advantages of Gift Giving. 287
      B. General Requirements. 288
  XX. Special Considerations 289
      A. Gifts of Services 289
      B. Disclaimers 290
      C. Assignment of Income 290
      D. Delivery of the Gift 290
  XXI. Annual Exclusion and Split Gifts 291
      A. Annual Exclusion. 291
      B. Gift Splitting 292
  XXII. Income Tax Basis in Gift Property 292
XXIII. Transfers Not Subject to Gift Tax 293
      A. Marital Deduction 293
      B. Charitable Deduction 293
      C. Tuition and Medical Expenses. 293
  XXIV. Gifts for the Benefit of Children 294
  XXV. Special Situations 294
      A. Net Gifts 294
      B. Gift Subject to an Indebtedness. 295
  XXVI. Introduction to Generation-Skipping Transfer Tax 295
XXVII. General Rules 295
      A. Skip Person 296
      B. Transferor 296
      C. Taxable Distribution 297
      D. Taxable Termination. 297
      E. Direct Skip. 298
XXVIII. Tax Apportionment 299
Appendix A: Tax Rate Schedule 300

I. Overview

There are not very many tax issues facing the attorney when working with most elder clients. This chapter provides a brief overview of individual income taxation with an emphasis on several areas of taxation that are of the most importance to elder clients. Those are covered in Section XII. For most elder clients the current income tax law with a larger standard deduction and limitations on itemized deductions makes for a relatively simple income tax return. Those clients are most often interested in issues of taxation of their social security benefits, taxation of distributions from their retirement accounts, tax consequences of selling property or giving property to loved ones. Thus a brief overview of those concerns is found in Section XII.

The federal estate and gift tax laws used to be of considerable concern to attorneys when working with elder clients. The current high exclusion amount results in fewer clients being concerned with the so-called death tax. The excluded amount in the current year (2019) is $11,400,000 per individual. A married couple has an exemption of $22.8 million dollars for the surviving spouse with no estate tax owed when the first spouse dies owing to the marital deduction. In 2026 the exemptions are scheduled to be reduced in half. Whether that occurs or other changes are made in the estate tax law is certainly not determinable at this time. For those clients who do have larger estates, this writing does not include planning for those situations. In those larger estates you may wish to see the author's publication, *A Lawyer's Guide to Estate Planning*, 4th edition, published by the American Bar Association (2018).

Many clients are confused about the effects of the new law on gift giving. Most clients are familiar with the fact that they can make an annual gift of $15,000, or a gift of $30,000 if married. They are not aware of the fact that the $11,400,000 estate tax exclusion amount can be used in part or in full for large lifetime gifts. The only requirement is the filing of a gift tax return. Thus most clients can make any lifetime gifts they chose to make without concern for the federal estate or gift tax.

The final section of this chapter deals with the generation-skipping tax exemption. For the sophisticated estate planning attorney there is little in this chapter that will benefit you in planning with that exemption. The purpose of the brief discussion is to make the attorney aware of this tax so that there is not an inadvertent generation skip subject to a 40 percent tax with the client nor the attorney being aware of the tax. The good news is that the exempt amount is the same as the estate tax exclusion. Thus, most of your clients will not be concerned with the generation-skipping transfer tax, as their entire estate will be less than the $11,400,000 exclusion in 2019. It is important to note that there is no portability without more sophisticated planning of the exclusion from the first spouse to die and the second spouse. In other words while the estate tax exclusion for the surviving spouse can be as high as $22,800,000 in 2019, it is only $11,400,000 for the generation-skipping transfer tax. About all the attorney needs to be aware of is that when writing wills and trusts that skip a generation, whether by trust or by life estates, generation-skipping transfers are subject to the tax unless the transfer is within the exempt amount. Thus, at least a cursory understanding of the tax is important for the elder lawyer. Keep the "skip" below the exclusion and you are safe.

II. Introduction to Federal Income Tax

Lawyers who plan to advise their elder clients on income tax matters should find this chapter a helpful starting point. Obviously, a portion of a one-chapter treatment of such a difficult and technical area of the law can only "hit the high points." Thus, the lawyer who plans to master this area of law has more work ahead. The income tax section of this chapter provides a working outline of individual income taxation, including the pertinent Internal Revenue Code sections, followed by a more in-depth treatment of those areas of income taxation that specifically affect elder clients.

Income taxation speaks in its own technical language. The ensuing discussion must of necessity lapse into the terminology of gross income, adjusted gross income, deductions, exclusions, exemptions, tax rate schedules, filing status, tax credits and other "tax-speak" words, but it will be kept to a minimum. The all too familiar 1040 will be used as a working model for discussing individual income tax.

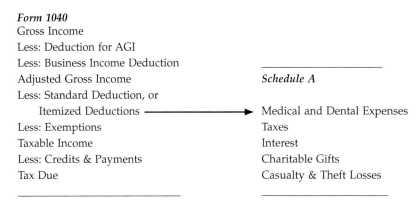

Form 1040
Gross Income
Less: Deduction for AGI
Less: Business Income Deduction   _____
Adjusted Gross Income   *Schedule A*
Less: Standard Deduction, or
     Itemized Deductions ⟶ Medical and Dental Expenses
Less: Exemptions   Taxes
Taxable Income   Interest
Less: Credits & Payments   Charitable Gifts
Tax Due   Casualty & Theft Losses

_____   _____

Before exploring the exciting world of gross income, let's take a quick glimpse at who must file an income tax return.

III. Filing Status

An individual must file an income tax return if he or she received a minimum amount of gross income during the calendar year. Basically, a tax return is required for all persons who have gross income that equals or exceeds the sum of their exemptions and standard deduction.[1] A significant exception requires a return for a self-employed person who has net earnings of $400.[2] Obviously, a return also must be filed to receive a tax refund or the benefits of the earned income credit.

Filing Status	Minimum 2019 Gross Income
Single	
Under 65	$ 12,200
65 or older	13,850
Married, filing joint return	
Both spouses under 65	24,400
One spouse 65 or older	25,700
Both spouses 65 or older	27,000
Married, filing separate return	
All, including 65 or older or blind	5
Head of Household	
Under 65	18,350
65 or older	20,000
Qualifying widow(er)	
Under 65	24,400
65 or older	25,700

IV. Gross Income Exclusions

Gross income is defined as all income from whatever source derived, except specifically excluded items.[3] The principal exclusions from gross income follow; however, the tax code section cited must be read. Some of these exclusions are available only if specific requirements are met and a few others are only partially excluded from gross income.

PRINCIPAL EXCLUSIONS FROM GROSS INCOME

Accident, health & sickness benefits in some situations	I.R.C. Sections 104, 105
Child support payments	I.R.C. Section 71(c)
Damages for personal injury or sickness	I.R.C. Section 104(a)(2)
Educational savings bonds	I.R.C. Section 135
Employer provided benefits	
Accident & health care plan contributions	I.R.C. Section 106
Athletic facilities	I.R.C. Sections 132(a)(3), 132(j)(4)
Cafeteria plans[4]	I.R.C. Section 125
Child care	I.R.C. Section 129
De minis benefits	I.R.C. Section 132(a)(4)
Employee discounts	I.R.C. Section 132(a)(2)
Group life insurance to $50,000	I.R.C. Section 79
Meals & lodging required by employer	I.R.C. Section 119
Moving expense reimbursement	I.R.C. Section 132(a)(6)
No-additional cost services	I.R.C. Section 132(a)(1)
Transportation	I.R.C. Section 132(a)(5)
Foster parent reimbursement	I.R.C. Section 131
Foreign income (partially)	I.R.C. Section 911
Gifts	I.R.C. Section 102
Improvement by lessee to lessor's property	I.R.C. Section 109
Income from discharge of indebtedness	I.R.C. Section 108
Inheritances	I.R.C. Section 102
Insurance reimbursement for living expenses due to casualty	I.R.C. Section 123
Interest on state or local bonds	I.R.C. Section 103
Life insurance paid on death	I.R.C. Section 101(a)
Military combat & uniform allowances	I.R.C. Sections 112, 113, 114
Minister's dwelling provided excludes rental value	I.R.C. Section 107
Sale of personal residence by older taxpayers	I.R.C. Section 121
Scholarship in certain situations	I.R.C. Section 117
Social security benefits (partially)	I.R.C. Section 86
Tuition reductions to employees of educational institutions	I.R.C. Section 117
Worker's compensation benefits	I.R.C. Section 104(a)(1)

V. Gross Income Inclusions

The list of items included in gross income that follows is based on the tax code definition of gross income, but this list is not exclusive. Generally, gross income includes income from any source that is not specifically excluded;[5] and you have just read the list of most all of those exclusions. So, if you can't exclude it, you must include it.

PARTIAL LIST OF INCLUSIONS IN GROSS INCOME

Alimony (Pre-2019 agreement)	I.R.C. Section 71
Annuities	I.R.C. Section 72
Awards	I.R.C. Sections 74, 117
Bartered services	I.R.C. Sections 61(a)(1), 6045
Bonuses	I.R.C. Section 61(a)(1)
Business income	I.R.C. Section 61(a)(2)
Capital gains	I.R.C. Sections 61(a)(3), 1221
Commissions	I.R.C. Section 61(a)(1)
Compensation for services	I.R.C. Section 61(a)(1)
Debts cancelled (if not excluded)	I.R.C. Section 61(a)(12)
Dividends	I.R.C. Section 61(a)(7)
Employee benefits (if not excluded)	I.R.C. Section 61(a)(1)
Estate and trust income	I.R.C. Section 61(a)(15)
Farm income	I.R.C. Section 61(a)(2)
Fees	I.R.C. Section 61(a)(1)
Gains from sale of property	I.R.C. Section 61(a)(3)
Gambling winnings	I.R.C. Sections 61(a)(2), 165(d)
Illegal transaction gains and payments	I.R.C. Sections 61(a)(2), 162(c)
Imputed interest	I.R.C. Section 7872
Interest	I.R.C. Section 61(a)(4)
Military pay (if not excluded)	I.R.C. Section 61(a)(1)
Partnership income	I.R.C. Section 61(a)(13)
Pensions, profit-sharing, IRA	I.R.C. Section 61(a)(11)
Prizes	I.R.C. Section 74
Professional fees	I.R.C. Section 61(a)(1)
Rents	I.R.C. Section 61(a)(5)
Rewards	I.R.C. Section 61(a)(1)
Royalties	I.R.C. Section 61(a)(6)
Salaries	I.R.C. Section 61(a)(1)
Social security (partially)	I.R.C. Section 86
Tips and gratuities	I.R.C. Section 61(a)(1)
Unemployment benefits	I.R.C. Section 85
Wages, including current, back and severance pay	I.R.C. Section 61(a)(1)

VI. *Adjusted Gross Income*

Adjusted gross income[6] is a concept only found in individual income taxation. Its sole utility is for computing certain deductions, credits, and other tax benefits that are based on, or limited to, a percentage of "adjusted gross income." The list of deductions is both specific and limited. The most common of those deductions follow.

PRINCIPAL DEDUCTIONS FOR ADJUSTED GROSS INCOME

Expenses attributable to a trade or business	I.R.C. Section 162
Expenses incurred by a taxpayer in connection with the performance of services as an employee if the expenses are reimbursed by the employer and other conditions are satisfied	I.R.C. Section 161
Expenses paid or incurred by a qualified performing artist for services in the performing arts as an employee	I.R.C. Section 162
Losses on the sale or exchange of property	I.R.C. Section 161
Expenses attributable to property held for the production of rents and royalties	I.R.C. Section 212
Alimony payments under agreement executed before 2019	I.R.C. Section 215
Certain contributions to pension, profit-sharing, and annuity plans of self-employed individuals	I.R.C. Section 404
IRA retirement savings	I.R.C. Section 219
The interest penalty imposed on premature withdrawal of funds from time savings accounts or deposits	I.R.C. Section 165

VII. *Standard Deduction*

A standard deduction is a specified amount allowed a taxpayer, depending on the taxpayer's filing status.[7] In addition to the basic standard deduction, taxpayers who are 65 years of age or older, or blind, qualify for an additional standard deduction that depends in amount on their filing status.[8] The effect of the standard deduction is to exempt a taxpayer's income from federal income taxes up to the specified amount. The current standard deductions follow. For tax years after 2019, see www.irs.gov.

Filing Status	Standard Deduction 2019	Additional Standard Deduction 2019
Single	$12,200	$1,650
Married, filing jointly	24,400	1,300
Married, filing separately	12,200	1,300
Qualified widow(er)	24,400	1,300
Head of household	18,350	1,650

The additional standard deduction is doubled if the individual is both 65 or older and blind. Thus, for a 65-year-old blind single or head of household filer, the additional deduction is $3,300. For a married or qualified widow(er) filer who is both 65 or older and blind, the additional deduction is $2,600; or if both spouses are 65 or older and blind the additional deduction is $5,200.

A person who can be claimed as a dependent on another taxpayer's return is limited to a smaller standard deduction. The dependent's standard deduction may not exceed the greater of $1,100 (2019) or the sum of $350 and the dependent's earned income up to the applicable standard deduction, which in 2019 is $12,200 for a single person.

VIII. Itemized Deductions

Individual taxpayers are allowed a limited number of itemized deductions for personal expenses in lieu of claiming a standard deduction. These deductions include medical expenses, certain taxes, interest, certain losses, and charitable contributions. Among the itemized deductions are the following:

PRINCIPAL ITEMIZED DEDUCTIONS

Medical expenses in excess of 7.5 percent of AGI (2019 and thereafter)	I.R.C. Section 213
State and local income taxes or state and local sales tax (maximum $10,000)	I.R.C. Section 164
Real estate taxes	I.R.C. Section 164
Personal property taxes	I.R.C. Section 164
Interest on home mortgage (up to $750,000 mortgage)	I.R.C. Section 163
Charitable contributions (within specified percentage limitations)	I.R.C. Section 170
Casualty and theft losses from federally declared disasters in excess of 10 percent AGI	I.R.C. Section 165(h)

IX. Tax Rate Schedules

The tax rate is based on one of several statuses, a single taxpayer, a head of household taxpayer, a married taxpayer filing either a separate return or a joint return.[9] Some clarification will be helpful. An unmarried taxpayer or one separated from a spouse by a decree of divorce or separate maintenance is a single taxpayer and must use those rates. A married taxpayer who qualifies under the abandoned spouse rules also may file as a single taxpayer.

Married taxpayers file as either married filing a joint return or married filing a separate return. The joint return status exists to create equity between married taxpayers in common law and community property states. Before joint return rates were established, taxpayers in community property states split income between them and thus owed less tax due to the progressive nature of the income tax rate schedule. This is similar to the inequity that existed in the estate tax area that caused the enactment of the marital deduction. Enough of tax history. Basically, the progressive rates and the joint return schedule are based on the assumption that the income is earned equally by the two spouses. If they so elect, married taxpayers may also file separate returns. Normally, this option is not advantageous, but in some circumstances separate returns may be appropriate.

Unmarried taxpayers who maintain a household for a dependent are entitled to use a head of household status. Generally, a head of household is one who provides more than one-half of the cost of maintaining a household in which a dependent relative lives. The head of household tax rate falls between the married joint rates and the single rates.

The tax brackets change yearly; for the current brackets and rate schedule, see www.irs.gov and in the search box in the upper right-hand corner of the IRS web page insert "1040 Tax Tables."

X. *Tax Credits*

Once the income tax is determined, the taxpayer may be entitled to one or more tax credits. The most obvious credit is for taxes withheld or estimated taxes paid. There are several other credits to which the taxpayer may be entitled. Only one of which, the earned income tax credit, results in a payment to the taxpayer. The other credits offset taxes, but do not result in a refund even though the credit exceeds the taxes owed. The principal tax credits are as follows:

TAX CREDITS

Taxes withheld on wages	I.R.C. Section 31
Earned income credit	I.R.C. Section 32
Credit for child and dependent care expenses	I.R.C. Sections 21, 24
Credit for adoption expenses	I.R.C. Section 23
Credit for the elderly or disabled	I.R.C. Section 22
Foreign tax credit	I.R.C. Section 27

XI. *Alternative Minimum Tax*

The alternative minimum tax is a rather odd addition made to the tax code in 1986. Generally, it is an additional tax aimed at thwarting the efforts of high income earning taxpayers to reduce their taxes by taking advantage of all of the tax incentives found in the tax code. The intent of the tax is to ensure that no taxpayer with substantial economic income can avoid significant tax liability by using exclusions, deductions, and credits, thus paying little or no income tax and undermining respect for the entire tax system. Of course, if the tax benefits do not represent good public policy, then they should be repealed or modified. The alternative minimum tax simply accomplishes through the back door what Congress is unwilling to do through the front door.

Generally, in computing the alternative minimum tax the beginning point is taxable income which is then increased by various tax preferences[10] and increased or decreased by certain required adjustments to income.[11] The adjustments are largely due to timing differences between the computation of income on the individual income return and income as determined under the alternative minimum tax. The real focus of the tax is on the tax preference items which include the following:

1. Percentage depletion deduction in excess of the property's adjusted basis
2. Excess intangible drilling costs reduced by 65 percent of the net income from oil, gas, and geothermal properties
3. Tax exempt interest on certain private activity bonds
4. Excess of accelerated over straight-line deprecation on real property placed in service before 1987
5. Excess of accelerated over straight-line depreciation on leased personal property placed in service before 1987
6. Excess of amortization allowance over depreciation on pre-1987 certified pollution control facilities
7. Seven percent of gain realized on sale of certain small business stock and excluded in I.R.C. section 1202.

Once the alternative minimum tax income is determined, an exemption is subtracted based on the taxpayer's filing status. For individual taxpayers in 2019 the exemption is $71,700, for married taxpayers filing jointly it is $111,700, and for married taxpayers filing separately it is $55,850. A tax rate of 26 percent is applied in 2018 to the first $194,800 (or $97,400 if married filing separately) of AMT income with the rate increasing to 28 percent for all amounts over $194,800 or $97,400.[12] The exemptions are phased-out by 25 percent of the amount AMT income exceeds a threshold based on the filing status.[13] The 2019 threshold and the point at which the phase-out begins is set forth here:

Filing Status	Exemption	Threshold
Single	$71,700	$510,300
Married, joint	111,700	1,020,600
Married, separate	55,850	510,300
Head of household	71,700	510,300

XII. Common Tax Issues for Elder Clients

A. Tax Credit for the Elderly or Disabled[14]

An individual who is 65 or older, or under age 65 who is retired on permanent and total disability when retired, may be entitled to a tax credit. The credit is 15 percent of an amount that depends on the filing status of the taxpayer. If the individual's exceeds either of the following amounts, the credit is not available. Those amounts at this writing are as follows:

Filing Status	Adjusted Gross Income	Non-Taxable Income
Single	$17,500	$5,000
Married, joint one spouse qualifies	20,000	5,000
Married, joint both spouses qualify	25,000	7,500
Married, separate	12,500	3,750

The credit is figured on Schedule R or the IRS will figure it for the individual. The actual computation is a bit confusing and results in a modest credit, but it may be of a help to a low income elderly client. For the seriously interested go to www.irs.gov and insert "Publication 524" in the search box in the upper right-hand corner of the IRS web page.

B. Social Security Exclusion[15]

A portion of an individual's social security or railroad retirement benefits may be taxable. If an individual's only income is from social security, those benefits likely are not taxable. But if the individual has other taxable income, including income from tax deferred retirement savings, other work, or tax-exempt interest, then 50 percent or 85 percent of the individual's social security benefits may be subject to federal income taxes.

To determine the percentage, calculate what is termed *provisional income*, which is the individual's gross income, excluding social security benefits, plus any non-taxable interest and one-half of the individual's social security benefits. If the total is less than $25,000 for a single taxpayer, or $32,000 for a married taxpayer filing jointly, the social security benefits are not taxable. If it is between $25,000 and $34,000 for a single taxpayer, or $32,000 to $44,000 on a joint return, then up to 50 percent of the person's social security benefits may be taxable. If the provisional income is more than $34,000 for a single taxpayer or $44,000 on a joint return, then up to 85 percent of the benefits may be taxable. For more information on this computation, see www.irs.gov, and insert "Publication 915" in the search box in the upper right-hand corner of the IRS web page.

C. Sale of Personal Residence[16]

Internal Revenue Code section 121 permits an unmarried taxpayer to exclude from gross income up to $250,000 of the gain from the sale of a personal residence. The taxpayer must have owned and used the home as his or her main home for two years or more during a five-year term ending on the date the home was sold. Thus, the exclusion can be used on a continuing basis, but not more frequently than once every two years. For married individuals filing jointly, the excludable amount is increased to $500,000 as long as one of the spouses owns the property, both spouses use the property as their main home, and neither spouse is ineligible for exclusion due to a sale of a home within the last two years.

D. Medical Expense Deduction[17]

Internal Revenue Code section 213 permits medical and dental expenses to be treated as itemized deductions to the extent they exceed 10 percent of adjusted gross income, in 2019. This deduction may become more important for elder clients as their income is often reduced and medical expenses increase during these later years. If there is uncertainty as to the deductibility of certain medical expenses, IRS publication 502 found at www.irs.gov is quite helpful.

An area that is often of concern for the elder client is the deductibility of nursing home care expenses. Treasury Regulation section 1.213-1(e)(1) should be consulted when there are questions about deductibility. Basically, the Treasury Regulation permits full deductibility for medical care, including meals and lodging that are furnished as a necessary incident for such care, provided the individual's condition is such that the need for medical care is the reason for being institutionalized. When this is not the case, only that part of the cost attributable to medical care is deductible, thus causing meals and lodging to be non-deductible.

E. Retirement Plan Distributions

Treatment of distributions from qualified retirement plans and IRAs is complex, involving the income tax questions of the amount that must be withdrawn annually and how that amount is taxed, as well as, the various payout elections that may be made to receive these payments. This subject is covered separately in Chapter 8 at Section XII.

F. Cost Basis

An income tax issue that is important for the elderly client is the determination of the cost basis for property that an individual owns that will result in income taxes owed when the property is sold. It is not our purpose to go into the intricacies of ordinary income taxation versus capital gains taxation, but rather to remind the reader that under I.R.C. section 1014 an individual's income tax cost basis is changed to the date of death value for assets held at death. Many elderly clients want to give assets to their children or other loved ones not realizing that the recipient of a gift must use the donor's income tax cost basis. Generally, this is the purchase price less depreciation, if any. This is also discussed in the gift tax section of this chapter at Section XIX. It is mentioned in this section to serve as a reminder that from an income tax savings perspective it is almost always better for the property to be received at death rather than the elderly donor making a gift during his lifetime. Of course this is only a consideration if the property has increased in value since it was first purchased.

XIII. Introduction to Federal Estate Tax

Tax advice to elder clients often involves questions about the federal estate and gift taxes. To advise one's elder clients a good knowledge of this area of the law is essential. The federal estate tax is an excise tax levied on the estate owing to the transfer at death of an individual's property. It differs from an inheritance tax, which many states impose, because an inheritance tax is levied on each beneficiary's inherited share rather than on the estate itself. The federal gift tax is also an excise tax and is levied on the transfer during an individual's lifetime of that individual's property. Before 1976, the estate tax and the gift tax were separate taxes, with the gift tax rate being 75 percent of the estate tax rate. The Tax Reform Act of 1976 merged these two taxes into one unified transfer tax. Now, owing to the unification of the two taxes, a transfer during lifetime or at death generally results in the same tax assessment. Yet the two taxes are not quite the same because the estate tax is tax-inclusive and the gift tax is tax-exclusive.

EXAMPLE: Assuming a taxpayer in the 40 percent estate and gift tax bracket bequeaths $100,000 to a child, the bequest is taxed $40,000 leaving the child $60,000 (tax-inclusive since the bequest includes the tax); however a lifetime gift also results in a $40,000 tax, but the tax is paid by the donor and not from the gift (tax-exclusive as the gift excludes the tax). Stated differently, a lifetime gift of $100,000 costs a gift tax of $40,000 for a total cost to the donor of $140,000. If the gift tax is to be paid by the donee to have a net gift of $100,000 the donor must gift $166,667 ($166,667 – $66,667 gift tax).

The Tax Cuts and Jobs Act of 2017, referred to herein as the 2017 Act, makes a substantial change in the estate and gift tax laws. The act increases the amount of an estate that is exempt from federal estate tax to $11,400,000 in 2019, which amount is adjusted annually for cost of living increases. The 2017 Act preserves the concept of portability discussed at Section XVII, reduces the top tax rate to 40 percent and permits any part or all of the estate tax exempt amount to be used for lifetime gifts.

The federal estate tax can be best understood by considering four concepts: (1) gross estate, (2) adjusted gross estate, (3) taxable estate, and (4) net estate tax. These concepts will now be discussed.

XIV. Gross Estate

The gross estate is the beginning point in determining what property is subject to the federal estate tax.[18] The gross estate includes both probate and non-probate property and certain gifts made during one's lifetime. Probate property includes all property, real or personal, tangible or intangible, owned at death by the decedent, either in his or her sole name, or in which the decedent owned an undivided interest. Included are such properties as real estate, stocks, bonds, cash, vehicles, equipment, and household items. Non-probate property and gift property includes various types of property in which the decedent had an interest at death, but that do not technically pass from the decedent to another by will or intestacy. These types of properties require further explanation.

A. Gifts

Prior to 1982, any gift made by a decedent to another within three years of death was subject to being included in his or her gross estate. The gift was presumed to have been made in contemplation of death and was taxed as part of the gross estate. The only exception was when the executor could establish sufficient lifetime motives for the making of the gift, in which event the presumption was overcome and the gift was not included in the gross estate. When included in the gross estate, the gift was valued at its value at the death of the decedent's death, rather than the earlier date-of-gift value. Thus, for assets that had appreciated in value, this treatment negated all tax advantages of the gift. The Economic Recovery Tax Act of 1981 significantly changed the tax treatment of gifts. Now, with only those few exceptions discussed in this section, a gift is not included in the gross estate, even if made within three years of death.[19]

Although a gift made within three years of death is not included in the gross estate, it is considered in the estate tax computation. Such a gift, and any other lifetime gifts made after 1976, are considered in the estate tax computation due to the unified nature of the present estate and gift tax law.[20] Regardless of when made, however, the gifts are valued in the estate tax computation at the earlier date-of-gift value and not the date-of-death value. Thus, appreciation between the date of the gift and the date of death is not included in the estate tax computation.

EXAMPLE: If a decedent made a $30,000 taxable gift in 2000 and died in 2018 when the gift property was valued at $50,000, the decedent's estate would consider the gift at its 2000 gift tax value in computing the current estate tax. Because the gift was reported earlier and gift tax paid on it, credit is given on the estate tax return for the previously paid gift tax. The effect of considering the gift in the estate tax computation used to be to push the estate higher up the progressive rate schedule due to the earlier gift. That is no longer the case as the current larger exemptions offset the lower tax rates. As a practical matter, once taxes are owed all estate taxes are owed at a flat rate of 40 percent.

Now for the exceptions. Transfers within three years of death will be treated as part of the gross estate for the limited purpose of determining if the estate qualifies for one of the following special tax elections:[21]

1. The 35 percent of adjusted gross estate requirement for a section 303 stock redemption to pay death taxes and administrative costs without unfavorable dividend income tax treatment to the estate;
2. The 25 percnt and 50 percent of the adjusted value of the gross estate requirement of the section 2032A special use valuation for farms and closely held businesses; and
3. The 35 percent of adjusted gross income estate requirement of the section 6166 extension of time to pay the estate tax for estates consisting of a large interest in a closely held business.

These three tax code sections are intended to aid individuals whose estates consist of a large interest in a farm or closely held business. To qualify for each election the farm or closely held business must represent a certain percentage of the gross estate or the adjusted gross estate. The exceptions are designed to prevent an individual whose estate does not meet these percentage requirements from qualifying by making gifts shortly before death.

EXAMPLE: Section 303 permits a decedent's stock in a corporation to be redeemed by the corporation and used by the estate to pay death taxes, funeral expenses, and administrative costs without the distribution being treated as a dividend, which would have less favorable income tax consequences. The principal requirement for the election is that the stock must represent more than 35 percent of the value of the decedent's adjusted gross estate. Assume a $15,000,000 adjusted gross estate in which the decedent's stock in a family corporation is valued at $4,500,000. This represents 30 percent of the adjusted gross estate, thus section 303 is not application. If the decedent makes a $3,000,000 gift within three years of death, his or her stock will then represent 37 $1/2$ percent of his or her adjusted gross estate; however, this exception causes the gift to be treated as part of the gross estate for the sole purpose of the percentage computation only. Thus, the percentage test of section 303 is not met.

It would not be the tax code if there were not yet another series of exceptions that also must be recognized.[22]

1. Any gift tax paid within three years of death is included in the gross estate;
2. Life insurance proceeds received from a policy owned by the decedent and given by him or her to another within three years of the decedent's death is included in the gross estate; and
3. Property which would be includable in the gross estate under the following sections of the Internal Revenue Code is included in the gross estate when the property rights are relinquished within three years of death: Sec. 2036 - transfers with a retained life estate; Sec. 2037 - transfers taking effect at death; Sec. 2038 - recoverable transfers; and Sec. 2041 - powers of appointment.

B. Transfers with Control Retained by Decedent

Transfers made by the decedent during his or her lifetime may be included in the gross estate if the decedent retained control of the transferred property. Sections 2036, 2037, and 2038 of the Internal Revenue Code are the sections that cause such transfers to be included in the gross estate. A transfer included in the gross estate due to the application of one of these sections is usually included at the full value of the property. Reductions in value due to intervening interests, however, may be appropriate, depending on the nature of the particular interest involved.[23] Also, the relinquishment of these retained controls by the decedent within three years of death will still result in the inclusion of the property in the gross estate at the full value of the property on the date of the decedent's death.

Section 2036 includes in the gross estate gratuitous transfers in which the decedent retains, by trust or otherwise, a life interest in the transferred property to:

1. Receive the income from the property;
2. Possess or enjoy the property; or
3. Designate, either alone or with another, who will receive the property.

Typical of these type of transfers are a life estate retained by the grantor in a conveyance of real estate to another, or a transfer of property into a trust in which the settlor has retained the right to income for life or the right to designate who among a group of beneficiaries shall receive the income.

A tax trap is laid for the decedent who retains the right to vote, directly or indirectly, shares of stock in a corporation the decedent controlled. This will result in the entire stock interest being included in the gross estate as a retention of possession or enjoyment of the property.[24] A corporation is considered controlled by the decedent if he or she owns 20 percent or more of the voting stock in the corporation. Worse still, the attribution rules in I.R.C. Section 318 apply which treat ownership by a spouse, parent, child, grandchild, and certain controlled entities, such as a partnership, estate, trust or corporation as if owned by the decedent.

Section 2037 includes in the gross estate gratuitous transfers in which the decedent retains a reversionary interest in the transferred property.[25] The section applies to transfers in which the transferee must survive the transferor-decedent to continue in possession of the property. It also includes any transfer that may revert to the decedent from the transferee during the decedent's lifetime or to his or her estate, or be subject to a power of disposition by the decedent. For administrative convenience and to avoid overly harsh tax treatment of taxing remote reversionary interests, this section applies only if the value of the reversionary interest immediately prior to the decedent's death exceeds $5,000 or 5 percent of the value of the transferred property.

EXAMPLE: The decedent irrevocably transferred property in trust with the income payable to his 55-year-old wife and with the remainder payable to the decedent or, if he is not living at his wife's death, to his daughter or to her estate. The daughter cannot obtain possession or enjoyment of the property without surviving the decedent. Therefore, if the value of the decedent's reversionary interest immediately before his death exceeds 5 percent of the value of the transferred property, the value of the property, less the wife's outstanding life estate, is includable in the decedent's estate. Thus, if the decedent died when his wife was age 70, and assuming a 7 percent interest factor, her life estate would represent 53.86 percent and the remainder 46.14 percent at the time of the decedent's death. Obviously, the remainder interest exceeds 5 percent, resulting in inclusion in the estate under 2037; however, the value of the property would be reduced by the wife's outstanding interest (53.86 percent) because the wife's life interest was not subject to surviving the decedent, as was the daughter's interest.

Section 2038 includes in the decedent's gross estate any transfer of property in which the decedent retains, in trust or otherwise, the right to alter, amend, revoke, or terminate the transferee's possession and enjoyment of the property.[26] Obviously, a transfer by the decedent into a trust for the benefit of another is included in the gross estate if the decedent retains the right to alter, amend, revoke, or terminate the trust. This is still the result, even though the trust could not revert to the decedent or his or her estate.

Similarly, a transfer by the decedent into trust for the benefit of another is included in the gross estate if the decedent acts as trustee of the trust and has the right to withhold the distribution of income and principal. Section 2038 is broad in its application because it applies to any power reserved by the decedent which affects the time or manner of enjoyment of transferred property or its income.

C. Annuities and Retirement Benefits

Annuities purchased by the decedent will be included in the gross estate under I.R.C. Section 2039. Inclusion occurs if (1) prior to death the annuity was payable to the decedent or to the decedent and other, and (2) after death any payment is made to a beneficiary who survived the decedent. Simply stated, if because of a contractual obligation to the decedent payment is made to a beneficiary who survived the decedent, the payment is included in the gross estate. This includes not only commercial annuities and private annuities but also the various types of qualified employee benefit plans, such as pension plans, profit-sharing plans, and 401(k) and 403(b) plans, SEPs, and IRAs.

Frequently, the beneficiary of an annuity has the payment option of receiving a lump sum, in which event the lump sum payment is included in the gross estate. If instead payment is receivable as a periodic payment, then the present value of the income right of the beneficiary is included in the gross estate of the decedent. This computation is made according to regularly published Internal Revenue Service valuation tables.[27]

D. Joint Interests

Joint interests as the term is defined in Section 2040 of the Internal Revenue Code refers to property owned jointly with right of survivorship by the decedent and any other person or persons. It also refers to property held by husband and wife as tenants by the entirety in those states that permit such tenancies.

For all individuals other than spouses, the gross estate includes the entire value of all jointly owned property and not merely the decedent's proportionate interest. The full value of the property can be reduced, however, by the actual consideration furnished by the surviving tenant or tenants. A tempting "end run" around this rule is for one tenant to give funds to the other to purchase an interest in the joint tenancy. But the IRS is savvy and considers actual consideration furnished by another joint tenant not to include consideration that was given to the joint tenant by the decedent.[28] Therefore, one tenant cannot give money to the other tenant and the tenants then purchase jointly owned property and treat the purchase as if each furnished consideration for the property.

If jointly owned property was received by the decedent and other tenants by gift or inheritance, the gross estate only includes the decedent's proportionate part of the gifted or inherited joint property. For example, if the decedent and his two brothers received property as joint tenants by will, inheritance or gift, the decedent's gross estate would include only one-third of the value of the property.

Jointly owned property held by spouses as joint tenants with right of survivorship or as tenants by the entirety is treated more simply. Such property is treated as if one-half were owned by each spouse, irrespective of the actual consideration furnished. This simplification comes with some loss associated with it. Because only one-half of the property is included in the decedent's gross estate, only one-half of the income tax basis in the property receives a stepped-up basis to the date-of-death value of the property. This is particularly unfortunate because in most estates the unlimited marital deduction will preclude any estate tax being owed by the surviving spouse.

E. Powers of Appointment

The gross estate includes property over which a decedent holds a general power of appointment. Generally, a power of appointment is a device through which owners of property reserve to themselves or to others the power to designate a transferee of a property or the shares or interests a transferee may receive. A general power of appointment, as the term is used in estate tax law, refers to a power that may be exercisable in favor of decedents, their estates, their creditors, or the creditors of their estates.[29] The value of the property over which a decedent possesses a general power of appointment is fully includable in the gross estate. This result applies even if the power is never exercised. Yet another trap lies for those who release a general power of appointment within three years of their death. This will result in the property subject to the power being included in the gross estate at the date-of-death value of the property.[30]

EXAMPLE: A wife's estate passes into a trust for the benefit of her husband and children with the husband named trustee and being directed to pay income and principal as deemed appropriate in his sole discretion. The husband is also given the right to direct at his death without restriction who receives the trust property and in what percentages. Because each of these powers could be exercised in favor of the husband, his creditors, his estate, or the creditors of his estate, these powers are each general powers of appointment that will cause the property to be includable in the husband's gross estate.

EXAMPLE: If the husband's power of appointment in the above example was limited to an ascertainable standard relating to "health, education, support or maintenance" and he cannot direct who receives the property at his death, the power is not a general power of appointment.[31] Therefore, the wife could pass her estate into a trust for her husband's lifetime benefit and name him as trustee with the estate passing to their children at his death. If the husband's discretion as trustee in spending income and principal for his own benefit is limited by the preceding standard, the power will not be a general power and will not cause the trust property to be included in his gross estate.

F. Life Insurance

The gross estate includes the full value of any life insurance on the decedent's life, the proceeds of which are payable to the decedent's estate or any other beneficiary, provided the decedent possessed at death any incidents of ownership in the life insurance policy.[32] Incidents of ownership include:

1. Being the owner of the policy;
2. Having the right to change beneficiaries;
3. Having the right to cancel the policy;
4. Having the right to assign the policy; and
5. Having the right to borrow against the cash value of the policy or to pledge the policy as collateral.[33]

Another three-year rule trap exists when the incidents of ownership in a life insurance policy are transferred by the decedent to another within three years of his or her death.[34] This results in the entire proceeds of the insurance policy on the life of the decedent being includable in the gross estate.

Insurance owned by the decedent on the life of another is included in the decedent's gross estate under the general taxing statute I.R.C. Section 2033. The amount included in the decedent's gross estate is the replacement cost of the policy which approximates the cash value of the policy.[35] Term life insurance provides death protection only and no cash value, therefore, term insurance owned by the decedent on the life of another will result in minimal, if any, value being included in the gross estate.

An easy gift tax trap to fall into exists with policies owned on the life of another. If the owner of a policy on the life of another names a third party as the beneficiary of the policy a gift tax problem exists because on the death of the insured, the owner has inadvertently made a gift to the third party in the amount of the insurance proceeds. To avoid this consequence, the owner and beneficiary of the policy should be the same.

XV. *Adjusted Gross Estate*

The adjusted gross estate is determined by subtracting several type of estate-related expenses from the gross estate.[36] The only importance of the adjusted gross estate is to calculate the percentage requirements to determine if the estate qualifies for a Section 303 redemption or a section 6166 extension to pay the estate tax. The adjusted gross estate had greater significance in earlier years when the marital deduction was limited to 50 percent of the adjusted gross estate. Now that the marital deduction is an unlimited deduction, the adjusted gross estate has significance only for computing entitlement to these two elections.

The permissible deductions include the actual expenses incurred for funeral expenses, costs of administration, debts and unpaid mortgages of the decedent, and losses incurred during estate administration.[37] The deductible funeral expenses include not only the funeral home expenses, but other funeral-related expenses such as grave markers, transportation, and lot maintenance.[38] Administrative costs is a broad category of estate settlement-related costs and includes such expenses as executor, legal and accounting expenses, appraisal and brokerage fees, and court costs.[39]

Any debts, including accrued but unpaid taxes, owed by the decedent at the time of death that are enforceable under state law are deductible.[40] Mortgages are likewise deductible, provided the decedent's interest in the under-lying property is included in the estate.[41] Losses incurred during the administration of the estate are also deductible expenses to the extent not reimbursed by insurance.[42]

XVI. *Taxable Estate*

In estates in which the election under Internal Revenue Code section 303 and 6166 is not used, the above-discussed deductions are allowed in determining the taxable estate. Two additional deductions are also allowed. The first deduction is allowed for the value of any property passing to public, charitable and religious organization.[43] The deduction is permitted for a bequest, devise, or transfer to (1) federal, state, or local government for public purposes; (2) corporations or fraternal organizations whose exclusive purpose is religious, charitable, scientific, literary, educational, fostering national or international sports competitions, prevention of cruelty to children or animal; or (3) qualified veterans organizations. The estate tax deduction is allowed for the fair market value of the property passing to the charity to the extent such property is included in the gross estate.

The second deduction, a marital deduction is allowed for qualified property passing from the decedent to his or her surviving spouse.[44] The marital deduction, just as the charitable deduction, is allowed for the full value of the property passing to the surviving spouse to the extent such property is included in the gross estate. It is immaterial whether the property passes by the decedent's will, by intestacy, by beneficiary designation on a life insurance policy or retirement plan, by right of survivorship, or in some other manner. The basic requirements for entitlement to the deduction are that:

1. The property must pass from the decedent to the surviving spouse;
2. The survivor must be the decedent's spouse at the time of death; and
3. The property must pass outright to the surviving spouse, unless the qualified terminable interest property (Q-TIP) election discussed below applies.

A couple of precise rules must be followed for the property to be considered passing to the surviving spouse. First, property passing from the decedent to the surviving spouse that is conditioned upon the spouse surviving for a limited period of time will not qualify for the deduction if the time period from the decedent's death exceeds six months.[45] Second, property passing into trust or consisting of proceeds payable under a life insurance or annuity contract in which the surviving spouse receives only an interest for life will not qualify for the deduction unless the surviving spouse:

1. Receives all of the income from the property at least annually;
2. Receives a lifetime or testamentary general power of appointment over the property; and
3. The power of appointment is exercisable (whether or not it is exercised) by the surviving spouse alone and in all events.[46]

An important exception applies when the qualified-terminable interest property (Q-TIP) election is made. Because of this election, property that does not pass outright to the surviving spouse may still qualify for the marital deduction if certain requirements are met. Examples of typically non-qualifying property are (1) a life estate to the surviving spouse with the remainder passing to the children, or (2) a trust for the survivor's lifetime benefit in which he or she does not receive a general power of appointment. These types of property will qualify for the martial deduction under the so-called Q-TIP election if (1) the property qualifies for the marital deduction for reasons other than its being a terminable interest, and (2) the executor elects on the decedent's federal estate tax return that the property qualifies for the marital deduction.[47]

The effect of this election is the decedent's estate receives a marital deduction, but to qualify for the election, the property will be taxable in the surviving spouse's estate. Without the Q-TIP election the property will not qualify for the marital deduction in the estate of the first spouse and will thus be taxable; however, the property will not then be taxable in the estate of the surviving spouse.

XVII. Net Estate Tax

The net estate is increased by gifts made by the decedent. Any gifts made by the decedent after 1976 that are not includable in the gross estate are added to the taxable estate.[48] The amount "added back" is the date-of-gift value of the gift, less any applicable gift tax exclusion, marital deduction, and charitable deduction. This is termed the *adjusted taxable gift*.[49] The adding back is required because of the unification of the estate and gift taxes.

The federal estate tax is then computed.[50] The rate schedule is shown in Appendix A at the end of this chapter. The tax is then reduced by the gift tax previously paid on the "added-back" gifts.[51] Previously, the net effect of adding back the post-1976 gifts was to increase the estate tax owed on the estate because of the progressive nature of the estate tax rates. The corresponding deduction for the gift tax was payable on the added-back gifts is allowed to give proper credit for the tax paid on the earlier gifts. Today's higher estate tax exemption precludes any estate tax at the lower rates. Thus, when an estate tax is owed, it is a flat tax rate of 40 percent.

The resulting estate tax is then reduced by any of the three credits that are applicable to an estate. The application of these credits results in the net estate tax payable. The first is the *unified credit* (now termed applicable exclusion amount), which in 2019 exempts from estate taxation an estate up to $11,400,000. This amount increases annually because it is indexed to future cost of living increases.

The amount of the exclusion is further increased for the amount of the unused exclusion of a deceased spouse. For example, assume a husband died in 2014 when the exclusion amount was $5,430,000. He passed his entire estate to his wife and his estate utilized the marital deduction to eliminate the federal estate tax in his estate. Current law allows the $5,430,000 exclusion amount from the husband's estate to be added to the $11,400,000 exclusion amount for the wife's estate. Her estate now has an exclusion in 2019 of $16,830,000. This concept is termed *portability* in the estate tax laws; it was first added to the law in 2011 and made permanent in 2013.[52]

The second possible credit is a credit for the federal estate tax paid on a prior estate.[53] If a property was subject to the federal estate tax in a prior decedent's estate, the property passes to the present decedent, and the property is included in the present decedent's estate, then the present estate is entitled to a credit. The credit is limited to the lower of the estate taxes paid on the transferred property in the first decedent's estate or the estate tax attributed to the transferred property in the second decedent's estate. Also, the credit is further reduced by 20 percent at two-year intervals, beginning with the third year after the date of death of the first decedent. Therefore, after ten years the credit ceases.

The third credit is for any foreign death tax that is paid.[54] This credit is available for estates of both U.S. citizens and resident aliens and is allowed for the amount of any foreign death taxes paid on property situated in a foreign country that is also included in the gross estate.

XVIII. Filing and Payment

The federal estate tax return, which is filed on IRS Form 706, is due nine months after the date of death of the decedent, provided the gross estate exceeds the applicable exclusion amount.[55] No return is required for estates equal to or less than the applicable exclusions amount because no estate tax is owed on such estates owing to the unified credit.[56] The exclusion amount is $11,400,000 in 2019. The exclusion amount increases annually based on cost of living increases. An extension of time to file the return may be obtained from the IRS district director's office for the decedent's service area for an additional six months on filing an application and establishing reasonable cause for the extension.[57] An extension of time to file does not result in an extension of time to pay.

Normally, payments must be made within nine months of the death of the decedent. In situations in which there is a reasonable need or an undue hardship will result if the payment is made within nine months of death, the district director can permit extensions of time to pay from twelve months to a maximum of ten years.[58] Typical situations meriting an extension include (1) an illiquid estate that would suffer a loss in value if a forced sale was required to pay the estate taxes; (2) an estate consisting largely of assets that will result in value being realized in the future, such as royalties or pending litigation claims; or (3) estate assets consisting largely of a farm or closely held business that does not qualify for the section 6166 extension.[59] Section 6166 provides for payment of estate taxes and a reduced interest rate over a period of 15 years for certain farms and closely held businesses when certain requirements are met.

XIX. *Introduction to Federal Gift Tax*

Since many elder clients are desirous of making gifts to children, grandchildren and public charities, a thorough understanding of the federal gift tax law is essential. The gift tax is an excise tax imposed on the transfer of property by a donor during his or her lifetime to a recipient-donee. The donee of a gift may be an individual or other entity, such as a trust, partnership, corporation, or charity. However, donees of gifts to a trust, partnership or corporation are deemed to be the individual beneficiaries, partners, or stockholders to the extent of their proportionate interest.[60] The gift tax is obviously a necessary complement to the estate tax. Otherwise, avoidance of the estate tax could be easily accomplished if individuals could give property away during their lifetime without any tax consequence.

Before 1977 the gift tax rate was 75 percent of the estate tax rate. Now the tax rate is the same for both gifts and estates. The gift and estate taxes have been unified so the two taxes are now basically one tax, which could more properly be referred to as a transfer tax. In 2019, the exempt amount is $11,400,000 which may be used to offset taxable gifts,[61] with any balance available for future offset against estate taxes. In addition most gifts qualify for the annual gift tax exclusion which is currently $15,000 per year, per donee, and is discussed at Section XXI.

A. *Advantages of Gift Giving*

Although the advantages of gift giving are not as great as in prior years, there are still several significant tax advantages. There also are several non-tax reasons for making gifts. The advantages of gift giving merit brief review.

1. Gift giving may accomplish the donor's purpose of assisting the donee with some special needs, such as educational, medical, or charitable needs.

2. Gift giving will reduce the size of the donor's estate, which may, in turn, reduce the amount of probate expense, such as executor and legal fees when these fees are calculated as a percentage of the estate.

3. An individual may give $15,000 per year to as many different donees as he or she chooses without any gift tax being owed on such gifts.[62] Over a number of years this may enable a donor to reduce his or her estate significantly, thus reducing the estate tax owed at death.

4. The $15,000 annual gift tax exclusion can be doubled to $30,000 per year per donee when the donor's spouse joins in the gift.[63] This technique, known as gift-splitting, is permitted even though the gift has been made from the assets of only one of the spouses. Obviously, gift-splitting permits more rapid gift giving.

5. When the donee is in a lower income tax bracket than the donor there is an overall income tax savings when gifts are made. This advantage is not as great for lower-bracket taxpayers (10 percent and 12 percent), but is an advantage for higher-bracket taxpayers (32 percent, 35 percent, and 37 percent).[64] This savings is not available when the donee is under 18 years of age or between 19 and 23 years of age and a full time student due to the so-called kiddie tax.[65]

6. When the donated property has increased in value from the time of the gift until the death of the donor, the appreciation is not taxed in the donor's estate when he or she dies. This is obviously a tax savings, compared with the tax that would be owed if the property had been held until death and was subject to the estate tax. However, the appreciation is subject to income tax if a subsequent sale of the property by the donee takes place.

7. In estates that consist largely of stock in a closely held business, farmland or other business property, a stock redemption pursuant to section 303 of the Internal Revenue Code to pay death taxes, funeral expenses, and administrative costs is a possible estate tax savings to the estate. Also, the special-use valuation permitted under I.R.C. section 2032A and the installment payment election under I.R.C. section 6166 are other estate tax benefits. Each of these code sections requires certain percentage tests to be met to qualify for the tax benefit. A gift of property reduces the size of the estate, which may then enable these percentage limitations to be met, although any such transfer must not be made within three years of the decedent's death.

B. General Requirements

A gift tax is not owed until a complete gift has been made. A gift has three basic elements (1) the intent of the donor to give the property, (2) delivery of the property to the donee, and (3) the acceptance of that property by the donee. Although these three elements must be satisfied for there to be a complete gift on which a gift tax is owed, the gift tax law tends to minimize these elements. For example, donative intent is determined based on the objective facts of the transfer, not the subjective motive of the donor.[66] In addition, the focus is not so much on delivery and acceptance as on the cessation of the donor's control.[67]

The gift is tax imposed based on the fair market value of the transferred property.[68] A present interest transfer subject to the gift tax is entitled to a $15,000 per donee annual gift tax exclusion.[69] The exclusion is indexed for inflation. Further, the donor's spouse may join in the gift, thus creating the possibility of so-called gift-splitting and increasing the annual gift tax exclusion to $30,000 per donee, or higher once the inflation adjustment begins.[70]

An unlimited marital deduction is allowed for transfers between spouses, thus eliminating any gift tax for most such transfers.[71] Additionally, transfers to charities receive a charitable deduction, thus eliminating gift tax for most of these transfers.[72] A final exclusion is allowed for certain tuition and medical expenses paid on behalf of another.[73]

Under prior law, gifts made within three years of the decedent's death were included in the donor's gross estate for estate tax purposes. This is no longer the law. The three year rule has not been applicable since December 31, 1981; thus, any transfer subject to the gift tax will not be included in the gross estate.[74] However, the gift is considered in the estate tax calculation as the gift is added to the gross estate based on the date of gift value of the gift.

Since this is the tax code, there are exceptions. A donor who within three years of death (1) relinquishes a life estate, (2) makes transfers taking effect at the donor's death, (3) makes revocable transfers, or (4) makes transfers in which the donor retains a general power of appointment will have such property included in his or her estate.[75] The transfer of a life insurance policy within three years of death will still result in the insurance proceeds being included in the estate, even if the policy value at the time of the gift was within the $15,000 annual exclusion.[76] Also, the three year rule still applies in determining qualification for the percentage requirements of a 303 redemption and a 6166 installment payment of the estate taxes.[77]

The donor is required to file a gift tax return and pay any resulting gift tax by April 15 following the calendar year in which the gift or gifts are made.[78] The return is not required for gifts with a value below the $15,000 annual gift tax exclusion, gifts for certain educational or medical expenses, and gifts to a spouse that qualify for a marital deduction.[79] The tax rates are the same as those for the estate tax.

XX. *Special Considerations*

A. *Gifts of Services*

Several types of gifts are not subject to the gift tax. For example, a donor who gratuitously renders services for the benefit of another has not made a taxable gift. This includes the gratuitous use of a donor's time for the benefit of a donee, such as a donor donating his or her services for the benefit of a charity, a friend, or family member. Other examples include an executor who chooses not to charge an executor's commission.[80]

B. Disclaimers[81]

When a donee has received property and then disclaims the property within nine months, as required for a qualified disclaimer under the Internal Revenue Code, the subsequent transfer of the property to the next donee is not subject to an additional gift tax.[82] In those situations in which a disclaimer is properly used a transfer can be made without the imposition of a second gift tax. Of course, a gift tax is still owed by the initial donor of the gift.

EXAMPLE: A widow makes a $600,000 gift to her son, to be used by him to pay for the college education of his eighteen and nineteen year old children. The gift is taxable to the widow as she is the donor of the gift. The income subsequently earned from the $600,000 gift will be taxed to the son, and gifts by him to each child in excess of the $15,000 annual exclusion will be subject to gift tax, except to the extent the tuition exclusion applies or the applicable exclusion amount is used.[83] If the son disclaims the gift, it will pass equally to his two children. There is no gift tax owed by the son due to the disclaimer, and the future income will be taxable to the children because they now own the gift property.

C. Assignment of Income

The assignment-of-income doctrine should also be considered.[84] This doctrine can create unintended income tax consequences when a donor is giving income-producing property to a donee. In a typical situation a parent gives his or her right to future income, such as future rentals from a building or future royalties from a mineral ownership, to the children. These transfers constitute completed gifts and are subject to the gift tax; however, for income tax purposes the assignment of the gift has no effect, and the income is still taxed to the parent. The only way the income tax can be shifted to the children is for the underlying asset to be given. In this example, the ownership of the building or minerals must be transferred to the children not just the income from the asset.

D. Delivery of the Gift

The concept of delivery to the donee is simplistic, but several points need to be recognized. For example, a gift of a check is not a gift until it has either been certified by the donor or cashed by the donee.[85] This makes a significant difference because the annual gift tax exclusion is a calendar year exclusion. Thus, a check given on December 31 should be cashed immediately; if this is not possible, the donor should certify the check.

A similar situation is involved when a donor executes a deed, but does not have the deed recorded. This is not a completed gift until the deed is recorded, because the deed can always be destroyed during the donor's lifetime.[86] A possible alternative to recording the deed is to irrevocably transfer it to an escrow agent with direction to record the deed at some future date. The gift is then regarded as having been completed at the time the deed was delivered into the hands of the escrow agent.

A gift of stock is completed on the date it is delivered to the donee, to the corporation for transfer, or to the corporations' transfer agent.[87] A transfer of a U.S. government bond is a completed gift when the bond is presented for registration.[88]

A transfer to a joint bank account is not a completed gift. The transfer is completed at such time as the donee withdraws funds from the account.[89] Similarly, a transfer by the settler to a revocable trust he or she created is not completed until such time as the settler relinquishes control of the trust. This occurs when principal or income is transferred to a beneficiary or when the settler amends the trust to make it irrevocable. At that point a gift occurs.[90]

XXI. Annual Exclusion and Split Gifts

A. Annual Exclusion

As discussed previously, every donor is entitled to an annual exclusion of $15,000 per year per gift for gifts to as many different donees as the donor chooses.[91] In future years, the exclusion will be indexed for inflation in $1,000 increments. The exclusion is allowed only for a present-interest gift, as opposed to a future-interest gift. A present-interest gift is one in which the immediate use of the property is available to the donee. A gift of a future interest, such as a reversionary or remainder interest, is not allowed an annual exclusion.[92] The requirement creates a problem when a gift is made to a trust for the benefit of the trust beneficiary.

EXAMPLE: A transfer of assets to a trust that pays income for the life of the life tenant and then distributes the remainder to the remaindermen on the life tenant's death is a gift of both a present interest and a future interest. The life tenant's interest is a present interest that can be valued and for which the annual exclusion is available; however, the remaindermen do not come into possession of the property until the death of the life tenant. The remainder interest is a future interest, for which no annual exclusion is available.

If the trustee may withhold annual payments of income, such as the typical discretionary trust, no annual exclusion is allowed for the gift to both the life tenant and the remaindermen.[93]

B. Gift Splitting

Gift splitting is an option in which a husband and wife join together in making the gift.[94] This election is made on IRS Form 709. The effect is that the entire gift is treated as though made one-half by the husband and one-half by the wife. This option is available even though one of the spouses made no financial contribution to the gift. Gift-splitting has two advantages. First, the amount of the available annual exclusion is doubled from $15,000 to $30,000. Second, by splitting the gift a better use is made of the progressive nature of the gift tax rate schedule because one-half of the gift is taxed to the husband and one-half to the wife. To qualify for gift-splitting, the spouse who does not actually contribute to the gift must consent to this tax treatment by signing the gift tax return.[95] This is necessary even if the combined annual exclusion results in no gift tax being owed and no unified credit being used, such as when making a $30,000 gift to a child.

XXII. Income Tax Basis in Gift Property

When property is given to a donee, it is required that the donor's adjusted income tax basis be used by the donee as his or her own income tax basis in the property.[96] The adjusted basis can be increased for any federal gift that is attributable to the portion of the gift that represents appreciation in the value of the gift property.[97]

EXAMPLE: Property valued at $1,000,000 is given to a donee. The donor's adjusted income tax basis in the property is $100,000 and the gift tax paid on the gift is $400,000 (assuming a 40 percent rate). The donee will have an adjusted basis of $100,000 plus the gift tax on the $900,000 appreciations which is $360,000 resulting in a basis of $460,000.

When the donor later sells the gift property at a gain, he or she then will pay income tax on the difference between the sales price and the adjusted basis of the property. In the event the property is sold at a loss, the donee's adjusted basis is modified somewhat, to the lesser of either the donor's adjusted basis or the fair market value of the property at the time of the gift.[98]

EXAMPLE: The donee in the above example later sells the property for $1,100,000. The taxable gain for income tax purposes is $640,000.

EXAMPLE: The donor gives property with a fair market value of $500,000, in which the donor has an adjusted basis of $1,000,000, to the donee. The donee's basis for purposes of a gain is $1,000,000, but for purposes of a loss the basis is $500,000. A subsequent sale of the property for $1,100,000 will result in a $10,000 gain, but a sale for $450,000 will result in a loss of only $50,000. A sale between $500,000 and $1,000,000 will result in neither a gain nor a loss.

XXIII. Transfers Not Subject to Gift Tax

A. Marital Deduction

Under current law a marital deduction is normally allowed for the full value of any property transferred from one spouse to another. The requirements for the gift tax marital deduction are generally the same as for the estate tax marital deduction. Basically, the property must be given outright to the donee-spouse, or if in trust, the donee-spouse must have the absolute right to income for life from the property coupled with a general power of appointment. Another option is that the gift meet the requirements to be treated as qualified terminable interest property. This option requires that the donee receive a lifetime income from the property without having to receive a general power of appointment. It also requires an irrevocable election on a timely filed gift tax return. If these requirements are met, the marital deduction is available for the entire interest given, and no gift tax is owed on the transfer.[99]

Transfers incident to a divorce can create a gift tax problem but will not if the specific rules are followed. If the transfer is made before entry of the decree of divorce there is no gift tax, owing to the unlimited gift tax marital deduction.[100] To avoid gift taxation for a transfer after entry of the divorce decree, however, (1) the transfer must be made pursuant to a written agreement relating to the property transferred and (2) the divorce must occur within a three-year period beginning one year before the date of the agreement. The transfer must be to one of the spouses in exchange for marital or property rights or to provide support for one or more of the children during their minority.[101]

B. Charitable Deduction

A gift tax deduction is allowed for the full value of any property passing to charitable, religious, governmental and certain other nonprofit organizations.[102] This deduction is similar to the estate tax deduction, and, as with that deduction, it is not limited solely to tax-exempt organizations under the income tax law.

C. Tuition and Medical Expenses

Payments to an educational institution for an individual's tuition are excluded from the gift tax. The payments must be made directly to the institution and not to the donee. Also, the exclusion is available only for tuition and does not include other educational-related expenses such as housing, meals and books. A similar exclusion is available for medical expenses that are paid to the institution or the person providing medical care.[103]

XXIV. Gifts for the Benefit of Children

The "kiddie tax" creates some difficulty in transferring assets to an individual's children to create an educational fund for their benefit. This was often done in the past since the children's income tax bracket was usually lower than the parent's, thus allowing a larger after-tax fund to build up over the years. This was particularly good planning for establishing educational funds for the donor's children. The current income tax rules provide that all net unearned income (investment income) of a child in excess of $2,100 is taxed at the estate and trust rates and brackets.[104] This tax result applies to all net unearned income without regard to the source of the income, when it was transferred, or by whom. Generally, the tax applies to children under 19, or under 24 if a full-time student.

XXV. Special Situations

A. Net Gifts

A net gift is a gift in which the donor requires the donee to pay the gift tax attributable to the gift. Such a gift often is made when the donor lacks liquidity with which to pay the tax or wants to shift the tax burden to the donee. The taxable amount is not the gross amount of the gift; it is the gross amount of the gift reduced by the amount of gift tax the donee must pay. The formula for determining the amount of the gift is "tentative" tax divided by (1.00 + donor's gift tax bracket).

EXAMPLE: A donor who has made sufficient lifetime gifts to use his entire exclusion amount, desires to give a donee property that has a fair market value of $1,000,000, but wants the donee to pay the gift tax. The donor is in the 40 percent gift tax bracket. Therefore, the gift tax is determined as follows: tentative tax ($400,000) ÷ (1.0 + 0.40) = $285,714.[105]

A net gift does have possible income tax consequences to the donor.[106] Such a gift is treated as a part sale and part gift transaction, due to the donor being relieved from paying the gift tax liability. The income to the donor is the amount of gift tax paid by the donee less the donor's basis in the property. Thus, the greater income tax problem is created when low basis property is given. In the preceding example, if the property given had a basis of $100,000, then the income to be reported by the donor is $185,714; however, no income tax is reported if the basis equals or exceeds the gift tax.

B. Gift Subject to an Indebtedness

In making a gift the donor must be aware of the adjusted income tax basis of the property and the effect of any indebtedness on the property. A gift of low basis property that is subject to an indebtedness can create an unintended income tax result. Income tax is owed on the difference between the indebtedness assumed by the donee and the basis of the transferred property.[107]

EXAMPLE: The donor gives rental property that is valued at $100,000 in which the donor's income tax basis is $10,000. This property is subject to a $70,000 mortgage. If the donee assumes the indebtedness, an unexpected income tax will result. The difference between the $10,000 basis and the $70,000 debt that has been assumed by the donee is treated as taxable income to the donor. Thus, the donor has made a $30,000 gift, but also must recognize $60,000 in additional income. Both a gift tax and an income tax will be owed, making this an unexpectedly costly gift.

XXVI. Introduction to Generation-Skipping Transfer Tax

Just as understanding gift tax laws is important, a working knowledge of the generation-skipping transfer tax is important as many elder clients want to make lifetime or testamentary gifts not only to their children, but also to more remote descendants. The generation-skipping tax and its 40 percent tax rate will apply to most of these gifts. Thus, a knowledge of the tax is essential.

The generation-skipping transfer tax creates a minefield for the unwary. The tax was first enacted in 1976, was significantly revamped in 1986, and appears to be a permanent part of the Internal Revenue Code, in spite of periodic optimism that it might be repealed. Thus, it appears necessary for lawyers to be familiar with the tax.

The "evil" the tax seeks to end, if an "evil" at all, is illustrated in the situation of a father creating a trust for his daughter, which terminates on the daughter's death and is distributed to her children. The trust for the daughter could permit income and principal to be spent during her lifetime as needed for her health, education, and support or maintenance. She could withdraw annually the greater of 5 percent or $5,000 from the trust principal. She even could have a power to appoint the trust at her death to anyone she chooses other than her own estate and her creditors. Such a trust does not result in any estate tax to the daughter's estate, because she never owned a vested interest in the trust. The estate taxes on the assets in the trust were skipped. Now a tax will be imposed.[108] Unfortunately, the tax laws that accomplish this result are rather technical.

XXVII. General Rules

A flat tax equal to the maximum federal estate tax rate, presently 40 percent, is imposed on all generation-skipping transfers.[109] Every individual is allowed a $11,400,000 exemption for any generation-skipping transfers, whether made during lifetime or at death.[110]

Additionally, transfers that are not subject to a gift tax owing to the $15,000 annual gift tax exclusion or the unlimited exclusion for the direct payment of medical and tuition expenses are not subject to the generation-skipping tax, thus the GST exemption is in addition to these exclusions. To determine when a generation-skipping transfer has occurred, consideration must be given to whether the transfer is considered to be (1) a taxable distribution, (2) a taxable termination, or (3) a direct skip. It is also helpful to define the technical terms skip person and transferor.

A. Skip Person

A skip person is a person assigned to a generation which is two or more generations beyond the generation of the transferor. A skip person may also be a trust, if all interests in the trust are held by the skip persons.[111]

EXAMPLE: A father establishes a trust for his daughter which terminates at her death and is distributed to the daughter's children. The daughter's children (transferor's grandchildren) are the skip persons.

In the normal case of lineal descendants there is no difficulty in determining to which generation each individual is to be assigned. Parent, child, grandchild, and great-grandchild is a simple enough concept, even in the tax law. As would be expected, spouses are treated as being in the same generations. Adopted individuals and relationships of half-blood, such as stepchildren, are treated the same as full-blood relationships.[112]

In the case of non-lineal (unrelated) descendants, a fixed numerical rule is imposed. An individual who is within twelve and one-half years of the age of the transferor is assigned to the transferor's generation. An individual more than 12 $\frac{1}{2}$ years to 37 $\frac{1}{2}$ years younger than the transferor is assigned to the next younger generation. Generation-skipping assignments continue thereafter at 25-year intervals.[113]

B. Transferor

The meaning of the term transferor is rather obvious. It is the decedent when a testamentary transfer is involved and the donor when the transfer is an inter vivos gift.[114] In the prior example, the father is the transferor.

As with the skip person some of the finer points are more technical. The holder of a general power of appointment becomes a transferor on the exercise or lapse of the power, including a lapse due to the holder's death. If a married couple utilizes the gift-splitting option so that a gift is treated as made one-half by each spouse, then each spouse is a transferor. That is, gift-splitting for gift tax purposes creates two transferors for generation-skipping transfer tax purposes.[115]

Also, when a qualified terminable interest property election is made by the executor of the transferor's estate, the estate may also elect to be treated as a transferor for generation-skipping transfer tax purposes. If the election is not made, the surviving spouse will be treated as the transferor.[116] This becomes important when trying to maximize both spouse's generation-skipping tax exemption.

C. Taxable Distribution

A taxable distribution is any distribution from a trust of income or principal to a "skip person."[117] The tax is paid by the skip person[118] and must be paid by April 15 of the year following the taxable distribution.[119]

EXAMPLE: In a trust which permits the payment of income or principal among a group of beneficiaries including both the children and grandchildren of the transferor, the trustee distributes $10,000 of income to a grandchild. The grandchild is a skip person and owes a generation-skipping tax of $4,000. The grandchild only receives a net of $6,000.[120] If the tax is paid by the trust, the payment is treated as an additional distribution in the amount of the tax. Thus, to net $10,000 a distribution of $16,667 is required.[121]

It must be remembered this tax is imposed on distributions of both income and principal. Before the Tax Reform Act of 1986, distributions of income were not taxed. But, now a distribution of income will be subject to both income tax and the generation-skipping transfer tax, although an itemized income tax deduction is allowed for the generation-skipping transfer tax.[122] This can be quite costly.

EXAMPLE: A $10,000 income distribution that is a taxable distribution results in a generation-skipping transfer tax of $4,000, plus an additional $2,220 in income taxes, assuming a 37 percent income tax bracket applies and the $4,000 generation-skipping transfer tax is deducted as an itemized deduction for personal income tax purposes. This leaves a net distribution after both taxes of only $3,780.

D. Taxable Termination

A taxable termination is the termination—by death, lapse of time, release of a power, or otherwise—of an interest in property held in trust. Before the termination is taxable there must be no skip persons having an interest in the trust.[123] The tax is paid by the trustee[124] and must be paid by April 15 of the year following the taxable termination.[125]

EXAMPLE: A father establishes a trust for his son and following the son's death, the trust continues for the grandchildren until the youngest becomes thirty-five years old, at which time the trust terminates and is distributed to the grandchildren. A taxable termination occurs upon the son's death. The generation-skipping transfer tax is paid by the trustee. Thus, if the trust held $1,000,000 on the death of the son, the trustee would be required to pay $400,000 in generation-skipping transfer tax. The trust is reduced to $600,000.[126]

E. Direct Skip

A direct skip is a transfer subject to estate or gift taxes which is made to a skip person.[127] Direct skips were not taxable prior to the Tax Reform Act of 1986. A tax is now imposed on the transferor.[128] The tax must be paid by the due date for the federal estate tax return if the transfer is testamentary, or by April 15 of the year following an inter vivos gift.[129]

EXAMPLE: Grandfather dies and bequeaths $1,000,000 to his grandchildren because his son already has a large estate of his own and does not need the additional inheritance. This is a direct skip for which a tax of $400,000 is owed.[130]

There is a significant tax trap for the unwary. Absent directions in the will to the contrary, the typical tax clause in a will that charges all taxes to the residue will cause the grandchildren in the above example to receive the $1,000,000 bequest and the $400,000 generation-skipping transfer tax will be paid by the estate. Obviously, this could cause a significant problem in the distribution of the other estate assets. Additional consideration must be given to the fact that the bequest is subject to the estate tax. A will that directs all taxes be paid from the residuary estate could result in the $1,000,000 bequest passing to the grandchildren, but the residuary estate being reduced by $800,000 for both the generation-skipping transfer tax and the federal estate tax.

For example, an estate in the highest estate tax bracket of 40 percent would pay 80 percent in combined taxes because the generation-skipping transfer tax is also 40 percent. The obvious intent of the law is to discourage direct skips. Nonetheless, if it is desired to make a generation-skipping transfer in excess of the exemption amount consideration must be given to the apportionment of the estate and generation-skipping transfer taxes.

XXVIII. *Tax Apportionment*

The generation-skipping transfer tax specifies who is liable for the tax. The trustee is liable for the tax in a taxable termination or if there is a direct skip from a trust. A direct skip, other than from a trust, must be paid by the transferor or estate. In the case of a taxable distribution, the tax must be paid by the skip person (transferee).[131] In the case of a taxable termination or distribution, the tax is paid from the transferred property. The transferor or estate is liable for the tax on direct skips, but it is charged to the property transferred[132] unless the will or trust specifies to the contrary.

A disclaimer can also create an unintended result. If a child inherits property from a parent and then disclaims the property so that the property passes instead to the next generation, a direct skip has resulted. This will cause both the estate tax and the generation-skipping transfer tax to be imposed on the transfer. In larger estates this will result in both the 40 percent generation-skipping transfer tax and the 40 percent maximum estate tax being imposed upon the same property. Thus, the total tax could be 80 percent of the value of the property. To further compound the problem, if the will provides for all taxes to be paid from the residuary estate, the disclaimed property then passes without reduction for either tax, thus creating a potentially disastrous result.

Yet another tax trap can cause double taxation owing to the interplay of the generation-skipping transfer tax and the gift tax. The following example shows the need to consider the generation-skipping transfer tax before making any transfer.

EXAMPLE: Assume grandfather makes a $1,000,000 gift to his grandson. A generation-skipping transfer tax must be paid by him of $400,000. However, a gift tax is also due, not only on the $1,000,000 gift, but also on the $400,000 generation-skipping transfer tax paid by the grandfather. If the grandfather is in the 40 percent gift tax bracket, $560,000 in gift taxes is owed. Thus, total taxes of $960,000 are owed on a $1,000,000 gift.

Appendix A: Tax Rate Schedule

TRANSFER TAX RATE SCHEDULE AFTER DECEMBER 31, 2012

(A) Amount subject to tax more than——	(B) Amount Subject subject to tax equal to or Less than——	(C) Tax Amount in column (A)	(D) Rate of tax on excess over amount in column (A) Percent
. . . .	$10,000	. . . .	18
$10,000	20,000	$1,800	20
20,000	40,000	3,800	22
40,000	60,000	8,200	24
60,000	80,000	13,200	26
80,000	100,000	18,200	28
100,000	150,000	23,800	30
150,000	250,000	38,800	32
250,000	500,000	70,800	34
500,000	750,000	155,800	37
750,000	1,000,000	248,300	39
1,000,000	. . . .	345,800	40

Notes

1. I.R.C. § 6012.
2. *Id.* § 6017.
3. *Id.* § 61.
4. These are plans sponsored by an employer that provide employees a choice between taking cash and various qualified benefits, such as group life insurance and accident and health insurance. The cash choice is included in gross income, but the qualified benefits are not.
5. I.R.C. § 61.
6. *Id.* § 62.
7. *Id.* § 63(c)(2).
8. *Id.* § 63(c)(3).
9. *Id.* § 1.
10. *Id.* § 57.
11. *Id.* § 56.
12. *Id.* § 55.
13. *Id.* § 55(d)(3).
14. *Id.* § 22.
15. *Id.* § 86.
16. *Id.* § 121.
17. *Id.* § 213.
18. *Id.* § 2031.

19. *Id.* § 2035(d).

20. *Id.* § 2001(b).

21. *Id.* § 2035(c).

22. *Id.* § 2035.

23. Treas. Reg. § 20.2036-1(a), (b)(1)(ii); § 20.2037-1(e)(3), (4); Notice 89-60, Int. Rev. Bull. 1989-22 (May 1, 1989).

24. I.R.C. § 2036(b).

25. Treas. Reg. § 20.2037-1(c), (d), (e).

26. *Id.* § 20.2038-1.

27. Valuation tables and interest factors are available at www.irs.gov.

28. Treas. Reg. § 20.2040-1(c)(4).

29. I.R.C. § 2041(b)(1).

30. *Id.* § 2041(a)(2).

31. Treas. Reg. § 20.2041-1(c)(2).

32. I.R.C. § 2042.

33. Treas. Reg. § 20.2042-1(c)(2).

34. I.R.C. § 2035(d)(2).

35. Treas. Reg. § 25.2512-6.

36. I.R.C. § 303(b)(2); 6166(b)(6).

37. Treas. Reg. § 2053-1.

38. Treas. Reg. § 20.2053-2.

39. *Id.* § 20.2053-3.

40. *Id.* § 20.2053-4.

41. *Id.* § 20.2053-7.

42. *Id.* § 20.2054-1.

43. I.R.C. § 2055.

44. *Id.* § 2056.

45. *Id.* § 2056(b)(3).

46. *Id.* § 2056(b)(5).

47. *Id.* § 2056(b)(7).

48. *Id.* § 2001(b).

49. *Id.* § 2001(b)(2).

50. *Id.* § 2001(c).

51. *Id.* § 2012.

52. *Id.* § 2010(c).

53. *Id.* § 2013.

54. *Id.* § 2014.

55. *Id.* § 6017.

56. *Id.* § 6018.

57. *Id.* § 6081.

58. *Id.* § 6161.

59. Treas. Reg. § 26.6161-1(b).

60. *Id.* § 20.2511-1(h)(1).

61. I.R.C. § 2505.

62. *Id.* § 2503(b).

63. *Id.* § 2513.

64. *Id.* § 1.

65. *Id.* § 1(i).

66. Treas. Reg. § 25.2511-1(g)(1).

67. *Id.* § 25.2511-2.

68. I.R.C. § 2512; Treas. Reg. § 25.2512-1.
69. I.R.C. § 2503(b).
70. *Id.* § 2513.
71. *Id.* § 2523.
72. *Id.* § 2522.
73. *Id.* § 2503(e).
74. *Id.* § 2035(d)(1).
75. *Id.* § 2035(d)(2).
76. *Id.* § 2035(b)(2).
77. *Id.* § 2035(d)(3), (4).
78. *Id.* § 6075(b).
79. *Id.* § 6019.
80. Rev. Rul. 56-472, 1956-2 Cum. Bull. 21; Rev. Rul. 66-167, 1966-1 Cum. Bull. 20.
81. A helpful resource is C. Cline, *Disclaimers in Estate Planning*, 2d ed. (American Bar Association).
82. I.R.C. § 2518; Treas. Reg. § 25.2518-1(b).
83. I.R.C. § 2503(e).
84. Lucas v. Earl, 281 U.S. 111, 50 S. Ct. 241, 74 L. Ed. 731 (1930).
85. Rev. Rul. 67-396, 1967-2 Cum. Bull. 351.
86. Whitt v. Commissioner, 751 F.2d 1548 (11th Cir. 1985).
87. Treas. Reg. § 25.2511-2(h).
88. Rev. Rul. 68-269, 1968-1 Cum. Bull. 339.
89. Treas. Reg. § 25.2511-1(h)(4).
90. Commissioner v. Guggenheim, 288 U.S. 280, 53 S. Ct. 369, 77 L. Ed. 748 (1933).
91. I.R.C. § 2503(b).
92. Treas. Reg. § 25.2503-3.
93. *Id.* § 25.2503-3(c)(1).
94. I.R.C. § 2513.
95. *Id.* § 2513(b).
96. *Id.* § 1015.
97. *Id.* § 1015(d).
98. *Id.* § 1015(a).
99. *Id.* § 2523.
100. *Id.* § 2323.
101. *Id.* § 2526.
102. *Id.* § 2522.
103. *Id.* § 2503(e); Treas. Reg. § 25.2503-6.
104. I.R.C. § 1(i).
105. Rev. Rul. 75-12, 1975-1 Cum. Bull. 310.
106. Diedrich v. Commissioner, 457 U.S. 191, 102 S. Ct. 2414, 72 L. Ed. 77 (1982).
107. I.R.C. § 61(a)(12), 1015.
108. *Id.* § 2601–2663.
109. *Id.* § 2641.
110. *Id.* § 2631.
111. *Id.* § 2613.
112. *Id.* § 2651(b)(3).
113. *Id.* § 2651(d).
114. *Id.* § 2652(a).
115. *Id.* § 2652(a)(2).
116. *Id.* § 2652(a)(3).

117. *Id*. § 2612(b).
118. *Id*. § 2662(a)(1).
119. *Id*. § 2662(a)(2)(B).
120. This example assumes the GST exemption has previously been used.
121. I.R.C. § 2621(b).
122. *Id*. § 164(a)(5).
123. *Id*. § 2612(a).
124. *Id*. § 2603(a)(2).
125. *Id*. § 2662(a)(2)(B).
126. This example assumes the GST exemption has previously been used.
127. I.R.C. § 2612(c).
128. *Id*. § 2603(a)(3).
129. *Id*. § 2662(a)(2)(A).
130. This example assumes the GST exemption has previously been used.
131. I.R.C. § 2603(a).
132. *Id*. § 2603(b).

INDEX

401(k) plans. *See* employer-provided 401(k) plans

ABA Model Rules of Professional Conduct, 5–10
  Rule 1.5, 9
  Rule 1.6, 6
  Rule 1.7, 7
  Rule 1.8(f), 8–9
  Rule 1.14, 10
adjusted taxable gift, 286
administrative law judge (ALJ)
  social security, 91
  Supplemental Security Income (SSI), 165
advance directives. *See directives*
Advance Health Care Directives (Krohm and Summers), 34
Affordable Care Act of 2011, 177
age, SSI eligibility, 145
aid and assistance (A&A) benefits, 102, 107, 108
Aid to the Blind, 145
Aid to the Permanently and Totally Disabled, 145
Alaska Native Claims Settlement Act, 159
alcoholism, 76, 88, 90
alternative minimum tax, 273–274
American Bar Association (ABA), Commission on Law and Aging, 2
AmeriCorps NCCC, 148
AmeriCorps State and National, 148
annuity purchase, Medicaid for married couple, 187–188
Appeals Council
  expedited process, 92

social security, 91–92
Supplemental Security Income (SSI), 165
appeals procedures
  Medicare, 136–137
  Medicaid, 192–194
  social security, 90–92
  Supplemental Security Income (SSI), 164–165
applicable exclusion amount, 286
application procedure, Supplemental Security Income (SSI), 162–163
Assessment of Older Adults with Diminished Capacity (ABA), 10
assets
  joint ownership of, 46–47
  questionnaire, 16–20
assignment
  limiting charge, 131
  Medicare, 130–132

benefit period, definition, 125
Black Lung program, Medicare and, 134
blind individuals, substantial gainful activity (SGA) for, 89–90
blindness, SSI eligibility, 146
Board of Veterans' Appeals (BVA), 117
borrowing transactions, power of attorney, 51
burial benefits veterans, 115–116
burial funds, term, 160
burial space, term, 160
business operations, power of attorney, 51

charitable deduction, transfers not
     subject to gift tax, 293
checklist(s)
   Medicare for new beneficiaries,
        140–141
   social security retirement, 93–96
   Supplemental Security Income
        (SSI), 168–170
   VA benefits, 118–119
Checklist for Family Caregivers (Hurme),
     3, 4, 5
Checklist for Family Survivors (Hurme),
     3
Checklist for My Family (Hurme), 3
child's benefits
   dependency requirement, 86
   qualifying for, 86
   qualifying for DIC benefits, 110,
        111–112
   rule for adopted children, 86–87
   rules for grandchildren/step–
        grandchildren, 87
   social security, 85–88
   surviving, qualifying for survivors
        pension benefits, 114
   termination of, 87–88
claims
   power of attorney, 51
   veteran benefits, 116–118
client(s). *See also social security*
   accepting payment of fees from
        non-client, 8–9
   asset questionnaire, 16–20
   basic drafting information for, 2–3
   competency of elder, 9–10
   engagement letter for couple, 23–24
   engagement letter for individual,
        21–22
   estate planning conflicts, 8
   ethical considerations, 5–10
   family questionnaire, 11–15
   interviewing, 1–2
   limited capacity considerations, 3–4
   living arrangements, 4
   maintaining confidentiality, 5–7

multiple representation, 7–8
paying for housing, 5
setting fees for elder, 9
social security benefits, 68–69
Clinton, Bill, 78
Code of Federal Regulations, 106
Commission on Law and Aging,
     ABA, 2
competency, of elder client, 9–10
confidentiality
   attorney-client, 5–7
   patients' rights, 29
conflicts, engagement letter, 21, 24
Conroy, Claire C., 30
conservatorships, health care, 44–46
Consumer Price Index, 74
Court of Veterans' Appeals (CVA),
     117–118
creditor protection, retirement,
     257–258
critical access hospital (CAH),
     Medicare Part A, 125, 126
Cruzan, Nancy, 30–31
   U.S. Supreme Court, 29, 65n1

death pension, veterans, 112–114
death tax, 56, 60, 195–196, 266, 278–
     279, 286, 288
deductions. *See also federal income tax*
   itemized, 272
   standard, 271–272
deeming of income, 151–152
   Supplemental Security Income
        (SSI), 151–154
   term, 151
Deficit Reduction Act of 2005, 181, 187
defined benefit, 262
defined benefit plan, pension, 247,
     260, 262
Department of Veterans Affairs (DVA),
     102–103. *See* also veteran
     benefits
   income types, 106
   Social Security Administration
        (SSA), 155

dependency and indemnity
compensation (DIC) benefits,
102, 120n56
amount for surviving spouse, 111
amount of benefits for dependent
children, 111–112
amount of benefits for surviving
dependent parent, 112
child qualifying for benefits, 110
eligibility requirements, 110–111
parent qualifying for, 110
surviving spouse qualifying,
109–110
dependents, medical benefits for
veterans', 115
DIC. *See* dependency and indemnity
compensation (DIC) benefits
directives, 31–39. *See also* health care
appointment of an agent, 39
durable health care power of
attorney, 32–34
durable health care power of
attorney form, 34–39
revocation of durable health care
power of attorney, 39
second state residency, 39
disability
grades of, 104
SSI eligibility, 145–146
term, 88
disability insurance benefits,
88–90
alcoholism, 90
drug addiction, 90
qualifying for, 89
SGA (substantial gainful
activity), 89
SGA for blind individuals, 89–90
termination of, 90
Disabled Adult Child (DAC), 167
Disaster Relief and Emergency
Assistance Act, 149
divorced spouse(s)
qualifying for husband/wife
benefits, 79–80

qualifying for mother/father
benefits, 83–84
qualifying for widow/widower
benefits, 82
DNR. *See* Do Not Resuscitate (DNR)
Domestic Volunteer Service Act, 107
Do Not Resuscitate (DNR), 31, 41–44
Kentucky Emergency Medical
Services DNR Order, 42–44
revocation of, 44
Don't Let Dementia Steal Everything
(Peck and Law), 3, 10, 176
drug addiction, 76, 88, 90
durable health care power of attorney.
See also health care
advance directive, 32–34
appointment of agent, 39
form, 34–39
revocation of, 39
second state residency, 39
durable power of attorney, 31
health care, 47–48
sample, 49–52

earned income, self-employed
plans, 249
Economic Recovery Tax Act of
1981, 278
elder clients' tax issues, 274–276
cost basis, 276
medical expense deduction,
275–276
provisional income, 275
retirement plan distributions, 276
sale of personal residence, 275
social security exclusion, 275
tax credit for elderly or disabled,
274–275
Elder Law and Later Life Legal Planning
(Frolik), 4, 176
Employee Retirement Income Security
Act of 1974 (ERISA), 257
employer-provided 401(k) plans,
259, 261
retirement, 248–249

employer-provided 401(k)
    plans, (*continued*)
  Roth 401(k), 248
  Safe Harbor 401(k), 260, 261
  SIMPLE plan, 249
engagement letter for couple, 23–24
engagement letter for individual,
    21–22
estate
  definition, 190
  planning, 246
  planning conflicts, 8
  power of attorney for
      transactions, 51
  recovery and Medicaid, 190–192
*An Estate Planner's Guide to Qualified
    Retirement Plans* (Mezzullo),
    246
Estate Planning Forms (Hunt), 2, 59
estate taxation. *See also* gross estate
  distributions at death, 257
  federal, 276–277
  net estate tax, 285–286
  taxable estate, 284–285
ethics
  accepting payment of fees from
      non-clients, 8–9
  competency of elder client, 9–10
  confidentiality, 5–7
  estate planning conflicts, 8
  multiple representation, 7–8
  setting fees, 9
Ethics in Practice of Elder Law (Flowers
    and Morgan), 5

fair hearing procedure, Medicaid, 184
family maximum rule, social security
    benefit, 75
family questionnaire, 11–15
Federal Benefit Rate (FBR), 180
federal Black Lung program, Medicare
    and, 134
federal court
  judicial review of social security, 92
  Supplemental Security Income
      (SSI), 165

federal estate tax, 276–277. *See also*
    estate taxation; gross estate
  filing and payment, 286–287
federal gift tax, 287–289
  advantages of gift giving, 287–288
  general requirements, 288–289
  special considerations not subject to
      gift tax, 289–291
  transfers not subject to gift tax,
      293–294
federal income tax, 267–268
  adjusted gross income, 271
  alternative minimum tax (AMT),
      273–274
  basis in gift property, 292–293
  common tax issues for elder clients,
      274–276
  filing status, 268
  gross income exclusions, 269
  gross income inclusions, 270
  itemized deductions, 272
  standard reduction, 271–272
  tax credits, 273
  tax rate schedules, 272–273, 300
fee(s)
  accepting payment from non-client,
      8–9
  attorney's, for social security
      case, 92
  engagement letter, 21, 24
  setting, 9
financial institution transactions,
    power of attorney, 49
financial qualifications, Medicaid
    eligibility, 179–180
First Party Special Needs inter vivos
    trust, 220–228
First Party Special Needs trust,
    3, 188
five-year look-back rule, Medicaid,
    184–186
Flowers, Roberta K., 5
Food Stamp Act, 149
form(s)
  durable health care power of
      attorney, 34–39

Kentucky Do Not Resuscitate (DNR) Order, 42–44
  living trust, 55–59
  living will, 40–41
  power of attorney, 49–52
  sample pour-over will, 54–55
  simple will, 59–64
Frolik, Lawrence A., 4, 28
The Fundamentals of Guardianships (ABA), 44

generation-skipping transfer tax, 295
  direct skip, 298
  general rules, 295–298
  skip person, 296
  taxable distribution, 297
  taxable termination, 297–298
  tax apportionment, 299
  transferor, 296–297
gift(s). *See also* federal gift tax
  annual exclusion, 291–292
  assignment of income, 290
  for benefit of children, 294
  delivery of, 290–291
  disclaimers, 290
  income tax basis in gift property, 292–293
  net gifts, 294
  power of attorney for gift giving, 50–51
  services, 289–290
  special considerations not subject to gift tax, 289–291
  splitting, 292
  subject to an indebtedness, 295
  transfers not subject to gift tax, 293–294
gift tax. *See* federal gift tax
Goldberg v. Kelly (1970), 184, 192
grandchildren, rules for child's benefits, 87
gross estate, 277
  adjusted, 284
  annuities and retirement benefits, 281
  gifts, 277–279

joint interests, 281–282
  life insurance, 283–284
  powers of appointment, 282–283
  transfers with control retained by decedent, 279–281
gross income. *See also* federal income tax
  adjusted for elderly or disabled, 274
  exclusions, 269
  inclusions, 270
  principal deductions for adjusted, 271
guardianship, health care, 44–46

health care, 27–28. *See also* directives
  advance directives, 31–39
  case law on withholding medical treatment, 30–31
  do not resuscitate (DNR), 41–44
  durable power of attorney, 47–49
  durable power of attorney (sample), 49–52
  factors determining life-sustaining treatment, 31
  guardianship and conservatorships, 44–46
  joint ownership of assets, 46–47
  living trust, 53–59
  living will, 40–41
  patients' rights, 29
  right to be informed, 28
  simple will, 59–64
  unwanted medical treatment, 28–29
health insurance. *See* Medicare
Health Savings Account (HSA), signing up for, 95–96
home health care services, Medicare Part A, 126–127
hospice services, Medicare Part A, 127–128
hospital insurance. *See* Medicare Part A
housebound benefits, 102, 107, 108–109
housing, clients paying for, 5

Housing Act of 1949, 160
Housing Act of 1959, 160
Housing and Urban Development Act
    of 1965, 160
HR-10 plans, retirement, 249
Hunt, Lara Rae, 59, 202, 215
Hunt, L. Rush, 59, 202, 215
Hurme, Susan Balch, 2–3
husband/wife benefits
    deemed valid marriages, 79
    divorced spouses qualifying,
        79–80
    social security, 78–80
    spouse qualifying, 79
    termination of, 80

impairment, 88
income. *See also* federal income tax;
        Supplemental Security Income
        (SSI)
    deeming of, 151–154
    definition of, 179–180
    earned, 147–148
    Social Security Administration
        (SSA) considerations, 154–156
    taxation distributions during
        lifetime, 256–257
    treatment for SSI, 146–156
    unearned, 148–149
income-capped states, Medicaid, 180
Income Diversion Trust, Medicaid, 180
Income Only Trust, 3–4, 180, 189,
        235–242
individual retirement accounts. *See*
        IRA (individual retirement
        account)
in-kind support, 150
insurance and annuity transactions,
        power of attorney, 49–50
insured status
    currently insured individuals, 73
    disability insured individuals, 73
    early credits, 73–74
    fully insured individuals, 72–73
    insured individuals, 72
    social security, 72–74

Internal Revenue Code (IRC), 147, 156
    annuities, 281
    death taxes, 288
    federal income taxation, 267
    generation-skipping transfer tax, 295
    income taxation of distributions,
        256–257
    joint interests, 281–282
    Medicaid resources, 181
    medical expense deduction, 275–276
    retirement benefits, 281
    sale of personal residence, 275
    taxable estate, 284–285
    top-heavy retirement plans, 253
IRA (individual retirement account),
        156, 250
    creditor protection, 257–258
    estate taxation, 257
    income taxation of, 256–257
    Roth IRA, 251
    SIMPLE (Savings Incentive Match
        Plan for Employees) IRA,
        251, 261

judicial review, social security, 92

Kentucky Emergency Medical Services
        (EMS), Do Not Resuscitate
        (DNR) Order, 42–44
Keogh plans, retirement, 249
kiddie tax, 288, 294
Korean War, 105
Krohm, Carol, 34
Kruse, Clifton B., Jr., 195, 209, 229

Law, Rick L., 3
*The Law of Later Life Health Care
        Decision Making* (Frolik), 4,
        28, 176
Lawyer's Guide to Estate Planning (Hunt
        and Hunt), 59, 202, 215, 267
Life Expectancy Calculator, 95
life expectancy factor, minimum
        distribution tables, 254, 255
life insurance, gross estate, 283–284
life-sustaining treatment, 31

limited capacity considerations, elder clients, 3–4
limited objective standard, 30
limiting charge, Medicare, 131
living trust, 53–54
   sample, 55–59
   sample pour-over will, 54–55
living will, 31, 40–41
   form, 40–41
   revocation of, 41
long-term care benefits, Medicaid eligibility, 179
lump sum death benefit, social security, 72

maintenance, 150
marriage, deemed valid, 79
married couples
   gift splitting, 292
   planning Medicaid for, 186–188
   promissory note, 187–188
   purchase of annuity, 187–188
   spend down, 186
   transfers not subject to gift tax, 293
Medicaid, 3, 145
   appeals procedure for, 192–194
   community spouse resource allowance, 184
   definition of income, 179–180
   eligibility for long-term care benefits, 179
   estate recovery, 190–192
   fair hearing procedure, 184
   financial qualifications, 179–180
   First Party Special Needs Trust, 220–228
   five-year look-back rule, 184–186
   income-capped states, 180
   Income Only Trust, 235–242
   introduction to eligibility, 176–177
   mandatory covered services, 177
   non-income-capped states, 180
   optional services covered by, 178
   overview, 176
   patients' rights, 29
   planning for married couple, 186–188

   Qualifying Income Trust (QIT), 229–234
   resources and resource exemptions, 181–182
   services covered by, 177–178
   spousal impoverishment rules, 182–184
   Third Party Special Needs Trust, 209–219
   transfers to trusts, 188–190
   Will with Testamentary Third Party Special Needs Trust, 195–208
Medicaid asset protection trust, 4, 189, 235–242
Medicaid Compliant Trust, 235–242
Medicaid eligibility rules, 5
Medicaid Qualifying Trust, 188
medical benefits
   veteran enrollment, 114–115
   for veterans' dependents, 115
medical expenses, transfers not subject to gift tax, 293–294
medical insurance. *See* Medicare Part B
medical treatment. *See also* health care
   case law on withholding, 30–31
   right to be informed, 28
   unwanted, 28–29
Medicare, 3, 124
   Advantage plans, 134–135
   appeals procedures, 136–137
   assignment, 130–132
   checklist for new beneficiaries, 140–141
   federal Black Lung program and, 134
   limiting charge, 131
   Medigap insurance, 132–133
   no-fault insurance and, 134
   overview of benefits, 138–139
   Part A, 124–128
   Part B, 128–130
   Part C, 134–135
   Part D, 135–136
   patients' rights, 29
   as primary payer, 133, 142n54
   private contracts, 131–132

Medicare, (*continued*)
  as secondary payer, 133
  signing up for, 95–96
  Supplementary Medical Insurance
      program (SMI), 132–133, 139
  worker's compensation and, 134
Medicare & You 2019 (DHHS
      publication), 141n4, 142n32,
      142n60
Medicare Advantage plans (Part C),
      134–135, 138
Medicare and Home Health Care (DHHS
      publication), 141n17
Medicare Choosing a Medigap Policy
      (DHHS publication), 142n47
Medicare Hospice Benefits (DHHS
      publication), 141n21
Medicare Part A, 124–128, 138
  home health care services covered
      by, 126–127
  hospice services covered by,
      127–128
  hospital services covered by, 125
  skilled nursing facility services
      covered by, 126
Medicare Part B, 128–130, 138
  additional services by, 130
  preventive services covered by,
      129–130
  services covered by, 129
  services not covered by, 130
Medicare Part C, 134–135, 138
Medicare Part D, 135–136, 138
Medicare Resource Center, 140
Medicare summary notice (MSN), 137
Medicare Supplementary Medical
      Insurance program (SMI),
      132–133, 139. *See also* Medicare
      Part B
Medicare Supplement Insurance
      (Medigap), 139
Medigap insurance, 132–133, 139
Mezzullo, Louis A., 246
military service benefits, power of
      attorney, 50
Miller Trust, 180, 190, 229–234

minimum monthly maintenance needs
      allowance (MMMNA), 182
mirror wills, 8
Missouri Supreme Court, 30–31
money-purchase plans, retirement,
      247–248
Morgan, Rebecca C., 5
mother/father's benefits
  divorced spouse qualifying for, 83–84
  social security, 83–84
  termination of, 84
multiple representation, 7–8

National Hospice and Palliative Care
      Organization, 128
National Housing Act, 149, 160
net gifts, 294
net worth, term, 106
New Jersey Supreme Court, 30, 65n2
no-fault insurance, Medicare and, 134
nondiscrimination, retirement
      plans, 252
non-income-capped states,
      Medicaid, 180

Old Age Assistance, 145
old-age benefits, social security, 76–78
Omnibus Budget Reconciliation Act of
      1993 (OBRA 93), 188
one-third reduction rule,
      Supplemental Security Income
      (SSI), 150–151
original Medicare, 139

parent's benefits
  qualifying for, 85
  qualifying for DIC benefits, 110, 112
  social security, 84–85
  termination of, 85
participation, retirement plans, 252
Patient Self-Determination Act
      of 1990, 34
patients' rights, 29
Patients' Rights Condition of
      Participation (CoP), 29
Payback Trusts, 188, 189

Peck, Kerry, 3
penalty taxes
    minimum distributions, 254–256
    premature distributions, 253–254
    retirement, 253–256
pension benefits
    aid and attendance (A&A) of, 108
    death pension, 112–114
    election of benefits, 109
    eligibility for, 105
    excluded resources, 106
    exclusions from income, 107
    household benefits for, 108–109
    improved survivors, 112–114
    non-service connected, 106
    resource limits, 106
    retirement, 247
    treatment of income, 106
    veterans, 104–109
    wartime service, 105
pension funds, definition, 156
Persian Gulf War, 105
PIA. *See* primary insurance amount
    (PIA)
pooled trusts, Medicaid, 189
portability, 286
power of attorney
    durable health care, 32–39
    sample, 49–52
Practical Tools for Lawyers (ABA), 10
presumed value rule, Supplemental
    Security Income (SSI), 151
primary insurance amount (PIA)
    alternate methods of calculating, 75
    determining, 74–75
    family maximum rule and benefit
        amount, 75
    grounds for reduction of
        benefits, 76
private contracts, Medicare, 131–132
profit sharing, 260, 262
profit-sharing plans, retirement, 247
promissory note, Medicaid for married
    couple, 187–188
provisional income, calculation, 275
pure objective standard, 30

qualified terminable interest property
    (Q-TIP) election, 285
Qualifying Income Trust (QIT), 180,
    190, 229–234
questionnaire(s)
    asset, 16–20
    family, 11–15
Quinlan, Karen Ann, 30, 65n2

Railroad Retirement Act, 79
Railroad Retirement Board (RRB),
    96, 124
Railroad Retirement System, 125
real estate transactions, power of
    attorney, 49
representation, engagement letter, 21,
    23–24
resources
    assets not considered as, 158–160
    definition, 156
    disposition of, 160–161
    Medicaid, 181–182
    rules for jointly held assets, 157–158
    timing for counting, 157, 172n91
    transfer, 161–162
    treatment by Supplemental Security
        Income (SSI), 156–162
retirement, 245–246
    401(k) plans, 248–249
    background of, 246
    comparison of plans, 259–262
    creditor protection, 257–258
    IRA (individual retirement
        account), 250
    Keogh or HR-10 plans, 249–250
    money-purchase plans, 247–248
    nondiscrimination, 252
    participation, 252
    penalty taxes, 253–256
    pension plans, 247
    power of attorney for plan
        transactions, 50
    profit-sharing plans, 247
    Roth IRA, 251
    SEP (simplified employee pension)
        plan, 250

retirement, (*continued*)
  SIMPLE 401(k) plans, 249
  simple IRA, 251
  social security, 76–78
  taxation of distributions, 256–257
  top-heavy plans, 253
  types of plans, 247–251
  vesting, 252
Rosenblatt, Carolyn L., 2
Roth 401(k) plans, 248
Roth IRA (individual retirement
      account), 251, 257–258

safe deposit box transactions, power of
      attorney, 49
self-employed, retirement planning
      for, 249–250
Senior Citizens' Freedom to Work Act
      of 2000, 78
SEP (simplified employee pension)
      plan, 250, 259, 261
  estate taxation, 257
  income taxation of, 256–257
SIMPLE (Savings Incentive Match
      Plan for Employees) IRA,
      251, 259
SIMPLE 401(k) plans, 249
skilled nursing facility, Medicare Part
      A, 126
social security
  appeals procedure, 90–92
  basics of, 69–72
  benefits, 3
  calculating benefits, 74–76
  child's benefits, 85–88
  disability insurance benefits, 88–90
  family maximum rule, 75
  grounds for reduction of benefits, 76
  husband's and wife's benefits,
      78–80
  insured status, 72–74
  lump sum death benefit, 72
  mother's and father's benefit, 83–84
  parent's benefits, 84–85
  payment procedures, 70
  persons eligible for, 69–70

power of attorney, 50
primary insurance amount (PIA),
      74–75
retirement checklist, 93–96
rules for overpayments, 71
rules for representative payee,
      70–71
rules for underpayments, 71–72
widow's and widower's benefits,
      81–83
Social Security Act, 69, 96n1
  Medicaid, 188, 243n1
  Medicare, 125
  Supplemental Security Income
      (SSI), 152–153, 159, 170n2
  trust agreement, 230
Social Security Administration
      (SSA), 69
  administering Supplemental
      Security Income (SSI), 144–145
  administrative law judge (ALJ)
      stage, 91
  appeals council stage, 91–92
  attorney's fees, 92
  earning credit, 73–74
  expedited appeals process, 92
  initial determination stage, 90–92
  insured status, 72–74
  judicial review in federal court, 92
  overpayment rules, 71
  payment procedures, 70
  reconsideration stage, 91
  rules for representative payee,
      70–71
  social security retirement checklist,
      93–96
  underpayment rules, 71–72
Social Security Disability Insurance
      (SSDI), Supplemental Security
      Income (SSI) and, 166–167
social security retirement
  age of retirement, 77–78
  checklist, 93–96
  excess earnings and, 78
  monthly benefit rate, 77
  old-age benefits, 76–78

special monthly compensation (SMC), 104
special needs trust, 3
speech language pathology, Medicare Part A, 127
spouse(s)
impoverishment rules and Medicaid, 182–184
qualifying for husband/wife benefits, 79
qualifying for widow/widower benefits, 81–82
remarriage of, and DIC benefits, 111
SSA rules for changes in status of, 154
surviving, qualifying for DIC benefits, 109–110, 111
surviving, qualifying for survivors pension benefits, 113–114
SSI. *See* Supplemental Security Income (SSI)
standby trust, 53
step-grandchildren, rules for child's benefits, 87
stock and bond transactions, power of attorney, 49
substantial gainful activity (SGA)
for blind individuals, 89–90
definition, 89
Summers, Scott, 34
supplemental care trust, 3
Supplemental Security Income (SSI), 144, 166–167, 170n1–2, 177, 180
appeals procedure, 164–165
application procedure, 162–163
assets not considered resources, 158–160
benefits, 3, 144
deeming of income, 151–152
disposition of resources, 160–161
earned income, 147
earned income that does not count, 147–148
eligibility requirements of, 145–146
income types that SSA does not deem, 152–153

in-kind support and maintenance, 150
introduction to, 144–145
one-third reduction rule, 150–151
overpayment of benefits, 163–164
persons who are ineligible for benefits, 146
presumed value rule, 151
resources defined, 156–157
rules for changes in status of a spouse, 154
rules for deeming income, 153–154
rules for jointly held assets, 157–158
Social Security Disability Insurance (SSDI) and, 166–167
transfer of resources, 161–162
treatment of income, 146–156
treatment of resources, 156–162
underpayment of benefits, 163
unearned income, 148
unearned income that does not count, 148–149
what is not considered income, 154–156

tangible personal property transactions, power of attorney, 49
tax. *See also* federal income tax
power of attorney, 50
tax rate schedule, 272–273, 300
taxation of distributions
estate, 257
income, 256–257
retirement, 256–257
Tax Cuts and Jobs Act of 2017, 277
Tax Reform Act of 1976, 277
Tax Reform Act of 1986, 297, 298
Third Party and Self-Created Trusts (Kruse), 195, 209, 229
Third Party Special Needs Trust
inter vivos trust, 209–219
will with, for couple with handicapped child/person, 195–208

transfers to trust, Medicaid, 188–190
tuition, transfers not subject to gift tax, 293–294

Understanding the Four C's of Elder Law Ethics (ABA), 2, 7
undue hardship, 192
unemployment benefits, power of attorney, 50
unified credit, 286
Uniform Durable Power of Attorney Act 1979, 47
Uniform Health-Care Decisions Act (UHCDA), 34
Uniform Power of Attorney Act 2006, 47
Uniform Statutory Form Power of Attorney Act 1998, 47
Uniform Transfers or Gifts to Minors Act, 51
U.S. Court of Appeals, federal circuit, 117, 118
U.S. Housing Act of 1937, 160
U.S. Supreme Court, Cruzan case, 29, 31

VA (Veterans Administration) benefits, 5
vesting, retirement plans, 252
veteran benefits, 5, 119n1
    burial, 115–116
    checklist for, 118–119
    claims for, 116–118
    death pension, 112–114
    dependency and indemnity compensation (DIC) benefits, 109–112, 120n56
    disability compensation, 103–104
    eligibility for pension, 105

exclusions from income, 107
improved survivors pension benefits, 112–114
introduction to, 103
medical, 114–115
pension, 104–109
resource limits, 106
treatment of income, 106
wartime service, 105
Vietnam War, 105

wartime service, definition, 105
When to Start Receiving Retirement Benefits (SSA publication), 93, 96
Why Am I Left in the Waiting Room? (ABA), 7
widow/widower benefits
    divorced spouse qualifying, 82
    spouse qualifying for, 81–82
    termination of, 83
wife. *See* husband/wife benefits
will(s)
    living, 31, 40–41
    mirror, 8
    sample pour-over will, 54–55
    simple, 59–64
    testamentary third party special needs trust for couple with handicapped child/person, 195–208
workers' compensation, Medicare and, 134
Working with Aging Clients (Rosenblatt), 2, 4
World War II, 105

Your Retirement Benefit (SSA publication), 75